The Past and Future of America's Economy

'I know of no way of judging the future but by the past.'

Edward Gibbon

The Past and Future of America's Economy

Long Waves of Innovation that Power Cycles of Growth

Robert D. Atkinson

Vice President, and Director of the Technology and New Economy Project, Progressive Policy Institute, Washington, DC, USA

Edward Elgar
Cheltenham, UK • Northampton, MA, USA

Published by
Edward Elgar Publishing Limited
Glensanda House
Montpellier Parade
Cheltenham
Glos GL50 1UA
UK

Edward Elgar Publishing, Inc.
136 West Street
Suite 202
Northampton
Massachusetts 01060
USA

A catalogue record for this book
is available from the British Library

ISBN 1 84376 955 7 (cased)

Printed and bound in Great Britain by MPG Books Ltd, Bodmin, Cornwall

Contents

Figures and Tables

FIGURES

TABLES

Acknowledgments

Undertaking to research and write a book while working full time is not a task that I undertook lightly. The motivation for doing so was the frustration I felt that the full and complete story of what the New Economy is and how it is transforming the economy and society was not widely being told. Yet, my preoccupation, or perhaps obsession, with this book on the countless weekends and evenings during the last several years was not without its toll on my family as I was too often locked away in my study in front of my computer. As a result, I am immensely grateful for the patient support of my wife, Anne-Marie, and son, David, without which this manuscript would never have been written. My heartfelt thanks and love to them both.

I am also grateful to my friends and colleagues at the Progressive Policy Institute and the Democratic Leadership Council who have helped me refine many of the ideas in this book. In particular, I want to thank Chuck Altson, Ed Kilgore, and Will Marshall for their helpful feedback and thoughts, particularly on the material relating to the politics of the New Economy. Shane Ham provided lively and thought provoking interchanges over much of the material on e-commerce and the Internet. I would also like to thank Randolph Court, my collaborator on PPI's *The New Economy Index*, a precursor to this book. In addition, my appreciation to my research assistants who have helped track down materials and data, including David Atkinson, Rick Codori, Julie Hutto, Brian Newkirk, Jacob Ulevich, and Joe Ward. I also want to thank Joan Sherry for editing parts of the manuscript.

If any errors remain, they are my sole responsibility. Moreover, the views and positions expressed in this book are my own, not necessarily those of the Progressive Policy Institute or the Democratic Leadership Council.

PART I

How Technology Drives Economic and Social Transformations

1. Introduction: A New Economy?

Given all the hype, do we really have a New Economy? It is true that the economy has steadily grown bigger, more prosperous and more modern. Yes, there has been a stream of innovations. Productivity growth has accelerated and, by historical standards, unemployment rates remain low. But do these changes reflect the emergence of a New Economy or just the old economy getting bigger? Is productivity likely to continue to increase? Is this New Economy confined to places like Silicon Valley, or does it represent a more profound shift in the nature and structure of the entire society? What, if anything, are the implications for how people live and for how government conducts our business? These are not simply academic questions. They go to the heart of the question of what life will be like for Americans over the course of the next few decades.

The conventional view held by most economists is that technological change and the periodic ups and downs of the business cycle are part and parcel of the continuous process of evolution in capitalist economies. According to the adherents of this view, there has been no recent economic disjuncture, no transformation in economic structure, no New Economy. *Newsweek* economic columnist Robert Samuelson even tells us that 'the New Economy was mainly a mood, a feeling of irrepressible optimism,' adding 'We can be sure that the economy will always be "new". We can be less sure it will be always be better.'[1]

But drawing on the work of mid-twentieth century economist Joseph Schumpeter and other 'long-wave' theorists, it is possible to construct a competing and more compelling story of how change takes place in the economy and, by extension, in society. Adherents of this story have long been lone voices toiling in the wilderness of economic doctrine, but over the last decade their views have become increasingly heard. According to this analysis, economic history is best understood as a set of fundamental transformations from one kind of economy to another. At their heart these transformations are propelled by, on the one hand, the stagnation of the existing new techno-economic production system and, on the other hand, by the emergence of a new production system that enables a new period of robust growth and innovation. Moreover, because society itself is organized to reflect and support the underlying techno-economic system, the transformation of the latter has profound implications for a nation's overall political economy, organization of business, labor force, legal system, urban structure, and even culture as they all transform to fit the new realities.

According to this story, four great waves of technological change have broken over the United States in the last century and a half, each leading to major transformations and the demise of one kind of economy and the emergence of another. Each in turn changed the nature of work, the organization of enterprises, the role of government, the shape of urban form, and even the structure of social organization and attitudes. And as each transformation from an old economy and old society to a new one was underway, each spread confusion and conflict, but each ultimately led to vast improvements in the quality of life for Americans. As noted economic historian Robert Wiebe argued: 'Americans have responded to each wave of technological advance in similar stages of protest and reform: diffuse criticism, attempts to patch the old order, [and] then efforts to modernize the social and political framework.'[2]

Wiebe goes on to say that these transformations are 'the motive forces in a century of American history.'[3] Indeed, the coming together of the rapid economic, social and political change that we are in the midst of today is by no means unprecedented. This series of transformations, occurring roughly every fifty years, from one kind of economy and society to another has in fact been the dominant, if unappreciated, story of America.

One of these transformations, fueled by the development of cheap steel, precision machine tools, and electricity, enabled the rise of a factory-based manufacturing economy in the 1890s, a fundamental change from the preceding agricultural and small merchant/craftsman economy. But contrary to the host of pundits and corporate gurus who argue that there was just one industrial revolution that replaced the prior agricultural era, the real story is more complex. Rather, there were transformations before and after the so-called industrial revolution. In the 1840s a host of local small-firm manufacturing industries such as iron and textiles began to emerge, but differed significantly from the regional factory-based system that was to come in the 1880s and 1890s. Likewise, the rise of the national corporate, mass production economy in the 1940s and 1950s, fueled by industries such as electronics, chemicals, and mass consumer goods, represented a turning point from the regionally based, manufacturing economy of the first half of the century. Indeed, that 'mixed economy' was so different from the one that preceded it that an issue of *Fortune* magazine in October 1955 was devoted to the 'New Economy' and dealt with the 'American breakthrough,' and the 'new management, and new economy.'

Another new economy began to emerge in the early 1990s, powered by the information technology revolution, including the Internet, software, the microprocessor and telecommunications. This New Economy represents a fundamental change from the national corporate, mass production economy that was in full force from the 1940s to the 1970s. Instead, it is a global, entrepreneurial and knowledge-based economy in which the keys to success lie in the extent to which knowledge, technology and innovation are embedded in products and services. This New Economy is as different from the old corporate economy as the prior two economies were different from the economies they preceded. And just as these prior economic transformations led to major changes in the organization of industry, work, governance, and politics, today's New Economy is doing the same.

Part I of this book explains how we got here, examining economic transformations over the last 160 years and how institutions and people responded to them. Chapter 2 discusses the concept of long cycles in economic growth and the relationship between the technical systems that underpin an economy and the organizations, policies, and other factors that combine to form the superstructure that makes an economic system work. Chapter 3 examines the last two major economies: the regional, small-firm factory economy of the 1890s to the 1930s, and the national, corporate mass production economy of the late 1940s to 1970s. Chapter 4 examines the contours of today's New Economy, including the underlying technology system and the effects on organizations, markets, and governance. Chapter 5 examines how the New Economy has led to a turnaround in productivity and how the emerging digital economy holds the key to continued robust productivity growth. While the prospects for sustained productivity growth from the new production system are strong, they can be derailed if resistance to change grows. Therefore, Chapter 6 examines both opposition to past economic transformations and the wide array of opponents of today's New Economy.

Taking into account the implications of the historical record, Part II focuses on what public policy needs to do to maximize the inherently progressive forces of today's New Economy. The last chapter outlines some of the implications for the lives of ordinary people, in particular, the potential of the New Economy to create the conditions for an economy much more centered on enhancing human potential and meeting higher-order human needs.

IS THE NEW ECONOMY A FLASH IN THE PAN?

Before jumping back in time, it is worth first addressing the question many will ask about any book about the 'New Economy': is what happened in the last decade a major, permanent structural transformation? Or was it, as new economy skeptics argue, simply an unsustainable bubble.

If this book were published in 2000 there would not be much convincing to do. For in the days before the stock market bubble burst and many dot-coms turned into dot-bombs there was, to use Alan Greenspan's term, much irrational exuberance. One could not open up a business magazine or turn on the news without hearing about the amazing New Economy and how it was transforming not just the economy but society. The expectations – some might say hype – were high. Kevin Kelly, editor of *Wired Magazine*, opined that 'The network economy will unleash opportunities on a scale never seen before on Earth.'[4] Futurists Peter Schwartz and Peter Leyden wrote 'we are watching the beginnings of a global economic boom on a scale never experienced before ... a period of sustained growth that could eventually double the world's economy every dozen years ...'[5] Such gushing enthusiasm at the beginnings of economic transformations is not new, in fact, as discussed in Chapter 3, optimism is always high at the beginning stages of a new economic period. When Henry Adams viewed the huge dynamo for producing electricity at the 1900 Great Exhibition in Paris he was so in awe that he described the sensation of having his 'historical neck broken by the sudden irruption of forces totally new.'[6] Indeed, this was all part and parcel of the 'New Century Fever,' that resulted from the turn of the century technology revolution.[7]

Contrast the excitement of the 1990s to today's gloom and doom. A parade of books and pundits tell us it was all hype and we, including

Alan Greenspan, were dupes to believe it.[8] It is fashionable, even the norm, to dismiss talk of a New Economy, believing that the events of the last few years prove that the New Economy was a flash in the pan, or a myth spun by an over-imaginative media. Stephen Roach, chief economist at Morgan Stanley, once a New Economy cheerleader, now sees it all as 'bubble-induced excesses.'[9] Dean Baker, an economist at the Economic Policy Institute, tells us that 'There is little basis for the claim that the technological innovations of the current period are qualitatively different than the technological breakthroughs of previous eras.'[10] In a widely touted article, Harvard Business School's Nicholas Carr tells us that 'IT Doesn't Matter' because 'As for IT-spurred industry transformations, most of the ones that are going to happen have likely already happened or are in the process of happening.'[11]

Given the turmoil of the last three years, including the drawn out recovery, it is tempting to think that the skeptics may be right. The NASDAQ stock market index fell from its commanding heights of roughly 5000 in 2000 to roughly 1850 in March 2002. The dot-com mania turned into the dot-com bust, most Internet firms saw their stock prices plummet,[12] and dot-com failures increased from 225 in 2000 to over 535 in 2001.[13] Corporate scandals of Enron, Global Crossing, Adelphi, MCI-World Com and others dragged down investor confidence. After being in surplus in the late 1990s, the federal budget deficit exploded. Investment in information technology fell sharply. Unemployment went up. In short, things went from great to seemingly pretty bad.

However, as I will argue in Chapter 4, there is a fallacy in making the leap from bad news in high-profile technology sectors, and even the overall economy, to the death of the New Economy. The key is to remember that the New Economy was never just about the Internet and the 'next new thing.' Rather, as Chapters 2 and 3 discuss, the transformation to today's New Economy is equivalent in scope and depth to the rise of the factory economy in the 1890s and the mass production economy in the 1940s and 1950s. In fact, most forget that following a new economy growth boom following World War II, the economy suffered a severe slump in the late 1950s, only to rebound for 15 years of further robust growth. As we pass through these ground swells that regularly but infrequently reshape the economy (and society), there are sure to be occasional bumps along the way – such as the current economic slowdown – but these are the negative phases within what are longer growth periods.

But there is a second reason not to be pessimistic. This negative phase is not nearly as bad as the naysayers would have us believe. First, while jobs are down (almost 3 million private sector jobs were lost during the first three years of the Bush administration), productivity has remained remarkably robust. Unlike past slowdowns, productivity has continued to grow, at a stunning annual rate of 4.9 percent in 2002 and 4.2 percent in 2003. One reason is that companies are just beginning to fully exploit the potential of the new information technology system to allow them to do more with less.

Second, one reason why things look so bad, especially in the technology sector, is that things were so good. It is a bad idea to compare the present performance to the bubble, and the last half of 1999 and the first three quarters of 2000 were indeed a bubble of massive proportions. More money was invested in venture capital in those two years than in the prior 20 years combined. The NASDAQ went up 57 percent between January 1999 and its peak in March 2000. Information technology (IT) investment exploded.

However, if we take slightly longer view, things are not so bad. As of mid-2004 the NASDAQ was still 43 percent higher than when Alan Greenspan warned of 'irrational exuberance' in 1996.[14] Notwith-standing some noted bankruptcies of Internet high fliers, venture capitalists continue to have faith in the nation's entrepreneurs, and invested more in 2002 and 2003 than in any year prior to 1998.

Moreover, it is not as if much of the shakeout was unexpected. Even though the Internet market was steadily growing, it was not big enough to support every money-losing dot-com spending millions to gain 'eyeballs.' Sure, some dubious businesses, like BBQ.com, pets.com and Webvan.com were launched, only to crash and burn soon after. This doesn't mean that e-commerce was a high-tech tulip bulb craze. While almost 110 000 jobs were lost at dot-coms in 2001, many due to failures, the total number of dot-com domains was 8 percent higher in March 2002 than it was at the end of 2000.[15] Moreover, while Hoovers, a business information service, listed in August 2001 72 dot.com companies that had bitten the dust, by December 2003 over 60 percent of those web companies were back in business, either as redirects to another web site (pets.com redirects to petsmart.com) or as the brand name of other companies (allwall.com became art.com).

In fact, despite what the naysayers may tell us, the Internet revolution has actually exceeded the heady expectations of the late 1990s. In 1997 Forrester Research estimated that by 2001 business-to-business (B-to-

B) e-commerce would total $186 billion. By 2001 it was almost four times as much at $715 billion. In 1999 B-to-B e-commerce was projected to range from $131 billion to $842 billion by 2003 while business to consumer (B-to-C) was estimated to grow to $97 billion.[16] In fact, by 2003 B-to-B e-commerce was worth $1.8 trillion and B-to-C $143 billion. One reason is because since the third quarter of 2000 to the middle of 2004, e-commerce retail sales have grown 68 percent while traditional retail sales have grown just 10 percent.[17] By early 2004, two-thirds of Internet users had purchased a product online.[18] Deployment of high-speed, broadband Internet access has also exceeded expectations, although to listen to the media, one would believe that the take up rate is slower than molasses. In 1998, the Progressive Policy Institute's *New Economy Index* projected that by 2003 9 million American homes would subscribe to broadband.[19] By the end of 2003, approximately 20 to 25 million households subscribed. Other indicators of health are that the number of web sites worldwide grew 20 percent in 2003, with nearly 7 million added, more than the number that existed in 1999.[20] Moreover, between July 2000 and February 2002, almost 8 million Internet domain names and 54 million Internet hosts (an address one can go to on the Internet) were added.[21]

Even in the IT capital sector things are not as cataclysmic as people think. Some of the slowdown resulted from a correction due to accelerated spending to address the feared Year 2000 (Y2K) crisis. The falloff in telecom investment was due to the artificially induced competition brought on by the 1996 Telecom Act that gave investors and entrepreneurs false hope that what is essentially a natural duopoly of local telephone and cable service would accommodate a multitude of players. Even though investment in IT fell relative to the peak 2000 levels, in 2003 it was still 5 percent higher than 1999 levels and is increasing. Moreover, as a host of new technologies become ready for the market, IT investments are likely to remain robust.[22] In the longer term, technologies like the Next Generation Internet, intelligent cars, optical computing and switching, and new technologies based on genomics and nanotechnology, suggest that technology innovation will also remain robust.

There is one final reason why we have been riding a roller coaster, plummeting from initial utopian and exuberant visions to today's doom and gloom. That is because almost everyone overestimated the rate of change, as in fact, is usually the case when it comes to predicting the growth of new industries.[23] Most investors, entrepreneurs, and the public mistakenly thought that the Internet was not like past innovations that took time to mature. As IT expert David Moschella notes 'history says that the promise of IT is almost always farther off than it initially appears.'[24] Most expected the economy to be transformed overnight, and when it was not the bubble burst. The reality is that the Internet and the digital economy are poised to fulfill all their original promises, though not solely through the dazzling dot.com startups, but rather through their integration into existing industries and companies.

In short, those skeptics who think the New Economy was some late-1990s flash in the pan staked to the emergence of dot-coms are roughly equivalent to the great wits who shouted 'Get a horse!' at early motorists broken down on the side of the road. In the late 1920s and 1930s people might have said that the auto era was over because scores of auto companies went bankrupt.[25] But that was just the beginning. In short, the stock market may have been a bubble, but the New Economy was real. To paraphrase Mark Twain, reports of the New Economy's demise have been greatly exaggerated. The New Economy is here to stay.

THE COURSE OF PRODUCTIVITY GROWTH

Some economists argue that the New Economy is new principally because productivity growth has revived relative to the lagging levels that dragged down growth from the late 1970s to the mid-1990s. While this confuses the outcome (productivity) with the process (structural change) it is true that productivity growth has rebounded significantly since 1996. The last time we experienced such rapid productivity growth was in the 1960s when the average worker saw real, inflation-adjusted income grow by over 30 percent. Yet, in relatively short order the productivity miracle from the mid-1940s to the 1960s fell flat. During the transition period from the mid-1970s to the mid-1990s the average worker would be lucky if his income went up 10 percent in a decade. Some workers, particularly blue-collar men, saw their incomes go down. As Chapter 5 details, economists have struggled to figure out the causes of the productivity slowdown, postulating everything from oil price shocks, to too much government regulation, to the entry of the baby-boom generation into the workplace. While we still do not know definitively why productivity fell off, I argue that it was largely because the old corporate, mass production, consumer economy had exhausted its potential for innovation and growth, while today's more entrepreneurial, customized, technology-driven economy had not yet emerged.

Part of what made the mid-1970s to early 1990s so difficult was that the deceleration happened so fast. It was as if the economy was a high-speed bullet train expecting to continue to travel at 200 miles per hour, but all of a sudden it slowed down to 60 mph. If the slowdown caught the passengers of the American economy off guard, it really surprised the experts. In his ambitious 1967 book forecasting what the world would be like in *The Year 2000*, Herman Kahn, noted futurist and founder of the Hudson Institute, thought that the high-speed train would keep roaring down the track. He stated:

> We shall simply postulate that recent rates in such things as increases in productivity will at least be equaled or increased in the future ... There is an almost general expectation that the United States ought to average between 2.5 and 3.5 per cent a year (productivity growth) or even more over the next 33 years. Indeed some expect that as soon as automation reaches its stride it will be 1 or 2 percent higher than this ... Very likely 3 or 3.5 percent is a good figure on which to focus.[26]

As a result, he predicted that inflation-adjusted gross domestic product (GDP) per capita would grow from $3557 in 1965, increasing to $10 160 by 2000. Instead, it was only $6355 (1965 dollars), while productivity rates were about one-third of what Kahn had predicted. Moreover, Kahn predicted we would have all this extra income while work hours would drop from 2000 per year to 1600, and even as low as 1100. Taking into account that Americans today are working more hours than before (including due to increased workforce participation rates), we are about 50 percent poorer than we would have been if the economy had been able to grow at the rate that not just Kahn, but most experts thought was in the cards.[27]

Since 1996 we have regained the kind of productivity growth we enjoyed in the heyday of the old economy and the potential for sustained robust productivity growth for at least the next decade looks strong. If we are in fact in the early phases of the emergence of a new techno-economic system, analogous to the periods of the 1910s and early 1960s, then, if history is any guide, we can expect strong productivity and economic growth as the new technology system expands throughout the economy.

In spite of all the talk about the 'productivity paradox' and the debate about the impact of IT on productivity, there has been little examination of just exactly how IT could boost productivity of a large share of industries and occupations. Just as the driver of productivity in the old economy was mechanization, Chapter 5 makes it clear that by automating a large share of functions involving the routine processing of information, including face-to-face transactions, phone transactions, and paper transactions, digitization promises to be the major engine of productivity. It is the application of information technologies to the service sector (and to service processes in sectors like manufacturing) that will be the critical factor driving continuing productivity and income growth.

As the realities of the New Economy sink in, most Americans will get used to them, and even embrace them as ultimately liberating and empowering. As more Americans take control of their own careers, are focused on knowledge work and see their incomes go up due to the doubling of the productivity rate, what is currently seen by many as threatening is likely to be seen by many as progressive. However, this does not mean that economic transformations, including this one, do not threaten entrenched interests and established ideologies. Indeed, as Chapter 6 shows, there has developed a disturbing anti-progress trend in America and other developed nations that, unless checked, threatens to derail New Economy progress.

SINCE IT IS A NEW ECONOMY, WHAT SHOULD WE DO ABOUT IT?

As new techno-economic production systems emerged during the prior two major economic transformations of the late 1800s and mid-1900s, they changed more than the economy, they changed economic policy. The progressive reforms of the early twentieth century were a response to a factory economy that presented a vast new array of challenges. The creation of the New Deal and later Great Society reforms of the 1960s were a response to a new mass production, managerial economy that required a stronger and more centralized federal government role. Today, we are at a similar point: in order to prosper in this New Economy, we need to develop a new approach not just to economic policy, but also to the organization of government itself.

For starters this means abandoning the outdated legacy economic policy systems and thinking. John Maynard Keynes once wrote that 'practical men, who believe themselves to be quite exempt from any intellectual influences, are usually the slaves of some defunct economist.'[28] As Chapter 7 details, that is exactly the situation among today's economic policymakers on both the left and the right who remain rooted in earlier eras. Many liberals remain in a reactive mode defending the old economy Keynesian, Great Society economic framework. Conservatives are even more backward looking, seeking though their doctrine of supply-side economics to resurrect the economic policy system of the early 1900s factory era.

Chapter 8 argues that breaking free from these legacy policy frameworks will require embracing a new economic framework, what is termed 'growth economics.' This requires government to move beyond its almost exclusive focus on managing the business cycle and economic prescriptions rooted in the old economy. Instead, the true measure of economic success in growth economics is productivity growth. As Chapter 9 details, the tools by which government boosts productivity are not the traditional ones, fiscal and monetary policy, relied on in the old economy to manage the business cycle. Rather, they are policies that support the digital revolution, boost technological innovation, enhance workforce skills, promote entrepreneurship and ensure competitive and open markets. The New Economy also requires a fundamentally new approach to government, one that relies more on networks than hierarchy, more on civic and private sector actors than bureaucracy, and more on technology than on rule-based, bureaucratic programs.

Finally, as the New Economy gets more productive, companies become more knowledge-driven and people get more prosperous, Americans will increasingly expect more rewarding work, more leisure, and more livable communities. Just as we moved from a economy in the first part of the twentieth century focused on production and investment, to one in the last half of the twentieth century focused on mass consumption, it is possible that we are moving to an economy in the first half of the twenty-first century focused on enabling people to live good lives. Chapter 10 examines these developments and discusses what government can do to accelerate them.

Philosopher George Santayana once counseled that 'those who cannot remember the past are condemned to repeat it.'[29] Indeed, the prevailing view is that history does not repeat itself, or at least should not. To be sure, we must remember the Holocaust and other atrocities so we do not repeat them. However, understanding past economic transformations will help provide a road map, albeit a somewhat rough and patchy one, but still a better road map than just flying blind. To the extent that societies go through similar types of processes at similar stages of economic transformation, understanding the course of past transitions allows us to better understand today's context as we yet again enter into a New Economy and new society. As a result, because of the cyclical nature of economic change, it may be more accurate to paraphrase Santayana as 'those who understand the past realize that they will repeat it.' Navigating this New Economy though, will not be easy, for it will require new policies and new choices. This book is an attempt to articulate the path forward.

NOTES

1. Samuelson (2002) pp. 32 and 41.
2. Wiebe (1989) p. 3.
3. Ibid.
4. Kelly (1998) p. 156.
5. Schwartz and Leyden (1997) p. 48.
6. Adams (1973) p. 382.
7. http://abcnews.go.com/sections/us/DailyNews/newcentury001231.html.
8. Henwood (2003).
9. www.wired.com/wired/archive/10.07/Myth.html.
10. Baker (2000). Madrick (1995) sees the sewing machine as a more important invention than the Internet.
11. Carr (2003) p. 10.
12. From February 2000 to February 2002 stock prices of Internet pure-plays CMGI fell from $129 to $1.38, AOL from $58 to $23, and Yahoo from $156 to $15.
13. Seven thousand to 10000 Internet companies are still in business (webmergers.com).
14. The Dow Jones Industrial Average is 65 percent higher. Even the NASDAQ computer index rose from $94 in 1997 to $144 in the middle of 2003, while an index of Internet stocks rose from $80 to $137 (Adkinson et al., 2003, p. 53).
15. Challenger, Gray and Christmas, Inc. (2001).
16. *Business 2.0*, September 1999, p. 109.
17. www.census.gov/mrts/www/current.html.
18. The Pew Internet & American Life Project, February 2004 Tracking poll.
19. Atkinson and Court (1998).
20. Netcraft, web server survey (http://news.netcraft.com).
21. www.zoonik.com; http://www.isc.org/ds/WWW-200201/index.html.
22. These include voice recognition, voice over Internet protocol, expert systems, smart cards, e-books, cheap storage devices, new display devices and video software, intelligent transportation systems, Wi-max and 'third generation' wireless communication systems, robots, and fiberoptic broadband deployment.
23. Nairn (2002).

24. Moschella (2003) p. 18.
25. Such industry restructuring and consolidation is in fact quite common at the beginning phases of a new industry. For example, while the British railroad industry collapsed in 1847, leading to massive bankruptcies and failures, many more miles of rails were built in the 20 years after this than in the 20 years before. Likewise, while there were 253 auto companies in the US in 1908, by 1920 there were just 108, and by 1929 80 percent of cars were produced by the big three of Chrysler, Ford and GM.
26. Kahn (1967) p. 118.
27. Kahn was also overly optimistic when it came to predicting the growth of other nations. He predicted that by now the Soviet Union would be in an early post-industrial phase, and countries like Argentina, Malaysia, and Poland would be mass consumption societies with a prosperous middle class.
28. Keynes (1935) p. 122.
29. Santayana (1905) Chapter 12.

2. Technological, Economic and Social Transformation

To understand today's economic transformation it is important to first examine how others have viewed the relationship between technology, the economy and society. Within the economics and history professions there is a longstanding debate about how and whether technology and the economy determine society. Some argue that economic and social structures are relatively independent. In contrast, economic determinists argue that because the economy drives and determines virtually all the rest of society, as economies undergo transformations then societies must as well.

Karl Marx was the first well-known economic determinist, arguing that an era's technology and economic structure not only shape society and politics, but in fact determine them. In *Das Kapital* he argued: 'Technology discloses man's mode of dealing with nature, the process of production by which he sustains his life, and thereby also lays bare the mode of formation of his social relations and of the mental conceptions that flow from them.'[1] Thus, Marx differentiated between the economic structure (the prevailing technology system) and the superstructure (institutions and government) and argued that not only did technology determine the shape of society, but that when it changed, society itself had to change.

In contrast to the independent school, this was no 'great man' theory of history. In fact, Marx railed against competing German philosopher Hegel, who argued that the evolution of the West was driven by a competition of ideas. Marx would have none of this. Instead he argued that 'in acquiring new productive forces men change their mode of production, and in changing their mode of production they change their way of living – they change all their social relations.' Show Marx the technology a society is using, and he believed he could tell you the type of society. As he stated pithily: 'The hand-mill gives you society with the feudal lord; the steam-mill, society with the industrial capitalist.'[2] It is not clear what he would say the society with the electric motor or semiconductor gives you. While Marx mistakenly predicted capitalism's demise, to ignore his views on technology and society would be to throw out the baby with the bath water. To illustrate his point consider that advanced industrial nations in the 1950s and 1960s, whether communist, socialist, or capitalist, had much in common. Though the Soviet Union lagged behind the United States in its technology, in general it relied on the same technology system – industrial factories, automobiles, electricity production, chemical plants, etc. Both relied on mass production hierarchical organizations, and both focused on stability and continuity. And both economic systems were transformed in the 1980s and 1990s. However, while the technology system is important, it is not all-determinative. The Soviet Union, after all, had a different political system. Robert Heilbroner may have got it right when he states that: 'the general level of technology may follow an independently determined sequential path, but its areas of application certainly reflect social influences.'[3] One sees this in how different the Japanese, European and American economies are, even though all are powered by the same techno-economic system.

If technology is not absolutely determinate, neither is it irrelevant. Societies are not independent pastiches painted in whatever patterns their inhabitants choose. One is hard pressed to imagine how a society at one level of economic development and technology use could be similar to one at a different level. India is different from the United States not just because of a different cultural and social history, but because its level of development is different from ours. Perhaps the most accurate assessment of the relationship between technology, the economy and society comes from Heilbroner: 'I think we can indeed state that the technology of a society imposes a determinate pattern of social relations on that society.'[4]

Why is technology so important in determining how we live and work? At heart societies are organized to facilitate efficient production. How we work, learn, are entertained, and even live in the built environment is shaped by an overriding economic imperative. This does not imply, as some Naderite liberals would have us believe, that this tight linkage between the requirements of the economy and the society is the result of a process of corporate control and conspiracy. Rather, it stems from a more simple fact: throughout history society has itself been a technology humans employ to attain their goals, and the 'hard' technologies of machines, tools, and techniques must work in tandem with the 'soft' technologies of work organization, education, the built environment, politics and even the family. For example, it does no good to educate people to operate in a world in which they will do manual labor and be required to follow orders if the economy is a knowledge-based one that requires innovation and creativity. Likewise, cities cannot support a dispersed production system if the transportation system is centralized and organized around rails and ships. Similarly, in 1860, when large organizations generally had not yet been developed, save the railroad, it was difficult for people to imagine a government organized as it is now. In short, at any one time the features of a society and economy are more or less part of a larger self-reinforcing system of production. Organizations are attuned to the environment (technology, social attitudes, skill levels) and so resemble one another.

If the prevailing technology system indeed sets the parameters in which a society operates, how does technology, and by extension society, change and evolve? If, as the majority of economists believe, the economy evolves at a relatively steady pace (albeit undergoing short business cycles of growth and recession), with modest and sustained changes leading to constant improvement, then this would suggest that economic history should also be relatively linear, changing incrementally. In fact, most conventional economists hold to this position and reject the notion of technology-driven long waves. For example, as economic columnist Robert Samuelson notes, 'There are no long cycles driven by technology ... technology is always advancing.'[5] So are rivers, but once in a while there is a flood.

If most conventional economists have not looked beyond the short business cycle, there have nevertheless been a few maverick economists and an even larger number of economic historians who think that distinct transformational periods and cycles in the economy are the norm. They believe that technology does not advance incrementally, but rather bursts onto the scene irregularly with clusters of breakthrough technologies, and resultant transformations from one kind of society to another.

TECHNOLOGY AND ECONOMIC CYCLES

One of the first to propose the theory that economies undergo technology-induced transformations was the Russian economist Nikolai Kondratieff. Writing in the midst of the Great Depression, Kondratieff argued that the Depression was not the first step to the decline of the capitalist order, as Stalin and the Communist party power structure hoped and believed.[6] Instead, Kondratieff broke with Stalin's rigid orthodoxy and argued that the Depression was in fact the trough of a long 50-year cycle of boom and bust of the kind that industrial economies go through with surprising regularity. Because this was only the downturn of a 'long-wave' cycle, and not the death knell of a rotten capitalist order, Kondratieff argued that the Western economies would not only recover but would enter a new, long upward cycle of profound growth. Kondratieff got as far as suggesting that these long business cycles were caused by long cycles in business investment. But he never was able to get beyond this to speculate on what were behind these longer-term waves of investment. Perhaps if he had not been banished to the Gulag by Stalin, he would have developed an explanation.

As it was, it was up to Joseph Schumpeter, an Austrian economist who migrated to the United States in the 1930s and later became president of the American Economics Association, to take the next step. Like Kondratieff, Schumpeter was also seeking an explanation for the Depression. In fact, it was difficult for any economist then to not be obsessed with figuring out what had gone wrong. At the time, the economics profession was split by severe disagreements. On one side were the traditional classical economists who had dominated economic thought since the 1890s who argued that the nation would emerge from the Depression when prices and wages declined far enough so that consumers could afford to buy more goods and employers could afford to hire more workers. And indeed, as a believer in the conventional view, President Herbert Hoover waited for prices and wages to fall enough. They fell enough for voters to elect Franklin Roosevelt.

In contrast to the classical economists, a new wave of economists, Keynesians – named after British economist John Maynard Keynes – posited a fundamentally different explanation for the Depression. Keynes agreed with the classical economists that in the long run prices and wages would adjust and lead to the reemergence of growth. But he believed that this would take so long that the human suffering in the interim would be extreme. As a result, in response to the classical economists who counseled that 'in the long run, the market will adjust' he acerbically stated 'in the long run, we are all dead.' Keynes and his followers believed that the government, through its taxing and spending authority, should act to raise aggregate consumer demand, thus counteracting any decline in demand. This notion of relying on fiscal policy to moderate business cycles held sway among most economists and policymakers until the experiences of stagflation in the late 1970s, when the corporate mass production economy began to fall apart.

Though classical and Keynesian economists differed fundamentally on what to do, surprisingly they both agreed in their analysis of the problem – the United States was in the midst of a downturn, albeit severe, in the business cycle, caused by macroeconomic and monetary factors, not by technological and organizational ones. And while most economists today are neoclassicalists (they acknowledge the impact of government spending on business cycles but also recognize the role of prices, particularly interest rates), their focus remains almost exclusively on the business cycle. To this day their explanation of the Depression reflects this orientation, as they blame it on all sorts of factors – high tariffs, poor fiscal policy, the British decision to abandon the gold standard, and the like – but largely ignore technology. It is in this context that Schumpeter's work is all the more important because he was one of only a few voices arguing that the terrible economic times of the 1930s were caused by something other than a particularly bad downturn in the normal workings of the business cycle. Like Kondratieff, Schumpeter argued that the Depression was something more and different – it represented not just a normal business downturn, but the trough of a longer and more profound economic cycle that they termed 'long waves'. But where Schumpeter went beyond Kondratieff was in explaining how and why these long waves occurred. In his classic 1942 book *Capitalism, Socialism and Democracy*, Schumpeter explained:

> The essential point to grasp is that in dealing with capitalism we are dealing with an evolutionary process ... the fundamental impulse that sets and keeps the capitalist engine in motion comes from the new consumers' goods, the new methods of production or transportation, the new markets, the new forms of industrial organization that capitalist enterprise creates.[7]

Schumpeter focused on the constant innovation which is at the heart of the successful workings of the capitalist enterprise, stating:

> The opening up of new markets, foreign or domestic, and the organizational development from the craft shop and factory to such concerns as US Steel illustrate the same process of industrial mutation – if I may use that biological term – that incessantly revolutionizes the economic structure from within, incessantly destroying the old one, incessantly creating the new one.[8]

It is one thing to recognize that successful capitalist economies are driven by innovation, not just in technology but in all aspects of production and distribution, and that this innovation fundamentally reshapes economies. It is quite another to argue that these innovations come in waves that lead to economic transformation. But that is what Schumpeter argued when he wrote that 'each of the long waves in economic activity consists of an "industrial revolution" and the absorption of its effects.'[9] He went on to state:

> These revolutions periodically reshape the existing structure of industry by introducing new methods of production – the mechanized factory, the electrified factory, chemical synthesis, and the like; *new* commodities, such as railroad service, motorcars, electrical appliances; *new* forms of organization – the merger movement; new sources of supply – La Plata wool, American cotton, Katanga copper; *new* trade routes and markets to sell in and so on. This process of industrial change provides the ground swell that gives the general tone to business; while these things are being initiated we have brisk expenditure and predominating prosperity – interrupted, no doubt, by the negative phases of the shorter [business] cycles that are superimposed on that ground swell.[10]

The key to his analysis was the insight that innovation is not a regular process bringing steady incremental improvements but rather a discontinuous process that occurs in waves. He noted that:

> these revolutions are not strictly incessant; they occurred in discrete rushes that are separated from each other by spans of comparative quiet. The process as a whole works incessantly, however, in the sense that there is always either revolution or absorption of the results of revolution, both together forming what are known as business cycles.[11]

One reason technology changes in these waves, is because the prior technology system establishes firmly committed ways of doing things which are not easily disrupted. It takes the exhaustion of existing systems before institutions look to whole new approaches.

This process of technological change has two other critical characteristics that make it an important determinant of economic and social change. First, long waves are not a large collection of incremental improvements in the existing system. Rather, they are waves of radical innovations that disrupt the current production system. For example, the steam engine and the automatic spinning and weaving mill were not improvements on existing technology, but fundamentally new ones that reshaped British, and later European and American, economies in the first half of the nineteenth century. The microchip is a similarly radical and disruptive technology. It performs the same function as a vacuum tube, but in a fundamentally different way.

Second, these 'disruptive' technologies do not just emerge one or two at a time, but rather burst on the scene as an entire array that forms a mutually reinforcing technology system. The emergence of cheap steel in the 1880s transformed not just the steel industry, but also almost all manufacturing, since many industries could now take advantage of high-strength steel. These new technology systems periodically emerge and sweep through and transform the entire economic order.

This is not to say that innovation ceases after these revolutionary new technology systems emerge. Rather, it takes on a more incremental character, reinforcing and gradually improving, rather than disrupting the newly formed technology system. Thus, while hard drives, microprocessors, fiber optic cables, memory, and other devices will continue to get cheaper and more powerful, it is unlikely that any new disruptive technologies will gain wide acceptance during the next 20 years. Therefore, it is not necessarily the rise of individual industries or technologies that give rise to new economic periods. Rather, it is the rise of new technology systems, based on a concurrent rise in clusters of invention and innovation, that have the power to transform the production system both in terms of what things are made and how. This clustering of technically related systems of innovations not only leads to the rise of new industries, but also transforms existing ones.

In each period, a new key technology factor emerges, not 'as an isolated input, but rather at the core of a rapidly growing system of technical, social, and managerial innovations.'[12] Schumpeter goes on to state that the new 'techno-economic paradigm involves a new best-practice form of organization, a new skills profile in the labor force, a new product mix ... a new pattern in the location of investment ... a tendency for new innovator-entrepreneur-type small firms to enter the new rapidly expanding branches of the economy.'[13] Perez defines a techno-economic paradigm as 'a best-practice model made up of a set of all-pervasive generic technological and organization principles, which represent the most effective way of applying a particular technological revolution and of using it for modernizing and rejuvenating the whole of the economy.'[14]

Because these innovations create a web of interlocking products and firms producing them, they create secondary wave effects. Powerful new developments in a few core technologies have major ripple effects on a wide range of industries. British students of technological innovation, Christopher Freeman, John Clark, and Luc Soete stress 'the importance of the diffusion process and the way in which a series of further innovations are generated as a swarm of imitators move in to invest in a new technology, attracted by the exceptionally high profits achieved or anticipated by one or more of the pioneers.'[15]

One need look no further than the recent Internet and information technology investment boom to get a sense of this process. A core technology system (microelectronics, telecommunications, and Internet software protocols) led to a diffusion process whereby a worldwide swarm of tens of thousands of entrepreneurial firms in software, hardware, telecommunications, service providers and content providers emerged. As the last few years have so ably demonstrated, the results of such swarming are certainly not that all new entrants thrive. Indeed, a central factor of the early periods of the emergence of new systems is the overabundance of new entrants, as the 'animal spirits of capitalism' lead to a frenzied rush by many firms and entrepreneurs to take advantage of the new technology system. Many die and are left by the wayside, but the survivors thrive and drive the new wave of growth.

Such swarms of technology-led entrepreneurship built around new technology systems are not unique to the Internet age. They have occurred several times before in America's economic history. In the late 1860s about 10 percent of America's non-farm paid labor and 50 percent of the production of its capital goods industries were involved in railroad construction. Like the Internet, the railroad industry was a 'propulsive' industry that generated an economic boom, both through the investment wave it generated and the economic benefits railroads brought. In the late 1890s and early 1900s, during the next major economic transformation, the steel industry played a similar role. Again, in the early 1950s the technology systems of chemical processing, electronics and mass production powered an economic boom, with consumer goods industries like automobiles and appliances propelling the economy to new heights.

It is characteristic of these technology waves that rapid and dramatic reductions in cost and improvements in quality propel their widespread diffusion throughout the entire economy. Applied to today's technology revolution, this process is referred to as Moore's law. Named after Intel founder Gordon Moore, it refers to the prediction Moore made in the early 1970s that the cost of computing power would decline by half every two years while the power would double.

Yet, every major new technology system has undergone rapid and dramatic price decline/quality improvements. For example, in 1817 freight moved from Buffalo to New York via wagon at a cost of 20 cents per ton mile. By the 1850s freight on railroads cost less than 1 cent per ton mile.[16] In the late 1800s, lower steel costs created benefits that rippled throughout the economy, including lower rail transport costs, steel buildings, and machine-tool based industries.[17] For a time Moore's law reigned supreme in the telegraph industry. In 1872 Joseph B. Sterns invented a telegraphic duplex that made it possible to transmit two messages simultaneously over a single wire, doubling its capacity. A few years later, a young engineer working for Western Union, named Thomas Edison, invented the quadruplex, which let four messages be transmitted at once, two in each direction.[18] But we should be clear, it is not just falling price that leads to propulsive, transformation technology system. Indeed, as economist Brad Delong has pointed out 'The real price of light fell by a thousandfold over the past two centuries, yet we do not speak of the "illumination revolution," or of a "new economy" based on streetlights and fluorescent office and store lights.'[19] For a technology to be system transforming it has to form the core of a broader array of technologies, products and processes.

THE PROCESS OF TRANSFORMATION AND CONSOLIDATION

If technology is the skeleton upon which an economy is formed, and if that technological skeleton changes in waves every half century or so, then this suggests that the economy transforms from one type of economy to another, and that these changes are not steady, but rather are intensely clustered in particular periods. In fact, it is not just the economy that transforms, it is the whole of society – politics, social relations, how and where we live, how we organize our education system, and how our culture shapes our beliefs and attitudes. This is because, as Perez points out, 'the logic of a [techno-economic] paradigm reaches well beyond the economic sphere to become the general and shared organizational common sense of the period.'[20]

Just as Thomas Kuhn talked about the emergence of paradigms in science, we can speak of paradigms in the economy and society. Christopher Freeman describes the emergence of new techno-economic paradigms as a 'combination of interrelated product and process, technical, organizational and managerial innovations, embodying a quantum leap in potential productivity in all or most of the economy and opening up an unusually wide range of investment opportunities.'[21] When these technology systems, and their accompanying social, organizational and managerial innovations, develop momentum they lead to the development of whole new economic systems.

Thus, in each period of American history, a new key technological factor has emerged at the core of a new system of technological, organizational, and social innovations. As we will describe below, the 'techno-economic paradigm' involves not just new technologies, but also new products, new and better forms of economic organization and managerial practices (in the private and public sectors), the dominance of new sets of skills in the labor force, and even dramatic changes in where and how we live.[22] But this is not a period of permanent revolution, to use Leon Trotsky's term. These transformations ebb and flow, as transformation occurs, only to be followed by a period of consolidation and then exhaustion.

When a new technology system begins to transform the economy, an increasing share of people and institutions recognize the disconnection between it and current practices, organizational forms and attitudes, and a growing number of people struggle to adapt these to the emerging new economy. However, as the new techno-economic system becomes a current system, most people take it for granted and come to see the system as the natural order of things. The 'new economy' then is no longer the 'new' economy, but rather 'the' economy.

It is at this point that the danger of complacency sets in. For example, in the 1960s, during the heyday of the corporate, mass production economy, most economists expected the economy to continue along the path it was on, in spite of the fact that the old techno-economic system was about to reach the end of its limits. Because economists, political scientists, and even futurists, were caught in the forest of the old system, they could not foresee that it would break down due to internal contradictions and exhaustion of the technology system, and that a new one would eventually emerge to take its place. As a result, they wrongly extrapolated into the future the trends of the current system. They could just not conceive that the managerial, large corporate, 'mixed' economy of the time would not continue to get bigger and even more extensive. For example, writing in 1977, liberal economist Robert Heilbroner stated, 'the surrender of society to the free play of market forces is now on the wane. The pressures in the future will be toward a society marked by a much greater degree of organization and deliberate control.'[23] As a description of the mass production economy with its growth in large corporations, unions, and government, this was accurate. However, Heilbroner failed to see that most of what the economy and society had been built on was about to collapse.

Liberal economists were not the only ones to extrapolate the current trends. In his 1967 book *The Year 2000*, Herman Kahn extrapolated from the current increase in the role of the federal government in funding technology and predicted that by 2000, 'business firms would no longer be the major source of innovation, and the market would play a diminished role compared to public sector and social accounts.'[24] In actuality, private sector R&D grew 4.5 times faster than federally supported R&D over that period so that corporate-funded R&D is now twice as much as government.

These observations are not meant as criticisms of Heilbroner, Kahn or other forecasters of the period. After all, as Mark Twain pointed out, 'Prophesy is a good line of business, but it is full of risks.'[25] Rather it is to show that while prediction may not be too risky during periods of stability, it is extremely risky during periods when the economy is shifting from one kind of system to another. Few of the assumptions about how the economy and society work apply in the next economy. That is why virtually all the futurists of the 1960s and early 1970s got it wrong. They did not expect that the innovations of the 1940s and 1950s would have reached their limits by the early 1970s. Nor did they predict that a whole new techno-economic system would emerge.

New economic systems do not just easily and quickly pop into place with the old system going gently into the night. New technology systems take time to mature and diffuse, and the resulting institutional, political and personal transformations left in their wake take even longer. Before a new economic system can take the place of an old one, there has to be a transitional period during which the old system loses its propulsive force and progressive energy. The technology system becomes 'played out' and it becomes increasingly difficult to wring advances and innovations from it, since most have already been figured out. Yet, during the transitional period the new economy technology system has not yet gained the critical mass needed to generate robust growth; it is too small, expensive, and weak, just as computers and telecommunications were in the 1980s.

Moreover, in each transition period there is a lag between the speed of technological transformation and the corresponding institutional,

cultural, political, societal, and individual transformatio
engineers, and entrepreneurs are often driven to change
through rapid development of new technologies and deve
new business models. The rest of society takes longer to
being committed to old ways of doing things, old investm...ns, old
skills, old institutional arrangements, and old attitudes. As a result,
during the periods when a new techno-economic system is emerging,
organizations, institutions, laws, governments, the built environment,
and attitudes and culture lag behind. But some do not just passively
wait, many actively resist the change as it threatens entrenched ways of
doing and established economic positions. Moreover, old economy
stakeholders, whether in business and government or as consumers and
workers, usually have more power than innovators. That is one reason
these periods of transformation generally take between 15 and 20 years,
during which time economic growth usually stagnates. That is also why
these transitional periods bring forth strong debates and arguments
about the future and what kind of society is desirable. Usually these
debates are between those who view the new order with fear and
trepidation and seek to hold onto an idyllic past, and those who
embrace the changes and promote the future. Today's debates about
globalization, technology and the New Economy are no different in
their flavor or motivations. Thus, as described in Chapter 6, the critical
task of our time is to modernize these systems to match the
requirements of the new knowledge economy.

During the new economy periods of consolidation, all aspects of the
system are generally in synch. As Harvard social scientist Daniel Bell
stated, 'Societies have tended to function reasonably when there is a
congruence of scale among economic activities, social organization,
and political and administrative control units.'[26] However, as transition
periods begin there is an increasing mismatch between the new techno-
economic system and the old institutional framework. The institutions,
rules, skills, attitudes, and physical environment that had been created
to match the former techno-economic system no longer fit the new one.
Freeman notes that as the new technology system emerges it produces
'major structural crises of adjustment, in which social and economic
changes are necessary to bring about a better match between the new
technology and the system of social management of the economy.'[27]

This is what happened from 1974 to 1993. The economy underwent a
major slowdown, with productivity growth declining from about 3
percent per year that it sustained from 1947 to 1974 to about 1.2

percent a year. The stock market and wages stagnated, as inflation and unemployment increased. Many regions underwent painful economic decline and restructuring as established industries and occupations either declined or faced increased competitive threats from overseas.

Just as most economists during the 1930s were baffled by the causes of the Depression, conventional neoclassical economists struggled to come up with an explanation for this unexpected long-term slowdown. They constructed elaborate models to figure out what went wrong, but made little progress. This is because the causes, in the words of student of technological innovation Nathan Rosenberg, were inside the 'black box' of organizational and technology systems and, therefore, outside the scope of conventional economic analysis.[28]

A perspective grounded in long technology cycles suggests that the 20-year stagnation period was due to an exhaustion of the techno-economic system that emerged after World War II: the managerial, national economy with big corporations, big government and big labor, and mass market acceptance of consumer-oriented industries like automobiles and appliances. Powering these was an electro-mechanical and chemical technology system that boosted productivity in both manufacturing and many service sectors. By the 1970s these propulsive industries and their underlying technology systems had run their course. Growth in demand for the products had slowed as the market was saturated and innovation stagnated. For example, patents issued fell from a high of 78 000 in 1971 to 48 000 in 1979 and did not exceed the 1971 levels until 1987 (see Figure 2.2 below).[29] Eking out further productivity gains from the electro-mechanical production system proved difficult, as the technologies had been taken as far as they could go, particularly in the 75 percent of the economy not involved in goods production. Big, inflexible institutions were increasingly unable to cope with the new realities of a diverse and volatile market environment.

While the old economy was reaching its limits, there was no 'new economy' to replace it. Microchips, computing, the Internet and telecommunications were still too costly, slow, and limited to drive a revolution. It is easy now to forget how feeble these technologies were as late as the late 1980s. For example, desktop computer processing speed in 1990 was only about 25 MHZ, compared to over 3200 MHz today. It was only by the mid-1990s, when these technologies coalesced into a powerful and networked information technology and telecommunications system, that the New Economy began to emerge.[30]

PERIODS IN AMERICAN ECONOMIC HISTORY

Given that the history and future of the economy can be understood as undergoing fundamental structural revolutions approximately every 50 years, and that these revolutions are powered by technological innovation, it is appropriate to examine history through this lens. As one economic historian noted when describing the new economy of the 1890s, 'The economy did not merely become a magnified version of its mid-century self ... [it] was a vastly different institution than that which existed at the time of Civil War.'[31]

While most economists do not admit the existence of longer periods of transformation, business and economic historians are more likely to classify economic history into periods. If we take the Schumpeterian view that economies undergo periodic technology-driven transformations, then it is possible to categorize the economic history of the last 150 years into distinct periods. One historian who did this was Alfred Chandler, who saw three distinct phases in American economic history: the colonial period to 1840, the mercantile period until 1880 and the industrial period from 1880 to 1920.[32]

However, many who recognize the notion of economic periods simply assume that there was the agricultural era, the industrial revolution of the 1890s and now the New Economy of the 1990s. A common view is that the rapid changes we are experiencing today have not been seen since the days of the industrial revolution. Futurist Alvin Toffler perhaps best popularized this view. According to Toffler, the world's economy has gone through two great transformations: from agricultural to industrial in the early 1800s, and now the 'third wave' powered by the IT revolution.[33] Toffler talks about the Meiji reformers winning in Japan as the triumph of the second-wave modernizers over the first-wave traditionalists. The Civil War represented the battle between the first and second waves forces in the United States.

However seductive such a view is as we experience dazzling new technological innovations, it is vastly oversimplistic. First, Toffler and others misread history to conclude that there was only one industrial revolution. Clearly, the 'pre-industrial' mercantile economies of seventeenth-century Europe were quite different from the more rural economies of the early part of the second millennium. The shift from an agricultural to an industrial society did not occur over a short period of time; it took hundreds of years, from at least the 1200s to the 1800s.

Moreover, today's economic transformation in no way compares with the magnitude of the shift from agricultural societies to industrial, with the concomitant dramatic shifts from rural to urban life, and shifts in ownership and technology. Today's shift is much more in keeping with the kinds of transformations the United States has experienced every 50 or so years. In fact, as Table 2.1 shows, there have been four distinct economic periods in the last 150 years: mercantile/craft, 1840s to 1890s; factory-based industrial, 1890s to 1940s; corporate mass production, 1940s to 1990s; and the new entrepreneurial, knowledge-based economy, from 1990s to sometime into the future. As we will see, each era brought with it a new economic vitality, new kinds of industries and jobs, new kinds of business and work organization, a new spatial organization of production, a new kind of public governance and politics, and even a new kind of popular culture.

Table 2.1   Periods in American economic history

Period	Years
Mercantile/craft	1840s to 1890s
Factory-based industrial	1890s to 1940s
Corporate mass production	1940s to 1990s
Entrepreneurial, knowledge based	1990s to –

In each of the four periods, economic growth flourished in the early and middle part of the period, and as the economic, technological, and organizational drivers lost steam at the end of the period, growth slowed. At the beginning and middle of the eras, the economy enjoyed a 'long boom.' Schumpeter described the results of booms: 'Now the results each time consist of an avalanche of consumer goods that permanently deepens and widens the stream of real income although in the first instance they spell disturbance, losses and unemployment.'[34] For example, the industrial revolution of the 1840s led to an economic boom that lasted until after the Civil War. But during the period between the depression from 1873 to 1878 and the recessions of the early 1890s, the economy struggled with relatively slow growth and frequent downturns. As factory-based industrialization and mechanization finally emerged and became widespread, the economy boomed from the late 1890s until 1929.

The Great Depression cut short the Roaring Twenties, and it was not until the late 1940s that per capita incomes recovered to their pre-Depression levels. However, as the new economy of the 1950s emerged, driven by large corporations and mass production consumer industries, a boom led to the incredible prosperity of the 'golden era' 1950s and 1960s. The title of a 1953 *Fortune* magazine article said it all, 'Productivity: The Great Age of 3 Percent.' Indeed, during the 1960s the average household's real income increased almost one-third.

Once more though, as that period's new economy exhausted its growth possibilities, a long period of economic slowdown transpired from the mid-1970s to the mid-1990s. Because policymakers knew so much more about managing the business cycle, and because a host of 'Keynesian' fiscal policies were in place (such as unemployment insurance and a progressive tax system), the transition did not result in a depression, as it had in the earlier periods. But still growth slowed significantly, with productivity and per capita income growth slowing to about a third of their rate in the postwar boom period, while unemployment increased. However, as had happened at least three times before in American economic history, a new economy powered by the new technology system emerged and began to ratchet up growth rates. Since 1996, productivity growth has been more than double that of the prior two decades. In 2001, a year of economic slowdown, when historically productivity growth falls off sharply, productivity actually grew 1.9 percent. In 2003, annual productivity growth was a robust 4.2 percent, almost four times as fast as the 1974 to 1994 rate.

Figure 2.1 illustrates how productivity growth changes during periods of transformation and consolidation. During the transformation from the factory economy to the corporate, mass production economy productivity dipped to almost 1 percent, while steadily increasing during the new post-war economy. Again, during the transformation from the corporate economy to the entrepreneurial, knowledge-based economy, productivity again fell as the old economy's technology system had reached its limits. With the rise of the new IT-based technology system, productivity has rebounded to the kind of levels seen at the peak of the old economy.

A key component of these rebounds is the emergence of powerful new general purpose technologies that provide the platform for new industrial processes and products. Indeed, each of the boom periods has been powered by a core technology system and the propulsive industries that use it. At the time, these technologies and industries seem larger than life, capturing the excitement of the entire society. In the boom period of the mercantile period 1840 to 1973, the railroad was at the center of the national imagination. As one economic historian described it, 'Stories about railroad projects, railroad accidents, and railroad speed filled the press, the fascinating subject was taken up in songs, political speeches, and magazine articles.'[35] In 1880, sociologist Charles Fraser stated, 'an agent is at hand to bring everything into harmonious cooperation, triumphing over space and time, to subdue prejudice and unite every part of our land in rapid and friendly communication ... and that great motive agent is steam.'[36] The rhetoric of the late 1990s was not too different. One enthusiast expounded that: 'The expansion into cyberspace now underway parallels the expansion of European civilization into North and.South America that followed Columbus's discoveries, exactly 498 years before Tim Berners-Lee discovered, or rather invented, the Web.'[37] Another marveled, 'The Internet should be as important as the invention of cities ... The arrival of the network economy, the gurus say, should be like the transition from an agricultural economy to an industrial one.'[38]

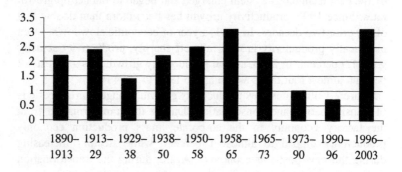

Source: Brenner (1998) p. 4.

Figure 2.1 Annual percentage change in GDP per hour worked

Each era also brought with it the rise of new fast-growth industries that either produced the new technologies or used them. In the mercantile economy textiles and woolen goods and a wide range of iron goods, including the railroad, took off. In the factory-based industrial era, the core industry was steel, with many rapidly growing industries in producer-oriented steel-using industries, such as mechanical reapers, machine tools, and transcontinental railroads. With the rise of the postwar corporate economy, the propulsive industries were based on the new petrochemical, electrical and mass production technologies, cranking out a dizzying array of consumer goods, from cars to toasters, to televisions. Of course, the core technology of our New Economy is information technology, with robust growth in computer, software, Internet, and telecommunications industries.

One of the reasons economic periods eventually lag and transform to new economies is that the existing technology systems mature and eventually exhaust their propulsive potential. For example, in the early stage of the corporate, mass production economy from 1953 to 1959 36 percent of major US innovations were considered radical breakthroughs while 60 percent were considered improvements or imitations. However, later in this economic era from 1967 to 1973, only 16 percent of the innovations were radical, while 60 percent were incremental or imitations.[39] This is one reason why innovation appears to go in cycles. Figure 2.2 provides one indicator of this cyclical process of innovation. Patenting dipped during each transition period, from the mercantile/craft economy to the factory economy, at the end of transition period to the mass production, corporate economy in the 1930s, and again from the 1970s to mid-1990s.

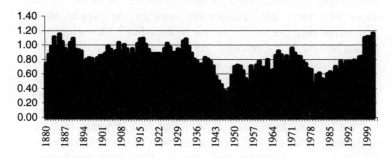

Source: US Patent Office.

Figure 2.2 Patents per 1000 workers: 1880 to 2001

Because the available system of production technology enables and shapes the dominant form of business organization, it should be no surprise that each economic period brings with it a new form of business organization. During the mercantile/craft period, most firms were small, run by individuals or family members and had modest levels of capitalization. Until the 1890s, Dupont Chemical, for example, was a small regional gunpowder firm owned entirely by the Dupont family. Often formed by combining many smaller family-run enterprises into one large corporation controlled by a dominant personality, the subsequent factory era saw the rise of the corporation in its legal form. By 1900 Dupont had become a national, and even international company, issuing stock and expanding into a wide range of chemical products. The experiences of companies like Swift, Ford, Standard Oil, and others all fit this pattern. However, unlike the kinds of corporations that were to dominate the post-World War II era, these firms were generally run by founders employing a small corporate headquarters staff. Moreover, most manufacturing firms, and almost all service firms, remained small and family owned. With the rise of the postwar economy the large, multidivisional, managerially controlled corporation became the dominant business form. In fact, a major change from the 1920s to the 1950s was the shift in control of corporations from owners to managers, what some termed the rise of 'managerial capitalism'. The emergence of the New Economy in the 1990s has seen several changes in business organization, including the shift of control from managers to shareholders and the rise of entrepreneurial, fast-growing small and mid-size companies. Clearly corporations still dominate the economy, but the rise of the shareholder value movement has dramatically reduced the former scope of managerial prerogative (Enron not withstanding). Moreover, even the largest of today's corporations seek to organize themselves so they are decentralized, entrepreneurial and fast moving.

Each new economic era produces also new kinds of business and labor organizations. In the industrial economy, the fastest growing and dominant business organizations were the US Chamber of Commerce and the National Association of Manufacturers. However, with the rise of the large 'Fortune 500' corporations who sought to make peace with the labor unions, and what Harvard economist John Kenneth Galbraith called the 'new industrial state,' business organizations like the National Planning Association and the Corporation for Economic Development emerged as the leading voices of business. As John Judis documents, these 'peak-associations' declined in influence and power during the transitional period of the 1970s to the early 1990s.[40] In the entrepreneurial New Economy the dominant form of business organization has become the specialized trade association lobbying for narrow and short-term advantage.

The rise of each new economic era also changes the dominant skills and occupations. During the mercantile/craft period, over half of Americans worked on the farm, and of those who were in production, virtually all were craftsmen. The industrial era saw the rise of the unskilled blue-collar factory worker. The workers employed in Ford's River Rouge plant, seen standing in long rows all doing the same repetitive task, became the prototypical worker. Charlie Chaplin's movie, *Modern Times*, memorialized this kind of job and it became etched into the American imagination, so much so that its image in the popular culture as the prototypical job has only recently given way to a new reality of office jobs. With the rise of the corporate mass production economy, the prototypical job became the white-collar paper-pushers with their in-boxes on desks arrayed in row after row. In today's New Economy, the prototypical worker is the higher skilled 'knowledge worker', working in a cubicle in a suburban office park.

In each new period, the rapid growth of new industries with new skill requirements creates skill shortages. Because technology changes faster than people's skills, new occupations expand faster than supply. In the transition to the factory economy, unskilled workers to man the machines were not in short supply, rather clerks to take the orders and keep the books were. During the first decade of the twentieth century, the number of clerical workers grew 127 percent, the fastest rate of growth of any decade since. As the managerial corporation became dominant during the 1950s, corporate America struggled to find qualified college-educated white-collar managers to fill the rapidly growing middle ranks of accountants, salespeople, human resources specialists, and other white-collar workers. It was only the fact that the GI Bill of Rights gave millions of returning American servicemen the ability to go to college that the supply was able to stay close to the demand. In the 1990s, the rise of today's IT-driven economy created a similar shortage of workers with the skills to work in the expanding information technology field. This is one of the main reasons why the nation turned to foreign immigrants under the H1-B visa program to fill these positions. However, if history is a guide, these shortages will be temporary, as the labor market responds to the new conditions.

As the underlying production system transforms and new skills are needed, the education system also undergoes transformation. Indeed, each economic period has led to significant hand wringing over the state of the education system, followed by calls for far reaching education reform. As the mercantile economy emerged in the 1840s, the movement for compulsory elementary schooling, led by Horace Mann, took hold. In 1852 Massachusetts became the first state to pass a law requiring mandatory attendance for children between the ages of eight and fourteen for at least three months a year. As the factory economy emerged in the 1890s, school reform again emerged with the focus on extending mass schooling through high school.[41] Moreover, schools began to be modeled on the modern factory.[42] The transformation to the corporate economy in the 1950s brought yet another transformation, as a greater share of schools now focused on preparing students for college and for social adjustment to the mass society. The threat of Sputnik also spurred change, leading Congress in 1958 to pass the National Defense Education Act (NDEA) that appropriated federal funds to improve instruction in those areas considered crucial to national defense and security. Federal financial involvement was expanded still further with the passage of the Elementary and Secondary Education Act (ESEA) of 1965. As the corporate economy began to fall apart in the late 1970s and shift to a more knowledge-based economy, calls for reform were once again heard. Perhaps most notable was the issuance in 1983 of the report *A Nation At Risk* issued by the National Commission on Excellence in Education that stated American education was in crisis and recommended that education focus on basics and establish standards. With the passage of the '3R's' legislation in 2002, federal funding was used to hold schools accountable for meeting quantitative standards of learning. Moreover, a wide array of alternatives to traditional public schools have emerged including magnet schools, charter schools, and increased home schooling.

Each new period also brings with it new organizational forms for workers. In the mercantile era, unions were largely non-existent. However, in the transitional period of the 1880s, through the efforts of union organizers such as Terrance Powderly and others, workers tried to organize unions, most notably the Knights of Labor. It was not until the emergence of the industrial economy in the 1890s that the first real unions emerged, organized along craft lines (e.g., barrel-makers, horse-shoers, plumbers). Formed in 1886 and led by Samuel Gompers, the American Federation of Labor had over 275 000 members by 1893. As the large mass production corporation expanded in the 1930s, unions began to organize more along industrial lines. Led first by John L. Lewis, head of the United Mine Workers, and aided by leaders like the Reuther brothers of the United Auto Workers, these labor leaders formed their own union, the Congress of Industrial Organizations. In 1935 the joined-up AFL-CIO set the stage for large industrial unions, matching the large corporations of the postwar economic era. During the transitional period between the corporate mass production economy and the entrepreneurial knowledge economy, union membership declined significantly. It is unclear whether unions can revive themselves and find a vital role in the New Economy. If there is a role, new models of unionism emerging in places like Silicon Valley that focus on organizing workers by occupation and providing them with services such as training and health-care policies, may point the way.[43]

As new industries and occupations emerge, the composition and relationship between social classes also change. During the mercantile /craft economy, the largest social group was the farming class (free landholders in the North and slaves in the South). With the rise of the industrial economy, the blue-collar working class became the largest and most significant group. With the emergence of the corporate economy in the 1950s, the new suburban middle class became the modal class in America. In today's New Economy, the modal class is perhaps the newly rising knowledge worker, what political commentator David Brooks calls 'bourgeois bohemians.'[44]

The rise of different social and occupational groupings reshapes the politics of each period. In the mercantile period politics was divided between Southern agricultural interests and Northern urban craft and trading interests. With the rise of the industrial era, the central political conflict was between owners and workers, who Marx termed capitalists and proletarians. Not surprisingly, this was the only time in our history that a viable socialist party emerged when Eugene Debs, candidate of the Socialist Party of America, won almost 1 million votes for President in 1920. In the postwar corporate economy, the key political battleground was between big corporations with their ties to the Republican party on one side, and big unions with their ties to the Democratic party on the other. With such a division, it was no surprise that Democrats dominated the postwar political landscape. With the decline of unions and the rise of a new class of 'wired workers' without the same animus toward the corporation and the wealthy, the traditional Democratic lock on 'working Americans' has diminished. Likewise, the concurrent rise of a class of New Economy entrepreneurs with a more tolerant social outlook who do not reflexively vote Republican means that these old divisions have become less relevant.

Just as the prevailing technological and economic system shapes the institutional system of an era, so too does it shape the policies and governing philosophy. Organizations, whether public or private, are attuned to the technological, social, and organizational environment and so resemble each other in any era. As technology and society changes, so too does government change to reflect the underlying social structure. As Gordon Brown, the UK Chancellor of the Exchequer, puts it, 'in each decade the relationship between individuals, markets, and communities will evolve as technology and rising expectations challenge each generation's vision of what is possible and best.'[45] As a result, each phase of economic development has produced a new organizational paradigm, in the corporate world and in government.

In the heydays of each of the major periods there has been a dominant governing approach and system that shapes how government works and how political parties express their aspirations. However, as old economies lose steam and begin to fall apart, so do political governing philosophies. While making sense during the economy's boom period, they fail to produce results during the transition period. At this point the minority party usually rejects the old governing model and forges a new one, more suited to the new economic and institutional realities, and in so doing, becomes the majority party. Over time, both parties coalesce around the new governing philosophy until such time as the economic system once again is transformed.

Indeed, given the limitations in transportation, communication and information processing in the mid-1800s, it would have been difficult to forge a New Deal-type governance system then. How would the federal government exert its will on businesses in far-flung states like California and Washington when it took weeks to get there and the Pony Express was the best communication? The creation of a strong federal government to tie the nation together and offset growing corporate power required the rise of new technologies (e.g., telephones and typewriters) and organizational forms (e.g., managerialism). Conversely, the rise of the corporate national economy required the development of the managerial state. As a result, in spite of conservative opposition to the New Deal in the 1930s and 1940s, there was really no viable alternative governance system to manage the large, corporate mass production economy of the time. As one historian noted, 'The government's evolution toward enhanced social control through bureaucratic means only paralleled, albeit with a considerable lag, the evolution of corporations.'[46] The organization of government is not simply the result of citizens' wishes, interest group pressures, or even Presidential intentions, but rather, a reflection of the organizational, technological, and social factors in the broader society.

Each period also brings with it new forms of urbanization. Indeed, one would expect such transformations since urbanized areas have always been organized to maximize economic efficiency, and as a result are a reflection of the dominant mode of production. The growth of the manufacturing economy led to the rapid ride of urbanization, predominantly in the Northeast and Great Lakes regions. The postwar mass production economy brought about the rise of the automobile-based residential suburb and the rise of dominant national metropolitan areas (e.g., New York, Chicago, Los Angeles), but also secondary metros in other parts of the nation (e.g., Dallas, Atlanta, Denver). The New Economy has once again reordered urban form, creating edge-cities and exurban suburban sprawl, as well as booming mid-size metropolitan areas (e.g., Austin, Raleigh-Durham, Seattle).

Each period also differs in the spatial locus of the economy. In each transitional phase, the economy expanded its geographic scope. The mercantile economy was essentially a local economy, with most production and consumption taking place in areas relatively limited in geographic scope. However, as the factory economy spread, partly enabled by the railroad, economic regions expanded, but the nation was still composed of distinct and somewhat isolated regional economies. Particularly noticeable were differences between the agricultural and resource-based economies of the South and West and the manufacturing economy of the East coast and Midwest. With the emergence of the corporate mass production economy in the 1950s and the rise of air travel and the interstate highway system, the economy became tied together into a national economic system. Companies bought and sold from suppliers and customers throughout the nation. Factories and offices that were once concentrated in the Midwest and Northeast began to migrate to the lower cost South and West. Today's information technology driven economy, facilitated by advances in global shipping and logistics and telecommunications, means that many companies can locate almost anywhere and serve customers throughout the globe. The recent rise of offshored services to places like India and Eastern Europe, is just the latest manifestation of how new economies change the spatial locus of economies.[47]

Finally, each period brings about a transformation in culture with a more open and permissive culture emerging during periods of growth.

For example, in the early twentieth century the auto, radio and motion pictures all broke down rural isolation. Not surprisingly, it was during this time that the first major attack on traditional puritan cultural values came from a group of young intellectuals at Harvard. A similar but more far-reaching cultural homogenization was to happen again after the emergence of the corporate, mass production economy. Television and pop music created a national culture where standards were set by national forces, not the local community. For the first time someone in a small town was getting the same news and cultural entertainment as someone in a major metropolis. Now with the rise of the Internet and global telecommunications, a similar phenomenon is happening again, although on a global scale. Tom Friedman's *The Lexus and the Olive Tree* details how foreign nations are immersed in American culture and, in the case of Muslim fundamentalists, are often reacting violently against what they see as a threat to their way of being.

As with Muslim fundamentalism, while new cultural modes emerge during periods of growth, a backlash tends to develop during transitional periods. For example, in the 1890s, in the face of a new industrial society that was more cosmopolitan, vibrant, and sexually oriented, small-town America reacted and formed the nucleus of what became the temperance movement. Nixon's silent majority reacted against the free-thinking, counter-culture movement of the 1960s. The Christian right has responded to this period's more permissive culture with a similar moral outrage and attempts to resurrect a simpler and more understandable past. However, as new economies mature and the changes are seen as inevitable, such movements lose much of their moral and political force, and are relegated to the political sidelines. Whether today's Christian right will lose their current political potency remains to be seen.

In order to understand how these technological, organizational, political and social forces evolve, it is worth examining the two major economic eras before today's New Economy. It is to the emergence of the factory-based industrial economy that we now turn.

NOTES

1. Quoted in Plant (2001).
2. Quoted in Heilbroner (1996) p. 54.
3. Heilbroner (1996) p. 63.

4. Ibid. p. 59.
5. Samuelson (2002).
6. Kondratieff (1935).
7. Schumpeter (1975) pp. 82-3.
8. Schumpeter (1975) p. 83.
9. Ibid. p. 67.
10. Ibid. p. 68.
11. Ibid. p. 83.
12. Freeman (1982) p. 48.
13. Ibid. p. 21.
14. Perez (2003) p. 14.
15. Freeman (1982).
16. Ibid. p. 33.
17. By the 1890s the cost of rails was one-tenth their cost two decades prior. This helped push rail transportation costs down 40 percent.
18. John (1998).
19. Summers and DeLong (2002).
20. Perez (2003) p. 16.
21. Freeman and Perez (1988) p. 47.
22. As urban historian John Borchert (1967, p. 18) states, 'the pattern of urbanization in this country has not been a smooth evolution to the conditions of the present, but has been marked by major transformations from one kind of city to another.'
23. Heilbroner (1977).
24. Kahn (1967).
25. Twain (1897) p. 44.
26. Bell (1976) p. 42.
27. Freeman and Perez (1988) p. 47.
28. Rosenberg (1983).
29. US Patent and Trademark Office (2002).
30. Technology often runs its course and must wait for new innovations. The mercantile/craft economy that emerged in the 1830s powered a new era of growth, but by the 1870s it had largely run its course. As a result, between the 1870s and the mid to late 1890s, the American economy underwent several major depressions combined with rapid urbanization and social hardships.
31. Gray and Peterson (1974) p. 312.
32. Chandler (1977).
33. Toffler (1980).
34. Schumpeter (1975) p. 68.
35. Heilbroner (1996) p. 52.
36. Bar (2000).
37. Goldhaber (1997).
38. Maney (1998) p. 1E.
39. Haustein and Maier (1980).
40. Judis (2000).
41. By 1880 there were 800 high schools in the United States and 2500 by 1890.
42. Elwood Cubberly, a turn-of-the-century historian, stated that schools should be like factories with teachers as factory workers and students as raw material.
43. Herzenberg et al. (1998a).
44. Brooks (2001).
45. Brown (2003).
46. Graham (1976) p. 80.
47. Atkinson (2004a).

3. Economic Transformations from the 1840s to the 1990s

As new technology systems emerge, they lead to profound changes in how economies, and indeed societies, are organized. This happened during the mercantile/craft economy from the 1840s to the 1890s, as the steam engine powered by coal and made of iron transformed a wide range of manufacturing processes, from glass-making to printing. The discovery of anthracite coal in Pennsylvania in the 1830s and 1840s fostered the iron industry and steam production. The development of a commercial legal code facilitated the growth of commerce. The emergence of the telegraph as a means of long-distance communication helped link together an expanding nation. The building of regional railroads transformed transportation. Yet, with the exception of the railroads and some textile mills, most firms were single establishments run by their owners that could utilize innovations with relatively little capital. Thus, up until after Civil War the economy was dominated by small, craft-based enterprises using the new technologies to produce largely for regional markets. This was an economy that was still largely agrarian, with the leading industries principally involved in clothing, food, and shelter.[1]

Until the Civil War, much of America's manufactured output was made by hand and much of that in the home – craftspeople making shoes, quilts, and furniture. Coopers, silversmiths and blacksmiths, carriage-makers and cabinet-makers, cobblers and tailors were ubiquitous in 1860. With the exception of a few goods, most notably cloth, the factory system – the idea that goods were made in factories with scores of workers under supervision – was still not the norm. However, just as the seeds of today's Internet economy were sown in the 1960s and 1970s through the Defense Department's work on computers, software, and networks, so too were the seeds of the manufacturing era sown, in part by government, during the Civil War. The demands of an all-out war fought on increasingly modern terms led to a significant increase in industrial production and new innovations. But it was to take at least two more decades for these and other seeds to mature into the beginnings of the factory-based industrial era.

In the intervening period, the nation stumbled from one economic downturn to another. The period between the early 1870s and the mid-1890s was fraught with deep economic downturns. For those living at the time, it must have seemed that the American economy was taking two steps forward, only to fall back one step. From 1873 to 1878, the nation underwent the severest depression in its young history. But this was not the end. Four years later it was again plunged into depression, this time lasting until 1885, with yet one more final downturn lasting from 1893 to 1897, brought on in part from overinvestment in railroads and tracks. Overall, unemployment exceeded 10 percent during five years in the 1870s and six years of the 1890s. It was not until the full-fledged emergence of the factory-based industrial economy toward the end of the 1890s that growth took off once again.

THE FACTORY-BASED INDUSTRIAL ECONOMY: THE EARLY 1890S TO THE EARLY 1940S

This long difficult period was not due any particular failure in public policy, although it is perhaps no coincidence that the era is noted for its lackluster Presidents. Rather, the new industrial system was still too nascent to power a new economy, while the old system had exhausted its potential. When the pieces finally began to fit in place in the late 1890s, the economy once again fired on all cylinders. By then, not only were the key technologies inexpensive enough and ubiquitous enough, but the industrial-era corporation capable of assembling the capital (financial and human) needed to take the technologies to scale came fully onto the scene. The result was that from these traumatic, transitional two decades came a fully-formed regionally based factory economy that would lead the nation to unparalleled prosperity and, eventually, world supremacy.

The Technology System

Metals and machines – 'the mechanical arts' – were this economy's technological engine. Most of the major new processes and products of the era (e.g., steel processing, mechanical reapers, machine tools, mechanical mining drills, and transcontinental railroads) were based on breakthroughs in metallurgy and the ability to shape and mold metal to tolerances and qualities unknown in the past. Just as the Internet provides the common technology platform on which a growing share of economic activity is based today, this period's core technology system was steel. Hardened steel enabled machine tools to cut metal parts to low tolerances, which boosted the use of interchangeable parts. That in turn enabled the development of assembly line production. Just like Moore's law relating to today's computing power, steel enjoyed rapid declines in price and improvements in quality, in part because of the introduction of the Bessemer converter in the mid-1870s. In 1873, steel was selling for $100 a ton. By 1885 it had fallen to $20 per ton, and by the mid-1890s it was down to $12.[2] This is why books on the American economy written as late as 1957 would usually begin with a chapter on the iron and steel industry, since 'they serve a vital position ... in civilization.'[3]

The rapid decline in the prices and the dramatic improvements in quality (e.g., hardness, resistance to corrosion) meant that steel could be economically useful in a host of new applications. Between 1870 and the early 1900s, steel overtook iron in production, rising from virtually no production in 1870 to almost 40 million tons in 1915. These developments were at the heart of the mechanical revolution, with cheap steel underpinning the development of automobiles, bicycles, sewing machines, typewriters, machine tools of every description, reapers, steel girder-based skyscrapers, elevators, and a host of other innovations.

Take steel's role in the transformation of railroading, what used to be known in the prior era as the 'iron horse.' In the prior economy railroads had grown, but limitations in metallurgy and machining meant that they were slower, smaller and less powerful. Cheap steel made more durable tracks, more powerful locomotives, and better brakes all possible. New steel technology enabled coal cars to carry up to 100 tons by 1920, up from 10 tons in 1870. Organizational changes complemented technological ones. In 1871, 23 different track gauges were in use. By 1886 the nation enjoyed just one. And by 1900 a national railroad network was in place in virtually every state. Rail miles grew from about 32 000 in 1860 to about 180 000 in the mid-1890s. Such a rail network was critical to the support of a factory-based manufacturing economy. Factories were successful largely because they were able to produce large quantities. But they needed to find ways to get that output to market, and the railroad was that way. This self-reinforcing cycle of railroads helping foster a manufacturing economy, which in turn led to greater demands for rail, meant that railroad employment increased significantly, from 750 000 in 1890 to 2.1 million in 1920 – a number not achieved since.[4] Like Silicon Valley of today's New Economy, regions producing steel (like Pittsburgh) or using steel (like Cleveland) boomed. For example, by 1880 Cleveland boasted 23 metal firms, capitalized at between $200 000 and $1 million and its prosperity was based on making metal products (ships, bridges, houses, conveyers, pumps, compressors and bicycles).

While other innovations, such as the telephone, electricity, chemical processing, and the automobile, emerged during this period, they did not take off and become truly national, widely adopted industries until the postwar mass production economy.[5] From 1890 to 1904 the telephone infrastructure spread from New York and a few northeastern cities to virtually the whole non-rural nation. However, it was not until the next major economic period in the 1950s that it would be possible to speak of truly universal telephone service penetration. One indicator of this is that telegraph traffic grew steadily until the 1940s when telephone costs finally fell enough to make it a more competitive long distance alternative.

Similar patterns were true as well with respect to electricity. During the factory-based economy before World War II, the dominant application of electricity was in urban homes, factories and offices for electric lighting, and to a limited extent in factories for electric motors. While just 5 percent of factories used electric motors in 1900, by 1920 over half the power in factories came from electricity. Even so, it was not until the emergence of the corporate mass production economy in the 1940s that a whole host of industries and products based on electro-mechanical goods become widely available (e.g., television, electric appliances, etc.).

Unlike the prior era, which was largely dominated by small-scale craft production and agriculture, this era was dominated by larger scale factory manufacturing, at least for many sectors that focused on commodity processing. By 1885, manufacturing income exceeded farming income for the first time. In 1919, the ten largest manufacturing industries were, in order of value-added, iron and steel, textiles, lumber, paper and printing, food, miscellaneous, chemicals, liquors, stone clay and glass, and metals and metal products.[6] In spite of the growth of manufacturing, this industrial economy was not, as the economy of the later half of the twentieth century was to be, based on production of consumer goods. With a few notable exceptions (e.g., cigarettes, textiles), it was an economy based on natural resource and capital goods production.

But even to the extent that consumer goods manufacturing industries grew, they reflected the technology system of the time. For example, it was not until after World War II that a truly consumer-oriented automobile industry emerged, with a wide choice of models and more rapid new model introduction. Prior to that, the dominant car producer, Ford, succeeded by following the principles of that era's manufacturing economy, focusing on engineering and production innovation to drive down costs and prices. As Ford once said, 'You can have a Model T in any color as long as it is black.' It would take Alfred Sloan at General Motors in the 1930s and 1940s to pioneer a different approach based on marketing, style, rapidly changing models, and cars tied to status and moving up the socio-economic ladder.

There was a second, and just as important structural change and that was on the farm. Though many agricultural inventions had been developed before 1900, it took until then for a large numbers of farmers to use them. For example, it was not until after 1910 that the worth of agricultural machines and equipment exceeded the value of horses and mules on farms. The diffusion of new agricultural technologies, including the mechanical reaper, the combine, and other tools, combined with technologies like the railroad and the refrigerated train car, opened up large areas of more productive Midwestern farm land. These developments boosted agricultural productivity. As a result, between 1865 and 1929, the share of the nation's workforce employed on the farm declined from 50 percent to 20 percent.

New Forms of Business Organization

The industrial era not only led to the rise of new industries, it led to new kinds of business organizations. Large corporations and financial institutions rapidly came into their own. For example, in 1860 Pittsburgh boasted 17 foundries, 21 rolling mills, 76 glass factories, and 47 other manufacturing establishments, but none were incorporated and almost all were small.[7] Before the Civil War there were few manufacturing plants with more than 500 workers. In fact, the corporation was not widely adopted as the legal form of business.

By 1900 this had all changed. Half the world's glass and iron and two-thirds of the steel now came from Pittsburgh's factories, most of them medium to large in size. The largest company of the day, US Steel, was formed from a plan hatched by J.P. Morgan and Carnegie Steel's president to merge Carnegie Steel with Morgan's number two-sized Federal Steel to make US Steel the nation's first billion-dollar company. Due to the unprecedented size of this new corporation, financiers on Wall Street gave it the nickname 'the Corporation.' By 1920 there were over 10 000 manufacturing plants with more than 500 workers and they accounted for more than two-thirds of manufacturing output. The value of physical capital per plant doubled from 1880 to 1900 and doubled again from 1900 to 1920.

Firms did not get bigger because their owners acquired a new taste for wealth and power, although the robber barons enjoyed exercising their power. Rather, the new technology let establishments, in fact required establishments, to grow to hitherto unprecedented size. The larger the factory or the corporation, the more efficient it could become and the more it could drive down costs, put its competitors out of business, and grow even more. The cost reductions resulting from factory operations and geographic concentration of production overwhelmed made-to-order and small-volume production in industry after industry.[8]

Until the emergence of the factory economy, there was no straightforward legal form that dealt with this concentration. Indeed, with the exception of the railroad, the prior technology system did not enable such concentration, so there was little need to develop a new legal form. As the technology system made it possible for industry to become larger, companies initially turned to trusts as a way to become big. Trusts were made up of stockholders of individual smaller firms who gave their stock to a central board in trust. The emergence of these large 'trusts' dominated the imagination of friends and foes alike. Ida Tarbell, of muckraking fame, stated that the rapidly changing economic landscape and the rise of monopolistic trusts was 'disturbing and confusing people.'[9] Though trusts were sometimes used to engage in anti-competitive behavior, they nevertheless reflected an underlying reality that efficient production required increased size.

However, as is true in all new economic periods, law had to catch up to the economic system. After the enactment in 1889 of the New Jersey corporation law that allowed companies to buy stock in other corporations, trusts gave way to mergers between separate corporations. By 1904, one or two giant firms, usually put together by merger, controlled at least half the output in 78 different industries. In 1896 there were fewer than 12 firms worth $10 million, but by 1904 there were over 300. To cope with the emergence of large firms with complicated balance sheets, the profession of public accounting arose. In 1896 New York State enacted the first public accountant licensing law. By 1915, 39 states had similar laws.

Many see the rise of industrial era companies as one development that lasted until the entrepreneurial 1990s. The reality is that while they represented a significant evolution from the merchant era family enterprise, they were still a far cry from the large managerial corporations that became the standard after World War II. In the former, most decisions continued to be made in informal ways, with owners and top managers acting on their own intuition and limited information. Strict and clear lines of authority were not laid out, and decisions depended on personal priorities and discretion. Unlike the corporation of the 1950s with its large masses of middle managers and supervisors, a small group of managers oversaw thousands of workers. As Chandler notes, the Carnegie Corporation did little to coordinate its various mining, shipping and manufacturing units, which remained separate companies under independent management.[10] Most corporations were one-product companies run by their owners and a small executive cadre. It was not until the emergence of the next economy that the practice of management became the standard.

In fact, in the early stages of industrialization in the 1870s, the new enterprises were often family groups. They drew capital from family and friends' wealth and expanded by self-financing. Indeed, many of the big names in American industry began as family names (e.g., Dupont, Swift, Armour, Grace, Ford, Olin, Dow, Heinz, Firestone, Dodge). As these firms accumulated capital and their demands for more capital grew, a new more organized and systematic finance system emerged by the early 1900s. As a result, a national securities market came into place, and investment banks, operating as financial 'wholesalers,' emerged. Perhaps best known was J.P. Morgan's house, which specialized in underwriting (i.e., buying newly issued corporate stocks and bonds and then reselling them at a profit to investors). This change in financing is reflected in the fact that as late as the late 1880s only one manufacturing company's stock was listed on the New York Stock Exchange and daily shares per day did not exceed 1 million. By 1928, 5 million shares per day were trading and most big companies were listed. Finance capitalism, where financiers (or owners) controlled companies, lasted until the 1930s when managers slowly began to gain real operational control. The forced separation in the New Deal of investment and banking functions through the Glass-Steagal Act limited further the investment bankers' control of the market.

Finally, the new organization and technological system led to the emergence of a new organization of work. In this era, work was tough. Workers were expected to obey orders. Companies wanted workers who could work hard, not think well. As one of Andrew Carnegie's managers said, 'I always had one rule: if a workman sticks up his head, hit it.' This economic era's industrial relations were epitomized by what is called 'Taylorism,' named after the famous industrial operations engineer Frederick Taylor. Taylorism was based on the notion that only management had the knowledge and skills to organize work, and therefore machine speeds, choice of tools, and methods of work were to be decided by the industrial engineer. In one of his very first consulting jobs to Andrew Carnegie's steel mill, Taylor examined how work was done and decided that, in place of individual workers deciding how to shovel coal or run a machine, the engineer should decide it. Such a management attitude did not place much faith in the worker's ability to self-govern his work. Given this attitude, it is not surprising that Taylor said, 'one of the very first requirements for a man who is fit to handle pig iron as a regular occupation is that he shall be so stupid and so phlegmatic that he more nearly resembles in his mental make-up an ox than any other type.'[11] This new kind of work environment was a major reason why the era saw the rise of organized labor, with the formation in 1886 of the American Federation of Labor to organize the new industrial craft workers.

The New Urban System

This new economy did not just require the reorganization of company production systems and organizational forms, it led over the period of 1870 to 1920 to the reorganization of the spatial production system of cities and regions. As the factory revolution unfolded, railroads and steam-powered ocean vessels broadened the national market. Moreover, the factory organization of production beyond the textile industry, new communications technologies (telegraph and telephone); new energy sources (electricity), and replacement of a self-sustaining rural economy by commercialized agriculture emerged. This enabled the industrial economy to reach out along the Northeastern and Midwestern industrial belt that lay at the heart of a national rail network, with processing centers at rail nodes. Because the new capital-intensive manufacturing was almost exclusively an urban phenomenon, cities exploded in response. Urbanism shifted from one made up of mill towns and mercantile ports to one characterized by the classic core-oriented industrial city (e.g. Detroit, Pittsburgh, Chicago, St Louis).

At the beginning of the period, 1870, about one-fourth of Americans lived in urban places – near the end, 1920, over half did. Migrants streamed from rural to urban areas, as early-stage agricultural mechanization (such as the mechanical reaper) boosted productivity and industrialization proceeded at a rapid pace. This flow of displaced farm workers, plus European immigration, produced a concentration of population in the urbanized core of young metropolises, and population in the surrounding rural areas declined in many places. Some immigrant groups, such as the Scandinavians, went west to work the land, but most immigrants went to cities: Germans to Milwaukee, Cincinnati and Chicago; Irish to Boston and New York; Italians to Providence and Philadelphia; and Jews to New York.

Within cities, there were also dramatic changes. Production and circulation became concentrated around central business districts, and the introduction of steel led to the first 'skyscraper' office buildings. Land uses were specialized, leading to distinct separations between production and residential areas. Within residential functions, high-status groups moved outward in new residential areas, first to country estates and later to garden suburbs, leaving behind the working classes in the inner city. Electric streetcars and train lines contributed to this suburbanization. New kinds of water and sewer systems and advances in public health made high urban densities safer.

In contrast to the older mercantile/craft economy in which rural life was considered to be superior to urban life, as a majority relocated in cities, cities became seen as places of progress. Popular disdain for the farm grew, reflected in the fact that it was during this period that terms like 'hick' and 'yokel' came into use. Someone living a rural life was seen as stuck in the old economy and not at the cutting-edge of change, now centered in the city. The factory era also marked a change in the attitudes of Americans, not just about rural life, but about progress and the future itself. Until the 1890s the notion of the frontier actually meant the geographical frontier that beckoned people to go west and open up new lands. Frederick Jackson Turner's famous thesis on the end of the frontier in 1893 struck a cord because he articulated what most Americans only sensed, that an era of American history was passing irrevocably and that a fundamentally new one was upon them. Progress was no longer seen in the exploration and settlement of new lands and the opening up of new territories for exploitation. Rather, it now became inextricably caught up with the machine itself. As Henry James noted, Americans' quest now became divorced from nature, and tied to the great man – the inventor, the builder, and the architect.

Governance

Not surprisingly, as an economic system transformed, so too did the governance system, and indeed the reigning public philosophy. In the mercantile/craft economy made up largely of farmers, merchants, and self-owned enterprises, the task of managing the public sphere was quite simple. Individuals were on their own, responsible for their own health care, retirement security, and even education. Government did little more than engage in canal and road building, national defense, mail delivery, and currency management. In fact, up until 1880, the Postal Service employed over 80 percent of the civilian federal workforce. The role of government was quite limited.

The dominant social philosophy of the 1870s and 1880s, social Darwinism, reflected this reality as it justified a limited role for government as the natural order of things. Social Darwinism, whose main proponent was English sociologist Herbert Spencer, celebrated the survival of the fittest. Yet, as an industrial economy and society began to emerge, a new public philosophy based on a new conception of the role of the individual and society was taking shape. For example, when the American Economics Association was created in 1885, its founders explicitly rejected the old laissez-faire, liberal view of the state and the social Darwinist philosophy that went with it.

It was not that people became more enlightened. Rather the prevailing social philosophy was found to be increasingly out of step with new realities. Just as the emergence of an industrial production system required the creation of a new form of corporate organization, so too did it require the creation of a new form of government organization and a new governing philosophy. Government policies and organization that had sufficed for an agricultural nation were no longer adequate for an emerging industrial nation. Robert Wiebe wrote that from 1870 to 1920 the nation created a managerial government 'derived from the regulative, and hierarchical needs of urban-industrial life.'[12] This was the period of the rise of public administration as both a discipline and a way to organize government.

The new public philosophy and governance that it supported did not come on the scene fully formed. At first, reformers resisted change and hoped to put in place piecemeal solutions to emergent problems, rather than attempt to come to grips with the need to fundamentally change the governing system. Such resistance to the new factory-based industrial economy was epitomized by the Populist movement that sought a host of legislative 'fixes' to the problems, including the nationalization of railroads (see Figure 3.1).

Source: http://history.smsu.edu/wrmiller/Populism/2pcartoon/pcartoon17.htm.

Figure 3.1   Populist Party poster calling for nationalization of the railroads and telegraph[13]

As the old economy stagnated, and the new, more complex economy began to create a whole host of problems, Wiebe notes that the first responses were:

simple means of preserving a competitive, individualistic, society without sacrificing the material benefits for technological progress. Civil service, anti-monopoly, the single tax, the earliest cooperatives, and schemes for inflation were all presented as panaceas which at one stroke would free the individual and ensure prosperity and justice for everyone ... a single act, properly executed and enforced would readjust society's machinery.[14]

By the time the new factory economy emerged in the 1890s, reformers were beginning to come to grips with the fact that they were in the midst of a transformation of significant proportions, and that a more complex society demanded a stronger and more sophisticated role for government. This new role encompassed a much broader set of regulatory activities. However, in contrast to the more activist government role to come in the postwar corporate economy, the chief role of government became one of restraining the excesses of an industrial economy and protecting those left behind or hurt by change.

Congress soon passed a host of legislation to do just that. The Interstate Commerce Act of 1887 addressed issues of regulating railroad rates. The Sherman Antitrust Act of 1890 declared that 'every contract, combination in the form of trust or otherwise, or conspiracy in restraint of trade among the several states ... was illegal.' In 1903 Congress established the Department of Commerce and Labor, and created a separate Department of Labor in 1913. The Hepburn Act of 1906 provided the Interstate Commerce Commission with authority to regulate railroads. The Federal Reserve Act of 1913 sought to bring stability to the banking system. The Clayton Antitrust Act of 1914 extended the powers of the government to control monopoly practices. The Federal Trade Commission was created in 1914 to prevent fraud and misleading practices by businesses, as was the Food and Drug Act of 1906. In 1913, the sixteenth amendment authorized the federal income tax in order to help pay for this expansion.[15]

Reformers placed many of the responsibilities for these new duties in the hands of independent regulatory agencies (e.g., the Interstate Commerce Commission and the Federal Trade Commission). But by the 1920s most of these organizations operated as a means for business self-regulation, as opposed to the regulatory state that would emerge in the next economy.

The political force for the creation of this new form of governance, Progressivism, represented the culmination of America's response to this wave of technological innovation. Progressive reformers sketched a new relationship between government and society, one that gave government responsibility to regulate economic abuses, keep order and preserve morality. Once it was clear that the new economy was there to stay, and with it big corporations, the debate shifted from breaking up or nationalizing big businesses to making sure they served the public interest. Progressivism took hold quickly in many states and cities. During its heyday, a robust institutional framework was created that enabled experts to give advice and carry out policies, particularly at the local and state level. For example, the New York Bureau of Municipal Research was formed in 1907 and by 1910 had a staff of 46.

While state and local governments expanded rapidly, the federal government was slower to grow. In 1869, Congress created the Bureau of Labor Statistics to keep track of the new jobs in the new industries that were beginning to appear. In 1883, Congress passed the Pendleton Act to create the federal civil service. Notwithstanding these developments and the reforms put in place by President Woodrow Wilson, the federal government remained relatively small and its role was limited. Just as the management cadre in big corporations remained small, so did the number of managers in the federal government. As late as 1931, Herbert Hoover had just four administrative aids in the White House. The federal government undertook no real planning or analysis on which it could base its actions. During the Hoover administration, private foundations largely funded the few studies of the economy and major social problems. The fact that state government spending increased three times faster than federal spending between 1860 and 1913 illustrates that the governance system was still predominantly at the state and local level. Explosive growth of the federal government would have to wait until the emergence of the national corporate, mass production economy in the 1930s and 1940s.

The political tenor of the time supported such a limited role for government. The major business organization of the era, the National Association of Manufacturers (NAM), in a letter to President Taft in 1912, stated that, 'it is not a function of government to regulate private industry, and that the ... relation of industry to government should be as remote as possible.'[16] Even during the Depression, which marked the disintegration of the factory economy, NAM remained committed to the old order. Its president, John Edgerton, blamed the workers, 'they do not practice the habits of thrift or conservation, but gamble away their savings in the stock market and elsewhere. Why blame our economic system, or government, or industry?'[17] Granted, NAM was expressing its own ideological and interest-driven perspective, but most in business and large numbers of Americans held the view that the role of the government should be tempered and limited. President Taft agreed, stating in 1912 that 'a national government cannot create good times. It cannot make the rain to fall, the sun to shine or the crops to grow.'[18] Calvin Coolidge agreed, proclaiming that 'it does not follow at all that because abuses exist, it is the concern of the federal government to attempt their reform.'[19]

As the period started, the political parties were far apart. Populists aligned with the Democratic standard-bearer Williams Jennings Bryant in the 1890s sought to resist the onslaught of industrialism and preserve small farms and merchants. In contrast, winning candidate Republican William McKinley placed his stake with the future industrial system.[20] However, after the Democratic party became reconciled to the permanency of these changes, they shifted from opposing industrialization to managing it. Just as Dwight Eisenhower and Bill Clinton each attempted to craft a 'third way' middle ground between liberalism and conservatism in the subsequent two economic eras, Woodrow Wilson sought to craft a middle ground between two major competing political positions of the day – socialism and corporate individualism. Under Wilson's leadership, workers' compensation was provided for federal workers, child labor was outlawed, railway workers were given the eight-hour day, and a host of other reforms were enacted.

In spite of these reforms, a public philosophy of limited government continued all the way into the Great Depression when the factory era economy began to break down. As he tried to react to the economic slowdown that would lead to the Depression, Herbert Hoover warned that government intervention would undermine the development of leadership. It would cramp and cripple the mental and spiritual energies of the people. For, as Daniel Bell described, the dominant economic philosophy still assumed that 'the market was a sufficient arbiter of the public weal; there were different utilities of individuals and the scarcity of different goods would come to an equilibrium that harmonized the intensity of desire and the willingness to pay the asking price.'[21] But it was not just the public and politicians who could not envision a stronger role for government. Neither could the dominant intellectuals. Before the Depression, social scientists had been uncertain about which institutions could make the economy work more efficiently and manage the business cycle. The consensus was that the mechanism that would work best was one based on voluntary cooperation between business, government, and labor.

Unlike today when virtually all agree that one of the federal government's roles is to manage the business cycle, in this era the government had neither the tools nor the mandate to do the job. In the face of an economy in free-fall, Hoover's Secretary of the Treasury, Andrew Mellon, declared that there was only one alternative: 'Liquidate labor, liquidate stocks, liquidate the farmers, liquidate real estate ... It will purge the rottenness out of the system ... People will work harder, live a more moral life. Values will be adjusted, and enterprising people will pick up the wrecks from less competent people.'[22] Easy for him to say.

As the factory economy began to break down, the public philosophy of limited government and reliance on private action became an increasingly poor compass with which to guide social progress. In response to the disintegration, first Hoover, and then Franklin Roosevelt, tried to save the system of self-control. Eventually Roosevelt was forced to shift responses, fundamentally reordering government's relationship with society and the economy.

In sum, America became a vastly different place between the end of the mercantile/craft economy in the 1870s and the emergence of the industrial economy in the early 1900s. As this revolution in the techno-economic system established itself, Americans' attitudes and beliefs changed and caught up to the new realities. As Digby Baltzell, author of *The Protestant Establishment*, stated:

> Slowly at first, but with increasing momentum in each decade after 1880, a naturalistic, urban, environmental, egalitarian, collectivist and eventually democratic ethic finally undermined the rural, heriditarian, opportunarian, individualist, and republican ethic which rationalized the Natural right of the old stock business-gentleman's rule in America between 1860 and 1929. What a rural Republican quite naturally blamed on heredity in the 1870s was confidently blamed on environment by his urban and Democratic grandson in the 1930s.[23]

THE CORPORATE, MASS PRODUCTION ECONOMY: THE MID-1940S TO THE MID-1970S

During the 1920s, America's economic future looked bright. A host of innovations, including the radio, automobile, and airplane burst onto the scene. In particular, 1929 was a boom year, capping off a decade of phenomenal growth in which real gross domestic product (GDP) grew by 42 percent.[24] Yet, within a year GDP fell a remarkable 15 percent. By 1933, the economy was operating at 60 percent of capacity, while GDP was down 31 percent. The stock market had lost about 80 percent of its value. Three successive waves of bank failures spread panic across the nation. By 1933 close to one-quarter of workers were unemployed. The production lost through idle capacity in the Great Depression was about equal to the government's expenditures on World War II. What had gone wrong?

The standard explanation offered by economists is bad economic policy. Some blame the increase in protectionism and tariffs, decrying Great Britain's adoption of a system of imperial preference for the importation of goods as the first spark of the breakdown, and the retaliatory passage of the Smoot-Hawley Act to raise tariffs as the fuel that fed the fire. Others point to a restrictive monetary and fiscal policy.

While these policy failures certainly exacerbated the depth and length of the Depression, they were in many ways symptoms and reactions to more fundamental economic problems brought on by the decline of one type of economy and the exhaustion of its technology system. The British established their imperial preferences program in response to lagging growth. The US government cut spending because tax revenues lagged as growth slowed. The real cause of the Depression lay in the fact that the techno-economic system that had emerged in the 1890s had run its course and the new system that would take its place was yet too nascent to be the needed growth engine.

At the time, economists looked at the turmoil quite differently. When Alvin Hansen made his presidential address before the American Economics Association in 1938, he postulated that long-term growth had leveled off and he wondered if society had finally reached its pinnacle of economic development and income. Writing three years later he continued, arguing that, unlike in the past when the railroad and electricity and the automobile had propelled growth, 'we cannot take for granted the rapid emergence of new industries as rich in investment opportunities.'[25] Indeed in the midst of such transitions, it is hard for most observers to envision just how, or even if, the next new growth cycle will occur. Witness the many pundits and economists in the 1980s and 1990s who argued that the glory days of the US economy were permanently over and that we had to learn to live with slow or even no growth.

The reality, however, was that by the end of World War II the US economy was poised to enter a boom period of unprecedented proportions. How could economists be so wrong? It was because they could not envision the structural changes that were working their way quietly through the economy. Thus, while the economy of 1929 looked very much like the economy of 1909 (albeit larger and with some new products and innovations), it looked dramatically different from the economy of 1949. The economy had been transformed. The new mass production, corporate, national economy had superceded the factory-based, smaller-firm, regionally based economy. As historian Robert Griffith states, 'By the middle of the twentieth century, corporate reorganization of the economy had taken place.'[26] By the 1950s, big corporations had become a way of life and Americans had grown used to them. Professional managers now ran corporations, so much so that the period became known as the era of managerial capitalism. Moreover, a new technology system emerged based on electro-mechanical and chemical technologies, and standardized mass production techniques applied to a wide range of different goods and services industries. The economy was linked together in a nationwide network of transportation and communication. In the new managerial state, as Dwight Eisenhower noted, 'big business, labor, professions and government officials [are] working together in the calmness of a nonpartisan atmosphere.'[27] Finally, what had largely been a production economy trying to provide the basic needs of a toiling working class transformed into to a consumption economy designed to meet the wants of a growing middle class.

The Technology System

The technological basis of the new mass production corporate economy that emerged in the 1940s was quite different from that of the prior economy. Whole new industries, in many cases ones that emerged in embryonic form in the 1920s and 1930s, 'took off' to achieve critical mass by the late 1940s and 1950s. Emblematic of this was the fact that in the factory era, people had spoken of 'mechanical arts' to refer to physical advances. By the end of the 1930s, people began to speak about technology, and a host of products and production processes based on that technology were about to burst on the scene.

Perhaps the best symbol of what that new economy was to look like was presented at the 1939 New York World's Fair. The fair depicted futuristic technologies such as the television and the interstate highway system, while offering a vision of a world brimming with new consumer goods. As Figure 3.2 shows, in one advertisement for the fair, featuring the fictitious Middletown family, the mother comments on the fact that the time capsule did not contain appliances, stating, 'Yes, like refrigerators, irons, toasters, and vacuum cleaners. If they do not have those things 5000 years from now I certainly would not want to be living then.'[28] The fair captured the imagination of Americans because it represented 'the world of tomorrow.' Americans sensed correctly that the world was changing, in no small part because of the incredible array of new technologies and products that corporate America was beginning to produce. The fair was the first organized glimpse into a future that, while it could be imagined, was not yet within reach for most Americans.

Source: www2.sjsu.edu/faculty/wooda/middleton/middleton5.html. Reproduced by kind permission of Westinghouse Electric Corporation.

Figure 3.2   A poster from the Westinghouse exhibit at the 1939 New York World's Fair

Of all the industries supporting the new corporate economy, none was more important than electronics. The development of new applications, coupled with near universal consumer acceptance, meant that by the

1950s, the electronics industry became the fifth biggest, behind auto, steel, aircraft and chemicals. Before this, electricity was used principally to generate light or to power large motors. In the new economy of the 1940s and 1950s electricity became part of everyday life, partly due to the invention of the transistor in 1947, which enabled the development of a myriad of new devices. While most urban homes had electricity prior to World War II, only 30 percent of farmers did. By 1959, this rose to 96 percent.[29]

Nowhere was the impact of this new electronic era more evident than with the introduction of television. In 1940, General Electric's Schenectady, New York station became the first to relay television broadcasts. Electricity also powered an array of new appliances and devices for the home. General Electric's first electric washing machine was sold in 1930, although it would not be for another 20 years, until prices came down and convenience went up, that many Americans would buy one.[30] Other electronic appliances, including air conditioners, garbage disposals, power tools, and kitchen appliances (mixers, coffee-makers, toasters, electric can openers, etc.) were first introduced during the late 1920s and 1930s, but did not take off until the late 1940s and 1950s. Colonel Schick had invented the electric razor in 1931, but it was not until the 1950s that many men began to use it instead of a blade. Air conditioning had been invented in 1902, but as late as the mid-1940s it was still a novelty that most people experienced only occasionally in movie theaters and department stores.[31] But by the 1950s air conditioning was touted as a technology 'for the millions, not the millionaire.' In order to get Americans to buy these new products, typical advertisements in the 1950s featured a well-dressed woman beside a display of new electronic appliances, touting the need to get into the modern world. And indeed, in the 1950s people bought televisions, movie cameras, tape recorders, hi-fi record players, and the like in droves. In 1950, only 1.4 percent of wired homes had clothes dryers, 1 percent had dishwashers, 7 percent had freezers, and almost none had air conditioning. Just nine years later, 22 percent had freezers, 90 percent had televisions, 18 percent a dryer and 13 percent an air conditioner.[32] New music technology including the '45' and '33 and 1/3,' aided by the invention of high fidelity, meant that record sales tripled in the 1950s.

Electronics also invaded the office. The first Xerox machine, invented in 1938 by Chester Carlson, was an electro-mechanical device. It was not until 1960 that Xerox produced the first plain paper copier. Other new office devices included the dictaphone, electric typewriter, electric adding machine, and even the first large, expensive and slow mainframe computers full of vacuum tubes. A 1954 *Fortune* article, entitled 'The Coming Victory Over Paper', reflected the optimism when it discussed the innovation of the electronic recording machine for processing checks electronically.[33]

A number of other key industries were part of the new technology system that powered growth. Most important was the revolution in materials. The discovery of new chemicals and new ways of processing them shifted from a mostly trial and error process to one based on complex mathematical modeling and a scientific understanding of chemistry.[34] The introduction of catalytic cracking in 1936 opened the way for a dramatic price decline in chemicals, and an array of new chemicals were introduced. The initial commercial development of today's major thermoplastics – polyvinyl chloride, low-density poly-ethylene, and polystyrene – was achieved in the 1930s. Indeed, plastics was the nanotechnology of its era, with one futurist predicting that: 'bathtubs and home equipment made of plastic will weigh so little that a child will be able to lift them.'[35] But it was not until the late 1940s and 1950s that these and other new chemical materials, including polypropylene, were widely produced and consumed. The loss of sources of natural rubber in World War II stimulated the industry to develop synthetic rubber. The war also stimulated the petroleum industry to learn to produce gasoline in new ways, using catalytic reforming, which allowed the production of high-octane fuel from lower grades of petroleum. Hydraulic fracturing was invented in the 1940s by scientists at a subsidiary of Standard Oil and led to the significant increase in yields from oil fields. New metals were developed as well, most significantly aluminum, which was instrumental in facilitating the growth of aviation. The boom in synthetic products after World War II meant some traditional materials industries were declining or experiencing slow growth, while 'new economy' industries such as plastics (growing 600 percent in the 1950s) and chemicals (growing 455 percent between 1947 and 1970) boomed.

The emergence of the pharmaceutical industry was based on similar developments. Before 1930 most drug companies sold things like laxatives, quinine, cold lozenges, and poison ivy lotion. Modern pharmaceutical products based on advanced chemistry were developed in the 1920s and 1930s, but it was not until the postwar period that they reached a mass market. For example, Beecham Research Laboratories was opened in 1943 to focus in a systematic way on drug discovery. The result of the shift to a science-based industry was that by the 1940s new drugs like streptomycin and other antibiotics, cortisone, ACTH, and antihistamines were put on the market. By the 1950s, a host of new drugs, such as Thorazine, Dexadrine, Purinethol (anti-leukemia drug), and Erythrocin (antibiotic) emerged.[36]

This was also the era when the automobile became a product of mass consumption. Until the 1930s, most cars came equipped with a toolbox to enable the owner to repair the car when it broke down. In the 1930s traffic lights and speed limits were few, and drivers had to watch out for horses and wagons. Until the 1950s cars were still quite difficult to use and, compared to later models, quite uncomfortable. But by the 1950s with the introduction of innovations like power brakes, power steering, automatic transmissions, V8 engines, automatic windshield wipers, torsion bar suspensions, padded seat backs, and radios, autos became something that everyone could drive. It was not until these developments, and the building of a national highway network, that car sales took off. As a result, motor vehicle miles traveled increased from about 100 million in 1940 to 1.6 billion in the late 1970s.[37] Autos, trucks and buses per thousand people went from about 225 between 1930 and 1945 to about 700 by 1980. By 1960 the number of autos sold in Los Angeles County alone exceeded all those sold in Asia or South America.[38]

Developments in the chemical and transportation industries paved the way for another transformation in agriculture. Specialized automated crop planting and harvesting machines began to be adopted in the 1950s and accelerated the decline in farm employment. By 1950 tractors had finally replaced horse and mules. Cotton harvesting was mechanized in the 1940s. The mobile green pea harvester/sheller was introduced in the mid-1950s and within three years had been almost universally adopted. Moreover, with the dramatic expansion of the chemical industry, new fertilizers, pesticides, herbicides, and seeds boosted yields dramatically, fostering the so-called Green Revolution in a number of developing nations. Chemical fertilizers and pesticides, unused in 1900, accounted for 5 percent of production costs in 1950 and 20 percent in 2000.[39] The result was that, while the number of farm operators stayed constant between 1900 (5.7 million) and 1945, they declined to 3.5 million by 1970.[40]

Change was also sparked by the application of mass production manufacturing to virtually all sectors of the economy. Numerous production innovations, including automated assembly lines, numerically controlled machine tools, automated process control systems, and mechanical handling systems, drove down prices in American manufacturing and led to production of a cornucopia of inexpensive manufactured consumer goods. In fact, the rise of mechanical automation was the truly great development of that era's economy. The term 'automation' was not even coined until 1945 when the engineering division of Ford used it to describe the operations of its new transfer machines that mechanically unloaded stampings from the body presses and positioned them in front of machine tools. But automation was not confined to autos, discrete parts and other durable goods industries; it became widespread in commodity processing. Continuous flow innovations date back to 1939 when Standard Oil of New Jersey created the first of the industry's great fluid crackers. In these plants raw material flowed continuously in one end and out as product at the other end.

One of the distinguishing features of the postwar economy was standardized mass production itself. Because the production systems of many core industries were based on specialized, high-cost machines, it was only economical to produce very long production runs of the same items. For example, Ford would regularly produce 50 000 items, such as right door panels, and then store these for weeks at a time. In order to take advantage of the economies of scale of mass production systems, by the 1950s, Ford and Chrysler had two basic auto body designs, and General Motors had three. One 1957 book summed up the mass production system and its risks: 'The installation of too much special-purpose machinery may be dangerous because of style changes and changes in design, which may render highly specialized machines useless.'[41] The authors went on to complain that some industries mistakenly tried to mass-produce goods 'before the style and engineering features had been definitely and finally determined.'[42] Companies sought to find products that changed only slowly and that many consumers wanted to buy, and then to produce as many of these as possible. Daniel Bell wrote that:

> Today's fully automatic assembly is possible only when a large output of a single product is called for, but such inflexible, single purpose machinery is too costly for medium or short production runs, and consequently the adoption of such machines tends to 'freeze' the design and the technological

stage of the product. True automation ... would design products in terms of a multi-purpose machine, rather than a machine for each product. If such machines ever were produced, they would create a revolution not only in technology, but in aesthetics as well.[43]

It would not be until the next new economy of the 1990s and the digital IT revolution that such 'true automation' and customization became possible. In the meantime, the catchword for the era was standardization.

The mass production revolution was not confined just to manufacturing; it applied to other industries, including housing. Twenty miles from Manhattan in 1947, William Levitt pioneered the mass production of affordable homes. Levittown became famous for one reason: it epitomized the revolution that brought mass production to the housing industry. Levitt was able to break down the building of a house into 26 operations and hired 80 subcontractors efficiently doing the same narrow job over and over again (e.g., putting up drywall, which in turn was invented by US Gypsum in 1935). In addition, he used paint sprayers and other labor-saving devices previously banned by unions. Variations in the 17 477 houses were minor; each had two bedrooms, a bath, living room and kitchen on a 750-square-foot concrete slab. By standardizing the units, Levitt was able to put up more than 24 a day, helping fill the enormous postwar demand. The ability to build cheaper homes was a principal reason why the percentage that were mortgaged went from about 40 percent after World War II, to about 60 percent by the late 1960s.

Just as the industrial economy saw a revolution in transportation based on railroads and steamships, the corporate economy saw a similar revolution based on commercial aircraft, much larger ocean-going cargo ships, the construction of a national system of pipelines and a vibrant interstate trucking system that exploited the newly built interstate highway system. This new transportation system not only knit the nation together, it dramatically lowered transportation costs so that companies could easily serve national, and in some cases, international markets. For example, pipelines grew from about 1 billion ton miles carried in 1930 to about 500 billion by the late 1970s. Truck traffic went from 13 billion miles traveled in 1930 to 450 billion. In 1930 trucks carried 450 billion ton miles but by the late 1970s that had increased to 1950 billion. While airlines carried 24 percent of all combined airline-railroad passenger traffic in 1950, by 1960 they were carrying 61 percent.[44]

Communications also boomed. Telephone calls per capita per year had averaged around 250 between 1920 and 1945. After 1945 the number took off, averaging about 1400 by the late 1970s. Moreover, the vast majority of telephone calls were local until well after World War I. Prior to then virtually every phone call required a telephone switchboard operator to manually connect the call.[45] Indeed, it was not until after World War II, facilitated by generous federal subsidies, that a national telephone network was attained.

A 25-year postwar boom arose from the rapid decline in prices brought about by mass production technologies, the extension of the transportation system to create national markets, and the significant increase in new consumer products. In fact, the whole notion of regularly changing products and the need to 'keep up with the Joneses' was central to this economic era. If Henry Ford was the epitome of the factory era economy and its focus on an engineering and production approach to car production, Alfred Sloan and General Motor's approach of marketing style and cars tied to status and moving up the ladder was the epitome of the corporate industrial economy. Indeed, the economy shifted to a consumer-driven one. In 1959 *Time* magazine reported that, 'The US productive machine popped out more than 7 million television sets, almost triple 1949; 4 525 000 electric toaster sets, 4 212 00 washing machines, more than 1 million Hopalong Cassidy suits, and enough nylon stockings to give every woman in the US eleven pairs.'[46] They summed it all up saying, 'The strength of the nation lay in the fact that the US economy, which had tripled in size since it was formally pronounced "mature" by New Deal hare-braintrusters in 1936 was still capable of gigantic growth.' In 1956, Stevenson enthused that, 'the United States at mid-century stands on the threshold of abundance for all.'[47] The National Association of Manufacturers agreed, stating, 'Guided by electronics, powered by atomic energy, geared to the smooth, effortless workings of automation, the magic carpet of our free economy heads for distant and unrealized horizons.'[48] Indeed, it was a heady time.[49]

In short, while the old factory economy had largely been a producer economy trying to meet the basic needs of society, the postwar economy became a consumer economy designed to provide the middle class with a new array of goods and services.[50] Spurred in part by the automobile, this period saw a revolution in retailing as profound as the current e-commerce revolution. Before World War II there were virtually no shopping centers, big department stores, malls or supermarkets. The 1950s and 1960s saw their development, changing how America shopped. One innovation that was symbolic of the move to the mass consumer economy was the invention in 1936 of the shopping cart by grocer Sylvan Goldman, who would became the father of the modern supermarket. In order to encourage this spending, it was also an era in which consumer debt was developed. The credit card business started in 1950 with Diners Club, and American Express followed in the mid-1950s. As a result, private debt jumped from $73 billion in 1950 to $196 billion in 1960.

As big corporations became the predominate suppliers of consumer goods, they increasingly turned to advertising to gain competitive advantage. Between 1910 and 1950 advertising expenditures averaged about $225 per year per American (1999 dollars), but in the 1950s they rose to $450. Indeed, in the 1950s advertising more than doubled, rising from $6 billion in 1950 to $13 billion in 1963. In fact, the term 'marketing' itself was coined around 1950 to emphasize the need for business to focus beyond its own production concerns. The growth was so great that it propelled Vance Packard's book, *The Hidden Persuaders*, which documented the new advertising system, to bestseller status.

Finally, in the new corporate economy the sources of innovation changed from being based largely on a technical tinkering and trial and error by mechanics and inventors working in their garages to a science-based one in corporate laboratories where innovation was derived from a more fundamental understanding of underlying processes.[51] Schumpeter argued that in the new corporate economy, 'Technological progress is increasingly becoming the business of teams of trained specialists who turn out what is required and make it work in predictable ways.'[52] As a result, R&D expenditures skyrocketed by 400 percent between 1953 and 1964. For example, Dupont's R&D expenditures increased from around $1 million per year in 1921 to over $60 million by the mid-1950s.[53] Research and development laboratories increased from around 1000 in 1927 – with few doing basic research – to almost 5000 in 1956, with many, like Bell Labs conducting extensive basic research.[54] One reflection of this is the fact that in 1901 there were 20 896 patents issued to individuals, with only 4650 going to corporations. These balanced out by the 1930s, but by the mid-1950s the corporate rate took off. By 1980 corporations obtained about five times more patents than individuals. As the innovation process became systematized and corporatized, engineers became more important. In

1900 engineers made up only 0.5 per 1000 people, but by 1940, 2 out of 1000 people were engineers, and by 1970, 6 out of 1000 were.[55]

New Forms of Business Organization

As a new economy emerged after World War II, so too did a new organizational system. This became the era of the big organization – big corporations, big government, and big labor – all of which were governed by a new ethos of management. Activities in the prior factory era that were run largely by individual proprietors or small firms now became the province of large national corporations. In the 1960s, Galbraith captured the change:

> Seventy years ago the corporation was confined to those industries – railroading, steam boating, steel making, petroleum recovery and refining, some mining – where, it seemed production had to be on a large scale. Now it also sells groceries, mills grain, publishes newspapers and provides public entertainment, all activities that were once the province of the individual proprietor or the insignificant firm.[56]

As a result, by 1948, the corporate sector held almost 60 percent of national income-producing wealth, and the largest 200 employers accounted for 20 percent of private non-agricultural workers. By 1950, the 200 largest non-financial corporations accounted for 40.3 percent of value added. In 1901, only one corporation, US Steel, had over $1 billion in assets. By 1960, 638 corporations had more than $1 billion in assets (in constant dollars). Bigness was the order of the day.[57]

The rise of corporate America also meant a change in the way Americans looked at businesses. Bigness was seen as the ultimate achievement, while small firms were seen as ones that failed to become big. As Galbraith argued, 'Being in an earlier stage of development it [the entrepreneurial firm] did less planning ... it had less need for trained personnel that the state provided. Its technology being more primitive, it had less to gain from public underwriting of research and markets.'[58] Entrepreneurial firms were looked down upon as a second-class group where wages were lower, management quality less, and insecurity higher. This was the era of the manager, not the entrepreneur. As Galbraith argued, 'Nor has power passed to the classical entrepreneur – the individual who once used his access to capital to bring it into combination with other factors of production. He is a diminishing figure in the industrial system.'[59] Such a view prevailed throughout the period. A few years before Bill Gates started Microsoft one economic textbook stated, 'The era of the entrepreneur may be over in terms of the individual owner-manager who single-handedly built up a large firm.'[60]

As large corporations came to dominate the economic landscape, control and management of business enterprises also changed in a fundamental way. In the factory economy, corporations were largely instruments of their owners. Men like Carnegie, Harriman, Ford, Eastman, Dupont, and of course, Rockefeller were known throughout the nation as corporate titans. Yet, as corporations grew, became ever more complex, and had a vastly increased need for management and administration, they became controlled by a new class of professional managers. Scholars argued that control was now separate from ownership. Adolph Berle, the Columbia University 'New Dealer,' went so far as to conclude that the large corporation gave no rights to the owners of the enterprise, so it was up to a class of enlightened managers to guide the corporation. It was not just New Dealers who held this view: Republican Senator Robert Taft stated, 'The social consciousness of the great corporation is promoted by the glare of publicity in which they must operate, and by a management attitude now approaching that of trusteeship, not only for the stockholders, but for employees, customers, and the general public.'[61] As business professor Mariana Whitman notes, during the heyday of the corporate economy between 1950 and 1973, America's large corporations became private institutions endowed with a public purpose.[62] They provided stable jobs, supported the arts, encouraged employees to become involved in their communities, and assumed leadership positions in civic organizations. There was a widely shared sense that the corporation was committed to the community it was in, that the corporation's goals, the worker's and the community's were in not in conflict. The model of the 'good corporation' became the goal that all 'good' corporations sought to emulate. Because managers had almost unlimited discretion, with limited pressure from financial markets and global competition, they could afford to view their role this way. As Michael Useem observed, 'managerial capitalism tolerated a host of company objectives besides shareholder value.'[63]

In addition, as the capital needs of companies increased, they turned more and more to public markets for financing, thus diluting the financial control of original owners and enabling managers to gain control. And indeed, with but a few exceptions, who can remember the names of the heads of US corporations in the postwar era?

In the old manufacturing economy founder-owners made decisions based on instinct and rule of thumb. Most firms, even the biggest of the day, were run by a small executive cadre. For example, Rockefeller at Standard Oil and Alfred Sloan at General Motors employed relatively few people at their corporate headquarters. Information at the bottom was ignored, while only that information that could be quantified was acknowledged or seen. The old model whereby foremen and lower level managers had leeway to run their operations the way they wanted, gave way to a more controlled environment.

This was the era of the manager. One who epitomized the new model was Robert McNamara, who, before becoming John Kennedy's Secretary of Defense, was chief executive officer (CEO) of the Ford Motor Company. Under the leadership of the Ford family, the company had steadily floundered. By the late 1940s the company had come to the realization that it needed to bring in sophisticated professional management as its competitors Chrysler and GM already had. It so happened that McNamara and his colleagues, called at the time 'the whiz kids', had just come from reorganizing the nation's defense system, instituting new kinds of formalized, quantitative management controls. En masse they moved to Ford and installed their system there. The whiz kids were the epitome of the rational managerial system. By the late 1950s most major corporations had adopted the managerial and financial controls they fostered.

Corporations also now embraced formal planning. In a survey in the late 1940s, only 20 percent of large corporations could provide summaries of investment plans for four years into the future; by the early 1960s, 90 percent could.[64] Likewise, business strategic planning originated in the 1950s and by the early1970s had been widely adopted. Most large corporations had established separate planning divisions, with vice presidents in charge of planning, sometimes looking out as far as ten to 20 years. At the time, Galbraith spoke for most in the corporate world when he stated that 'advanced technology, in combination with high capital requirements make planning imperative. All planning seeks, so far as may be possible, to insure that what it assumes as regards the future will be what the future brings.'[65] While different forms went in and out of fashion, in the 1950s SWOT (Strengths, Weaknesses, Opportunities, and Threat) analysis was popular. The 1960s brought quantitative models of strategy relying on new mainframe computers. In short, planning was a central factor. The term said it all. One could plan reasonably well. One had to plan, and big organizations had to plan from the top down.

In order for management and planning to be effective, a new corporate organization in which the top managerial cadre was empowered with information that worked its way up the chain was necessary. When the large, multidivisional company became commonplace after World War II, CEOs put in place elaborate paper-based managerial systems to coordinate these sprawling companies. Millions of new white-collar middle managers were needed to make these behemoths work. This rise of a new managerial class was one of the most profound changes resulting from the rise of the corporate economy. Columbia professors Berle and Means' 1932 study of corporate governance was the first to recognize the emerging prominence of managers.[66] Galbraith also noted, 'The development of bigger corporations, with committee-like managements, has meant that second and third tier executives, by the hundreds and thousands, have had to be kept informed and coordinated.'[67] As a result, after World War II, the discipline of management emerged. James Burnham's 1941 book, *The Managerial Revolution*, argued that the world was witnessing the emergence of a new ruling class, 'the managers,' who would soon replace the rule of capitalists and communists alike. The book was an instant best-seller and was translated into most major foreign languages. It took less than 40 years, from 1945 to 1980, for the management revolution to take hold worldwide.[68] As a result, managers became the dominant class, the new elites.

The managerial society first began in the 1920s to permeate the heretofore hereditarily-based establishment, but it was not until the 1950s that it won the day. In the new managerial society, where the route to elite status was now dependent upon managerial and professional success, the right college degree became the main criterion for potential elite status. Digby Baltzell argued that the rise of the corporate managerial economy led to the decline of the upper class as the ruling class: 'As the seats of economic power have shifted from the local, home-grown institutions to national organization, membership in the elite of many a city or town is being determined less by hereditary ties, more by current functional rank.'[69] The old elites resented and resisted the rise of the new managerial elite, drawn as it was from people with sometimes distinctly middle and working class backgrounds. Writing in the late 1950s, Protestant elitist T.S. Mathews wrote that, 'this day belongs to the 100 percenters, the new-rich Texans, the Madison Avenue boys, the professional patriots, the organization men, the hard-eyed herdsmen of political yahoos, the dogs that eat dogs.'[70] In other words, the narrow, Protestant, hereditary-based, club-going elite was being joined, and sometimes supplanted by a new group of men (women were largely excluded) who gained power from their control of large organizations.

It was not just management that was rationalized, so was work. The rough, brutal foreman of the industrial economy, indiscriminately giving orders, gave way to the human relations-oriented supervisor, seeking to motivate workers. As part of this trend, wages and jobs were rationalized. By 1947 US Steel described over 1150 distinct jobs with 152 classifications that governed the wages of more than 75 000 workers. In the 1950s Alcoa took three years to develop a computer program that set wage differentials mathematically. The final equation was three pages long, with 59 variables, and took 35 hours to process on a Univac computer. For the most part, pay was not tied to performance, which was difficult to measure, but to seniority. In such a system, it was easy to get seniority and to get the gold watch at the retirement party. Though it was never common for workers to have a job for life, it was true that worker, and even top executive tenure was much longer than it is today. For example, of 800 highest paid executives in 300 corporations in 1952, three-quarters had been with their company for more than 20 years. Of 308 senior executives who were board chairmen or presidents in 1952, 265 continued with the same firm until death or retirement, and only five lost their jobs because the company failed or they were fired.[71]

As jobs were rationalized, work increasingly became routine, boring, and repetitive. In the corporate economy, office jobs were the equivalent of factory work in the manufacturing economy: filling in forms, keeping ledgers, typing letters, etc. Aldous Huxley stated, 'Today every efficient office, every up to date factory is a panoptical prison in which the workers suffer ... from being inside a machine.'[72] John Kenneth Galbraith concurred:

> On few matters is the image of the industrial civilization so sharp as on that of its labor force. This is a great mass – the word itself is ubiquitous – which streams in at the beginning of the shift and out at the end. It consists of comparatively unskilled operatives who guide or attend the machines and a smaller aristocracy ... when labor relations are tranquil, men pass peacefully through the gates. When they are not, a picket line appears and the plant

either shuts down or functions in the face of the threats of the milling crowd outside.[73]

A 1973 report from the federal Department of Health, Education and Welfare reiterated Huxley's and Galbraith's views:

> What is striking is the extent to which the dissatisfaction of the assembly line and blue collar worker is mirrored in white collar and even managerial positions. The office today, where work is segmented and authoritarian is often a factory. Secretaries, clerks, and bureaucrats were once grateful for having been spared the dehumanization of the factory. But today the clerk, and not the operative on the assembly line, is the typical American worker, and such positions offer little by way of prestige.[74]

As a result, ensuring worker motivation became a constant challenge. As Daniel Bell stated, 'If conspicuous consumption was the badge of the rising middle class, conspicuous loafing is the hostile gesture of the tired working class.'[75] Sociologist William H. Whyte wrote, 'the satisfactions of craftsmanship are gone, and we can never call them back.'[76]

As work became dehumanized and the number of large corporations increased, the organizational form of unions changed as well. Prior to the 1920s and 1930s, unions were largely organized around craft lines by the American Federation of Labor (AFL). As corporations became ever larger, a new form of industrial unionism emerged. Rather than follow the old AFL craft-based strategy where workers were organized according to their trade, the Congress of Industrial Organizations (CIO) chose to organize whole industries. But it was not without bitter struggles. At first unions were up against tough-minded capitalist entrepreneurs in the 1920s – like Henry Ford and Sewell Avery of Montgomery Ward who saw unions as an assault to their god-given capitalist authority. By the time of the new corporate economy, the big battles were largely a thing of the past. Most large corporations came to accept, albeit grudgingly, unions as a part of the new environment. Besides, if one's competitors were also unionized, and there was virtually no foreign competition, it was easy for managers to settle and make deals to achieve industrial peace. Eric Johnston, the President of the US Chamber of Commerce, a group that had been among the most vociferous in their opposition to government and unions, described collective bargaining as 'an established and useful reality.' AFL-CIO President George Meany predicted (incorrectly) in 1956, 'to some in management, any limitation of management's right to set the conditions of work is a challenge to its integrity. But this point is diminishing. I would expect that by 1980 it will have disappeared completely.'[77]

As a result, while union membership remained unchanged at approximately 3 million members from 1920 to 1940, from 1940 to 1960 it grew to around 19 million. As a share of non-farm employment, union membership grew from 11 percent in the mid-1930s to about one-third by the late 1950s. It is easy to forget, given how weak unions are today, how strong they once were. The election of a union president was national news. The media covered union conventions. What the United Automobile Workers (UAW), Teamsters, United Mine Workers (UMW), and other big unions did mattered. Americans knew who union leaders were and many Americans saw unions as respected institutions. As Galbraith stated, 'unions and their leadership were widely accepted and on occasion accorded a measure of applause for sound social behavior both by employers and the community at large.'[78]

As entire industries became unionized and wages and working conditions improved, unions came to be seen as part of a tripartite system of economic and social governance, with corporations and government making up the other legs of the stool. Galbraith noted:

> What we used to think of as the 'decentralized decision of the market place' has given way to various processes of large-scale private institutional decision-making remarkably like that of government in both its methods and results. We constantly see in such thing as labor unions, corporations and trade associations, and in the 'bargaining' that goes on between them, a reflection of the private institutional needs for government.[79]

The Rise of Planning and the Mass Society

The new technology system not only led to a new economic system, but also to a new society and outlook on life. This was an era of mass society – mass production, mass media, mass education, and mass government. It was an era of three television networks, three car companies, and one type of K-12 education system. It was an era in which Harvard sociologist David Riesman warned of the eclipse of the inner-directed man by the outer-directed man who took his cues from others and whose main goal was conformity. In an economy in which the production system specialized in cranking out large quantities of standardized, homogenous products it was no surprise that this was mirrored in the underlying culture and society. In his classic book, *The Organization Man*, William H. Whyte stated, 'people grow restive with a mythology that is too distant from the way things actually are, and as more and more lives have been encompassed by an organization way of life, the pressures for an accompanying ideological shift have been mounting.'[80]

As Daniel Bell put it, 'We have made conformity a religion ... The leading man no longer has the opportunity to fling himself into the fray. He is becoming just another office worker – and one who is not always difficult to replace.'[81] Computers were so good at dealing with masses of data that one futurist predicted that 'they undoubtedly will help to seduce planners into inventing a society with goals that can be dealt with in the mass rather than in terms of the individual ... the idea of the individual may be completely swallowed up in statistics.'[82]

This was a society in which people increasingly identified themselves not by where they were from, or who their families were, or even by what they did, but rather, what organization they worked for. As Galbraith said, 'The question automatically asked when two men meet on a plane or in Florida is, "who are you with". Until this is known the individual is a cipher.'[83] William H. Whyte comments on how college students viewed their future in terms of the organization, 'whether as a member of the corporation, a group medical clinic, or a law factory, they see the collective as the best vehicle for service.'[84] Not surprisingly, a typical advertisement in a 1950s business magazine might show a young company man ingratiating himself with the boss. To understand the mass society of the time just look at how men dressed. Pictures of men in the 1950s look remarkably dated today in that they all look alike; men in white shirts with dark suits and striped ties. People may not have liked the technostructure, but its very essence meant security. It was powerful and stable. In short, by the 1950s the 'Organization Man' had arrived.[85]

Governance and Politics

As the old factory economy began to fall apart in the 1930s, so too did that era's governing system. As John Judis writes, 'As a result of the New Deal, American politics shifted decisively away from the underlying assumptions about the limits of government that prevailed during the age of Mellon. It would be another four decades before these new assumptions would be effectively challenged.'[86] This shift actually began with Herbert Hoover, but because he was still rooted firmly in the governing precepts of the factory-based economy, his attempts at modest reform were not enough.[87] It took Franklin D. Roosevelt (FDR) to articulate a wholesale rejection of the past and a forceful embrace of the future.

Under FDR's leadership, in the 1930s, a raft of industry-regulating institutions and laws were established, including the Public Utility Holding Company Act, the Communications Act, the Social Security Act, the Civil Aeronautics Act, the Motor Carrier Act, the Natural Gas Act, the Securities Exchange Commission, and the Federal Housing Administration. Significant labor laws were passed including the 1938 Fair Labor Standards Act and its amendments in 1949 to prohibit child labor.

Big bureaucratic government became the norm. Between 1920 and 1970, government employment grew almost 14 times, with the lion's share of this at the federal level. Federal expenditures went up from 41 percent of all government expenditures in 1922 to 64 percent by 1956. In virtually all policy areas – urban policy and housing, transportation, employment and training, environmental protection, and others – the federal government had become the dominant actor that set the rules, provided the money, and made the decisions.

Unlike the prior era, there was widespread support for expansion of government. American business reversed its earlier opposition to the 'intrusion' of government, and made peace with big government, just as it had with organized labor. Business accepted a larger role for government, not just to smooth out the excesses of capitalism and maintain social peace, but also to lend stability to the entire economic system. The Corporation for Economic Development (CED) played a particularly important role in this change of attitude. Established in the early 1940s, the CED was a 'peak association' made up of the leaders of major corporations. Unlike the Chamber of Commerce and the National Association of Manufacturers, whose ideologies remained rooted in the old economy, the CED rejected the prior free-market fundamentalism. Organized labor, which had originally opposed a government-run social security system prior to the New Deal, also became a supporter of big government.[88] Finally, with the exception of a few lone conservative voices, most intellectuals embraced the new order. As Daniel Bell noted, 'In the western world there is a today a rough consensus among intellectuals on political issues. The acceptance of the welfare state, the desirability of decentralized power, a system of mixed economy and of political pluralism. In that sense, too the ideological age has ended.'[89] As literary critic Lionel Trilling, declared in the 1950s, 'In the United States at this time, liberalism is not only the dominant but even the sole intellectual tradition.'[90]

Government did not just get bigger, its entire role was re-envisioned as it became involved in all aspects of life. As a result, the terms 'mixed economy' and 'welfare state' were coined. Adlai Stevenson summed it up:

> nor in current talk of getting government out of business does there appear to be much recognition that government is in business to the tune of about $15 billion worth of military orders each year and is therefore playing, whatever the theory of the matter, a decisive part in keeping demand steady through the whole economy.[91]

Harvard sociologist Daniel Bell concurred, stating:

> The fundamental political fact in the second half of the twentieth century has been the extension of state-directed economies. In the last quarter of the century we now move on to state-managed societies. And these emerge because of the increase in the large scale social demands (health, education, welfare, social services) which have become entitlements for the population.[92]

Government had won World War II, built the Interstate Highway System, and sent a man to the moon. This was an age of government. Indeed, government service became a calling so much so that in 1955 futurist Ernst Morris predicted that by 1976 'civil service will share the highest prestige values with researchers and professions.'[93] Government grew in part because stronger public action was needed to cope with the complexities of the corporate mass production economy and also because a more prosperous economy could devote more resources to collective action. But it also flourished because most people now saw government as an essential agent of progress. As business guru Peter Drucker contended, 'Government became the appropriate agent for all social problems, in fact non-governmental activity became suspect.'[94] Otis Graham, a leading historian of the New Deal, agreed, 'Planning assumes that modern industrial society requires public intervention to achieve national goals, assumes that such intervention must touch all fundamental social developments, must be goal-oriented, and effectively coordinated at the center.'[95] If planning focused on centralized analysis, public administration focused on the advantages of carrying out public tasks through top-down, rule-driven bureaucracies. Unlike the old machine politics, the new public administration was based on the rational planning model by which government experts collected virtually all the relevant information needed to make the right decisions. This faith in big bureaucratic government was so strong that as late as 1974 the *New York Times* could write that 1975 'could usher in a fundamental transformation of the American economy toward increased government planning and controls.'[96]

This new confidence in the ability of government to be a progressive force was grounded in part in the emerging social science disciplines, including economics and psychology. The 1950s saw the rise of a new wave in social science based on imitation of natural science methods. Science would now guide our decisions. The Donald Fagen album, *I.G.Y.*, a series of songs about the musician's memories of the 1950s, epitomizes the widespread social attitude: 'we just need big machines to make big decisions, programmed with compassion and vision. We'll be clean when that work is done; We'll be eternally free, yes and eternally young.'[97] For the first time, operating through government, man could control his own destiny, or so the elites thought. Galbraith states, 'the emergence of the mixed economy is an assertion of intention to master our destiny.'[98] This notion of control from the top was characteristic of the managerial era. Heilbroner predicted that 'Planning will be the central political and economic necessity of all economic systems over the coming generations.'[99]

In the factory era economy, 'Liberal economics assumed that the market was a sufficient arbiter of the public weal; there were different utilities of individuals and the scarcity of different goods would come to an equilibrium that harmonized the intensity of desire and the willingness to pay the asking price.'[100] As the new corporate economy emerged from the wreckage of the Great Depression there was a growing consensus that the autonomic forces of the market and individual firm decisions were no longer adequate to manage a complex corporate economy. Historian Karl Polyani asserted, 'we are witnessing a development under which the economic system ceases to lay down the law to society and the primacy of society over that system is secured.'[101] Galbraith went so far as to state that:

> The market itself is suspended by vertical integration where companies control all phases of the production process. In this situation, the planning unit takes over the source of supply or the outlet, and the transaction takes place within the firm itself ... If the state is effectively to manage demand, the public sector of the economy must be relatively large.[102]

He went on to argue, 'The mature corporation depends on the state for trained manpower, the regulation of aggregate demand, for stabilization in wages and prices. All are essential to the planning with which it replaces the market.'[103] As a result, a new set of governing principles came to be accepted, partly through trial and error, partly through a slow, if not always conscious realization that the world had changed. These principles included a belief that top-down rational planning made sense, both in business and government; that in many industries government regulation of output and entry led to the most efficient outcomes; that 'command and control' government regulations were needed to protect people from the abuses of the marketplace; that the central goal of economic policy was to ensure full employment;[104] and that when confronted with problems, government programs managed by government agencies were the best solution.

Such a massive shift in governance could not occur without a similar shift in politics. Indeed, each new economy has brought about a shift in the political structure, with the dominant party of the old economy often failing initially to adapt to the new realities. As the old factory economy fell apart, the Republican party became the party of the past, fighting vigorously against the progressive reforms of the New Deal and for maintaining the factory era's small government governing system. So strong was the new Democratic vision and conversely so bankrupt the Republican one, that Al Landon, the Republican candidate for President in 1936 won just two states. By 1940 however, the Republicans had begun to come around to the new realities, as even the Grand Old Party (GOP) platform supported an extension of Social Security and important labor safeguards such as the right to collective bargaining. Indeed as one modern conservative has said, 'The GOP was mostly dominated by FDR wannabes like Thomas Dewey and Wendell Wilkie ... both parties essentially accepted the New Deal precept that modern society ... was too complex to be left to its own devices.'[105]

In a prelude to the current split in the Democratic party between 'old' and 'new' Democrats over whether to embrace a new governing philosophy inherent in today's New Economy, Republicans were also split. By the 1940s and 1950s, some conservatives were willing to accept the New Deal, but wanted to limit and constrain it.[106] This led the conservative right to attack these moderates. Echoing today's left-wing critics of the centrist Democrats, conservative author Russell Kirk complained:

The liberal, or anti-Taft, element of the Republican party (waxing or waning in strength, according to circumstance) acted upon the assumption that the New Deal was irrevocable ... concessions, therefore, must be made to public opinion, allegedly infatuated with Roosevelt's programs – large concessions, made with the best face possible; and presidential candidates must be secured whose personality and background would not remind the electorate overmuch that the Republican party's rank and file detested the assumptions of the New Deal. Victory at the polls, rather than the defense or vindication of principles, seemed to most of the liberal Republicans the object of their party.[107]

Kirk complained that liberal Republicans ran on a platform that they were better equipped to administer the New Deal programs. 'This amounted,' he felt, 'to a confession, perhaps, that the Democratic party was the party of initiative, of ideas, or new policies, of intellectual leadership.'[108]

Like the rise of the 'New Democrat' movement in the 1980s led by the Democratic Leadership Council to bring the Democratic party more in line with new realities, significant elements of the Republican party sought to embrace that era's new realities. Indeed, Dwight Eisenhower called his political philosophy 'New Republican'.[109] And just as liberals hoped that Bill Clinton would resurrect the liberal agenda when he was elected in 1992, as the Eisenhower administration and a new Republican Congress took power in 1953, Republican hard liners were hoping for a return to the kind of conservatism that was popular before FDR. To their disappointment Eisenhower supported the expansion of Social Security, unemployment insurance, internationalism and free trade. As political scientist Ken Baer notes: 'The Republicans could not ignore the consensus forming around the ascendant New Deal public philosophy and grudgingly began to accept the changes it had wrought on American society, differentiating their public philosophy from the Democrats based on their response to it.'[110]

In contrast, the conservative wing of the Republican party was in a constant state of frustration, not really believing that the world had changed in such a fundamental way as to make their governing ideology outmoded.[111] Vocal elements, like the Liberty League, opposed FDR and the New Deal. Perhaps the person who best epitomized this opposition was Senator Robert A. Taft, son of President William Howard Taft and Republican leader of the Senate. As Kirk notes, 'In 1939 Senator Robert Taft set out to rebuild his enfeebled party upon a foundation of principle, as an instrument of resistance to the New Deal.'[112] Taft argued that, 'The Republican party ... encourage men to go into business, to establish new industries, to enlarge existing

industries, through a reduction of taxation .... the whole tax system
should be revised to encourage and reward ingenuity, industry, genius,
and daring as those qualities have always been rewarded in the past.'[113]
He went on to state that:

> there is an underlying philosophy in the principal measures of the New Deal
> which desires to affect a complete revolution in the whole American business
> and constitutional system under which this country has prospered for 150
> years. Against that philosophy and the measures which attempt to carry it out,
> the Republican candidates must be wholeheartedly and violently opposed.
> That policy is one of a planned economy.[114]

Just as many on the Democratic left have never really accepted the
New Democratic philosophy of the Clinton administration, many
Republicans saw Eisenhower as a disappointment. Because Vice
President Richard Nixon was heir to the nomination in 1960 (as Vice
President Al Gore was in 2000), it was not until 1964 that the
Republicans could wage an intra-party fight over the direction of the
party. Frustrated over the 'tepid' Republicanism of the Eisenhower
years and rejecting Kennedy's New Frontier, Republicans coalesced
around Senator Barry Goldwater, a conservative who never accepted
the realities of the new era and who sneered at both parties for being
technocratic reformers.[115] Essentially looking backwards to the old
factory-based economy era, Goldwater declared, '[I have] little interest
in streamlining government or making it more efficient, for I mean to
reduce its size.' In his 1960 book *Conscience of a Conservative*
Goldwater made it clear that he aimed to return to the old economy
governing system, by restoring states rights (e.g., downsizing the
federal government), freedom to work (opposing unions), voluntarist
social services (by scrapping the welfare state), and regressive taxes (by
eliminating the graduated income tax[116]). After the Goldwater debacle
in which he lost 48 states, the Republican party finally accepted the
new reality, nominating moderate Republicans in the next three
presidential elections.[117]

The Mass Production Metropolis

There was one additional set of changes brought about by the new
corporate economy: new regional economic foci and form of
urbanization. Air travel, long-distance communications, and truck
transport began to recast regional relationships, allowing large-scale

urban development to spread farther south and west. With the building of arterial highways, then limited access parkways, then finally with the passage in 1956 of the National Defense Highway System, interstate highways, metropolitan regions and finally the entire nation were tied together. Just as information technology is enabling many companies to locate anywhere in the world today, highways and widespread electrification allowed industry greater locational freedom, stimulating industrialization in the South and West. In addition, the development of air conditioning made living and working in hot southern and western climes more tolerable. As a result, the new economy led to a boom in the South and West.

But the new economy did more than integrate all the regions into one economic system, it brought about a new regional homogenization. What was striking about the United States in the 1930s or 1940s is how very different the regions seemed. New England was more different from the South or the Pacific Northwest than it was from Eastern Canada. The architecture, food, culture and even vernacular differed significantly between regions. However, in the 25 years following World War II the United States became a national society in the sense that developments in one region had an immediate effect on all others. As Adlai Stevenson stated, 'an incredible linage of wires and roads and cooperative enterprise, public and private, has taken isolation (and now isolationism) from all but the remotest homes in America.'[118] As large corporations increasingly sold their wares in national markets, they imposed a new uniformity and homogeneousness on the nation. One could stay in a Holiday Inn in Maine or Montana and not tell the difference. With the rise of television and the major networks, for the first time all Americans were exposed to largely the same entertainment and news. In short, a set of distinct regional cultures was giving way to one national culture.

This was also an era of mass suburbanization. In 1920, about 20 percent of the population lived in suburbs. By 1980 approximately 60 percent did. 'Levittowns,' large, standardized bedroom suburbs, were the order of the day. 'Bedroom' suburbs dependent on the core city for most functions grew like wildfire, in part as increasing automobile use significantly expanded available residential locations. Congestion and rising land values in the urbanized core, the construction of an interstate highway system, Veterans Administration and Federal Housing Administration subsidies for single-family homes, tax incentives for new infrastructure, and a shortage of suitable development sites in the core city all encouraged firms and households to move outward. While people were moving to the suburbs, the new corporate office economy was locating downtown, building higher and higher monuments to power and grandeur – skyscraper office towers in all the major cities. Electric elevators and telephone communications facilitated and intensified their use in the central business district.

THE CALM BEFORE THE STORM: THE TRIUMPH OF THE SYSTEM AT THE END OF THE 1960S

If someone wrote in the 1960s that the American economy was about to disintegrate and fall into a 25-year period of stagnation with foreign firms challenging the competitive position of US firms, the writer would have been dismissed as a hopeless contrarian. After all, the nation had enjoyed an unprecedented period of prosperity and was the envy of the world.

As the United States excelled, its lead over other nations expanded, leaving Europeans fearful of being left behind. French author Jean-Jacques Servan-Schreiber wrote the best-seller, *The American Challenge*, which described an all powerful American economic system widening its technological lead and utilizing superior management ability and economies of scale to take over the European economy. Like the current European fears of American dominance in today's New Economy, Europeans struggled to adapt to the new economy of the 1960s.[119]

If the mood overseas was one of fear of US economic dominance, the mood at home was one of unbridled economic optimism. In *The Challenge of Abundance* Robert Theobald wrote that the problem now was an overabundance of goods and services and how to cope with increased leisure. As the 1960s boom kept going, it began to look as though America was finally on the cusp of solving the problem of production. Futurists studied how people would cope with all this free time (would they know what to do, or would they be lost without work?). University departments of leisure studies sprang up, and prestigious foundations gave grants to study how people would live in a society in which they had unprecedented wealth and never-before-dreamed-of amounts of leisure.[120]

Futurist Herman Kahn's writings typified this view. In his 1967 book *The Year 2000*, Kahn relied on the new 'science' of forecasting and ended up with a book that had the tone of 'you ain't seen nothing yet.' As discussed in Chapter 1, he vastly overstated the progress of the subsequent 33 years. One of the reasons for his optimism was that he thought the technology system would continue its dramatic improvements. Referring to the purported impact of automation on jobs, Kahn stated:

This seems to be one of those quite common situations in which early in the innovation period many exaggerated claims are made, then there is disillusionment and swing to over conservative prediction and a general pessimism and skepticism, and then when a reasonable degree of development has been obtained and a learning period navigated, many – if not all – of the early 'ridiculous' exaggerations are greatly exceeded. It is particularly clear that if computers improve by five, ten or more orders of magnitude over the next 33 years, this is almost certain to happen.[121]

The reality was that computers improved by many more than ten orders of magnitude and yet this level of automation did not happen. Of the 100 innovations Kahn said were very likely to occur by the year 2000 only 30 have been developed and 15 of these are IT related. For example, Kahn predicted a range of things that have yet to come about, including new airborne vehicles, widespread use of nuclear power, extensive centralization of computer power, control of weather, lunar settlements, and automated grocery stores. He did correctly predict developments like the use of lasers, more transplants of human organs, direct broadcasts from satellites, and personal pagers.[122]

Like the economic forecasters of the time, technology forecasters simply projected current technology trends forward. They assumed that current innovations in mastering the physical world (transportation, materials, etc.) would continue. Though Kahn was an optimist, he was not an outlier. Most Americans, from the working man on the assembly line to the ivory tower futurist, were bullish on the future. The expectations were not just that we would get richer, but that technology would transform our lives. The Organisation for Economic Co-operation and Development expressed the received wisdom in an early 1970s report which stated, 'The industrial and commercial exploitation of the existing body of scientific and technical knowledge will continue to generate increases in productivity for a long time to come.'[123]

In an era where technological innovations seem so revolutionary, it is hard to believe that from the perspective of the late 1960s, the innovations of the past 30 years and the level of economic growth would disappoint. Yet, this was a period in which man walked on the moon – anything was possible and everything was expected. The sky was the limit. So, what went wrong?

THE TURBULENT TRANSITION TO THE NEW ECONOMY: 1974 TO 1994

Fifteen years after Kahn rhapsodized on the wonderful future to come, Americans were waiting in line to buy gasoline and suffering through unprecedented rates of inflation and unemployment on a scale not seen since the Great Depression, rolling regional recessions as traditional heavy and natural resource industries shed millions of jobs, stagnant and even declining wages, growing income inequality, and the federal budget deficit spiraling out of control. Things got so bad that Jimmy Carter coined a new term, the 'misery index,' which was calculated by adding the inflation rate and the unemployment rate together. To the shock of almost everyone, robust growth had become stagnation. If productivity had in fact gone up from 1973 to 1995 as it had from 1955 to 1973, Americans would have been 50 percent richer, close to where Kahn predicted we would be. While US per capita disposable income grew 46 percent and real wages by 31 percent between 1963 and 1973, between 1985 and 1995 income grew just 13 percent and real wages 6 percent.[124] No wonder Americans were disgusted, angry and befuddled. Someone had taken their expected prosperity away from them, and they wanted answers.

Not only did the economy suddenly began to decelerate, but the nation's optimistic attitude also went into a nose-dive. Whereas most Americans in the 1960s felt that the nation could do anything, that government could solve a whole host of problems, and that technology was a force for progress, by the 1970s they had begun to question all three. By the 1970s, the rosy scenarios of the 1960s were being replaced by gloom and doom predictions. Daniel Bell argued, 'The sense remains that the period of American economic dominance in the world has crested and that, by the end of the century, the US, like any aging rentier, will be living off the foreign earnings on the investments its corporations made in the halcyon quarter century after WWII'.[125] Political scientist Samuel P. Huntington predicted that:

In the year 2000, the American system that has been developed in the last 20 years will be in a state of disintegration and decay. Just as American influence has replaced European influence during the current period, so also during the last quarter of this century American power will begin to wane, and other countries will move in to fill the gap.[126]

He suggested powerhouses such as Vietnam, Brazil, and China. The sense that the established order was falling apart extended to include all aspects of society, including technology. In the 1950s and 1960s, technology was seen as a positive force that would bring a better life. As the US chemical industry liked to boast, 'Better living through chemistry.' However, the large-scale technological failures of Bhophal, Chernobyl, and Three Mile Island, and environmental threats such as acid rain, ozone depletion, and global warming, led many to doubt that technology would lead to progress.

Americans began to doubt not only the ability of technology to deliver results, but the entire goal of the old economy, growth. During this transitional period, a vigorous anti-growth movement emerged. Where a rising standard of living was seen as the key to the good life in the old economy, in the transitional period wealth itself became indicted. Heilbroner stated, 'The Greek legend of Midas and the biblical estimate of a rich man's chances of entering heaven testify to a deep-seated psychological and moral wariness of riches ... All of this suggests deep reason why the quest for wealth has brought results that have so often disappointed us.'[127] And if wealth was no longer something we should strive for, that was just as well, since many, including the influential Club of Rome, believed that we had reached the limits of growth. Writing in 1977, Heilbroner opined that, 'A reasonable guess is that growth will have to be near zero – perhaps even negative – a century from now.[128] Americans were counseled to diminish their expectations and give up on the notion that their kids would live a better life.

If people were pessimistic about the economy, they were even more pessimistic about government. In stark contrast to the optimism of the 1960s, with its belief that social science and social policy could solve a host of intractable problems, by the 1970s, most problems were seen as too complex and our ability to solve them too limited. Not surprisingly, just as the political consensus around limited government fell apart as the factory economy broke down in the 1930s, the old economy political consensus around big government began to unravel around this time. By the early 1970s, the perceived failure of government to solve problems in areas such as crime, poverty, pollution, the economy, and transportation tarnished the image of planning and managerial government, and belied the notion that government could be made to work if it just brought in the 'best and brightest' experts. While government was able to solve what some called 'tame' problems like putting a man on the moon, it failed to solve 'wicked' ones like revitalizing decaying urban areas and reducing crime. Hence, the complaint, 'if we can put a man on the moon, surely we can fix the cities,' became commonplace.

Initially, as the failures emerged, the first reaction was to add technical fixes – encouraging citizens to be more informed, fostering stronger leaders, generating better information, and the like. Harvard sociologist Daniel Bell explained:

> In social policy, particularly in the United States, the record of social scientists is even more dismal. In the areas of education, welfare, and social planning, social scientists have reluctantly begun to admit that the problems are more complex than they thought. The failure of liberalism, then, is in part a failure of knowledge.[129]

More and better knowledge would provide the silver bullet, and once we got those 'great big machines programmed with compassion and vision,' bureaucratic government would once again work.

As the old economy continued to disintegrate by the 1970s, this reformist hope gave way, led by a re-energized conservative Republican party, to a pessimistic rejection of government and an inclination to leave problem-solving to the market and civil society. Many believed that government had overreached and had to set its sights lower. Budget cuts stemming from slower economic growth just exacerbated the trend toward smaller government. The watchwords of the day became deregulation, devolution, privatization, and retrenchment. The public's trust in government to effectively do the right thing declined from a high of 76 percent in 1964 to 21 percent in 1994.[130]

As this realization set in, politics rapidly pitted liberals who sought to preserve the New Deal and Great Society consensus, and its related governing apparatus, against conservatives who sought to destroy that governing framework which, like the underlying economic structure, had run its course. Goldwater's pre-New Deal conservative views of a reduced federal government, states' rights, and hostility to unions, had little chance of taking hold then, as they were sowed during the heyday of the old economy when big government was the dominant paradigm. It took the decline of the old economy and emerging cracks in the bureaucratic model before the anti-government, market model could be considered viable by more than the most hard-core ideologues. The minority party, led by Republican Ronald Reagan, articulated a forceful critique of the old economy governing system and politics. Reagan's proclamation that 'government is not the solution to our problem, government is the problem' reflected the view of many. In 1988, Democratic candidate Michael Dukakis argued that the election was not about ideology, but about competence. He was wrong; it was about ideology – in this case extending the Reagan revolution or bringing back the New Deal-Great Society revolution. Many voted for Reagan and later for Bush and their smaller government philosophy not because they rejected government, but because they instinctively understood that big bureaucratic government had run its course. As we will see in the next chapter, the rise of the New Democratic movement and the presidency of Bill Clinton was an attempt to modernize the Democratic party to fit the new economic realities.

In short, the pessimists in the transition period were just as wrong as the optimists at the end of the old economy. Both were extrapolating from the trends and forces of the day. The reality was that the old economy and its underlying technology system could not continue to generate robust growth and as such broke down in the 1970s. To those living through the breakdown, it was difficult if not impossible to see that this was a transitional phase between one techno-economic paradigm and another. If they could have seen this, they would have realized that in a relatively short time, a New Economy would emerge that would change everything. It is to this New Economy that we turn.

NOTES

1. The ten largest manufacturing industries in 1860 were, in order of output, cotton goods, lumber, footwear, flour, men's clothing, iron products, machinery, woolen goods, carriages, and leather.
2. Heilbroner and Singer (1977) p. 90.
3. Alderfer and Michl (1957) p. 25.
4. Today only approximately 200000 work the rails.
5. As late as 1920, the two places with the most horses in the United States were New York City and Chicago. (Huntington and Cushing, 1925) In 1944, only 10 percent of the German army was mechanized. The rest relied on horses and walking.
6. Gray and Peterson (1974) p. 301.
7. Ibid. p. 103.
8. However, it is important to realize as Philip Scranton (1997) has pointed out, that not all industries followed this mass production model. Many sectors, such as tools, jewelry, and printing, focused on specialized craft and batch production, in part because the production process did not enable mass production.

9. Tarbell (1904)
10. Chandler (1977).
11. Taylor (1911) p. 59.
12. Wiebe (1967) p. xiv.
13. Many populists considered railroads and telegraph systems to be natural monopolies that needed regulating, or even public ownership.
14. Wiebe (1989) p. 3.
15. Thus, the wealthy and powerful were not only subject to new regulations, they were being taxed to pay for them. This nexus explains much of the current Republican agenda to cut income taxes on the wealthy while hoping to force government to cut spending on regulatory enforcement.
16. Wiebe (1989) p. 112.
17. Leuchtenburg (1963) p. 21.
18. www.authentichistory.com/audio/1900s/19121001WilliamHTaft-TheAnti-TrustLaw.html.
19. Fred Seigel (undated) sums up the conservative world view: 'The GOP, a largely Protestant party, looked upon itself as the manifestation of the divine creed of Americanism revealed through the Constitution. To be a conservative, then, was to share in a religiously ordained vision of a largely stateless society of self-regulating individuals.'
20. This is similar to the politics that emerged in the prior industrial era that began in the 1830s, as Fred Seigel notes, 'Jacksonian democracy politically routed the Whig heirs of Federalism. It reduced the conservatism of the Founding Fathers to a literary temperament kept alive by writers like James Fenimore Cooper who warned that "the true theatre of a demagogue is a democracy"'.
21. Bell (1976) p. 26.
22. Chernow (1990) p. 322.
23. Baltzell (1987) p. 158.
24. www.korpios.org/resurgent/GDPreal.htm.
25. Griffith (1982) p. 79.
26. Ibid.
27. Ibid. pp. 88 and 89.
28. www.sjsu.edu/faculty/wooda/middleton/middleton5.html.
29. US Congress, Office of Technology Assessment (1993) p. 138.
30. This pattern of acceptance was repeated in the case of the underpowered and expensive personal computers that were introduced in the 1980s, but did not attain true mass market acceptance for at least ten years.
31. http://inventors.about.com/library/weekly/aa081797.htm.
32. Oakley (1986).
33. The Bank of America introduced magnetic ink character recognition to automate check reading (Van Deusen, 1955).
34. www.pafko.com/history/h_contrb.html.
35. Morris (1955) p. 39.
36. In 1956 over 80 percent of prescriptions drugs in use had been unknown in 1941.
37. Caplow et al. (2001) p. 234.
38. Oakley (1986) p. 239.
39. Caplow et al. (2001).
40. While in 1830, a farmer had to put in between 250 and 300 hours to grow a bushel of wheat, it fell to 40-50 hours in 1890 and by 1975 to 3-4 hours (Greenwood and Seshadri, 2002).
41. Alderfer and Michl (1957) p. 134.
42. Ibid.
43. Bell (1962) p. 266.

44. Oakley (1986) p. 396.
45. John (1998) p. 193.
46. *Time*, 8 January, 1959.
47. Stevenson (1956) p. 129.
48. Michael (1962) p. 10.
49. Like those who today argue that the Internet is leading to most things being free, the excitement with nuclear energy that was so palpable that it was widely repeated that power would be so cheap it would not even be metered.
50. One reflection of this is that travel and tourism took off. Visitors to national parks almost doubled. Disneyland, which opened in 1955, became an instant hit. The number of motels tripled, from 13 500 to 41 000 (Oakley, 1986, p. 260).
51. 'Inventor' was a separate occupation since 1900, but in 1940 the Census Bureau downgraded it to a title within professional workers not elsewhere classified.
52. Schumpeter (1975) p. 132.
53. Total private industrial research and development expenditures as a share of GDP grew 28 times from 1920 to 1960 (0.07 percent to 2.0 percent). By the mid-1950s over 3000 companies had R&D facilities. Public and private R&D expenditures grew from $3.6 billion in 1940 to $23 billion in 1967 (constant dollar) (www.nsf.gov/sbe/srs/seind00/c1/tt01-03.htm).
54. Low (1984).
55. The process was the same with scientists. The 1900 census had only one scientific occupation: chemical assayers and metallurgists.
56. Galbraith (1968) pp. 13-14.
57. Between 1939 and 1996, the share of business revenue going to corporations increased from 78 percent to 89 percent, while the share going to proprietorships declined from 14 to 5 percent.
58. Galbraith (1968) p. 311.
59. Ibid. p. 69.
60. Gray and Peterson (1974) p. 474.
61. Taft (1956) p. 176.
62. Whitman (1999).
63. Useem (1996).
64. Survey by McGraw-Hill. Cited in Graham (1976) p. 282.
65. Galbraith (1968) p. 244.
66. Berle and Means (1932).
67. Galbraith (1968) p. 131.
68. Ibid. p. 43.
69. Baltzell (1987).
70. Quoted in Ibid. p. 39.
71. Galbraith (1968) p. 105.
72. Huxley (1949).
73. Galbraith (1968) p. 243.
74. Cited in Ibid. p. 148.
75. Bell (1976) p. 239.
76. Whyte (1956) p. 244.
77. Meany (1956) p. 52.
78. Galbraith (1968) p. 272.
79. Ibid. p. 127.
80. Whyte (1956) p. 6.
81. Bell (1976).
82. (Michael, 1962). *Time* magazine Chairman Henry R. Luce wrote, 'The same wise and sensitive people who yesterday preached social consciousness to the individual are today trying to rescue individuality from a too-well-organized social conscience.

Poets and thinkers who earlier wooed the embrace of the downtrodden masses now flee the tread of the organized crowd' (Luce, 1956, p. 203).

83. Galbraith (1968) p. 164. In today's more individualistic New Economy, they are more likely to ask 'what do you do?'.

84. Whyte (1956) p. 85.

85. Henry R. Luce (1956), argued that 'Today, to a degree never before known, man is Organized Man.'

86. Judis (2000) p. 58.

87. During the 1932 presidential campaign Herbert Hoover (1932) argued that the opposition was 'proposing changes and so-called new deals which would destroy the very foundations of our American system.' And indeed it did, if one defines those foundations as the old way of doing things.

88. Meany (1956).

89. Bell (1976) p. 402.

90. Trilling (1950) p. ii.

91. Stevenson (1956) p. 129.

92. Bell (1976) p. 24.

93. Morris (1955) p. 234.

94. Drucker (1993) p. 123.

95. Graham (1976) p. 95.

96. Golden (1974).

97. Fagen (1982).

98. Galbraith (1968) p. 227.

99. Heilbroner and Singer (1977) p. 250.

100. Bell (1976) p. 26.

101. Polanyi (1944) p. 251.

102. Galbraith (1968) p. 269.

103. Ibid. p. 315.

104. One reason for the change in attitudes was that government was now seen as central to managing the business cycle. In the 1930s Keynes argued that government should use tax and spending powers to smooth out the business cycle. While Roosevelt stumbled towards Keynesianism as World War II put a large number of underutilized resources into play, it was John Kennedy with his tax cuts in 1961 in the face of a recession who gave explicit validity to this new role of government.

105. Garvin (2003) p. 62.

106. Eisenhower once told his brother Edgar that if any party tried to abolish the New Deal, 'you would not hear of that party again in our political history.' For this would mean returning to the politics of Hoover and pretending that the Depression and the transformation to the new mass production economy had never occurred.

107. Kirk and McClellan (1967) p. 47.

108. Ibid.

109. Eisenhower had trouble placing himself on the political spectrum, referring to himself as 'middle of the road' and his political philosophy as new republicanism, modern republicanism, or moderate progressivism.

110. Baer (2000) p. 13.

111. Taft (1956) acerbically stated, 'In striving for material things, we must not change those basic principles of government and of personal conduct which create and protect the character of a people … we cannot hope to achieve salvation by worshipping the god of the standard of living' (cover page).

112. Kirk and McClellan (1967) p. 129.

113. Ibid.

114. Ibid. p. 16.

115. One indication of the depth of resistance was the formation in 1958 of the John Birch Society with an emphasis on fighting a supposed communist conspiracy.
116. It is popular to view Goldwater as the vanguard of the new conservative movement of today. In actuality he represented the last gasp of the pre-New Deal governing philosophy. It was only the breakdown of the old economy that allowed the more conservative branch of the Republican party to gain power in the 1980s and 1990s.
117. One of the forces for modernization and moderation in the party was the Ripon Society, a group formed in the early 1960s. In a manifesto distributed to party leaders on 6 January 1964 they stated: 'We believe that the future of our party lies not in extremism, but in moderation. The moderate course offers the Republican Party the best chance to build a durable majority position in American politics. This is the direction the party must take if it is to win the confidence of the "new Americans" who are not at home in the politics of another generation: the new middle classes of the suburbs of the North and West – who have left the Democratic cities but have not yet found a home in the Republican party; the young college graduates and professional men and women of our great university centers – more concerned with "opportunity" than "security", the moderate of the new South – who represent the hope for peaceful racial adjustment and who are insulted by a racist appeal more fitting another generation. These and others like them hold the key to the future of our politics' (http://riponsoc.org/about.html).
118. Stevenson (1956) p. 130.
119. Robert Heilbroner (1983) stated, 'Fifteen years ago Jean-Jacques Servan-Schreiber sent a chill through the West with the opening words of *The American Challenge*: "Fifteen years from now it is quite possible that the worlds third greatest industrial power, just after the United States and Russia, will not be Europe, but American industry in Europe." We can now see that Servan-Schreiber was wrong about the continued predominance of American industrial power, but right about "multinationalization" as marking a new chapter in the economic history of capitalism. In much the same way, Joseph Monsen and Kenneth Walters, professors at the business school of the University of Washington, may be wrong about the nature of the "threat" of nationalization, but I believe they are right in calling attention to a striking change in the structure of economic life. This is the rise of state-owned companies, as perhaps the most rapidly expanding form of modern enterprise.'
120. For example, in the early 1970s the Rockefeller Foundation funded a series of studies on how to create the self-actualization society.
121. Kahn (1967) p. 93.
122. Of the 25 innovations less likely to happen, such as true artificial intelligence, room temperature superconductors, suspended animation, and complete control of heredity, few are here today. The areas they were closest to getting right were in medical and information technology. They were farthest off in the areas of control of the physical environment.
123. OECD, *The Growth of Output*. Cited in Brenner (1998) p. 236.
124. This slowdown was not confined just to the US economy; many European nations underwent a similar slowdown. In the United Kingdom, GDP per employee grew 2.65 percent per year from 1966 to 1974, but only 1.75 percent from 1984 to 1992.
125. Bell (1976) p. 215.
126. Quoted in Bell (1976) p. 216.
127. Heilbroner and Singer (1977) p. 236.
128. Ibid. p. 248.
129. Bell (1976) p. 129.
130. Hetherington (2004).

4. Today's Entrepreneurial, Knowledge-Based Economy

In his 1995 book, *The End of Affluence*, economic journalist Jeff Madrick warned of a future of stagnant productivity growth. A few years earlier, Paul Krugman had counseled Americans to have 'diminished expectations.' Madrick and Krugman were not alone; just as Alvin Hansen did in the 1930s, a host of pundits saw the economic stagnation in the transitional period of the late 1970s and early 1990s as a prelude of more of the same.[1]

The year after *The End of Affluence* appeared, productivity grew 2.8 percent and it has kept up its robust pace.[2] Just as the emergence of the corporate, mass production economy led to a turnaround after the Depression, today's New Economy has brought a new surge of growth after the 'quiet depression' of the transitional period. Indeed, productivity and wage growth averaged over 2.2 percent per year between 1997 and 2002. Twenty-two million jobs were created between 1992 and the end of 2001 and the unemployment rate fell from 7.5 percent to 4.2 percent, its lowest level in 20 years. Even the recession of 2001 was relatively mild, and while job growth since then has been exceedingly slow – in large part due to ill-advised fiscal policies of the Bush administration, and by the loss of jobs due to offshoring and a growing trade deficit[3] – productivity growth has remained strong, surging to 4.3 percent in 2003.

Why were the gloomy forecasts so wrong? The answer lies in the fact that as the old economy was playing itself out, new economic forces were finally gaining the critical mass needed to resurrect robust growth. It was just a matter of time before the new technology system, entrepreneurial ventures, organizational arrangements, and market environment took root and revived growth. Just as the transformations from the mercantile economy to the factory economy and later to the corporate, mass production economy each took around 20 years, the transformation to today's New Economy did not happen overnight.

Because the transformation took two decades, many neoclassical economists view today's economy and its driving forces – globalization, the IT revolution, entrepreneurialism and market dynamism – as simply extensions of the old economy, albeit a richer one. They see the stock market bust and the dot-bomb phenomenon as proof that the economy is the same as it ever was. In one sense, they are right: we still work at jobs for a living, and we still buy, sell and trade products and services. As Federal Reserve Chairman Alan Greenspan noted, the heart of the economy is, as it always has been, grounded in human nature, not in any new technological reality. In his analysis:

> The way we evaluate assets, and the way changes in those assets affect our economy, do not appear to be coming out of a set of rules that is different from the one that governed the actions of our forebears ... As in the past, our advanced economy is primarily driven by how human psychology molds the value system that drives a competitive market economy. And that process is inextricably linked to human nature, which appears essentially immutable and, thus, anchors the future to the past.[4]

Nonetheless, Greenspan admits that some of the key rules have changed, from the way we organize production, to our patterns of trade, to the way organizations deliver value to consumers, and to the role of technology. Indeed, during the 1990s these and other changes accounted to a structural transformation. If Schumpeter were writing about this transformation he might say, 'these revolutions periodically reshape the existing structure of industry by introducing new methods of production – the networked office, computer-aided manufacturing, biotechnology and the like; new commodities, such as the Internet, cellular telecommunications, the PC; new forms of organization – the venture capital movement, the rise of high-performance work organizations; the growth in business alliances and partnerships; and new sources of supply – high-skilled immigrants, nanotechnology; new trade routes and markets to sell in (NAFTA, Asia) and so on.'

As this paraphrase of Schumpeter's statement about the corporate economy (p. 21) suggests, the New Economy refers to a set of qualitative and quantitative changes that in the last 15 years have transformed the structure, functioning and rules of the economy. The economy has long been global. But something happened in the 1990s to make globalization big enough to change the economy in fundamental ways. Yes, ever since the invention of the telegraph, information technologies have played a role, but something happened in the 1990s when semiconductors, computers, software and telecommunications became cheap enough, fast enough, and networked enough to become ubiquitous. No question that the economy has always had managers and 'knowledge workers,' but by the 1990s knowledge workers became the dominant occupational category, enabling the economy to be powered by innovation and information. It is true that entrepreneurial growth, dynamism, 'churning' and competition have always been part of our economy, but in the 1990s the center of gravity seemed to shift to entrepreneurial activity, while at the same time the underlying operation of the economy accelerated to a new speed and became more customized and innovative. In short, the New Economy did not burst fully formed on the scene in one year, rather it emerged from seeds planted earlier, some, like the Internet, as far as back as the 1960s. But emerge it did, and we are now struggling to figure out what it means for management, economic policy, and even social policy and politics.

If the New Economy arrived on the scene like an adolescent who becomes a young adult ready to take his place in the world, there was one signal moment when it could be said that the New Economy had its coming out party – the release of the Netscape browser in 1994 that opened up the Internet for use by the masses. The Internet traces its origins back to work done by the Defense Department and later the National Science Foundation, but prior to the 1990s it was largely the province of academic researchers and a small group of computer aficionados. This began to change in 1991 when Tim Berners-Lee, a physicist operating at the European Center for Nuclear Research (CERN) in Switzerland, invented the World Wide Web computer and networking protocols to let people communicate more easily over the Internet. Even with the Web, however, the Internet was still used principally by nerds, hackers and scientists. It took the development of the Netscape browser, which added 'Windows'-like ease to the Internet experience, combined with graphics, to suddenly make it easy for everyone from a kid in the fourth grade to a grandmother to use. This basic platform of communications and software let a vast array of applications burst onto the scene, catalysing the digital revolution that has penetrated all aspects of the economy and society.

The New Economy is also about the change to a more dynamic and technology-based economy. Indeed, the story of how businesses are changing in today's economy has been told and retold with such frequency that it has become something of a cliché: the new rules of the game require speed, flexibility and innovation (see Table 4.1). New, rapidly growing companies are selling to global markets almost from their inception, and established companies are being forced to reinvent their operations to stay competitive in the new terrain. This is the part of the New Economy that was born in Steve Jobs's and Steve Wozniak's garage, at Bell Labs, Xerox PARC, and in the back of Michael Dell's car. It is Silicon Valley, eBay, Yahoo!, and the Next Big Thing.

The New Economy is about more than high technology and the Internet and frenetic action at the cutting edge. Most firms, not just the ones actually producing technology, are organizing work around it. The New Economy is a metal casting firm in Pittsburgh that uses computer-aided manufacturing technology to cut costs, save energy and reduce waste. It is an insurance company in Iowa that uses software to flatten managerial hierarchies and give its workers broader responsibilities and autonomy. It is a textile firm in Georgia that uses the Internet to take orders from customers around the world. It is a railroad that uses digitally directed DC current engines to power trains and transponders to automatically track cars. In short, the New Economy is a combination of a new technology system, a new global marketplace, a new organization of work and business, and a new workforce. These are inextricably linked, each enabling and driving the other.

The New Economy is not some strong strange manifestation of Yankee cowboy capitalism, as old economy defenders in Europe would comfortably like to believe, it is a worldwide development reshaping all advanced economies. And just like the transformation to the corporate, mass production economy in the 1950s, the United States is once again leading in the transformation. And just like Europe and Japan soon followed in the 1960s, today their economies are once again beginning to be restructured along new economy lines. One reason why growth in Europe and Japan lagged in the 1990s is because they experienced the breakdown of their old economic systems later. For example, Japan's old economy lost its steam in the late 1980s, just as America's did in the late 1970s. Yet, through much of the 1990s Japan resisted many of the fundamental forces of the New Economy. Its focus was on large stable companies, not disruptive entrepreneurial dynamism. Notwithstanding companies like Sony and Hitachi, it lagged behind in IT adoption, particularly Internet use. Japan kept its markets closed, resisting both foreign direct investment and offshoring.[5] It clung to its established systems of lifetime employment and seniority-based promotion, two bedrock aspects of its postwar economy.[6]

Table 4.1 Old and new economies' factors

Issue	Mass production corporate economy	Entrepreneurial knowledge economy
Economy-Wide Characteristics		
Markets	Stable	Dynamic
Scope of competition	National	Global
Organizational form	Hierarchical	Networked
Production system	Mass production	Flexible production
Key factor of production	Capital/labor	Innovation/ knowledge
Key technology driver	Mechanization	Digitization
Competitive advantage	Economies of scale	Innovation/quality
Importance of research	Moderate	High
Relations between firms	Go it alone	Collaboration
Workforce		
Policy goal	Full employment	Higher incomes
Skills	Job-specific	Broad and sustained
Nature of employment	Stable	Dynamic
Government		
Business-government relations	Impose requirements	Assist firm growth
Regulation	Command and control	Market tools/ flexibility

However, after a decade of a failed economy, the Japanese government has decided it can no longer fight globalization, and has begun a conscious policy of opening up Japanese markets and allowing, or even in some cases encouraging, foreign companies to purchase Japanese companies.[7] Internet and e-commerce penetration was initially lower in Japan, but in part because of smart and concerted government policies, Japan now significantly exceeds the United States in broadband deployment and use.[8]

The challenge of the New Economy may be greater for Europe and Japan because it more directly threatens established ways of being. Both regions want to manage the New Economy, not, as is the US pattern, to grab hold of the tiger's tail for the ride. In parlance, they want to make an omelet without breaking eggs. Yet, it is the embrace of creative destruction that has helped the US economy surpass Europe and Japan where entrepreneurship and dynamism are less vibrant and job protection more prevalent. Both regions have tried to retain stability, often with negative consequences of adapting and innovating less.[9] The legal, regulatory and social pressures against downsizing and the limits on entrepreneurship in Europe mean a more stable economy, but also one that is slower to let inefficient firms die and innovative firms grow. In France there are significant pressures on companies not to downsize, with CEOs equating downsizing to uncivilized behavior, and the government pressuring firms not to cut workers. Most European nations want to take an adaptive view of change, thinking and hoping they can avoid creative destruction. It shows in the fact that all of Europe's largest firms in 1998 were also large corporations in 1960.[10] They have also been reluctant to reduce restrictions on retail businesses that are required for e-commerce to flourish.

While these regions do not need to embrace the particular US style of capitalism to succeed, it is true that the New Economy is fundamentally reshaping economies no matter what policymakers and vested interests would like. At its heart, this reshaping is being powered by a new and powerful technology system.

THE NEW TECHNOLOGY SYSTEM

As Schumpeter noted, economic transformations are brought about by new technology systems. Just as the boom that began in the late 1940s was fueled by new electro-mechanical and chemical technologies, today's economic boom is being fueled by a new technology system based largely on information technology.

There may be no better testament to the fact that we have passed from the mass production, electro-mechanical era to a mass customization, digital era than the proliferation of semiconductor technology – the combination of integrated circuits (chips) and other discrete components found on circuit boards in everything from computers to phones, cars, appliances and medical devices. It is not an exaggeration to say that integrated circuits are everywhere. As the core material input of the New Economy, the world's appetite for semiconductors has been growing dramatically, a trend that despite recent market weakness is expected to continue. In 1984, worldwide shipments of semiconductors totaled 88 billion units worth over $20 billion but, by 2003, they exceeded 389 billion units worth over $170 billion.

Just as steel was the key material of the factory economy, semiconductors are the key material today. And just as the cost of steel declined precipitously while the quality went up, semiconductors and related information technologies have done the same. As Moore's law predicted, the price of computing power has fallen dramatically. In 1978, the price of Intel's 8086 processor was 1.2 cents per transistor, and $480 per million instructions per second (MIPS). By 1985, the 386 cost 0.11 cents per transistor and $50 per MIPS. Ten years later the Pentium Pro's introductory price amounted to 0.02 cents per transistor and $4 per MIPS, with a single wafer holding 55 million transistors. In 2003 the Itanium 2 processor cost 0.000002 cents per transistor and $2 per MIPS (Table 4.2).[11] This represents 22 doublings in 34 years, or about 1.6 years per doubling. Prices are expected to keep falling.[12]

This exponential progress is continuing across many core IT technologies (memory, processors, storage, sensors, displays, and communication). For example, hard drive storage capacity doubles every 19 months while the cost of a stored megabyte falls 50 percent per year. As a result, the cost of storing one megabyte of information – enough for this book – fell from $5257 in 1975 to 17¢ in 1999 to half a cent in 2002.[13] That is why sales of a whole array of devices based on stored data, from portable MP3 music players to digital television recorders, are taking off.

This rapid decline in cost has been accompanied with a rapid increase in power as computing power has grown 100 million times per unit cost since the first computers were invented 50 years ago.[14] As a result, the average US household contains more computer power than existed in the world before 1965. Smart cards (plastic cards with an embedded computer chip in them) have more computer memory then the first Commodore computers. A Palm Pilot has more computing power than the IBM 3083 mainframe computer of the early 1980s, while a new personal computer (PC) has 250 times more power than IBM's first PC, introduced in 1981.[15] IBM's new 'Blue Gene' supercomputer can make 360 trillion calculations per second, compared to around 2 billion calculations per second in the late 1980s for a typical supercomputer.

Table 4.2 Transistor growth in computer processor chips

Chip generation	No. of transistors
1978 Intel 8086	29 000
1995 Intel Pentium Pro	5 500 000
2000 Intel Pentium 4	42 000 000
2003 Intel Itanium 2	410 000 000

Source: Intel Corporation.

In a networked economy, it is not enough to have cheap computing and storage; cheap, high-speed data transmission and easy to use networking protocols are a must. One of the chief enablers of the New Economy is instantaneous and cheap global communications, the ability to easily send data – everything from documents to video and multimedia. The cost of transmitting data is going down and capacity is going up. Sending the *Encyclopaedia Britannica* over the Internet from New York to San Francisco would have taken 97 minutes in 1970, but today eight sets can be sent in one second.[16] Moreover, over the last 30 years the cost of sending 1 trillion bits of information has dropped from $150 000 to 17 cents.[17] Sending the *Encyclopaedia Britannica* coast to coast would have cost $187 in 1970. Today, the entire collection of the Library of Congress could move across the nation on fiber-optic networks for just $40. Moreover, these higher speed connections are coming to the home, as in 2004 almost 25 percent of households subscribed to broadband, either through cable, Digital Subscriber Lines (DSL) over phone lines, satellites, and increasingly fiber-optic cables.

Of course, there is the Internet. In 1995, there were 45 million Internet users worldwide; today there are 945 million.[18] Internet hosts (a web site where one can go to get information) have grown from around 30 million in 1998 to 233 million in 2004,[19] while the number of web pages has grown from approximately 2.1 billion in 1999 to 16.5 billion in 2003, with an estimated increase of 1.5 million web pages every day.[20] In spite of all the talk about 'dot-bombs,' Internet domain names (e.g., Yahoo.com) have grown from 10 million in 2000 to 35 million in 2004.[21] While it is safe to say that almost no American households had Internet access in 1992, today around 70 percent do.

There has been one other big development in IT and that is cheaper, easy to use off-the-shelf software. As recently as ten years ago, many companies relied on customized software to address key tasks like databases, accounting, and customer tracking. Today, most companies use off-the-shelf packages that are easily customized to particular applications and industries. For example, a dental practice can buy off-the-shelf software designed specifically for dentist offices to cover everything from accounting, billing, scheduling and patient relations. Finally, the increased ease of using software, pioneered by the commercialization of graphic user interfaces by Apple and then Microsoft has made using a computer something a novice can do.

The result of this dramatic reduction in price and increase in power and ease of use has meant that information technology is transforming businesses and industries. IT is increasing efficiencies, cutting costs, driving customization of products and services, and increasing the speed of commerce. The trend has enabled the emergence of completely new industries and products, as witnessed by the hundreds of thousands of new jobs created by the Internet and e-commerce. The core technology system has finally become small enough, cheap enough, and powerful enough to be part of virtually all sectors of the economy.[22] For example, in 1960, IT equipment or software made up only 12 percent of the value of business capital equipment. Today, this share is over one-third and is increasing as 46 percent of equipment spending is now on IT. As a result, the average worker has over $9800 of IT hardware and software at his disposal. Information technology is now the core technology system in a host of industries, not just in so-called technology industries. In 2002 over 80 percent of farms were online, giving them access to new markets, communities, and information on commodity prices and weather forecasts. Likewise, over 80 percent of manufacturers had Internet access. In 2000, 70 percent of companies had Internet access, while 57 percent had their own home pages, while by 2002 70 percent had their own web pages.[23] As a result, both business-to-business and business-to-consumer e-commerce have grown significantly.

While IT is at the heart of the New Economy techno-economic system, other key technologies, including biotechnology and nano-technology, are growing in importance. Biotechnology has already produced many important new products, but it has only begun to scratch the surface. Bio-engineered food (both plant and animal) and fiber will play an important role in boosting productivity in the agriculture, ranching, fishing, and timber industries. For example, scientists are working to identify the genome of tree species in order to develop trees that grow much faster. Cloning will also play an important role in boosting yields of animals. For example, the ability to clone cows that are the most prodigious milk producers will boost dairy productivity.

Nanotechnology represents a fundamental change in how humans make products. With nano, scientists and engineers have the ability to create materials and devices from the atomic level up.[24] Nano is all about making things smaller, faster or stronger, or making something completely new or with additional properties. Nanotechnology could transform medicine, computing, energy, food, and a host of other fields. It could power development of a new array of devices and materials with new properties.[25]

Unlike prior economic periods, today's prevailing technology system is driven not by machinery, skilled shop floor workers, or even capital – although these play a role – but rather by research and development. Just as capital- and machinery-intensive industries (autos, chemicals, steel) drove growth in the old corporate economy, knowledge-intensive industries, such as hardware, software and biotech, are the growth engines of the New Economy. One reflection of this is that more Americans work in the computer hardware, software, and service industry than in auto production.[26] More work in biotechnology than in machine tools.[27] As R&D is the key fuel of the engine of new economy growth, it is not surprising that business-funded R&D has almost doubled from 1.19 percent of GDP in 1980 to 2.02 percent in 2002. Moreover, the number of patents issued has almost doubled since 1984, with over 166 650 issued in 2002.

It is not just that the New Economy is more R&D intensive, it is that the nature of the innovation process has changed. In the old economy most R&D was conducted by laboratories of large manufacturing firms, usually separate from the rest of the corporation, sometimes physically, almost always organizationally. Moreover, innovation was often generated through a series of discrete steps in research, development and production. In the fast-moving New Economy companies have reoriented their research to more closely align with commercial requirements. For many companies research has become the central driver of competitive advantage. But firms do not just rely on in-house expertise. An increased share of research is done by companies in the service sector and by small and medium-sized firms in large firm supply chains. Indeed, with most industries affected by rapid technological and scientific change, external relationships have become a positive-sum game in which all firms in a collaborative network benefit.[28] As large firms have reduced, reoriented, or in some cases eliminated their central research laboratories and reduced their share of funding invested in basic research, the number and extent of industry ties with universities, industry consortia, and other entities have also multiplied dramatically.[29]

As we have become richer and more technologically advanced, we increasingly consume services and goods that have a higher value to weight ratio. Measured in tons, economic output is roughly the same as it was a century ago, yet in real economic value it is 20 times greater.[30] The weight of the GDP was less in 1997 than in 1977, while its dollar value was 70 percent higher.[31] Part of the reason is that physical goods have become lighter. Products that used to be made of steel are now made of lightweight, strong plastic. This is one reason why the average weight of a car has fallen about 20 percent.[32] But products do not just weigh more, they have much more embedded value, largely because they have been made smart by the inclusion of semiconductors. Obviously, computers' value has skyrocketed while their weight has remained relatively constant. But so have other products. One example is car brakes. The product of a generation of research and development, anti-lock car brakes are now loaded with electronics: they do not weigh any more than conventional brakes, but they certainly provide a great deal more value to drivers.[33] Finally, there is another big reason for what some have called the emergence of the weightless economy,[34] and that is the growth of services. For example, the weight of a legal service has not changed, but we consume twice as much.

INDUSTRIAL AND OCCUPATIONAL CHANGE

Past economic transformations have brought occupational and industrial changes, as some industries experience relative and sometimes
absolute decline while others grow. This has happened once again. Just
as producer goods manufacturing overtook agriculture in the 1890s as
the key industry, and consumer manufacturing overtook producer
goods in the 1950s, today services have superseded manufacturing.
Perhaps no better indicator of this is that for the first time in American
history, the largest company on the Fortune 500 list, Wal-Mart, is a
retail firm. This is not to say that the United States produces fewer
manufactured or agricultural goods, but we produce fewer as a share of
GDP. Higher rates of productivity growth have meant that 108 million
workers (82 percent) do not spend their days making or growing things
– instead, they move things and people, process or generate information, or provide services. As a result, manufacturing employment
fell from its high water mark of 21 million workers (23 percent of the
workforce) in 1979 to 14.3 million workers (10.8 percent) in 2004.[35]
Today, we are not the only country facing such a decline. Japan lost
more than 2 million manufacturing jobs in the 1990s, as their economy
shifted more to services, while manufacturing's share of GDP in
Germany fell from 33 percent in 1990 to 24 percent.

Traditional manufacturing is no longer the major driver of either
innovation or growth. One way to get a sense of this shift is to compare
the advertisements in a typical issue of *Fortune* magazine in 1954 and
2002. In 1954, 25 percent of advertisements were for industrial
machines, 12 percent for chemicals, 9 percent each for office
equipment and engineering services, 6 percent for metals, with 4
percent for mainframe computers. Readers could buy Ellicott dredges,
Cosco office chairs, Sunstrand mechanical lathes, Bower roller
bearings, General American vapor seals, Allied steel, Yale fork lifts,
and RB&W nuts and bolts. Looking through a 2002 issue of *Fortune*
makes it clear that a new economy based on services, information, and
IT had emerged. Twenty-two percent of the advertisements were
devoted to business finance and insurance, 17 percent to software and
16 percent to business services. Computer hardware and telecom
services came in at 6 and 5 percent respectively.[36]

If the shop floor was the modal place of work in the old economy, in
the New Economy it is the office cubicle. Since 1969, all the jobs lost
in goods production and distribution sectors have been replaced by

office jobs.[37] The tools most Americans use are now more likely to be the fax, copier, telephone or PC than the riveter, torch or lathe. When competitive advantage increasingly stems from customization, design, quality and customer service, more of the value-added is produced in offices. Even within manufacturing, fewer workers actually make things with their hands. As a share of manufacturing jobs, production jobs fell from 68 percent in the late 1970s to over 58 percent in 1997.

Partly because the new technology has let companies automate many production jobs and because the economy is more knowledge intensive, jobs whose principal function is the creation and management of knowledge have grown significantly. Because two-thirds of new jobs created from 1992 to 1999 were in managerial and professional occupations, these jobs increased as a share of total employment from 22 percent in 1979 to 28.4 percent in 1995 and to 34.8 percent in 2003.[38] Knowledge-based jobs (those requiring vocational, post-secondary, or higher education) have grown as a share of total employment. For example, there were fewer than 5000 computer programmers and other computer software workers in America in 1960, and there were over 2.5 million in 2002, 160 000 more than in 1999, in spite of the so-called IT collapse.

As a result, knowledge is now the key factor of production, a change that has significant implications. As Galbraith presciently noted:

> It will now be clear what accords power to a factor of production or to those who own or control it. Power goes to the factor which is hardest to obtain or hardest to replace ... capital is now accorded power in the enterprise and in consequence in the society. Should it happen that capital were to become readily abundant or redundant, and thus be readily increased or replaced, the power it confers, both in the enterprise and in the society would be expected to suffer. This would seem especially probable if, at the same time, some other factor or production should prove increasingly difficult to add or replace.[39]

His suspicion that capital might fall from its lofty place as the key factor in production has indeed been confirmed. It has now become comparatively easy to raise capital (initial public offerings, venture capital, junk bonds, factoring, etc.) and comparatively hard to get knowledge workers and entrepreneurial managerial talent. By any measure, the amount of capital available relative to 20 or 30 years ago is significant.[40] It is the innovation potential of the economy that matters, not the amount of capital.

As a result, as Galbraith sensed, competitive advantage has more to do with knowledge, skills, and the ability and willingness to innovate. The Organisation for Economic Co-operation and Development (OECD) reports that investment in knowledge (R&D, software and post-secondary education) equaled 6.1 percent of GDP in 2000, while growing 6.1 percent per year from 1992 to 2000.[41] Likewise, employment of highly skilled workers grew faster than total employment, 2.8 percent per year vs. 2.6 percent.[42] As a result, almost 42 percent of value added in the US economy comes from technology and knowledge-based industries, such as business services, finance, education, health and telecommunications and high-technology manufacturing.[43]

Skills are also becoming more important. Fifty-one percent of employers in the 1997 national employer survey report that skills needed to perform typical front-line jobs went up in the prior three years. More than half of the new jobs created between 1984 and 2005 require some education beyond high school.[44] This is why the percentage of Americans 25 years or older with four or more years of college increased from just 11 percent in 1970 to 28.6 percent in 2001. The United States is now only second to Canada among OECD nations in the percentage of the population with at least some college education.[45] According to Bureau of Labor Statistics (BLS) projections, the economy will get more skilled by 2012 with jobs requiring little training or skills growing 12.7 percent, while jobs with moderate skill requirements grow 14.9 percent and those requiring college degrees grow 21.5 percent.

In the factory era, industrial organizations were the antithesis of the human-centered work. Work life improved somewhat in the corporate mass production economy as for many workers the backbreaking work of the farm and factory was eased, although in many cases it gave way to the mind-numbing work of the office.[46] In the New Economy, old hierarchical, stultifying organizations (in business and government) are giving way to flatter, 'learning' organizations that rely more on individual initiative and creativity. While there are still work environments that are oppressive, stifling, and boring, an increasing share of organizations, particularly those that rely on individual employee initiative and knowledge, are creating more human-centered workplaces. Many employers realize that they can get more out of their employees by creating a more flexible work environment that empowers front-line workers. As Sidney Harman, CEO of Harman

Industries, stated, 'conventional management still functions in an obsolete manner that regards business operations as a linear, sequential set of mechanisms. By contrast, new organizations function in a more horizontal, interdisciplinary way with all units working fluidly together like a jazz quartet.'[47] To be able to perform in these jazz quartet companies, workers must be motivated, trust fellow workers enough to work in teams, and be committed to achieving goals. Treating workers as interchangeable cogs who are expected to follow orders creates a marching band, not a jazz quartet.

An increasing number of firms are reorganizing production processes in these new ways, implementing cellular production, use of teams, and other high-performance work organization methods that require higher levels and new kinds of skills.[48] More and more New Economy companies shift authority to front-line workers, replace bureaucratic 'assembly lines' with self-managed cross-functional teams, organize work in ways that rely on worker skills, and replace elaborate work rules with extensive cross-training, flexible work assignments, and broadened responsibilities. More than half of large corporations introduced new work designs in the 1990s. Massachusetts Institute of Technology economist Paul Osterman found that from 1992 to 1997 the percentage of companies employing quality circles grew from 27 percent to 57 percent, while total quality management practices increased from 24 percent to 57 percent, and job sharing from 26 percent to 55 percent.[49] Consulting firm Towers Perrin found that the highest performing companies put more emphasis on employees' knowledge and skills and the values and rewards that motivate them.[50]

In many ways, work and workers in the New Economy have much in common with workers in the mercantile/craft economy of the 1840s to 1890s. Both work in an economy dependent on specialized craft skills, although today the craft is knowledge, not mechanical skills. Just as workers in the pre-factory economy carried their own tools with them, so too, do an increasing share of today's workers. Whether it is the network systems administrator, the specialist in medical accounting systems, or the more traditional professional like the doctor or lawyer, individuals increasingly carry specialized knowledge. In knowledge organizations, many workers are specialists who know more about their work than anyone else in the organization does. If organizations in the old corporate economy employed essentially interchangeable workers, workplaces today require constantly evolving skills and skills tied to the enterprise, making workers less interchangeable.

These new work environments are emerging for several reasons. First, the United States is specializing in more complex, higher-value work as much routine, lower-skill work has either been automated or sent offshore. Second, it is easier to automate lower skill jobs (for example, pick and place robots can replace workers on assembly lines) than higher skill jobs. That is why the net loss in employment in manufacturing between 1970 and 1994 was in unskilled jobs, which declined 30 percent.[51]

Third, the new technology system is not only enabling work to be designed in new ways, it is requiring companies to do so if they want to compete. For example, the Miller brewery in Trenton, New Jersey, produces 50 percent more beer per worker than the company's next most productive facility, in part because a lean 13-member crew has been trained to work in teams with no oversight to handle the overnight shift.[52] Now instead of workers repeating one simple task, computers and computer-based machines let workers perform a variety of tasks. As a result, more workers are using technology and requiring more skills. For example, the percentage of workers who use computers at work rose from 25 percent to 50 percent between 1984 and 1997.[53] Moreover, 61 percent of manufacturing companies found that advanced equipment increased training costs because they required more skilled workers.[54]

The other reason for these changes is more straightforward: more workers are demanding that work be organized this way, particularly those who enjoy exercising creativity and believe their skills give them security. In the old economy, workers were more willing to accept less satisfying, more hierarchical work environments, in part because they could not conceive of work organized differently. Now companies must tap the loyalty and commitment of their workforces. An increasing share of Generation X and Generation Y workers who grew up without the stifling constraints of the hierarchical and bureaucratic organizations of the old economy chafe under the constraints of the old organizational models. If they find themselves working for a hierarchical, constraining employer, they are more likely to say 'take this job and shove it.' Jobs in participatory work systems provide more challenging tasks, more opportunities for creativity, and greater employee satisfaction.[55] As a result, employers are responding. Motorola has launched a program called 'Individual Dignity Empowerment,' which mandates regular reviews for all employees in which individuals and their managers explore whether or not the company has defined a 'meaningful' job for them. The Families and Work Institute found that work conditions are closely linked to how employees feel about their personal and work lives. Jobs that have more autonomy, flexibility, learning opportunities, and supervisory support lead to workers who are more satisfied, loyal, and committed. A Gallup study of employees at 700 companies found that most rate having a caring boss higher than money or fringe benefits. Workers are increasingly looking to be more in charge of their own time. That is the main reason more companies are supporting flexible working arrangements, such as flexible starting and ending times.

As knowledge workers have become a more important input, companies are tailoring compensation much more toward retaining and rewarding the most talented employees. World at Work, an organization that tracks employee compensation, reported that by 2001 about 77.5 percent of hourly union employees and 71 percent of salaried employees received profit-sharing payments or bonuses, up from 52 percent in 1997. The use of flexible pay increased significantly in the 1990s as companies compensated employees with stock options and bonuses. One study found that 66 percent of workers received variable pay in 2000, compared to 30 percent a year earlier.[56] The Federal Reserve Bank found that 95 percent of companies give stock options, year-end bonuses, profit-sharing or commission payments, up from 65 percent in 1996.

Finally, employment is less likely to be based on lifetime security. If the old economy was all about the Organization Man who was devoted to his company and vice versa, the New Economy is about temporary and utilitarian relationships between employers and employees. A recent study of California workers found that four out of ten workers have been at their jobs less than three years.[57] Only one-third of jobs conformed to the conventional view of employment – working outside the home at a single, full-time, year-round job as a daytime employee. The 'Leave It To Beaver' family, with one breadwinner in a family working full time from nine to five fits only 8 percent of all California households. But it is not just workers who face more risk, so do top managers whose level of performance is more apt to be subject to scrutiny. A CEO appointed after 1985 was three times more likely to be fired than one appointed before that date.[58]

THE RISE OF GLOBALIZATION

It has become a cliché to say that the United States is operating in a global economy. But it is true and it was not always this way. In the old economy, foreign products were an anomaly, something bought by esoteric or rich people who did not like good old 'Made in the USA.' One can occasionally find in attics wooden crates from the 1950s that have been used to hold a shipment from Europe. Getting an item from overseas was such a big deal that purchases were specifically crated and mailed. In the 1960s, a few people might have owned a Volkswagen or even a Mercedes, but by and large, people would point with surprise to foreign cars. While business people and well-to-do individuals might travel to Europe, and even perhaps Asia, few Americans ever left home, and still fewer foreigners visited here. There were a few multinational companies, like General Motors and Boeing, but most companies stayed close to home. When companies wanted to move production to low wage locations they did not move to Southeast Asia, they moved to the Southeastern United States, to places like Alabama or South Carolina.

That has all changed. The increased ease with which companies can move goods and services across borders has dramatically increased the ability of companies to source production anywhere in the world. Likewise, the opening up of formerly closed regions like Eastern Europe, Russia, China and India to global trade has significantly boosted trade and global investment. While exports and imports never exceeded 8.5 percent of GDP between 1929 and 1970, in the late 1970s they began to take off, growing to 16.9 percent of GDP in 1980 and almost 24 percent in 2000. With global communications and cheap jet travel, international travel has likewise grown rapidly. Before the September 2001 terrorist attacks, the number of international travelers and tourists exceeded almost 3 million people daily, compared to about 1 million in 1980.

As a result, US trade went from $19 billion in 1950, to $84 billion in 1970, to $466 billion in 1980 and to $2.5 trillion in 2000 (in constant dollars). Almost 18 million US jobs are now directly linked to international trade, investment, or tourism.[59] The value of world merchandise exports increased from $2 trillion in 1980 to $5.6 trillion in 1999 in constant dollars. In the last 50 years international trade increased fourteen fold – far faster than the five fold increase in world

GDP. Between 1978 and 1997, world trade in goods increased from 12 to 30 percent of global GDP.

Goods and services are not the only things that flow around the world, so does money. Currency traders and companies engaging in cross-border transactions move money around at the speed of light. Daily currency trading worldwide has grown from over $50 billion in the mid-1980s to over $1.5 trillion today.[60] As fewer currencies are pegged to the dollar, fluctuations in currency prices make the international marketplace more risky and volatile. But it also means that more and more people and companies are buying stocks and bonds in other countries. Between 1970 and 2000, cross-border purchases of bonds and equities grew 54 times in the United States, 55 times in Japan, and 60 times in Germany.[61] Companies also increasingly look to foreign markets for equity. Twenty years ago, most companies raised equity through their domestic equities markets. But as it became easier to enter other markets, the proportion of equity raised on foreign markets as a share of all global equity issues rose from 19 percent in 1985 to 27 percent in 1995.

The global imperative is also pushing companies to locate in foreign markets, and is blurring the distinction between companies and their nationality. When Michelin makes 35 percent of its sales in the United States and Johnson and Johnson earns 43 percent of revenues abroad, it is clear that these companies are global players. The result has been an explosion in multinational firms. There were about 7000 multinational companies worldwide in 1975; today there are approximately 40 000.[62] Moreover, in their quest to improve sales and market access and gain access to needed capabilities, companies are merging with and acquiring each other across borders. Between 1991 and 1999, the value of global cross-border mergers and acquisitions grew more than six fold, from $85 billion to $558 billion. Perhaps most noteworthy was Daimler's multi-billion dollar purchase of Chrysler, but there are many other examples.[63]

In order to access foreign markets, there has been a dramatic increase in foreign direct investment (FDI), including both investments in plants or subsidiaries and purchases of controlling stakes in foreign companies. Direct investment activity by US firms in other countries grew from $137 billion in 1979 to $451 billion in 1999 (in constant dollars), and from 2.3 percent of GDP to 4.9 percent. Private capital flows to emerging markets rose from $50 billion in 1980 to $200 billion in 1999.[64] While the net income of US companies derived from operations outside the US accounted for around 10 percent of income earned at home in the 1950s, today it is around half.[65] But not only are US firms are looking outward; so are foreign firms. From 1985 to 1998 FDI into the United States grew 19.2 percent per year. In Europe, which has pursued single market integration since 1992, FDI grew 27.7 percent. As a major driver of developing Asian economies, FDI grew 26.7 percent.

Some claim there is nothing new here, that the factory economy of the early 1900s was even more global.[66] It is true that as a percent of world output the level of international trade at the beginning of the twentieth century is almost comparable to the current level of trade in goods in today.[67] There is, however, a big difference. Then, most US exports were commodities and were exchanged for capital goods to build its emerging manufacturing economy. Globally, flows largely consisted of trade from dependent colonies to their colonial masters. As imports and exports declined as a share of the economy, their patterns remained unchanged. Our biggest import in 1950 was coffee, followed by rubber, newsprint, sugar and wool, while our biggest exports were cotton and grain. In contrast, most of today's trade is in finished goods and services traded between developed countries. Part of the reason for the changing composition of trade is the changing composition of the economy – cotton and grain are a smaller share. But it is also that in the New Economy the *raison d'être* of trading has shifted in fundamental ways. Today, the most traded goods are, in order of value, autos, oil, computer parts, clothes, and semiconductors. In other words, the basis of trade has shifted from what economists call factors of comparative advantage (e.g., coffee does not grow very well in the US; it does in Latin America) to factors of competitive advantage (the Japanese have figured out better than Americans how to make high-quality cars at a reasonable price). Because the United States is increasingly specializing in more complex, higher value-added goods and services, the average weight of a dollar's worth of American exports is less than half its value in 1970.

Globalization has boomed because changes in the structure of the economy have created opportunities. One of the most important is that the costs of shipping and communications have fallen significantly. With the deployment of global fiber optic networks and reform of the telecom sectors in many nations, the costs of transmitting information has plunged while the quality increased.[68] A three-minute telephone call between London and New York City cost $70 in today's dollars in

1964, but less than 50 cents today and probably close to zero as we move to Internet telephony.[69] In 1930 cross-Atlantic air travel cost 68 cents per passenger mile, compared to just 11 cents today (in constant dollars).[70] The rise of air transport has meant that an increasing share of high-value, low-weight products can be easily traded. As a result, the value of air shipped trade has grown from almost nothing in 1950 to nearly 30 percent of all international shipping in 1998.[71] Containerization also lowered the prices of ocean transport, particularly on long routes.[72] Finally, with the creation of the General Agreement on Tariffs and Trade (GATT) and other market opening efforts, global tariffs have fallen dramatically in the last 30 years.[73]

Not only is the cost of shipping a pound of pig iron from Australia to Zaire cheaper, but as the value-to-weight ratio of products has increased shipping costs as a share of total costs has declined. When most of the value of the economy was made up of heavy things that did not cost much (e.g., cement, wood, fish, commodity steel), it made little sense to ship them very far. But as the economy has become increasingly made up of lighter things that cost more (e.g., DVD players, airplanes, drugs) it is economical to ship them around the globe. That is why the inflation-adjusted value of our trade per pound has risen by approximately 4 percent per year on average over the last three decades.

Moreover, the weight of an increasing share of the economy is zero, since many services (e.g., insurance, software, media, call centers) can be now transported in bits, as opposed to atoms. A whole host of jobs that we once thought were tied to the local community in which they are consumed are now footloose. Retail can be conducted 5000 miles away over the Internet. Local business functions like banking, insurance, and securities brokering are now conducted by phone and net at a distance. A whole array of professional services, including law and accounting, can be conducted online. Indeed, the IT revolution has enabled an increasing share of information-based services to be physically distant from the customer (e.g., e-banking) or the other parts of the production process (e.g., back office operations) while remaining functionally close. By the end of the 1990s, IT, including computers, routers, and optical scanners, had become cheap enough, powerful enough and pervasive enough to begin to transform information-based industries.[74] In addition, the telecommunications system gained new powers as new switching and routing technologies allowed information, including telephone calls, to be easily routed throughout the globe. As a result, this new digital economy is transforming economic geography, enabling as many as 12 to 14 million once relatively immobile information-based jobs to now potentially be located virtually any-where across the globe.[75] In the New Economy, someone in Japan can just as easily purchase stocks on-line from E-Trade or Charles Schwab as someone in the United States. It is almost as easy to locate a call center in Hyderabad, India, as it is to put it in Hagerstown, Maryland. Indeed, this latest increase in offshoring of service jobs is just one factor in a quantum leap in global integration, as what was once a largely national economy as recently as 20 years ago has transformed into a global one.

All the evidence suggests that globalization will continue to transform national economies, including ultimately in the Middle East and Africa. Trade barriers continue to fall. More and more nations are becoming more linked to the global economy. And as it becomes self-evident to nations that a key to advancing standards of living is linking national economies to the global trading system, more nations will press to do so. As a result, the value of trade between nations is expected to exceed total commerce within nations by 2015.[76]

THE NEW ORGANIZATIONAL AND MARKET ENVIRONMENT

Globalization and the new technology system have reshaped the structure and functioning of business and markets, making them more dynamic, competitive, entrepreneurial, faster, and diverse. In many ways, this change in the underlying conditions and functioning of the market and its component organizations has been the most profound change in the economy, but it is also perhaps the one most overlooked. Have not markets always been competitive, diverse, and disruptive? The answer is yes, but at nowhere near current levels. While it is easy to hold overly simplistic views of the old economy, it is also true that that economy was less competitive, worked at a slower, steadier pace, and had a set of rules that most accepted. Many workers worked for the same corporation for their adult life and got to work at nine and left at five every day, year in and year out. They had stable, not too competitive jobs that did not require them constantly to put in that extra effort because all companies were in similar positions. Established companies in not very competitive markets could afford not to maximize profits every quarter, to be slower and to be less responsive to market pressures.

The New Dynamism

What used to be an oligopolistic economy with stable competition has transformed into an economy that is dynamic, constantly churning, and highly competitive. Take the auto industry for example. From the 1950s to the early 1970s, it was the epitome of the mass production economy. The Big Three, General Motors, Ford and Chrysler, held market shares that changed little over time. It was a staid industry in which profits could generally be assured. In fact, 1980 was the first year that General Motors ran in the red since 1921. Product markets were stable, with the Big Three producing a limited number of models, usually variations of the same kind of family sedan. Model changes were relatively limited. After the basic technological configuration of the car was perfected by the early 1950s, the technology changed little. The annual cosmetic model changes, with the tail fins getting a little bigger one year or a little smaller the next, were as big as the changes got. And, of course, competition was limited. German cars were a luxury some well-to-do bohemian types might drive, and Japanese cars were not even a presence.

Today, that industry is barely recognizable. Most obvious is the fact that the market is intensely competitive, with strong competitors from Japan, Korea, Germany, and Sweden. One of the Big Three, Chrysler, which was started in 1925 by Walter Chrysler, was bought by Daimler and is now a German company. Consumers contribute to this churning. In the old economy, it was typical for families to be 'Ford families' or 'GM families.' In fact, that is one of the main reasons auto makers had a range of car choices from inexpensive 'starter' cars to luxury cars; they wanted young buyers to buy their product so they would trade up as their incomes increased. Today, consumers have little brand loyalty and instead look for the best price and value. Product choices also abound. For example, in 1960, the best selling car was the Chevy Impala, selling approximately 900 000 vehicles. Today the market has tripled in size, and the best selling car sells approximately 400 000 vehicles. Just go to a car showroom these days to get a taste of how mass customization is transforming the economy. Americans can buy sedans, vans, light trucks, sport utility vehicles (SUVs) and Jeeps, two-passenger sport cars, hybrids, and a host of other kinds of vehicles, including Hummers. In fact, the number of SUV and crossover car models has increased to 60 from 37 just five years ago. Such product proliferation has become possible because car companies are increasingly able to build multiple models of cars on the same factory floor, allowing them easily to make more or fewer models as demand goes up or down. Technology is not standing still either. Beginning in the late 1970s, car companies have engaged in a continuous drive to upgrade cars, competing to incorporate advanced electronics, lighter materials, more powerful and efficient power trains, new safety features (e.g. airbags) and now, completely new fuel systems such as electric motors and fuel cells. Increasingly, cars are coming equipped with advanced electronics systems, including satellite positioning.

All told, it is a fundamentally different market environment, not just for cars, but for almost all industries. As Rosabeth Kanter noted in her 1984 book, *The Change Masters*: 'Nothing is forced on the corporation [GM] that it did not already want ... Thus, continuity is more important than change.'[77] Today it is virtually impossible to name a successful US corporation that thinks continuity is more important than change. The new keys to success have become an organization's ability to learn, adapt and innovate. As a result, companies are lucky if they are able to plan more than a few years into the future. It was no accident that in the 1980s business professors like McGill's Henry Mintzberg and Harvard's Michael Porter recognized the need for crafting business strategy in the face of uncertainty.[78] Companies now are showered with books warning them to be ever vigilant – or as Intel's Andy Grove warns, to be paranoid[79] – to be always on the lookout for new competitors, significant changes to markets, and radical new technologies that can destroy their business model, or government regulations that can blind-side them. In the old stable economy, paranoia would have probably been seen as a socially undesirable trait that a manager could straighten out by going to a Dale Carnegie course. However, when life and death competitive threats can come from any number of sources with virtually no warning, paranoia has become a needed survival trait.

This instability and difficulty in controlling, much less predicting, the future, is reflected not just in the short horizons of companies but in the underlying churning of the economy – the births, expansions, deaths and contractions of the over 24 million business establishments. Schumpeter called this 'creative destruction,' the continuous scrapping of old technologies and old ways of doing business to make way for the new. Such churning has become a central feature of the New Economy. Churning has accelerated as large numbers of new firms are born and others go out of business, while existing firms expand and still others contract. According to Dun and Bradstreet, from 1935 to 1981 around 15 000 businesses failed each year. By 1996, a year of strong growth, over 70 000 businesses went under. Only about 4 percent of Fortune 500 firms went under annually during the 1960s and 1970s; by the 1980s this was 8 percent.[80] In the 60 years after 1917, it took an average of 30 years to replace half of the 100 largest public companies. Between 1977 and 1998 it took an average of 12 years.[81] As a result, only one-third of America's 500 leading companies from 1970 still exist today. Most merged with other companies, but two went out of business. Only six of what had been the 25 biggest firms in 1970 were still on the list in 1997. Just 11 of the top 25 US firms in market capitalization in 1989 remained in the top 25 in 1999. From 1990 to 1998 two-thirds of major US corporations changed their names through mergers or acquisitions.[82]

Such churning is also reflected in the labor market. The addition of 100 000 private sector jobs in the third quarter of 2002 masks the fact that new firms created 1.6 million jobs and dying firms eliminated 1.5 million others. Likewise, expanding firms added 5.8 million jobs while contracting firms lost the same amount. About 10 percent of US jobs disappear annually due to business closures and contracting. Around 8.4 percent of US adults start a business every year (compared to around 2 percent in Europe). The rate of companies going out of business was at least three times faster in the boom years of the late 1990s than it was in the 1970s.

This more risky economy means that we have to rethink what business failure means. In the old economy when the government reported an increase in bankruptcies, one could expect that consumer demand was going south, weaker companies could not get enough revenues and the economy was headed for recession. Today bankruptcies just as often mean that companies are restructuring or being bypassed by innovators. For example, in the late 1990s in Silicon Valley the computer and telecom industries ranked third and fourth in the net amount of jobs lost, even though overall the industries added jobs. Growth in these sectors masked large numbers of layoffs and business failures. It was this very turbulence that led the Valley to be successful.[83] But it is not just high-tech industries that have been affected in this way. As Sears laid off tens of thousands of workers,

Wal-Mart added 624 000 workers between 1985 and 1996. In the 1990s as AT&T announced layoffs, MCI and Sprint and other long distance providers grew by 80 000 workers. More recently, MCI has laid off tens of thousands of workers while the local Bell companies added jobs. Even that last bastion of job security, government, has been undergoing its own restructuring, outsourcing, and downsizing. During the 1990s the federal government shed hundreds of thousands of jobs, while more 'entrepreneurial' state and local governments added millions. Risk is the new reality.

Churning has increased in part because entrepreneurship has increased. In the old economy, small firms were looked down upon and most economists had consigned entrepreneurship to the dustbin of history, in large part because the economy was dominated by establishment capitalism, with high barriers to entry that disadvantaged newcomers and new products. But today's faster pace of industrial evolution, combined with the ability of information technology to help smaller and mid-sized firms compete with large firms, has meant that larger firms are less dominant. Since 1980, the United States has added 34 million jobs, despite the fact that Fortune 500 companies lost more than 5 million jobs.[84] The total employment of America's 100 most valuable companies declined from about 9 million in 1989 to 8.7 million in 1999.[85] Since 1990, the share of industrial R&D spending by the largest companies (those with over 25 000 employees) has declined from 65 percent to 43 percent.

The economy is increasingly made up of fast-growing, entre- preneurial companies. Between 1993 and 1997, the number of these 'gazelles' (defined as companies whose sales have doubled in less than four years) has grown 40 percent, to over 350 000, and they were responsible for creating 70 percent of the new jobs added to the economy. One was Gateway Computer. In the early 1980s, Ted Waitt, a twenty-something fledgling entrepreneur, had the idea of selling computers by mail order, and turned that idea into Gateway, today one of the world's largest computer makers.

Financial markets have evolved to support this new dynamism. In the old economy sources of capital for entrepreneurs were limited. New firms were largely dependent upon investments from friends, family or angel investors, while existing firms could issue stock on the New York Stock Exchange and get bank loans. Perhaps one of the more important institutional developments has been the development of a robust venture capital industry.[86] Venture capital activity, which barely registered as a blip on the radar screen in the 1970s, grew steadily from an average of $6 billion in the early 1980s to $13 billion in 1997, and after booming in 1999 and 2000 has settled to around $18.2 billion in 2003.[87] This is a real competitive advantage for the US, which has seen its venture capital grow 70 percent faster from 1993 to 2000 than Europe.

It is also easier for entrepreneurial firms to get financing once they get past the first few rounds of venture capital. The number of initial public offerings (first rounds of companies' stocks sold when they make their debut in the public markets) grew steadily, by a total of some 50 percent between the 1960s and the 1990s. Initial public offerings (IPOs) grew in part because of the rise of alternative markets, most notably the NASDAQ, which was established in 1971. In 1999 there were 545 IPOs valued at $105 billion. By 2000 this had increased to 451 IPOs, valued at $112.5 billion. Though the number of IPOs fell in the subsequent three years as capital markets were reigned in, they were still valued at $30 billion in 2003.[88]

Companies can also turn to a wide variety of financing instruments. In the early 1980s Michael Milken believed that high-risk equity was undervalued and therefore a good investment if combined into a diversified portfolio. Thus was born junk bonds, which have financed an array of important start-ups, including Turner Broadcasting, MCI, TCI, and McCaw Cellular. Regulatory changes have also made it easier for small firms to raise capital. In the early 1990s the SEC adopted the Small Business Initiatives (SBI), which make it cheaper and easier for smaller companies to raise capital. The Securities and Exchange Commission (SEC) made it easier to raise funds without registering with them, and also significantly reduced paperwork requirements when firms do register. In addition, firms are now able to turn to a wide array of other financing tools, including loans from the Small Business Administration, factoring, supplier financing, mezzanine financing, and regional development loans from state and local governments. A new gamut of equity tools has also emerged. According to Tim Opler, Assistant Professor of Finance at Ohio State University, between the mid-1980s and the mid-1990s, more than 50 new financing vehicles were developed. For example, PERCS (Preferred Equity Redemption Certificates) allowed Texas Instruments to raise money in capital markets in 1991, even when it was losing money. In short, while the old economy provided a limited array of financing options for companies, which in turn limited what they could do, in the New

Economy companies have a vastly expanded toolbox of financing that lets them be more entrepreneurial.

The New Competition

The New Economy is also intensely competitive, driven by factors on both the supply side (more competitors) and the demand side (more demanding consumers). One measure of competition is how much companies can mark up prices over costs. The average price mark-up ratio over cost in manufacturing in the United States decreased from approximately 19 percent in the 1970s to 15 percent between 1980 and 1992 (among the lowest of all OECD nations), suggesting that increased competition held down prices.[89]

The widening of the global marketplace means that competitors now contest firms in more markets. The share of US production subject to foreign competition rose from 19 percent in 1985 to 28 percent in 1994.[90] Moreover, new technology enables allows new business models that can challenge long-held existing ones. It is not just that robust e-commerce competitors threaten 'bricks and mortar' companies, it is also that IT lets new companies develop new product offerings and consumer delivery channels. The experience of IBM reflects this more competitive marketplace. In 1965, IBM faced 2500 competitors for all its markets. By 1992, it faced 50 000.

IBM is not alone in feeling outside pressure; companies in most industries face it. Insurance was once a stable industry with a distribution system of local insurance agents. Now it is undergoing significant change and competition; from agent-less competitors like USAA that rely on phone, fax and the Internet to communicate with customers and offer lower premiums, to 'pure-play' insurance companies who only sell online. Grocery stores, like Kroger's or Safeway used to compete against each other, now they compete against super-store discounters (e.g. Costco and Wal-Mart) on one end, and specialty stores (e.g. Whole Foods and Trader Joes) on the other.

Twenty-five years of government deregulation has also boosted competition. The belief that unrestrained competition had ruinous results led to the passage between the 1930s and 1950s of a number of laws regulating industries. But as economists began to document the negative consequences for consumers, and as technology enabled new competitors to emerge, beginning with the Carter Administration, Congress and regulators began a deregulatory push. The deregulation of transportation (including trucking and airlines), natural gas and oil, financial and legal services, health care, power utilities, and telecommunications has meant more competition and innovation, with savings to consumers of billions of dollars. Between 1983 and 1997, the inefficiency costs of economic regulation borne by both industry and consumers fell almost 70 percent as a share of GDP.[91] What used to be stable, closely regulated industries with limited entry and exit and restrained innovation have turned into more dynamic and turbulent industries where survival is not assured and where moving forward and innovation are the keys to survival.

A good example is the telecommunications industry. In the old economy, telecom was the model of a stable, consistently profitable business and AT&T reaped the benefits. However, after the 1981 court-ordered breakup of AT&T and the passage of the 1996 Telecom-munications Act, today, it is anything but. It is not at all clear if AT&T will even survive in its present form, as cell phones, email, and increasing voice over Internet protocol (VOIP) substitute for long distance wireline calls, all for a fraction of the cost of the current long distance costs. The regional Bells also face competition from cable companies who not only provide cable television, but also broadband and telephone services.

Another factor driving increased competition is the ever-increasing pressure from securities markets to raise shareholder value. Just as we moved from an era of robber-baron and finance capitalism in the factory economy, to managerial capitalism in the corporate mass production economy, we have moved to investor capitalism the New Economy. In the old economy, there was a sense that the corporation was committed to the community, and that the goals of the corporation and the goals of the worker were not in conflict. Big corporations were relatively unconstrained by their competitors and relied on internal financing and passive stockholders, so they could afford to think 'beyond the bottom line.' Managers had considerable discretion in how they ran the company and how aggressively they focused on profitability, especially in the short term. As a result, companies had considerable slack. Economists even had a term for it, factor x, to explain the amount of costs companies carried and could easily have cut if they were focused solely on profit maximizing. Economists and business administration scholars developed elaborate models to explain why companies did not relentlessly cut these costs, coming up with terms like satisificing and incrementalism.

The priorities of the financial markets and the shareholder value movement, coupled with significantly more competitive markets, has changed all that. Maximizing shareholder value has become the overriding goal of most companies. Managers have much less discretion now that institutional investors and fund managers on Wall Street are demanding performance or else. Add to this the rise of new financing vehicles that let individual investors like T. Boone Pickens and Warren Buffet buy up firms that have excess cash and undervalued assets, and the environment is such that firms that do not cut costs and improve financial performance face swift action in equity markets. These new financial tools mean companies are more vulnerable to takeover. There were 12 hostile takeovers of companies valued at $1 billion or more during the last half of the 1970s. During the 1980s, there were more than 150.[92] As a result, competition has driven an increasing number of firms to restructure to cut costs and to become more nimble and responsive.[93] Not only are workers and companies less loyal to each other, but companies are less loyal to communities. Increasingly, hometown companies that were the mainstay of their communities have moved operations to cheaper locations or have been acquired by out of area firms.

There is one final spur to competition on the supply side and that is the decline of unions. In the old economy, unions played a key role in bringing stability. With the creation of industry-wide wage agreements in the 1940s, unions took wage competition out of the equation as most companies in an industry had to pay the same wages. Unions also limited downsizing, essentially taking this strategy off the table for economically healthy firms. The decline of unions has changed all of this. For example, in 1952, there were 470 reported work stoppages. In 2000, there were eight. Union membership went from 8.6 percent of the workforce in 1930 to 26 percent in 1940 and as late as 1983 it was still above 20 percent. But since then it has dropped steadily, and was down to 13 percent in 2003, with only 8.2 percent of non-governmental employees belonging to a union. Like it or not, companies are now much less constrained by unions and that has spurred competition.

Consumers are also driving the new competition as they have become more demanding and less loyal. In the old economy, brand loyalty was significantly higher and firms could use that to insulate themselves from relentless competition. As high-tech marketing guru Regis McKenna points out, consumers are significantly less loyal to brand. In fact, the brand that has the largest market share in many consumer markets today is 'other.'[94] Consumers are much more willing to look for bargains, constantly seeking sales and discounts. That is one reason why middle-class consumers, and not just low-income consumers, go to discount stores like Wal-Mart, Costco, and even second-hand stores like the Salvation Army and online auction sites. Consumers now relentlessly look for the best value, which in turn places increased competitive pressure on companies to constantly provide value.

One reason why consumers are so focused on value is that they have a surfeit of information to help them choose. The fact that companies like Consumers Union have grown to $200 million enterprises reflects the degree to which consumers value information. But the biggest factor is the Internet which allows consumers to educate themselves and re-balance the information equation between themselves and sellers. The Internet gives consumers more choices, especially with respect to consumer purchases that were previously made locally from local merchants and middlemen (e.g., contact lenses, books, electronics). Consumers can find more accurate information on prices (e.g., invoice prices for cars), better compare prices (e.g., airlines), find out how other consumers rank competing products, and even engage in reverse auctions, with companies bidding to sell to them.[95]

The Internet similarly enhances competition among business suppliers, who can no longer rely on existing relationships for continued business with original equipment manufacturers (OEMs) and other producers. B-to-B buying exchanges give companies increased power over suppliers to drive down prices. For example, the major auto companies banded together to create Covisint, a B-to-B Internet portal for purchasing auto parts from suppliers. Such systems will not only lead to a reduction in the number of auto suppliers, it will increasingly squeeze margins as buyers obtain more real-time information on prices and insist on more robust bidding and competition among suppliers for their business.

The New 'Coopetition'

While competition has been increasing, paradoxically so too has collaboration. Indeed, Peter Drucker suggests that the organizational dynamic of networks, partnerships, and collaborative ventures is a main organizing principle in the New Economy.[96] Some have called this new phase of capitalist development, 'alliance capitalism.'[97] Social capital, as fostered in collaboration and alliances, may actually be as important as physical capital (plant, equipment, and technology) and human capital (intellect, character, education, and training) in driving innovation. Firms are shifting from a model in which they operated as silos separated from each other to networked firms linked to suppliers, customers, and even competitors. Companies increasingly live in an ecosystem of alliance partners, spin-off enterprises, contractors, and free agents.

As a result, 'coopetition' in which competitors collaborate has become a structural feature of the New Economy, particularly in sectors on the frontier of innovation. Firms, through a proliferating array of partnerships, increasingly turn to suppliers, customers, users, universities, and federal laboratories for sources of technology and innovation.[98] While Europe and the United States had approximately the same number of industry technology alliances in 1985, in the 1990s alliances in the US boomed. The number of new inter-firm worldwide research partnerships set up annually increased from about 30 to 40 in the early 1970s to about 200 per year in the 1980s to 2000 in 1999.[99] Only about 40 percent of the partnerships were in the high-tech sector in the 1970s, but in 2000 more than 80 percent were.[100]

Such alliances are not just limited to research partnerships; they extend to joint production, marketing, and sales alliances. The number of new cooperative arrangements increased from just over 1000 in 1989 to over 7000 ten years later. As a result, the percentage of revenues of the 1000 largest firms attributable to strategic alliances of all kinds (e.g., joint ventures, research consortia, licensing arrangements) increased from 2 percent in 1980 to 18 percent in 1997.[101] The largest 1000 firms now draw nearly 6 percent of revenues just from alliances, up fourfold since 1987.[102] In addition to the rise of all sorts of formal alliances, the last decade has seen the rise of informal interorganizational collaboration. In fact, companies are also increasingly relying on collaborative knowledge networks to innovate.[103]

The Real-Time Economy

In a ruthlessly competitive environment, the ability to get to market rapidly has never been more important. Fierce competition coupled with a new wave of technology-based products and services have shortened cycles between market introduction and their eventual replacement by superior products and services. In some sectors, such as information technology, the pace of innovation causes such rapid obsolescence that firms have to run just to stay in place. Computer components, for example, lose about 1 percent of their value per week.

One study found that in 1990 new products or major product improvements took an average of 35.5 months to complete, but by 1995 companies were introducing new products in approximately 23 months. This trend affects a host of industries. Autos that took six years from concept to production in 1990 now take two years. Thirty percent of 3M's revenues are from products less than four years old. Similarly, 77 percent of Hewlett Packard's revenues are from products less than two years old. New products accounted for a third of corporate products in the 1980s, up from a fifth in the 1970s.[104] IBM had over 30 percent of its 1995 patents incorporated into products by 1996.

The need for speed is not confined to the high-tech sector; all sectors are under pressure to be swift. For example, 20 years ago, the boat-building industry produced a new hull design every three to four years. Today, because competition forces them and technology (e.g., computer-aided hull design) lets them, the industry is producing new hull designs every nine months to a year. The speed of processing goods and services has also gone up. Between 1979 and 1997, the ratio of unfilled orders to shipments for US manufacturers declined by 25 percent, suggesting that the speed with which goods flow through the production, distribution and retail systems is much compressed.[105] In the 1970s new products accounted for 20 percent of corporate profits; by the 1980s they accounted for one-third.

Mass Customization

The old economy was a mass production economy where the underlying technology system limited product diversity. The new technology system enables a mass customization economy. Companies now produce a dazzling array of products and services.[106] Perhaps the best way to see it is to go into a grocery store, which houses a cornucopia of products, with individual aisles devoted to nothing but cereal, frozen foods, or other items. The average number of products in grocery stores increased from 13 000 in 1980 to 40 000 in 1998. Product diversity is not confined to grocery stores and Wal-Marts; it is found in virtually every area of the economy. The number of new vehicle models rose from 140 in the 1970s to over 250, television channels from five to 185, running-shoe styles from five to 285, and new books from 40 000 to 77 000.[107] The average number of magazines increased from 2500 in 1987 to 4400 in 1997. Brands of carbonated soft drinks grew from 20 in 1970 to 87 in 1995. According to Regis McKenna, there are more than 500 different soft drinks on the market and 500 types of bottled water. In 2001 alone, there were 3487 new beverage products introduced, including 490 kinds of tea, 142 beers, and 181 bottled waters.[108] McKenna estimates that 30 000 new products are announced annually in America, up from only a few thousand in 1970.[109] In a broad range of product and service categories, Americans are offered an ever-expanding array of choices. For example, consumers can buy 24 different kinds of Tropicana orange juice and 19 000 different combinations of Starbucks coffee (Figure 4.1).

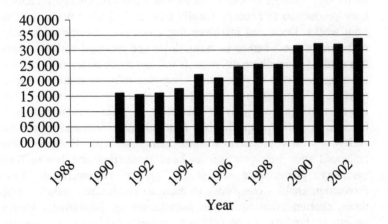

Source: Marketing Intelligence Service, Ltd, www.productscan.com/news/newsmouse 98.htm.

Figure 4.1   Number of new food, beverage, health and beauty aids, household and pet products introduced: 1988 to 2002

Companies have been driven to expand product and services offerings, in part because the competitive marketplace forces them continually to seek out narrower niches and in part because consumers are more demanding and less homogeneous. The corporate mass production economy led to the creation of essentially one large national market. People watched one of three television networks, drank one of four different brands of beer (Bud, Schlitz, Pabst, or Miller), and drove one of three kinds of car. In the New Economy, the number of distinct marketing sub-groups has exploded. Marketers now use highly detailed census and sales data to determine distinct market subgroups. Both factors have made companies more customer focused. In the old economy, large companies were often unresponsive to consumer demands. People railed against Detroit for producing cars Americans did not really want and against Ma Bell for poor telephone service. Now consumers have wide choice not just in cars and long distance telephone service, but in most privately provided products and services, and increasingly demand it in the provision of public services. In the New Economy, success depends upon being customer focused, because if one company does not do it, competitors will.

Market forces may lead companies toward customization, but new technology systems enable it. In the old economy, changing factory-floor production technology usually took skilled labor many days or even weeks. Dedicated machines that could only do one thing (e.g., stamp out a door) had to be taken down and replaced with new ones that could do something different. It was not much different in offices; to change software on mainframe computers software engineers had to reprogram complex and expensive proprietary software systems. Information technology is at the heart of 'mass customization.'[110] Companies can develop 'flexible' factories and offices and expand the variety of their products at little additional cost. Factories have embraced such new practices as Lean Production and Just-In-Time inventory management to enable greater customization. Lean Production enables companies to decrease batch sizes, reduce set-up times, shorten cycle times and manufacture an increasingly greater variety of products in an efficient, cost-effective manner. With the capability to produce more products in smaller quantities, companies can offer mass customized products, at close to mass production costs. The key is computer-controlled machinery that can be easily adapted through software changes. For example, computer-controlled molds in tire factories have let tire companies make and shift tire molds in molding machines much more rapidly, allowing them to produce much shorter production runs for different kinds of tires.

Dell Computer Company uses a flexible production process to configure each computer that it sells to meet the needs of individual buyers. Using the telephone or the Internet, customers describe the kind of computer they want, the size of the monitor, the speed of the microprocessor, the capacity of the hard drive and the type of other devices (e.g. keyboard, mouse, video cards, speakers) that they want. The number of possible combinations is almost 16 million for desktop models alone. Dell assembles the computer only after it receives the order and ships it to the customer within a few days. Though it is usually more expensive to make customized products, the price difference is now less, leading more companies to do so.

Such IT-driven customization is not confined to manufacturing, it is also growing in the service sector. In the credit card industry, MBNA uses computers to produce thousands of different 'affinity' credit cards. For example, colleges market their own credit cards to alumni through MBNA, with the college getting a small share of the transaction fee. Alumni have a choice of several images on the card (e.g., a picture of the campus clock tower, football stadium, etc.). The biotech and genome revolutions are leading to drug customization. Doctors have long struggled with the fact that the same drug reacts very differently in different patients, leading to cure in some cases and toxicity in others. The ability to identify patient characteristics at the genetic level, along with customization of drugs, is enabling doctors to tailor the medicine patients receive. The promise of therapeutic cloning has the potential to let individuals grow new body parts specifically with their own unique DNA structure. Medical researchers believe that the patient's body will not consider a stem-cell created organ as a foreign object. With no risk of rejection, there would be no need for dangerous immunological suppression.

At the extreme of customization is the capability to make production runs of one. In the old economy, only the rich could afford custom work. While customized goods are still more expensive, the price differential is declining. For example, by using computer-controlled cutting and sewing machines, Levi Strauss is able to custom-make women's jeans based on individual body sizes.[111] Nike lets customers customize their own shoes, while American Quantum Cycles lets customers customize bikes to fit their unique measurements.

On the Internet, of course, customization is already the norm. It is as cheap to have a web site serve up customized web pages unique to each viewer's particular interests as it is to provide the same pages to everyone. E-commerce leaders like Yahoo, Amazon, and others have discovered that to achieve higher levels of customer satisfaction, customization is the key. This is not just confined to the Web. A company called Vert has developed technology that lets the top of cabs display advertisements customized according to the zip code the cab is in. A Global Positioning System (GPS) receiver in the display knows the location of the cab and the demographics of the area, and feeds up an advertisement based on this information. E-commerce is also driving customization as it enables companies to stock a wide array of products. For example, the number of book titles available at Amazon.com is over 23 times larger than the number of books on the shelves of a typical Barnes & Noble superstore and 57 times greater than the number of books stocked in a typical large independent bookstore.[112]

SOCIAL, POLITICAL AND SPATIAL CHANGES

Just as past transformations changed not just the economy but the broader society, so too is today's New Economy leading to transformations in society, politics, and the spatial form of the economy.

The New Economic Geography

The same forces that are driving the New Economy – new industries and jobs, globalization, the information technology revolution, and competition and dynamism – are also driving a new reordering of the economic geography.

In the old economy most economic activity took place in large metropolitan areas. As the IT revolution gives companies and workers more locational freedom, a smaller share of employment is located in the largest, most expensive metropolitan areas than was the case just ten years ago. The share of employment located in the largest 61 metropolitan areas actually declined by 1.5 percent between 1988 and 1997, from 55.1 percent to 54.3 percent. In contrast, the share of jobs in mid-sized metros (between 250 000 and 1 million) increased by 4 percent, and the share in small metros (between 50 000 and 250 000) increased by 7 percent.[113] But so far the deconcentrating forces of the New Economy are not all powerful – the share of jobs in rural counties not adjacent to metro areas declined by 11 percent

These forces are also leading to decentralization within metropolitan areas. The old economy metropolis was like an atom – most of a region's economic activity was concentrated densely at the center like a nucleus, with residents spread out in rings around the city, poorer ones close in, richer ones farther out. Nothing epitomized this better than the skyscrapers located in the downtown areas and the large factories adjacent to the downtown areas. Corporations erected skyscrapers that, as monuments, were intended to be as lasting as the companies themselves. Manufacturers in the core city were housed in sprawling factories that spewed out thousands of workers at the end of each shift.

But fundamental New Economy forces have acted like an atom smasher, breaking the nucleus up into hundreds of pieces and strewing it across the countryside. An office is more likely to be located in an anonymous building in a remote suburban office park, while the typical manufacturer is a small operation located in a metal 'Butler' building located at the outer edges of a metro or in a small town.

In short, the common vision of the metropolitan area as a place with one economy, located among downtown skyscrapers and inner-ring factories, no longer describes the metropolis common to America at the beginning of the twenty-first century. By the early 1990s, 57 percent of office stock in America was located in the suburbs, up from 25 percent in 1970. Similarly, most high-tech jobs are in the suburbs as well.[114]

The bedroom suburb – little more than a home to workers commuting to the central city – is an anomaly, something to be experienced in reruns on Nickelodeon. Today, many people live and work in the suburbs and rarely visit the central city; others still commute to the core for work, but find any and all services needed for their daily lives available in the suburbs. These changes have proceeded to the point where even the terms 'cities' and 'suburbs' have become artifacts of the old economy.

The centripetal forces sending businesses throughout all parts of the metropolitan area mean that people can live farther from the center and not face inordinately long commutes. In the old industrial metropolis, when most jobs were downtown, few people wanted to live 25 miles from the center city. With edge cities and office parks 20 miles from the center city, people now live 30, 40, and even 50 miles from downtown and still have reasonable commutes. For example, the growth of the high-tech I-270 corridor in the Washington, DC, suburb of Montgomery County, Maryland, has meant that people who work there are increasingly commuting from as far away as West Virginia.

This kind of sprawl is not necessarily leading to lower population densities within the current bounds of metro areas. On the contrary, the fact that suburban areas are becoming urbanized accounts for much of the concern over sprawl. Residents who moved to the suburbs to get away from it all – to experience the equivalent of Frank Lloyd Wright's Broadacre City – are increasingly wondering what happened to their semi-rural good life. For example, while population density in the city of Chicago fell from 16 000 persons per square mile in 1950 to 12 000 in 1990, the density in already developed suburbs increased from 400 to 1200 as infill and multifamily homes increased. Between 1980 and 1990, population density of the built-up areas of the 40 largest metropolitan areas actually increased 14 percent, from 456 persons per square mile to 523. Thus, while many urban core areas are getting less dense, inner and outer suburbs are getting more dense.

But while inner and outer suburban densities may be increasing, development on the far fringes of metropolitan areas, which often leapfrogs existing metropolitan development by miles, has meant that overall population densities are declining as many metro areas encompass increasing amounts of land. For example, by the mid-1990s the population of the Philadelphia metropolitan area was only 100 000 more than it was in 1960, but it had spread out over a land area 32 percent larger than in 1960, representing the development of 125 000 acres of open space. It is this low-density development at the fringes of metro areas that is commonly referred to as sprawl.

These patterns of dispersal differ by region. Places like Phoenix and Los Angeles are sprawling outward, but because they are gaining population, overall densities are going up. In contrast to this 'dense sprawl,' places like Rochester, NY, and other slow-growth metropolitan areas can be characterized as 'thinning metropolises,' where low-density exurbs continue to develop even as the population remains constant (or, as in the case of places like Buffalo, NY, even declines). In the New Economy, dispersed development is the dominant spatial form in virtually all areas.

The New Governing System and Politics

Just as in past economic transitions, government and politics are also being transformed. In the old economy, big bureaucratic government was the order of the day. However, the concepts of hierarchy, bigness, management and bureaucratic rules – core pillars of the old big government paradigm – were based on four conditions that no longer apply: predictable processes, a stable environment, a fixed output and economies of scale. While the old economy was one in which top-down, hierarchical institutions could create value, in the New Economy they all too often create problems. Networks, rather than hierarchy, are the operative principle.[115] In addition, whereas large organizations were the only ones that could assemble the resources to tackle problems, today's technology system lets small and mid-sized organizations of all types effectively mount resources.

Moreover, in contrast to the mass production system of the old economy, with a government that provided little choice, we are now in a society where consumers and citizens expect mass customization. In contrast to the mass society of the old economy, we are now in an individualistic society of the New Economy. As former Clinton administration official Bill Galston states, 'The task of modern politics is not engage in a quixotic campaign against the spirit of individualism, but rather to devise principles and forms of vigorous public life that are consistent with it.'[116] Legal scholar Lawrence Friedman argues that 'the state, the legal system, and organized society in general ... seem more and more dedicated to one fundamental goal: to permit, foster and protect the self, the person, the individual.'[117]

There is one other fundamental change and that relates to the level of development and its effect on the role of government. The task of the factory economy and that era's government was to ensure a basic level of survival, to 'put a chicken in every pot.' The task of the corporate economy and that era's government was to help people obtain a solid middle-class existence, a house, a car, an education and retirement security. While by no means achieved by all, the prosperity of the New Economy enables a rising middle class to allow 'post-material' concerns to influence their political orientation. While Herbert Hoover stated in the late 1920s that the slogan of progress was changing from the full dinner pail to the full garage, today, it can as easily be said that it is changing to the 'full life.' This is one reason why the fault lines today in American politics have less to do with class, and more to do with culture and lifestyle differences.

As each New Economy has emerged so too has a new governing system and philosophy. Not surprisingly, as the old economy broke down in the 1970s, the old form of governance came under attack. Given the disillusionment with rational planning and bureaucratic government, conservatives argued that the old economy governing model forged by the Roosevelt's New Deal, Truman's Fair Deal, Kennedy's New Frontier, and Johnson's Great Society had failed. While Goldwater's attempt to resurrect the pre-New Deal Republican governing agenda failed in the 1960s, the conservative political mission did succeed 20 years later because the conditions in which large bureaucratic organizations thrived had changed fundamentally. Indeed, it was the breakdown of the old economy and old governing system that allowed the Republican party, first at the presidential level with the election of Ronald Reagan, and then in Congress in 1994, to regain power. Their goal, like Goldwater's to restore the old, factory-era governing system. Political writer Elizabeth Drew noted, 'Gingrich sought to destroy the entire force behind the idea of an activist federal government.'[118] Unlike Reagan, who largely reacted to the failures of the old economy and the old governing model, Gingrich understood that the nation was in the midst of a major economic and social transition. Unlike President George Bush, who was had one foot in the old economy governing philosophy shared by Presidents Nixon and Ford, his son, President George W. Bush, like Gingrich, seeks to overthrow the old governing system.

However, the governing system Gingrich and Bush seek to construct for this new 'third wave' society is informed more from an ideological embrace of the past governing system, than from a pragmatic view of the present and the future. In particular, they draw heavily from the Republican governing philosophy of the McKinley era at the turn of the twentieth century, where the federal role was much smaller.[119] The conservatives' answer to the breakdown of the old economy and the governing system that accompanied it was simple: go back to the much smaller government of the pre-New Deal factory era. William Kristol, former policy advisor to Vice President Dan Quayle, argued, 'The construction (or reconstruction) of a politics of liberty and sociology of virtue is at the core of the promise of post-progressive America ... Above all the politics of liberty does not imply that we reinvent government; it requires that we relimit it.'[120] James Pinkerton, advisor to President George Bush, concurred, proposing to reduce the size of federal government by two-thirds in the next 20 years, with most functions devolved to the states and localities. He contended that, 'The states today do not need federal G-people to tell them how to weatherize buildings or help kids go to college, they just need the money. Yet eventually, the foolishness even of this block grant process – sending money to Washington so that Washington can take its cut and then send most of the money back – will be so manifest that the states will decide to keep the money for themselves in the first place.'[121] Conservative commentator James Glassman summed up the right's take on the world, 'Americans are returning to values and ideas associated with the Republican Party, which dominated political life from the 1880s to the early 1930s.'[122]

The breakdown of the old economy also compelled Democrats to adjust. Just as Republicans could govern in the old mass production corporate economy only if they accepted the realities of that economy, as Presidents Eisenhower, Nixon and Ford did, Democrats could govern only if they came to grips with a changed economy and society. Running as a 'New Democrat' Bill Clinton presented an alternative form of governance for the New Economy that recognized the role of markets, choice, and personal responsibility, but also tempered those with appropriate public action. Emulating the New Democrat model, Tony Blair did the same in the United Kingdom. As Blair put it, 'New Labour (and New Democrats) have to fight conservatism on the right and conservatism on the left. The response of the right is to dismantle the welfare state. The response of the left cannot be to fight to preserve it.'[123] As third way expert Tony Giddens states, 'New Labour is a modernizing party. Modernization is not a meaningless term. It refers to the need to reshape the institutions of the country to respond to changes that are transforming the economy, sovereignty, cultural life, and the wider international system.'[124]

Just as the Taft wing of the Republican party resisted modernizing the party for the new realities of the corporate, mass production economy, the liberal wing of the Democratic party has also resisted such modernization. Just as Goldwater rejected the New Deal, and in many ways the entire new corporate mass production economy, so too do many on the Democratic left as they seek to take the country back to the high water mark of liberalism, the Great Society era.[125] Jeff Faux, president of the liberal Economic Policy Institute summed up the left's view: 'A vote for the Democrats is still a vote to preserve the major remaining protections of the New Deal against the marketplace. A vote for the Republicans is still a choice to close most of them down and let the market prevail.'[126] Just as the populists aligned with the Democratic standard-bearer Williams Jennings Bryant in the 1890s to resist the onslaught of industrialism and preserve small farms and merchants, the new populists on the left resist the changes stemming from the New Economy and seek to bring back the glory days of stable jobs at big corporations, blue-collar manufacturing, strong unions, dominant central cities, big national government, and a national, as opposed to global economy. They argue that the New Economy has failed

American workers, leading to declining wages, increased income inequality, and higher levels of uncertainty and risk.

Many liberals believe that the rise of the conservative movement and the falling fortunes of liberalism are unconnected to structural shifts in the economy. For them it is only a question of emulating the conservative movement's marketing, think tank, and money raising tactics to revive liberal fortunes. Yet, Republicans did not regain power in the 1980s simply because they had more charismatic leaders, better organizations, and more money. They came to power because the underlying economic structure had shifted and too many in the Democratic party were unwilling to respond and modernize the party for the New Economy.[127]

Neither the liberal or conservative view meets the realities of the New Economy.[128] Yet the stakes are great for both parties. For a party to become the majority party for the next 30 years it must be the one that best understands and articulates the changes making up the New Economy and promotes the most credible and effective policies to advance it. It is not clear which party will get there first. On the one hand, eight years of strong growth and solid New Economy policies from Bill Clinton and other New Democratic elected leaders have gone a long way in demonstrating to Americans that Democrats 'get' the New Economy and can be trusted to move forward. But as Democratic presidential nominee Al Gore in 2000 (and Democratic candidate Howard Dean in 2004) rejected the centrist New Democratic governing framework of the Clinton era it became clear that the party has much work still to do.[129] The challenge may be as great in the UK. In discussing the left's disinclination to take the third way seriously, Tony Giddens states 'there is something more going on – a willful refusal to face up to the change the left must make to adapt to the world in which we find ourselves. On this topic, many on the British left are in a state of denial'.[130] Chapter 10 examines how a new politics may emerge as the new economy potentially produces the kinds of income gains that could lead to Americans demanding not just more money, but more fulfilling work and more free time. However, to get there, we will need to boost productivity significantly.

NOTES

1. Princeton economist Alan Blinder (1997) stated 'Our highly productive future may be a long way off, in the meantime we may be condemned to a lengthy and uncomfortable transition period'.
2. President's Council of Economic Advisors (2003).
3. Atkinson (2004a).
4. Remarks by Chairman Alan Greenspan at the Haas School of Business, University of California, Berkeley, 4 September 1998 (www.bog.frb.us/boarddocsspeeches.19980904.htm).
5. For example, the import penetration rate (the share of total goods sold made up by imports) for the Japanese manufacturing sector is just 9.9 percent, compared to 20.6 percent for US manufacturing (OECD 2003, C.2.2).
6. Japan's Deputy Minister of Posts and Telecommunications, Yoshio Utsumi (1998, p. 11) wrote, 'Japan has not yet fully met the challenge of moving to an economy that is led by domestic consumption rather than a heavy reliance on exports; that bases business on strict cost-benefit analysis rather than personal ties; and, above all, that is dependent not on manufacturing but on knowledge and the skills of the information age.'
7. Japanese companies are increasingly investing overseas. The share of overseas Japanese production grew from 6 percent of GDP in 1992 to 13 percent in 1997.
8. Because phone service in Japan is priced by the minute, consumers have a distinct incentive to switch to broadband that is priced at a flat rate. Moreover, NTT, the partially government owned telecommunications provider, was given tax incentives and favorable financing to build a fiber optic network that provides broadband speeds of up to 100 mb per second (Taniwaki, 2003).
9. This is essentially what the European Union's 2000 Lisbon Declaration did. Recognizing that Europe was at risk of being left in the dust of the American New Economy growth, the declaration proposed to make Europe a leader in the innovation economy within a decade. But rather than tackle fundamental issues such as low levels of entrepreneurship, limited capital markets, closed borders, and overly strict regulations, they hoped to get there largely by government programs.
10. Britain is the leading exception, where entrepreneurial activity and churning is more pronounced. For example, in Britain in the 1980s, about 10 000 new manufacturing jobs were created every week, while 13 000 were destroyed, and the rate is even higher in the 1990s (Barnes and Haskel, cited in Corey 2001).
11. www.intel.com/pressroom/archive/speeches/moore20030210.htm.
12. A single memory chip now holds 250 000 times as much data as one from the early 1970s – the difference between one page of text and 1600 books. As Intel Chairman Andy Grove noted in 1999, 100 transistors cost the same as a grain of rice; and the world produces 1 million transistors every year for every person on earth. Within the next few years, single chip computing/communication devices will cost in the pennies, making it possible to attach them to a wide variety of objects and have those objects connected.
13. (*Business 2.0*, 'Numbers,' May 2003). IBM has been able to use nano tech to create microscopic punch cards that can hold one terabit of data per square inch, 20 times better than existing data storage rates. Blue violet lasers should increase CD and DVD capacity by a factor of five. IBM and GE are working on new nano-tech based hard drives, that could hold ten times more than today's hard drives. 'Magnetic Future', *MIT Technology Review*, July/August 2003, p. 23.

14. In 1955, a high-speed commercial computer weighed 3 tons, consumed 50 kilowatts of power and cost $1.26 million (adjusted for inflation). It could perform 50 multiplications per second, faster than any human or adding machine. In 1977 a handheld calculator could perform 250 multiplications per second and cost $300. In 2000 a low-end desktop computer can perform 100 million calculations per second and costs around $800 (www.howstuffworks.com/question54.htm).

15. http://www.c-i-a.com/pr1296.htm.

16. Total bandwidth of all US wireline networks was 1 terabit (1 trillion bits) per second in 1996, but rose to 100 terabits by 2003. The first transatlantic fiber optic telephone cable was installed in 1988 and could carry 40 000 conversations at once. By early 2001, a fiber optic cable could carry almost 50 million conversations simultaneously (Alcaly 2003, p. 58). In 1995, Wal-Mart computers held 6 terabytes of data. In 2002, they held 225.

17. 'Untangling e-economics,' *The Economist*, 21 September, 2000.

18. Adkinson et al. (2004) p. 10.

19. Ibid. The number of web pages now exceeds 2.1 billion according to the Internet firm Cyveilance.

20. www.marketresearch.com.

21. Adkinson et al, (2004) p. 10.

22. Consider the IT-based consumer technologies that have become widespread since the mid-1980s: the Internet and World Wide Web; cell phones, portable phones, pagers, wireless email devices, call forwarding, call waiting and voice mail; credit cards with magnetic strips and smart cards with chips on them; personal computers and PDAs; spreadsheet, word processing, and data base programs; satellite dishes, big screen televisions, video cassette recorders, digital video recorders, and compact disc players; video games and 'Game Boys;' laser printers and fax machines; camcorders and digital cameras; microwave ovens; global positioning systems; motion sensors; and cheap radio frequency tags for products.

23. www.techtv.com/callforhelp/features/story/0,24330,4570,00.html.

24. Traditionally, the nano-technology realm is defined as being between 0.1 and 100 nanometers, a nanometer is one billionth of a meter.

25. Micro-electromechanical systems (MEMS) are tiny devices that integrate motors, sensors, and other mechanical devices with computer capabilities. A new generation of smart MEMS technology has created micro-sized sensors of all kinds (pressure, temperature, light). These sensors now cost from 5 to 20 dollars, but they could drop to as little as $1 as volume ramps up.

26. In 1999 the semiconductor industry was larger than the iron, steel, and motor vehicle industries combined in terms of value added (Wessner 2003).

27. There were 191 000 employed in biotech in 2001 and 161 400 in metalworking and machinery.

28. One study of the sources of innovation found that more than 50 percent of technological innovations occur at the interfaces between organizations, rather than within the organization alone (Von Hippel 1988).

29. Although industry funding of university research is still small compared to federal sources, which in 1995 contributed 68 percent of all university R&D support, it has risen from $236 million in 1980 to approximately $2.3 billion in 2002.

30. Wolf (1998).

31. In 1977, each American accounted for $19 400 in output that weighed 5300 lbs. By 1997, the value had increased to $26 840, with the weight declining to 4100 lbs, a decline of 23 percent (Meyer 2000, p. 193).

32. The average weight of a Cadillac in 1977 was 4900 lbs. Today, that has dropped to 3900 lbs, excluding Escalade and CTS models (which were not made in 1977).

33. The economies of the past were measured by weight (bales of cotton, tons of iron). Through the 1970s, England measured the imports of computers by the pound. If things were priced by the pound it would be easy to see that the New Economy is a knowledge economy, and not a materials or commodity economy. Chris Meyer (2000) calculates that potatoes sell for 79 cents a pound, a car for about $5.95 per pound, computers for about $168 per pound, and drugs for $23 199 per pound.
34. Coyle (1998).
35. Between 1992 and 2003, manufacturing employment declined by 2.6 million. About half of this decline was due to the fact that manufacturing productivity was higher than non-manufacturing sectors, meaning manufacturing could produce more with fewer workers. For example, jobs in the steel industry dropped from 400 000 to 180 000 between 1980 and 1992, yet we make about the same amount of steel today as we did then. About 25 percent was due to slower growth in domestic demand for manufactured products relative to services. As we get richer, we tend to buy more services (e.g., health care, education, entertainment). Finally, one-quarter was due to an increasing trade deficit in goods (Atkinson, 2003b).
36. *Fortune*, 11 February 2002.
37. Carnevale and Rose (1998).
38. www.bls.gov.
39. Galbraith (1968) pp. 67-8.
40. Foreign direct investment totaled over $300 billion in 2000, up from just $45 billion in 1995. The market value of the Wilshire 5000, the broadest index for the US equity market, increased from 35 percent of GDP in 1982 to 75 percent in March 2002. The ratio of M3 (the broadest category of money, including bank deposits, money market deposits, and large time deposits) to GDP increased from 60 percent of GDP in 1960 to 81 percent today, while bank credit increased from 37 percent to 56 percent. Likewise, there is five times more venture capital under management today than there was in 1995. In addition, the amount of money invested worldwide in private equity funds (funds which buy businesses with the idea of reselling them after restructuring them) has skyrocketed, from around $25 million in 1992 to over 1.2 billion in 2002 ('Parting the Veil', *The Economist*, 20 December, 2003, p. 103).
41. OECD (2003) Figure A.1.1.
42. Ibid. Table B.2.3.
43. Ibid. Table D.6.1.
44. Packer (1987).
45. OECD (2003) Table A.8.1.
46. With respect to manufacturing Daniel Bell argued that, 'the most characteristic fact about the American factory worker today is his lack of interest in work. Few individuals think of the job as a place to seek any fulfillment' (Bell 1976, p. 391).
47. Quoted in Tremain (2000) p. 41.
48. Osterman (1999).
49. Ibid.
50. Towers Perrin (2001).
51. OECD (1995).
52. Davis and Wessel (1998).
53. US Census Bureau (1993).
54. Moreover, compared to manufacturers using fewer technologies, companies using more technologies employ almost half as many employees with a high school diploma or less (Brynjolfsson and Hitt, 1993, p. 222).
55. Appelbaum et al. (2000).

56. Flexible pay has let companies keep more workers while cutting back expenses during the recent downturn. While variable pay rose 9.5 percent in 1999, it grew only 3 percent in 2001.
57. Yelin (1999).
58. Khurana (2000).
59. Fry (2000).
60. International Monetary Fund (1998).
61. A.T. Kearny and *Foreign Policy Magazine* (2001).
62. Fry (2000).
63. The German cellphone company Vodafone bought Mannesmann. British Petroleum invested $7.7 billion to purchase Russia's TNK oil group. The US company Citbank invested $13 billion to take over Mexican bank Banacci.
64. Claessens et al. (2003).
65. *Business Week*, 28 August, 2000, p. 200.
66. Henwood (2003) p. 150.
67. Mercedes Benz opened a factory in Long Island, New York in 1905, while Ford established an auto factory in Britain as early as 1911 (Atkinson and Garner, 1987).
68. The cost of a T-1 dedicated phone line between the United States and Manila has dropped from $30000 a month to less than $10000 in the past few years. Moreover, technology advances have allowed the number of voice channels that can be put on a T-1 line to increase about five fold (http://knowledge.wharton.upenn.Edu/100902ss5. html).
69. Between 1987 and 1997 the cost of a US to London telephone call declined by 90 percent (Burnham, 1997).
70. Hufbauer (1991).
71. Hummels (1999) p. 6.
72. Hummels (1999).
73. Tariff reductions and free-trade agreements were responsible for 75 percent of the growth of trade (holding income constant), while transport-cost declines accounted for 25 percent, (Baier and Bergstrand, 1998).
74. Scanners can digitize documents at the rate of 200 pages per minute and then transfer that information to virtually any place for further processing. Moreover, imaging technology has come so far that smudges on documents can be detected.
75. Atkinson (2004a).
76. Fry (2000).
77. Kanter (1984) p. 348.
78. Mintzberg and Waters (1983) and Porter (1985).
79. Grove (1999).
80. Whitman (1999) p. 9.
81. Ibid. p. 123.
82. Zey and Swenson (2001).
83. Benner et al. (1999). According to the Public Policy Institute of California new Silicon Valley companies hired 258 000 workers in the 1990s while existing companies shed 120000 jobs.
84. National Commission on Entrepreneurship (2001).
85. *Business Week*, 28 August, 2000, p. 82.
86. One important change in the 1980s was reform of the ERISA to let pension funds invest in venture capital funds.
87. National Venture Capital Association.
88. Adkinson et al. (2004) p. 48.
89. OECD (1997) p. 70.
90. Ibid. p. 88.
91. US Small Business Administration (1995), Table 3, p. 28.

92. Reich (2001) p. 73.
93. In 1992, three-quarters of 531 corporations identified economic pressures from competitors as one of the primary factors motivating their restructuring efforts (Cappelli et al., 1996).
94. McKenna (1997).
95. Scott McNealy, CEO of Sun Microsystems, describes a world in the future when a driver whose car is running low on gas will be able to send out a message to ask gasoline stations in the area he or she is driving in to bid on the lowest price of gas.
96. Drucker (1995).
97. Dunning and Boyd (2003).
98. Fountain and Atkinson (1998).
99. OECD (2000).
100. Hagedoorn et al. (2000).
101. Whitman (1999) p. 134.
102. Reinicke (1998) p. l 22.
103. Deloite Research (2003) www.dc.com/Insights/research/crossind/cknworkforce. asp.
104. Cappelli et al. (1996).
105. President's Council of Economic Advisors (2003).
106. One indicator of expanding consumer choice is the number of trademarks filed by companies. Since 1989, the number of trademarks filings has taken off, increasing from about 80000 per year to 180000 per year in 1995.
107. www.dallasfed.org/htm/pubs/annual/arpt98.html.
108. *Beverage Industry*, December 2003, p. 16.
109. McKenna (1997).
110. Davis and Pine (1999).
111. Some even speculate that digital manufacturing will soon make it possible for consumers to download three-dimensional fabrication electronic files and make their own clothes by employing electro-mechanical devices (www.ennex.com /publish /200002-MB-MassCustom.asp).
112. Brynjolfsson et al. (2003).
113. Atkinson and Gottlieb (2001).
114. Atkinson (1998).
115. Atkinson (2003).
116. Galston (2003) p. 9.
117. Quoted in Galston (2003) p. 5.
118. Drew (1996) p. 26. Jude Wanniski, the father of the supply-side economics movement agrees, describing Gingrich and the conservatives who took power in 1994 as wanting to 'unwind the New Deal' (quoted in Judis, 2004).
119. Atkinson (2002) pp. 35-7.
120. Kristol (1995) p. 121.
121. Pinkerton (1995) p. 281.
122. Glassman (1995) p. A18.
123 Blair goes on to argue that the fundamental task is to recast the relationship between the citizen and the state, not abandonment or dependence, but mutual responsibility and partnership. ... The citizen and the state need to meet each other on different terms than in 1945 (Author's notes on remarks by Prime Minister Tony Blair, Progressive Governance Conference, Policy Network, June 2003, London).
124. Giddens (2002) p. 80.
125. Such longing for the old governing ideology was epitomized by the energetic presidential campaign of Howard Dean, which rejected the shifts of the last 20 years. Indeed, much of the Dean campaign has been styled as protest against the

politics of the last 20 years, including the Clinton Administration. Instead he wants to take the nation back to the 1960s when 'it was also a time of great hope. Medicare had passed. Head Start had passed. The Civil Rights Act, the Voting Rights Act ... we felt like we were all in it together, that we all had responsibility for the country ... that's the kind of country that I want back' (Farhi, 2003, A5).

126. Faux (1996) p. 105.
127. For example, liberal commentator E.J. Dionne (2004) makes the claim that the key to a Democratic party revival is less about message and policy and more about tactics and positioning, particularly in matching the Republicans in the aggressiveness of their rhetoric.
128. From and Marshall (1998).
129. It has become trendy in liberal Democratic circles to explain away the electoral success of the Clinton administration by stating that it was Clinton's unique personality that led to success. This is in fact a replication of what conservative Republicans did in the 1950s when explaining Ike's success as a function of his winning personality. It is much easier to ascribe success to idiosyncratic factors like this, than to consider that one's own ideology might be rooted in a prior era (Marshall, 2001).
130. Giddens (2002) p. 3.

5. The Key to Productivity Revival

Productivity growth, and by extension per capita income growth, is the most important measure and determinant of economic performance, far more important than 'input' indicators like the value of the stock market, the inflation rate, or the trade balance, and even more important than minimizing short-term fluctuations in the business cycle.[1] The United States enjoys the highest standard of living not because we grew in population – that simply increased GDP – but because from 1900 to 2000 economic output per person grew eight-fold.[2] If productivity grows 1 percent faster for the next 40 years than its 1980s' rate and if that growth is distributed so that all income groups see increases, the average American will earn $41 000 more per year. With this, Americans could afford better housing, universal high-quality health care, and more college education. They could also work fewer hours without reducing their incomes. The nation could pay Social Security benefits for the increased retirees without having to raise payroll taxes.

It is precisely because the New Economy is creating the conditions that lead to robust productivity growth that it is so important. The higher productivity of the mid to late 1990s meant that the economy now produces $1.9 trillion in output more every year.[3] Even in the face of the post-2000 slowdown in job growth, productivity increases show few signs of abating. Indeed, business sector productivity increased by a robust 4.3 percent in 2003.

Why did productivity growth fall so suddenly in the 1970s and 1980s? Why did it turn around in the 1990s? Is the recent surge likely to continue? What can we do to keep the productivity boom going? The answers can be gained from looking at the relationship between past economic transformations and productivity growth. Productivity tends to grow slowly when one techno-economic system is declining and another is emerging. That is when the old economy has exhausted itself and it is becoming increasingly difficult to eke out productivity gains from the prevailing technology system, organization of work, and managerial, organizational and market structure. Only when the new technology system becomes cheap enough and pervasive enough is it able to revitalize the engine of productivity and propel the economy to new levels of efficiency and innovation.

THE PRODUCTIVITY BOOM OF THE OLD ECONOMY

In the heyday of the old economy from 1947 to 1973, productivity grew on average 3 percent per year. This was indeed a golden age. During Eisenhower's two terms, real family incomes increased 24 percent. During the next eight years under Kennedy and Johnson, real incomes went up another 30 percent. Overall, for the five-year periods between 1950 and 1975, productivity grew no slower than 12.4 percent, and as fast as 22 percent in the first five years of the 1960s. Real compensation (wages and benefits) per hour grew no slower than 13.7 percent per five-year period between 1950 and 1970. All the while unemployment averaged less than 4.6 percent.

The mass production technology system was a key engine powering the boom. While the assembly line was first developed in a rudimentary form in the 1910s, it was not until the 1940s that it was diffused widely throughout factories and it continued to be refined and improved through the 1960s. There were other major breakthroughs, however, that became widespread after World War II. In a host of industries, including chemicals, refining, and cement, continuous flow came to replace batch processing facilities. Productivity-enhancing break-throughs were not confined to manufacturing. A host of sectors became more efficient. Productivity grew almost 2 percent a year in the harder to automate service sector. New technologies and new kinds of work organization were letting offices become more efficient. Moreover, the emerging corporatization of a whole host of sectors that previously had been run by relatively inefficient 'mom and pop' operations boosted productivity. In sectors ranging from grocery stores (Safeway), department stores (Sears, J.C. Penny, Montgomery Ward), gas stations (Standard Oil, Texaco) and lodging (Holiday Inn),[4] corporate establishments spread throughout the nation.

As the new production system propelled productivity growth there was a widespread sense that the future would be bright. In his 1950 State of the Union address, President Truman stated that:

If our productive power continues to increase at the same rate as it has increased for the past 50 years, our total national production 50 years from now will be nearly four times as much as it is today. Allowing for the expected growth in population, this would mean that the real income of the average family in the year 2000 AD would be about three times what it is today.

Little could he expect that this was not to be.

THE GREAT PRODUCTIVITY SLOWDOWN

Starting in 1973 the growth in productivity of all our economic assets (capital and labor – what economists call total factor productivity) slowed from 1.9 percent per year between 1948 and 1973 to only 0.2 percent between 1973 and 1995. Labor productivity growth – how much workers produce per hour of work – fell from 3 percent per year to about 1.3 percent per year. Three of the four five-year periods between 1975 and 1995 saw productivity growth under 8 percent and the peak was only 10.3 percent. As a result, the average worker's income stagnated. In the eight years following Nixon's first term (1973 to 1980) average family income did not grow at all, while from 1981 to 1996 it went up just 9 percent. In the three five-year periods between 1975 and 1990, median income grew no faster than 7 percent and in fact declined 2.2 percent during the so-called boom years of the late 1980s. Between 1982 and 1991, white-collar workers saw their incomes go up about 0.6 percent annually, while blue-collar and service workers saw a decline of 0.4 percent and 0.1 percent respectively. Economist Frank Levy sums up the reality of this period when he calls it the 'quiet depression.'[5] Unlike the Great Depression, the quiet depression saw unemployment rates go up only modestly, largely because of the automatic stabilizers that were built into the system (e.g., unemployment insurance). But productivity and income growth declined precipitously and income inequality soared.

If the productivity slowdown was confined to just the United States one might argue that it was due to factors, such as public policy, unique to it. But because it was related to the transformation of the underlying technology system shared by all advanced nations, the slowdown affected most countries, including Europe. European productivity growth slowed from 5 percent in the 1960s to 3 percent in the 1970s, and to 2 percent in the 1980s where it has remained.

(and innovation in new products and services) and therefore was harder to justify investing in. Related to the investment explanation, others, like *Newsweek* economic columnist Robert Samuelson, blamed higher levels of inflation, but this again begs the question of what caused inflation.[10] In reality, it is more likely that the slowdown in productivity caused the rise of inflation, as slow productivity limited corporate cost-cutting, just as high productivity in the last decade limited inflation.

Some economists pointed to the large influx of younger, less productive workers into the economy in the 1970s and 1980s.[11] But there is no reason why replacing old workers with young workers would lower productivity significantly, particularly in some physically demanding industries where the opposite effect might be expected. Besides, this new cohort of workers was more educated, suggesting that, if anything, productivity should have been increasing.

By and large, economists were grasping at straws.[12] Harvard economist Alan Dennison conducted the most comprehensive analysis of the productivity slowdown.[13] After looking at a host of factors, including changes in the labor force, government regulation, and oil prices, Dennison concluded that collectively these factors could explain at best only 40 percent of the productivity slowdown. The remaining 60 percent was a mystery.

Neo-Marxist economists had their own explanation. Ironically, like conservative supply-side economists, neo-Marxists attributed the falloff in productivity to the sharp drop in profit rates in the late 1960s and 1970s. But neo-Marxists were split into two camps in explaining why profits fell. The conventional camp held to the wage-squeeze theory, that rising wages cut into business income.[14] This theory holds that capitalists cannot introduce labor-saving technology fast enough to keep profits from falling because of the strength of labor. But there is no evidence that wage growth exceeded productivity growth. If anything, the strength of labor was eroding. The other neo-Marxist camp argued that profits were held down by the failure of business to scrap capital stock fast enough. Historian Robert Brenner argues that:

> The long downturn, from this standpoint, has persisted largely because the advanced capitalist economies have been unable to accomplish profitably sufficient reductions and reallocations of productive power so as to overcome over-capacity and overproduction in manufacturing lines, and thereby to restore profitability.[15]

But this explanation falls short on several counts. First, it begs the key question of why they needed to scrap old capital and why they could not do it fast enough then. Brenner argues that companies failed to scrap existing investment and shift it to new more profitable sectors. But the reason is that there were few new more profitable sectors to shift capital into until the emergence of the new technology system in the 1990s. In addition, if the problem was 'excess competition' then one could reasonably expect productivity rates to increase, as firms would be forced to cut costs even more aggressively as they have been in the last few years in the United States. But instead, productivity fell.

In short, to this day economists are not quite sure what happened. Alan Blinder, former Vice Chairman of the Board of Governors of the Federal Reserve System, states 'No one quite knows why productivity growth slowed down so much, although many partial explanations – higher energy costs, lagging investment, and deterioration in the skills of the average worker – have been offered.'[16] Robert Samuelson admits, 'hardly anyone foresaw the productivity slowdown and even after decades of study it has not been convincingly explained.'[17] Paul Krugman confesses, 'We do not really know why productivity growth ground to a near halt. Unfortunately, that makes it hard to answer the other question. What can we do to speed it up?'[18] For policymakers desperate for an answer, Krugman offers no consolation, pronouncing: 'Productivity growth is the single most important factor affecting our economic well-being. But it is not a policy issue, because we are not going to do anything about it.'[19] Blinder, likewise, counsels low expectations, stating, 'Nothing – repeat, nothing – that economists know about growth gives us a recipe for adding a percentage point or more to the nation's growth rate on a sustained basis. Much as we might wish otherwise, it just ain't so.'[20]

Try as it might, neoclassical economics simply does not have the tools or orientation needed to answer the central economic question of the last quarter of a century. Usually having never visited an automobile assembly plant, a check processing facility of a bank, a telecommunications central office, or any other production facility, most economists do not have a clear bottom-up understanding of the technology, work organization, and entrepreneurial activities that drive productivity and innovation. As Michael Mandel, *Business Week*'s chief economist states, economists 'grudgingly acknowledge the importance of technological change, but they do not understand it or trust it.'[21]

Even if they understood these factors and were interested in them, neoclassical economists have no way of including them using their predominant analytic methods. As a result, most neoclassical economists see no difference between the expected impact on productivity between a million-dollar investment in a mechanical lathe and an equivalent investment in a computer-controlled lathe, even though the latter is significantly more efficient. The key is that innovation changes the quality of capital. If all you can measure is quantity, you're going to miss the real story.[22] To understand how productivity changes over the moderate to long term we need to call upon other disciplines: economic history, urban planning, business administration, labor relations, and engineering. In short, we need to look at the real economy as it plays itself out over time in the millions of workplaces in the nation.

When viewed through the lens of economic cycles the puzzle of falling productivity begins to make more sense. In its heyday the mass production, corporate economy was able to take advantage of a number of key innovations in technology, scale economies, and the organization of enterprises to create significant new efficiencies. However, eventually engineers, managers and others who organize production were able to wring out only so much efficiency from the prevailing techno-economic system. Over time virtually all enterprises had adopted the new technologies and ways of organizing work and firms: most manufacturers that could used assembly lines, most chemical companies adopted continuous flow processing, most companies sold through department stores, etc.

Even if all establishments adopted the core technologies, productivity could still keep growing if technologies continued to get better. Indeed, this is what happened for many years after World War II until the early 1970s. But by the late 1970s the dominant technological path was exhausted and further gains came with increasing difficulty. Eventually, all the efficiencies had been wrung out both from achieving increased scale economies and from fully utilizing the existing technological system. In short, the mass production system based on electro-mechanical automation had been milked for all it was worth.

This trend can be seen in a number of industries. In banking, the limits to mechanical check reading became apparent. In the early 1950s, IBM invented an automatic check reading and sorting machine for use by banks. Every few years they and other producers would come out with a better and somewhat cheaper machine that would process checks just a little faster with a few less errors. But by the early 1980s, the improvements slowed, as it was only physically possible to move paper so fast. At that point efficiency gains were more difficult to achieve. The same trend can be observed in the auto industry. Numerically controlled machine-tools and other mechanically based metal-working tools could not be made much more efficient. The industry had gone about as far as it could in tweaking out efficiency improvements in a mechanically-based production system. As a result, auto sector productivity growth declined from 3.8 percent per year from 1960 to 1975, to 2.2 percent from 1976 to 1995.

By the end of the 1970s the only way to regain robust productivity growth rates was for the production system to get on a new path based on a new set of core technologies. But as late as the early 1990s, the new IT-based techno-economic system was not well enough developed, and was too expensive, too weak, and too limited to exert a noticeable effect on productivity and economic growth.

Once it emerged, however, in the mid-1990s a new set of productivity possibilities also emerged to be taken advantage of by organizations. With respect to check processing, the new technology system – electronic bill payment and electronic check handling – does away with checks completely and lets banks once again ride the wave of significant ongoing productivity gains. Likewise in the auto industry, the new technology and organization systems developed by the late 1980s allowed car-makers to control parts delivery in real-time systems, design cars on computers, machine parts with computer numerically controlled machines, control quality with automatic inspection systems, and do a host of other things to boost efficiency. The result was that auto productivity growth surged to 3.7 percent per year in the last half of the 1990s. New developments in the Internet B-to-B marketplace that promise to automate and reengineer the entire automobile supply chain system and the ability of consumers to be able to go online and customize their car and order it directly from the factory suggest that the productivity benefits are nowhere near exhaustion. This opening up of new technology has not been confined just to the automobile and banking industry but affects a host of industries.

THE PRODUCTIVITY PARADOX: 'WE SEE COMPUTERS EVERYWHERE BUT IN THE PRODUCTIVITY STATISTICS'

By the early 1990s some economists began to speculate that the new technology system represented by the personal computer held the potential to get the economy out of its productivity slump. But once again most economists were puzzled since we had this amazing new technology and yet productivity still slumped. Nobel Prize-winning economist Robert Solow famously quipped, 'we see computers everywhere except in the productivity statistics.'[23]

The fact that productivity measures did not seem to show any impact from new technologies was labeled 'the productivity paradox.' Because productivity growth had lagged since the 1960s while investments in IT grew, some mistakenly concluded that this meant that IT did not affect productivity. Liberal economists Barry Bluestone and Bennett Harrison argued that, 'the first Intel chip, produced in late 1971, was capable of processing about 60 000 instructions per second. The latest, introduced in 1998, is capable of 300 million. Yet over that same period, productivity nose dived.'[24] Conservative theorists had their own explanation – they defined productivity away, claiming that the very notion was an old economy relic. The Progress and Freedom Foundation, originally dubbed as Newt Gingrich's think tank, claimed in 'Tofflerian' fashion that, '"GDP" and other popular numbers do nothing to clarify the magic and muscle of information technology.'[25]

The real reason we were not seeing IT in the productivity statistics was that it simply was not cheap enough or powerful enough to move a $6 trillion economy. The experience most economists had with the IT revolution was their desktop computer and they could not understand why this marvelous device was not leading to gains in productivity. In fact IT was boosting productivity, but only in particular sectors. Sectoral studies found significant positive relationships between IT investment and productivity.[26] Since the 1970s, productivity grew 1.1 percent per year for sectors investing heavily in computers and approximately 0.35 percent for sectors investing less.[27] Between 1989 and 2001, productivity growth in IT-intensive industries averaged 3.03 percent per year, compared to only 0.42 percent per year in less IT-intensive industries.[28]

So, even if IT affected particular sectors, why did computers not show up in the overall productivity statistics? Stanford economic historian Paul David has advanced the most widely accepted theory, claming that it takes a long time to learn how to use new technology. He argued that it took over 30 years for electric motors to be fully utilized by factories after they were first developed in the early 1900s.[29] He analogized this to the computer by suggesting that it takes a long time for companies to figure out how best to use these technologies and reorganize their production systems.

While David's 'learning' hypothesis seems reasonable, it suffers from two key drawbacks. First, there is little evidence that these technologies are hard to learn. In fact, with 'Windows' functionality, off-the-shelf software, and the easy to use World Wide Web, information technologies are relatively easy for companies to adopt and use. Second, David assumes that electric motors came onto the scene fully formed and that it took 30 or 40 years for recalcitrant companies to finally adopt them. The actual process was much different. Electric motor technology, like today's information technology, took over 25 years to increase power output, functionality, versatility and ease of use to get to the point where they were widely used and had a big impact.[30]

Like the electric motor then, it is not that it took a long time for organizations to learn how to use IT, but that in the 1980s and early 1990s the technologies were rudimentary. Compared to today, PC technology of even the early 1990s seems antiquated, not to mention expensive.[31] As late as 1994, virtually no personal computers were networked to the Internet, and for the few that were, they lacked an easy to use web browser like Netscape. The first popular Microsoft Windows platform (3.0) was not shipped until 1990 and even this was nowhere near as easy to use as Windows95. 'Pentium' computer chips were not introduced until 1993 and even then were slow compared to today's chip speeds. The average disk drive storage was 2 gigabits compared to 80 gigabits today. Few machines came with modems, CD-ROMS, speakers, or graphics cards. In short, until the mid-1990s most Americans were working on Ford Model Ts, not Ford Explorers. Compared to the original Apple 2 computer with no hard drive and 560 KB of memory, the machines of the early 1990s looked pretty impressive and economists expected them to have a big economic impact. Yet, compared to today's machines, they are not even good enough to donate to schools. Moreover, semiconductors overall were expensive and weak and only as they have become cheap and powerful have they been able to be used in a range of devices, from automated call answering systems, to PDAs, to optical character recognition.

It was not just that the processing, storage, and memory of PCs (and a host of other IT enabled devices) was limited, it was that they were stand-alone devices. The power in the box is important but so is connecting the boxes. No matter how powerful desktop computers were, unless they were networked, widespread productivity advantages would remain a distant dream. It is the network that plays a key role in driving productivity gains, by allowing transactions, relationships, and information exchange to be reengineered. In arguing that policymakers should not look to IT to boost incomes, Bluestone and Harrison wrote in 2000 that the information age was in its fourth decade and had yet to show returns. It is more realistic to say that the IT revolution is only in its second decade, and that all the prior activity was just a warm-up.

There is one additional reason why economists were not seeing the productivity results – in many cases IT was not boosting productivity. The reason was that a significant share of IT investments in the 1980s and early 1990s were designed not to raise productivity but to improve customer relations and support a broader range of product and service offerings.[32] While some might argue that these improved functions should be included in measured productivity, they were not. According to a study of banks by the McKinsey Global Institute, 'The majority of post-1995 IT capital investments were associated with banks' focus on increasing revenues such as customer information systems, analytic tools, and technology to support product customization.[33] This is one reason why despite the fact that the service sector purchased 88 percent of all IT hardware sold in the United States in 1991 it did not see significant improvements in productivity.

Finally, many of the early Internet and World Wide Web applications were largely passive, with companies putting up web sites largely just to provide information. However, as electronic commerce began to become a bigger share of the economy, where customers (both business and consumers) could access information about their accounts, insurance policies, real-time airline schedules, etc. and actually fill out forms, apply for policies, buy tickets, and conduct other transactions on line, significant improvements in productivity became possible.

WHY DID PRODUCTIVITY GO UP IN THE 1990S?

No sooner did the idea of the productivity paradox become widely accepted than it disappeared. Between the fourth quarter of 1996 and the fourth quarter of 2003, productivity growth averaged 3.3 percent growth per year, almost three times as fast as during the stagnant transition period. Real wages increased annually 1.3 percent in the 1990s, compared to only 0.2 percent in the 1980s.[34] White-collar workers saw real wages go up annually about 1.4 percent, blue-collar wages rose 1 percent, and service workers gained about 1.1 percent per year between 1991 and the end of 2001.[35]

What happened? Some economists insist that this was largely a cyclical recovery and that the New Economy broadly, and computers and the Internet specifically, had little effect.[36] The most notable productivity revival skeptic is economist Robert Gordon who claims that the lion's share (0.54 percent) of the productivity pickup in the 1990s can be accounted for by the business cycle. But if this were true why did productivity grow even faster in the recent slowdown of 2001 when it typically falls? Gordon also argues that virtually all the rest of productivity gain is confined to one sector – computer and semiconductors – and when this is controlled for, the rest of the economy looks no different than it has for the last two decades.[37] In fact, McKinsey Global Institute found that productivity gains were spread among a number of sectors, including wholesale and retail trade. Likewise, the Conference Board found that US industries that were IT-intensive users contributed 1.4 percentage points to US productivity growth between 1995 and 1998.

Like other new economy skeptics, Gordon thinks e-commerce is mostly smoke and mirrors, arguing that we are unlikely to see continued growth in productivity because the Internet fails to qualify as a great technology breakthrough. He says that computer demand stems from cost reduction and not the growth of the Internet;[38] e-commerce substitutes for existing goods and services (e.g. catalogues); Internet investments are driven by old economy companies defending themselves; and much of e-commerce takes place during work time by employees buying personal items.[39] For him the Internet offers a more convenient ways of doing old things, and so is no real breakthrough.[40] But this is like saying in the 1880s that the new Bessemer furnace alone would not drive income growth. Of course it would not, but as part of a suite of technologies based on metallurgy it did. Morgan Stanley's Stephen Roach, another New Economy pessimist, argues that the productivity boom was all about mismeasurement, in this case not counting all the extra hours worked.[41] Yet, the Bureau of Labor Statistics examined this claim and found that it was without merit.[42]

Other productivity pessimists ascribe the productivity rebound of the last few years to one-time transitory factors completely unrelated to the new production system. Typical is the neo-Keynesian notion that consumer spending fueled the boom, instead of actually resulting from the boom. *Newsweek* declares, 'Our restaurant tabs and spending sprees have fueled the boom.'[43] It asks:

> what if the boom has been at least partly a classic episode of speculative excess – overpriced stocks, doomed investments in dubious startups and people spending beyond their means. Then the productivity gains will prove fleeting – more the result of high demand than high technology – and the boom will end grimly.[44]

This is simply a rehash of the old Keynesian thinking; that the economy is all about business cycles and that fiscal and monetary policies are the key to stability. Even if one were to concede that the speculative excess led to the economy operating at full employment, it cannot lead to the economy becoming more productive. That is due to underlying changes in the production system.

Other economists recognize that something has changed, but do not see it in terms of any kind of change in the underlying technology system. Economist Dale Jorgenson explains the productivity turnaround and growth in IT solely in terms of the commodity prices – in this case, the price of semiconductor technology and memory chips.[45] Since prices fell faster than Moore's law would have predicted, Jorgenson believes this caused the boom. Yet, saying that prices fell ignores the fact that quality improved. As Schumpeter stated in reference to the fact that technologies get better, not just cheaper, 'Add successively as many mail coaches as you please, you will never get a railroad thereby.'[46] Add as many Intel 086 chips as you please and you will never get today's Internet. Moreover, while price declines certainly contributed to investment, the much more important question is why did prices fall? One can make a compelling case that the quickening pace of innovation and investment led prices to fall, not the other way around.

Other economists recognize that something has changed, but are not sure where we are in the process. Alan Greenspan states that, 'the diffusion of technology starts slowly, accelerates and then slows down with maturity. But knowing where we stand now in that sequence is difficult, if not impossible, in real time.'[47] This is in fact the key question. Why did Moore's law speed up in the 1990s and why did the

IT revolution take off? What were the changes in the innovation system that let this occur? Are they likely to continue?

To answer these questions it is important to delineate productivity growth by sector. Productivity growth over the past two economies was powered in large part by two industries, agriculture and manufacturing, both of which involved processing physical things. It was easier to raise productivity in these sectors (e.g., better fertilizers on farms, more mechanical automation in factories) than it was in services. The fact that factory and farm productivity has grown approximately three to four times faster than productivity in the services sector over the last three decades has meant that even though we produce more food and manufacturing goods, we do it with relatively fewer farmers and factory workers. In the old economy productivity did go up in services, but at a slower pace. Starting in the 1970s, productivity in both manufacturing and services took a nosedive. Then a curious thing happened. As Table 5.1 illustrates, in the 1980s manufacturing rebounded to historical rates of growth, and even exceeded them in the 1990s. Relying on new technologies and new ways to organize production, companies found new ways to squeeze out more production with fewer workers. For example, Navistar's Indianapolis engine plant spent $285 million in new investments between 1995 and 2000 with the result that, while it took 900 people to produce 175 engines a day in 1994, in 2000 it took 900 workers to produce 1400 engines a day. Pirelli Tires developed its modular integrated robotized system that can manufacture a tire in 72 minutes as opposed to the six days needed previously. As a result, its productivity increased 80 percent. The running-shoe company New Balance's Maine factory is so productive its workers can produce a pair of shoes in 24 minutes, compared to three hours in China.

In contrast to manufacturing, service sector productivity growth stagnated. Since over 80 percent of jobs are in the non-goods sector, even the fastest productivity growth rates in manufacturing and farming are not enough to pull the overall economy along. If we want to find out the cause of the productivity slowdown, we have to look no further than the service sector.

In an economy that is increasingly made up of processing information and conducting transactions between individuals, being able to better cultivate, manufacture or transport things is simply less important to driving future prosperity. Yet, raising productivity in services is in many ways more difficult than in manufacturing. This is because in most manufacturing sectors companies are making multiple copies of the same good and can use ever more effective materials, machines and routines to reduce production costs. But how can companies automate processes like phone calls, paper forms, personal face-to-face service? Until the mid-1990s, it was quite difficult.

Table 5.1 Trends in annual productivity growth

	Manufacturing %	Services %
1947–73	2.6	1.9
1973–79	1.2	0.5
1979–90	2.6	0.4
1990–96	3.5	0.2
1996–2002	5.0	1.7

Source: US Bureau of Labor Statistics.

In an economy where most of what people do does not involve the production or movement of things, the electro-mechanical technologies of the old economy can no longer be the engine of progress. An automated assembly line is not much use in an insurance company. A forklift truck cannot do much for a restaurant. Better fertilizer does not make a bank more efficient. Luckily, the IT system has the ability to vastly improve efficiency and productivity in services.[48]

IT'S ROLE IN DRIVING PRODUCTIVITY GROWTH

It is not immediately obvious how IT will boost productivity. Some analysts think that its major role is to enable companies to better collect, analyze and act on information. Alan Blinder suggests that, 'the basic idea is that advances in IT make more information available faster and cheaper, and that better, more timely information leads to better business decisions.'[49] But while IT enables managers to have more information at their fingertips which in turn should lead to better decisions, to suggest that the productivity slowdown came about because of poor decisions and will revive because of better decisions makes little sense.

Among those who admit that IT boosts productivity, many claim that since these technologies are becoming mature the economy will soon return to 'normal' productivity stagnation. Given the IT devices people encounter in their daily lives – cell phones, personal digital assistants (PDAs), broadband Internet, and the like – most people think that the digital revolution is mature. Charles Fine and Daniel Raff argue that with regard to the auto industry the biggest savings will be in the order to delivery cycle and that the improvement is 'a one-shot improvement in forecasting, communication and co-ordination.'[50] Morgan Stanley's Stephen Roach agrees, arguing that the productivity boost from the IT revolution is transient.[51] In his view, IT-led automation yields a one-time productivity gain that is difficult to replicate and over time even erode productivity because of the IT overhead. Even Alan Greenspan succumbed to this notion when he argued that productivity growth cannot indefinitely remain at current levels.

It is true that the adoption of technologies have sometimes produced one-time productivity gains for the adopters but, as they diffuse to other adopters, productivity kept going up. Moreover, even within an existing technology system, technologies continue to improve. The IT revolution is only in its adolescence as a whole array of new technologies will be rolled out, some of which we can only barely imagine. In these and myriad other ways 'one-time' gains become continuous gains, at least until the technology system is mature and fully diffused.

Just as mechanization let companies automate manufacturing, digitization is enabling organizations to automate a whole host of processes, including paper, in-person, and telephone transactions. As a result, the animating force for productivity and wage growth over the next decade will be the pervasive use of IT, particularly in the up to now low-technology service sector and in those functions involving routine processing of information and face-to-face transactions. This 'digitization' promises to bring the kinds of economic benefits to Americans that mechanization brought in the early twentieth century. And this will be spurred by the 'network effect' – the more Americans use these technologies (e.g., Internet, smart cards, mobile wireless, broadband telecommunications) the more applications will be developed and the more value they will provide.

While most of the hype of the late 1990s was on the Internet, and in particular on a narrow segment of it (e-commerce retailing and Internet content sites), the Internet is not the only source of digital transformation. The same pundits who mistakenly thought that the personal computer was synonymous with the technology revolution of the early 1990s also thought that e-retailing and advertising-supported Web sites were the be-all and end-all of the e-commerce revolution. But no matter how much they grow, Internet retailing and Web sites built on advertisement revenues will be at best a modest part of the digital economy.

The digital economy is not simply an expanded version of Internet catalog sites, although this is certainly a part of it. Rather, it represents the pervasive use of IT in all aspects of the economy, including internal operations of organizations, transactions between organizations, and transactions between consumers/citizens and organizations. In particular, the major driver of the digital economy will be production applications that let businesses use IT to reengineer and automate processes. Moreover, the new IT system is turning individuals into 'prosumers' (consumers who also produce), a term futurist Alvin Toffler coined 25 years ago.[52] In fact, productivity in the economy in the future may depend as much on what goes on on the living room floor as on the shop floor. Just as companies invest in capital equipment, so too do prosumers invest in their own capital equipment: computers, broadband, wireless networks, displays, smart cards, etc. Information technology lets consumers play an increasingly important role in the production process, whether it is using a telephone keypad to enter information, buying a product or service over the Internet, or using a smart card to pay at a parking garage.

The digital economy promises to raise productivity in at least three key ways: (1) machine-to-machine communication will replace person-to-person interaction; (2) person-to-computer automation will lead to a significant increase in self-service applications like banking, applying for insurance, filing taxes, ordering goods and services, purchasing tickets, and buying groceries;[53] and (3) IT will reengineer internal processes and automate interactions with suppliers and business customers.

There are at least four things, however, that will have to happen to the technology system for it to achieve the full promise of the digital revolution. First, the technology will need to be easier to use and more reliable. Americans do not think twice about plugging in an appliance to the wall socket because they know it will work. They do not have to learn programming to place a wireline phone call. They do not get out a manual when they start their car. But in spite of considerable efforts to make them easier to use most digital technologies remain complicated and less than fully reliable. Technologies will need to be so easy to use that they fade into the background. Luckily, much of the IT industry is working on this challenge, and indeed, each new generation of technology is getting to be more 'plug and play.'

Second, all kinds of devices will need to be linked together. It is funny to see many 'road warriors' carrying around their cell phone, laptop, Blackberry and PDA. At home, it is just as bad, with a host of electronic appliances (e.g., stereos, televisions, phones, computers, printers and peripherals, and MP3 players) not hooked together. Moreover, an array of new convenient devices like smart cards, e-book readers, and ubiquitous sensors will need to be part of daily life. But again, the IT industry and consumer electronics industry are working hard on overcoming this challenge and pushing toward convergence and integration.

Third, new and improved technologies are still needed. Better voice, handwriting and optical recognition features would allow humans to better interact with computers. Better intelligent agents that routinely filter and retrieve information based on users preferences would make the Internet experience better. Expert system software would help in making decisions in medicine, engineering, finance, and other fields. Again, these improvements are being made.

Finally, we need more ubiquitous adoption. When we get to 75 percent online penetration and 50 percent usage of key applications (such as electronic bill payment) and high-speed broadband penetration, a critical inflection point will occur. At that point the cyber world will begin to dominate, whereas now both activities, cyber business and traditional business, exist in parallel worlds. It is not just online ubiquity we need, IT will need to be applied to all things we want to do, so that every industry and economic function that can employ digital technologies does.

While we have made considerable progress, we have got a considerable way to go. Most companies have only started to grasp the potential of networking everyone online, including employees, customers and suppliers. Most people still do not use the Internet to conduct business transactions. Yet past economic transformations should give us cause for hope. The enabling revolution of the steel age, the Bessemer steel process was in place by the 1870s and took 40 years for the technology to permeate the industry. The fundamental component of the digital revolution – the PC – has been available for only 20 years.

THE CONTOURS OF THE EMERGING DIGITAL ECONOMY

To understand how the digital technology system will continue to boost productivity, it is worth looking in detail at the kinds of processes, functions, and industries that are likely to be transformed. A good rule of thumb in considering what the emerging digital economy will look like is to assume that virtually all processes that convey information through physical media or human interactions will become digital.

Take music and films. Thirty years ago most people listened to music by rotating plastic discs and having a diamond-tipped needle transform the physical vibrations into an analogue electrical signal that was processed and put through speakers. Along came audio tapes that still used a physical analog format but read magnetic signals embedded on plastic tape. Then music was digitized (broken into ones and zeros) but still put on plastic discs (CDs) read by lasers. Only recently with digital music (e.g., the MP3 digital format) have we got rid of the physical component, downloading electrons over the Internet.

Music is not the only content moving to digital format. Within a few years, as people download movies over broadband connections and store them on massive hard drives, DVDs will be looked at the way we view LP records. Cameras are going the same way, as reflected by Kodak's recent decision to stop selling film cameras. Millions have purchased digital cameras and inexpensive, high-quality color printers. Within a few years chemical-based film cameras – what Kodak built 100 years of success on – will occupy a very small niche. People are also shifting from VCR analog devices to digital video recorders. When display technology improves to the point that it mimics the printed page, sales of e-book readers will likely take off. Even radio and television, which involve the transmission of analog electric signals over the air, are being transformed into digital format, with the rise of satellite radio services, Internet radio, and Internet-protocol video. In short, people will be consuming media in ones and zeros, not atoms.

This means that whole swaths of the media industry can be bypassed or transformed, including production, distribution, and sales, dramatically cutting costs. Take e-books. The entire process of printing a book, shipping it to a warehouse and then to a store where it is put on a shelf for weeks at a time, only to be sold by a clerk to someone who made a special trip to a bookstore would be eliminated with e-books. Instead, people would download the book to their e-book reader. This would produce dramatic savings considering that employee compensation in the book-printing industry amounts to over $1.6 billion per year and that there are over 667 book-printing establishments, 3883 book wholesalers, and 11 559 book stores in the US alone. E-book publishers save about $8 per book in printing, distribution, and return costs. Moving to digital format in other media would produce similar savings.[54] For example, movie studios estimate they can save tens of millions of dollars a year by sending movie theaters digital files to be shown on digital projectors.

Digital transformation could go even further and eliminate a host of other intermediaries. For example, the role of publishers could be reduced if authors were to sell 'e-books' directly to the consumer, as mystery writer Stephen King has attempted to do.[55] Why share the proceeds with a publisher if the writer can hire his/her own copy editor and put the content on his/her own web site? Why have almost 13 000 local radio stations employing hundreds of thousands of people if a couple of hundred could stream content over the Web?[56] Why have local television networks, when the Web could enable people to view any television episode from any time? Similarly, other content intermediaries such as movie studios and record companies could see significantly reduced business as some content producers (film-makers, authors, musicians) use the Internet to sell their products directly to consumers.

Reduction of Paper Transactions

Notwithstanding the fact that people have spoken about the emergence of a paperless society for over 40 years, the digital revolution promises a dramatic decrease in paper, particularly forms, bills, and publications.[57] Start with money. Like media, money is simply the expression of a certain kind of information, in this case that the money is backed by the government and is transferable for a certain amount of goods and services. But like media, there is no inherent reason why that information has to be held in physical form (e.g., paper bills and metal coins). Digital cash can play the same role. Pacific Northwest Indians used shells for currency. Our system of pieces of paper and round bits of metal is not much more efficient. Each year, the US mint produces over 27 billion coins, spending almost $800 million to do so.[58] The cost of handling and processing money is vastly greater, approximately half a percent of GDP.[59] Moving to e-cash would save each American $240 per year.

Consider a cash transaction. A clerk waits for a customer to get the money out of his wallet, takes the money, puts it in the cash drawer, counts the change and hands it to the customer. Merchants then count the money and deposit it in a bank, where the counting and storing begins all over again. E-cash streamlines much of this, but the savings from e-cash go much further.[60] Consider the scores of applications where consumers use cash for things like vending machines, parking meters, tollbooths, and casinos. For example, paying with digital cash (using either smart cards or wireless phones) at parking meters would allow cities to eliminate tens of thousands of parking meter coin collector jobs. In cases where an individual serves as an intermediary to collect the cash and make change, such as in parking garages, tollbooths, and ticket windows, these jobs could also be eliminated, saving consumers billions.[61]

It is not just government-issued cash that is costly, so is bank-issued cash (e.g., checks). In 2000, Americans wrote over 42.5 billion checks, down from 49.5 billion in 1995.[62] The process of collecting, sorting, reading, and transporting paper checks costs banks over 1 dollar per check. In contrast, electronic payments cost pennies. A growing share of Americans pay bills online. Given the savings, it is likely that within 15 years, paper checks will have been largely replaced by electronic forms of cash (e.g., credit and debit cards and electronic funds transfer).[63] A shift of 25 percent of paper checks to electronic payments over five years would yield an additional 1.8 percent annual productivity gain in the banking industry, which would contribute a 0.03 percent productivity boost for the economy.

Every year Americans fill out billions of forms, including tax returns, medical records, insurance and banking forms, and applications. In addition, billions of forms are sent as bills, reminders of appointments, applications, and stock prospectuses. This process requires large numbers of workers. For example, the telephone company Verizon has two factories to print, sort and mail telephone bills. In contrast, e-transactions (e-forms, e-bills, etc.) would dramatically cut costs. For example, switching from checks to electronic bill payment cuts the cost of each transaction from $1.40 to 8 cents.

One large use of paper forms is in dealing with government. E-government that lets more citizens and businesses interact with government through self-service online applications (e.g., filling out electronic forms) will cut government costs. Governments are moving ahead with online applications to let citizens do things like renew a driver's license; find information about parks and make camping reservations; order birth, death, marriage or divorce certificates; obtain hunting and fishing licenses; renew professional licenses on line; and pay their taxes.[64] For example, each year students file more than 2 million applications for college financial aid online. The US Patent and Trademark Office has implemented the use of digital signatures to allow more than 7000 registered patent attorneys and 4000 inventors to file patents electronically instead of with paper.

One of the big places to get rid of paper is within organizations themselves. Organizations can use IT to shift their internal transactions, such as travel reimbursements, changes of address, pension fund modifications and a host of other functions, to an Intranet system. Oracle recently implemented a system to process employee expense reports online, cutting the cost from $25 per report to $10, and saving the company over $6 million annually. Wireless technology can help organizations reduce the costs of paper. For example, St Luke's Episcopal Hospital in Houston uses wireless networks and has equipped doctors and nurses with laptops on which to enter treatment information. It cut data-entry time by 30 percent and allowed the respiratory therapy group to cut staff by 20 percent, saving $1.5 million per year.

Telephone Transactions

Digital technologies can also automate routine person-to-person transactions. There are hundreds of different functions that consist of a customer interacting with an employee to receive or process routine information. One is telephone operators. The major reason why telephone operator productivity has increased approximately 12 percent a year since 1950 is because customers, instead of operators, now place the vast majority of calls (through dialing). Now rather than talk directly to an operator, most telephone companies have the computer ask the customer to say the listing they want, saving the operator from asking that. Voice recognition technology is getting so effective that there is little need for the operator to be the go-between for the customer and the telephone company computer. The potential to automate routine telephone transactions goes far beyond telephone operators. Many company phone systems allow people to look up employees' direct phone extensions. Airlines use voice recognition technology to let people check on the status of flights. The company TellMe uses such systems to let people verbally surf the Web from a telephone. In 1999 55 percent of bank call inquires were served by voice recognition systems, and without these, call center agents would have had to grow by 86 percent.[65]

As voice recognition software continues to improve, it will be applied to more and more functions. In a decade we may look at an old keyboard entry system the way Scotty did in the Star Trek movie when he tried to talk into the computer mouse. Improved voice recognition software could automate functions like court stenography and medical transcription. For example, software is already good enough that many doctors and psychologists enter their notes directly by voice transcription.

Face-to-Face Transactions

Self-service is not new. As electronic control systems were developed, people operated elevators themselves, eliminating most elevator operators. Automatic pin setters eliminated the need for bowling ball boys. However, digital technologies are enabling a whole new array of self-service functions, including an increasing share of formerly face-to-face transactions as well. Given that there are over 60 billion transactions a year just in retail stores, 68 percent of which are in grocery, gas and convenience stores, the potential savings are significant. A large number of these transactions could easily be done with self-service applications. Pumping gas has become largely self-service. Automatic teller machines could take an even larger share of transactions if customers had more incentive to use ATMs. Police are using cameras to record cars that run red lights, saving money since they do not have to spend their time looking for people running lights.

Information technology lets self-service applications for routine transactions expand considerably beyond gas stations and banks. An increasing number of toll roads use E-Zpass systems employing wireless transponders in cars that automatically debit the customer's account. Airlines have moved to self-service check-in and ticket issuance at electronic kiosks and are experimenting with automated boarding pass checks.[66] The Metro subway system in Washington, DC was a pioneer in the use of self-service ticket machines, issuing paper tickets with a magnetic stripe holding the stored value. Metro recently introduced contact-less smart cards that can be passed over a reader at the turnstile, and is installing them on buses and Metro parking lots as well, reducing the time for people to board buses or leave parking lots. An increasing number of large retail stores are installing self-checkout systems allowing shoppers to scan their own products and pay by credit card, eliminating the need for a checker and bagger. Theaters are using electronic kiosks to enable movie-goers to buy tickets.

Opportunities for expanded self-service abound. The US Postal Service could slash costs if it installed computerized scales that accept credit cards and printed postage at all post offices. As Americans get smart cards (credit card-sized cards with computer chips on them) with electronic cash on them, they can use these for a host of self-serve applications, including paying at the drive-through window at their fast-food restaurant, eliminating the stop at the payment window. The same holds true at many retail businesses. People could buy theater tickets by inserting their smart card in a kiosk, touch on the screen the movie they want, and the kiosk would debit their smart card and electronically encode the ticket information to their smart card so they pass it over a turnstyle to enter the theatre. People could order food in restaurants by using a touch screen computer built into the tabletop. After the food is delivered and the meal is done, the total would appear on the tabletop screen and the customers would swipe their smart card and automatically pay, including leaving a tip for the server and cook. People could go to hotel web sites, choose a room, and download the key code information directly to their smart card which they would use to gain access to the room. Home utility (gas, electricity, water) meters could be wired directly into utility servers so that the meters are read electronically.[67] Radio frequency identification devices (RFID) – very small and very cheap wireless chips that will be attached to products – will allow a new level of supply chain automation and facilitate more self-checkout at stores. Wal-Mart plans to have RFID readers in all its distribution centers and more than 2000 stores by 2006.

E-commerce is the ultimate in eliminating the person from the transaction. E-commerce can cut costs dramatically but it can also cut inventory by 20 to 25 percent because firms can respond more rapidly to orders. According to A.T. Kearney, the consumer goods industry could save $40 billion per year if they could reduce the inefficiencies between retailers and customers' data. Business-to-business networks that link firms globally via auctions or buying cooperatives could cut raw material costs by up to 25 percent. Moreover, reducing incorrect orders, and other inaccuracies could save companies billions.[68] Wal-Mart's retail link computer system allows the company and its suppliers to monitor store sales constantly and automatically replenish stock. Home Depot uses electronic ordering to enable 85 percent of its merchandise to come directly to stores from manufacturers. By linking grain producers directly with grain buyers over the Web, sites like Cybercrop.com are able to cut prices by eliminating grain dealers. Cisco saves $360 million per year through using the Internet on e-business.[69]

Eliminating Intermediaries

Information technology-enabled transactions enable whole categories of economic functions to be eliminated with significant productivity benefits. Such 'disintermediation' – the reduction or elimination of the role of retailers, distributors, brokers, and other intermediaries in transactions between the producer and the customer – is a central aspect of the e-commerce revolution. E-commerce is enabling disinter-mediation in a wide range of industries and professions, including distributors and retailers of physical goods (e.g., wine and beer wholesalers, auto dealers, music and video stores); providers of transactional services (e.g., travel agents, stocks and bonds salesmen and traders, bankers, real estate agents, postal clerks, and auctioneers); and even providers of professional services (e.g., lawyers, optometrists, college professors).

Take the stockbroker industry. Not much more can be done to boost the productivity of these high-salary, labor-intensive jobs. Yet, the rise of Internet stock trading, through companies such as E-trade and Charles Schwab, has meant that the price of stock trading has declined by 90 percent. Stock trading can also be automated. Electronic communication networks (ECNs) are electronic markets that permit securities trades to be executed at low costs and in a fraction of a second.[70] Trading futures contracts through the Internet is at least 50 percent cheaper than through bricks and mortar exchanges such as the

Chicago Board of Trade. Selling corporate and municipal bonds directly over the Internet can eliminate most of the 2 to 5 percent commission charged by intermediaries. These exchanges and other online trading platforms are growing, but would grow faster if not for the chicken-and-egg problem of gaining sufficient liquidity and also because of restrictions erected by bricks and mortar exchanges.[71]

There are a host of other professional and semi-professional functions whose price could be lowered dramatically by digital technologies. Much of what lawyers and accountants do is complicated, but some is relatively routine and could be replicated by software. For example, Intuit's Turbotax software revolutionized the tax preparation business by offering a CD-ROM with as much tax expertise as a tax accountant, but at a considerably lower price. Using tax preparation software is much cheaper and more productive than hiring the services of an accountant. The same is true of many legal functions where drawing up a will, lease, or other simple contract online can be 75 to 80 percent cheaper than using a lawyer.

The travel services industry is another sector that is being disintermediated. Since travel agents increasingly charge a fee for their services, and airlines encourage online ticket purchasing through incentives such as bonus frequent flier miles, consumers are buying more tickets online. The savings are significant. The cost of processing a traditional airline ticket is $8; the cost for an electronic ticket purchased over the web is $1. As a result, travel agent employment fell by over 10 percent in 2002 and 2003.

Auctioneering is another function that the Web is disintermediating. Today, millions of Americans buy and sell goods on eBay and other online auctions, not only bypassing auctioneers and other sellers of used goods, but also enabling the more efficient allocation of goods in the economy.[72] E-banking can do an end run around tellers and check processing personnel. But beyond this a large share of other retail banking functions could be automated as well, from opening up an account, to buying a certificate of deposit (CD), to getting a loan. If individuals had biometric digital signatures they could open up a bank account over the Internet without a bank employee being involved in the transaction. They could buy CDs online that would be electronically deposited in their account. They could even get loans online with much of the work done automatically through loan approval software. Applying for a loan by phone costs $5.90; using a touchtone phone costs 45 cents; using the Internet costs 14 cents. The insurance industry promises similar productivity opportunities. Online insurance promises to dramatically reduce the agent function. Purchasing term life insurance online has already reduced prices by 8 to 15 percent.[73] Interactive online 'expert systems' software should be able to perform just as well, if not better than insurance agents on many types of coverage, allowing people to save considerably on their policy premiums. Digital technology can also automate live music. For example, the Opera Company of Brooklyn is now performing with only 12 musicians and one technician using a computer to play the parts of former musicians, reducing the company's wage bill by one-third and enabling the company to increase the number of performances.

Finally, no discussion of the effect of IT on service sector productivity would be complete without a focus on e-retailing. E-commerce retail sales continue to grow approximately six times faster than total retail sales and provide significant savings. For example, buying contact lenses over the Internet enables consumers to save between 10 and 40 percent of the cost of buying from an optometrist. Online retail will continue to grow, in part because the longer people are online the more likely they are to make online purchases.[74]

A number of companies are selling directly to consumers, bypassing even the e-retailer. Sony Electronics sells directly to consumers and corporate customers on the Web and of course Dell pioneered direct selling of computers. But the potential goes beyond just electronics to include virtually all items that are costly enough (no one is likely to buy office supplies costing $5 online), relatively cheap and easy to ship (no one is likely to buy cement online), and something that is easy to understand and have brand characteristics (no one is likely to buy a couch online). Items such as perfume, clothing, golf equipment, shoes, makeup, sailboats, and bicycles, just to name a few, could all be sold directly by the manufacturer, with increased efficiency and savings.

Other IT Applications

Information technology is not just transforming information-based functions, it is also transforming some physical functions. In particular, robotics will play an increasing role.[75] While robots are now mostly used for simple repetitive tasks in factories, more powerful integrated circuits mean that more autonomous robots are being developed. For example, Fanuc, the Japanese robot-maker, has a lights-out factory in Japan, where it can produce robots for 30 days without human supervision. In Connecticut ABA-PGT produces plastic gears in a lights-out factory. Workers arrive in the morning to pick up boxes filled automatically overnight. Robots are also being deployed in other settings. For example, the robot called TOBOR, is used at almost 100 hospitals to deliver drugs to nurses' stations around the hospital. The robot can navigate around the hospital, wirelessly 'push' elevator buttons and talk to people ('I have completed my mission, please examine my contents'). Pfizer uses a $30 000 robot as a security guard. Other robots could take on tasks like delivery of mail in offices and linens and food in hospitals, cleaning floors, and mowing lawns. Hans Moravec, a professor at Carnegie Mellon University, believes that robots could potentially operate many of the over 100 000 forklifts in the United States.[76]

IT advances are also leading to a rise in the use of mechatronics, the control of mechanical devices by electronics. First deployed in the latest generation of jet aircraft that 'fly by wire' with electrical as opposed to mechanical (e.g., hydraulics) controlling devices, it is beginning to spread to other applications, including cars. For example, Mercedes Benz is experimenting with brake systems that are engaged by electromechanical actuators, instead of hydraulics and mechanical devices.

Wireless data networks are also boosting productivity. For example, Wente Vineyards in California uses such a system to measure the microclimates in its 3000 hilly acres of vineyards. Being able to measure the real climate conditions allows them to respond better to powder dry mildew. The system works by deploying wireless weather stations that measure temperature, wind, rain, and humidity and even wetness on the plants. Wireless systems are also used to monitor fleets of trucks.[77] Companies that equip trucks use a geo-positioning system to allow truckers and dispatchers to find cargo within the range of their trucks, significantly reduce the share of trips made without cargo. Trains have wireless tags that are read by sensors and fed into centrally controlled facilities.[78] Restaurant staff increasingly use handhelds to communicate with the kitchen. Chefs can also beam the daily specials to the handhelds.

Because virtually any type of sensor can be plugged into a radio unit that sends data to the Web, the future will see a vast increase in wireless sensing networks. Wireless sensors are being used to remotely monitor air conditioning units and large pipelines. Wireless can also be used in machine-to-machine interactions. Thermo King Corporation, which makes cooling units for trucks and shipping containers has installed self-monitoring equipment. When a truck returns from a delivery a radio connected to the net contacts sensors on the vehicle to track performance of the unit. This can mean savings of up to $1000 per truck annually by reducing spoilage and cutting maintenance staff. Aramark, the snack supply company has given its drivers wireless handhelds to download the information about what vending machine products have been purchased. Driver productivity went up more than 40 percent during a two-year pilot program. The rise of cheap, networked wireless devices could lead to the creation of an 'Internet of things' whereby billions of things have unique Internet protocol addresses and are connected to the Internet wirelessly. In fact, researchers have developed extremely low-power wireless sensor networks, powered by a simply operating system termed TinyOS. From better software, easier to use devices, ubiquitous adoption, and new wireless networks, the IT revolution promises to lead to continued productivity improvements.

WHY IS DIGITAL TRANSFORMATION TAKING SO LONG?

The transformation to a digital economy is still in its early stages. In 2000, approximately 1 to 2 percent of hotel bookings were made online.[79] Ninety-five percent of companies in the auto industry communicate and transact by mail, fax and telephone while only 5 percent rely on EDI.[80] Only around 20 percent of warehouses have implemented automation tools like barcodes, scanners, automated picking machines, conveyers, and wearable computers. Only 17 percent of doctors use electronic records while just one in four interact with patients by e-mail. Only 15 percent of Americans paid a credit card bill online, and only 21 percent conduced a government transaction online.[81]

There are at least five reasons why progress has not been faster. First, it is important to understand that the interests of the overall economy are not necessarily the same as the interests of individual companies. Many companies focus more on gaining market share or on selling products or services with higher margins and less on cutting costs through digital automation. As a result, in many industries little of the technology budget of companies goes to directly improving productivity. For many companies it is easier to focus on boosting the top line than on cutting costs to reduce the bottom line. This is why most management gurus advise companies to focus not on cost-cutting but on innovation and gaining market share. This may make sense from the perspective of an individual company. However, in contrast to what free-market idealists would have us believe, in this case the collective result of decisions by millions of companies does not maximize the welfare of Americans by maximizing productivity.

Second, most companies still do not pass the savings of digital self-service back to consumers. By pricing goods and services the same, regardless of the delivery channel, companies are subsidizing consumers who choose the high-cost delivery channel. For example, it costs banks about a penny to conduct a transaction over the Internet, but over a dollar when a teller provides it. But many banks charge customers a monthly fee to use electronic bill payment services while making no charge for writing checks. The United States Postal Service (USPS) charges the same to buy a stamp at the postal counter as it does to people who download e-stamps, use postage meters, or buy stamps at kiosks, even though they cost USPS less.[82] Most companies using other applications, including self-service checkout, tollbooths, tax filing, and down-loaded music, fail to pass the savings to consumers, thereby reducing take-up rates.

Some companies and governments are beginning to give discounts to people who use online services. Gas stations have long done this, which is why self-service gas usage is so high. MCI and AT&T give a discount on customers' long-distance bills if they agree to do everything by email. They do this because it saves money to not have to print and mail bills and process checks. Some banks give online-only users free checking accounts. Some airlines give customers frequent flier points for using self-service kiosks to check-in at airports. The Massachusetts Department of Motor Vehicles offers a 5-dollar rebate to residents who renew their driver's licenses online. Yet most companies are slow to do this for fear of losing revenue, even though in the long run it will lower costs.

Anti-poverty and consumer advocates will argue that since the poor are less likely to be online, differential pricing benefits the affluent, further widening the so-called digital divide. Yet, if being online does not save people money, low-income Americans will be slow to get online. It is one thing for more affluent consumers to pay $800 for a computer and $20 to $50 a month to be online so they can surf the Web and send email. It is quite another for a low-income person to pay this if they are not saving money by doing it. If we want all Americans to be online, it is important to let them save money by doing so.

The third factor in the slower take-up is resistance by intermediaries. Those threatened with digital disintermediation are not sitting by idly; they are using all the judicial, regulatory, and legislative means at their disposal to thwart competitors who would like to use the Internet to sell a product or service. As discussed in Chapter 6, this 'revenge of the disintermediated' represents a significant threat to widespread digitization.[83] For example, optometrists and their professional association have worked to make it increasingly difficult for contact lens wearers to buy contacts online. Faced with a growing threat of online sales, the American Optometrist Association pressured manufacturers to distribute both contact lens and eyeglass frames only to licensed optometrists and not to Internet providers. Through their associations, optometrists pressured state legislatures to block legislation requiring optometrists to give the prescription to the patient. Because of such practices, optometrists are able to mark up lenses and glass frames from the manufacturer considerably more than if there were more robust competition. But the list of other professions is extensive, including insurance agents, real estate agents, mortgage brokers, title insurers, car dealers, and wine wholesalers.[84]

Those threatened with disintermediation do not just rely on government to stymie their competitors, they rely on hardball, and sometimes illegal, commercial practices. One of the main reasons many manufacturers have been slow to sell their products over the Web, particularly at a discount, is fear of retaliation from the retailers. In a survey of 50 consumer-goods manufacturers by Forrester Research, 66 percent indicated that conflict with retail channels was the biggest issue they faced in their online sales strategies.[85] In another survey of 42 retail and manufacturing companies, 74 percent of the manufacturers reported that they do not sell online due to worries about how it might affect their relationships with their retail channels.[86]

Retailers have punished manufacturers who did not play ball. For example, the Federal Trade Commission (FTC) successfully brought action against Toys-R-Us for threatening toy manufacturers with not carrying or promoting their toys unless they agreed to restrict the distribution of their products at low-priced warehouse club stores. Personal computer makers such as Compaq and NEC found that retailers resisted their efforts to sell direct by de-emphasizing those companies' products in their stores, resulting in a loss of sales for both companies. Levi Strauss closed its e-commerce site in 1999, mainly because of backlash from retailers. Manufacturers of such goods as autos, perfume, clothing, golf equipment, shoes, makeup, and bicycles have all delayed or scrapped plans to sell online due to fear of such retailer retaliation. Not surprisingly intermediary actions often lead to increased prices. One study found that in supermarkets with more wholesalers, prices fall and rise equally to a change in costs. In contrast, where there are few wholesalers, prices fall about half as much as they rise when there is a similar change in costs.[87]

The fourth reason for the slow transition is the system dependency of many applications. There are a host of 'chicken-or-egg' issues where the adoption of a technology (e.g., smart cards; digital certificates; radio frequency identification devices; and IP6, the next Internet addressing standard) is dependent upon the use of it by sellers, but sellers' use is dependent upon consumers' use. A case in point is online authentication. The full benefits of the digital era will not be realized until individuals can easily and securely authenticate themselves over the Internet. Yet, few Americans can do this; that is, they are unable to fully represent themselves over the Internet in a way that securely tells other people and companies that they are who they claim to be and that allows them to be taken seriously when they state their intentions. As a result, few companies or governments have developed applications that could use online authentication; and likewise, since few online applications require authentication, consumers have little reason to obtain the means to sign documents digitally. There are a host of other chicken-or-egg applications. Smart cards (cards with chips on them to store money and information) have diffused slowly, in large part because consumer value is limited as long as few merchants accept them, and few merchants accept them as long as few consumers have them. Likewise, few computers have smart card readers that would let people download or upload cash or information from the computer to the card. Intelligent Transportation Systems (ITS) are another area. Few people have on-board transportation monitors that display real-time traffic conditions because the infrastructure to detect disturbances in traffic flow and create real time traveler information systems has not been deployed yet by the public sector.

Broadband is another chicken-or-egg technology. Around 20 percent of American households have broadband, but the speeds offered are too low for advanced applications like robust video-conferencing and full-length, high-quality video. As a result, because broadband-dependent applications are limited, broadband adoption has been slow. Ensuring that a majority of Americans have high-speed broadband would lead to significant benefits. This is because broadband has the same kinds of 'network externalities' that investments in roads or electrical networks had 75 years ago. More broadband users would open up a host of new applications in distance learning, e-health, e-commerce and the like, such as being able to see virtual three-dimensional product demos online, or have your doctor monitor symptoms. Markets usually resolve these chicken-or-egg issues, but it can take a long time and be costly. As a result, government can help jump-start these 'chicken-or-egg' technologies, in part by adopting them first.

Finally, technological advances will accelerate the transition. For example, cheaper high definition displays would accelerate the adoption of e-book readers. Longer-life batteries and chips that draw less electricity would help speed adoption of more powerful mobile devices. Internet2, a consortium being led by over 180 universities working with industry and government, is working to develop advanced network applications and technologies, accelerating the creation of tomorrow's dramatically more powerful Internet. Research in a wide array of IT areas is needed, not just on the Internet. A recent National Institute of Standards and Technology report articulated a number of cross-cutting generic technology needs in areas such as monitoring and control of large networks, distributed databases, data management, systems management, and systems integration.[88]

SOURCES OF PRODUCTIVITY GROWTH IN THE NEXT ECONOMY

If the past two economies were about boosting productivity in manufacturing and agriculture and today's New Economy is about boosting productivity in information-based functions, the next challenge will be to boost productivity in human-service functions. While we can automate jobs like bank tellers and factory workers, it is hard to automate occupations like nursing, social work, and teaching. Because of their slow productivity growth, these occupations will make up an ever growing share of our economy. Between 2002 and 2012 12 of the 20 fastest growing occupations are projected to be in health and three in education. The two fastest growing occupations will be registered nurses (623 000) and post-secondary teachers (603 000). Other fast growing areas are security (security guards (317 000) and police officers (153 000)), and social service (social workers (70 000) and social and human service assistants (147 000)).

Boosting productivity in human service occupations is hard to do. Technology can play some role, but the best strategy is to find ways to eliminate the very need for the services.[89] For example, while IT can cut much of the costs of processing health-related information, more significant reductions in health care spending depends on improvements in people's lifestyles. Half of US deaths are estimated to arise from life-style choices made by individuals, including smoking, drug use, alcohol use, unhealthy diets and limited physical activity.[90] This means that health policy that shifts Americans' behavior to healthy ones will have to be a major part of a national productivity policy.

Likewise, a significant share of spending on social services, education, and criminal justice is related to treating (or incarcerating) individuals with mental health problems. These include not just mental illness per se, but psychological problems and social disorders stemming from having grown up with inadequate parenting.[91] America has long had an ethic that child rearing is largely a private matter, so long as the parents do not engage in sexual abuse or overt and sustained physical abuse or neglect. Yet, for many families, especially those beset by other difficulties, consistently providing top quality parenting can be a challenge. All too often, kids without good nurturing parenting end up with problems and needs that require societal resources to address. As a result, a public policy agenda that focuses on boosting the quality of parenting will also need to be a component of productivity policy. This means implementing better paid leave for new parents; more generous tax credits for stay-at-home parents of pre-schoolers so that parents can spend more time taking care of their pre-school children instead of placing them in long hours of often poor quality non-family care;[92] significant investments in parenting education in places like high schools, prisons, and community centers; and providing more active intervention to help at-risk families.[93]

Given the political resistance to making these kinds of long-term social investments coupled with the widely held view, particularly among conservatives, that decisions regarding the health and treatment of children are private ones, making significant progress here will be a challenge. However, as the entrepreneurial, knowledge-based economy runs its course over the next 20 years, and it becomes clear that the entire arena of human services is the next big area for productivity gain, it is likely that much more attention will be paid to these issues.

CONCLUSION

Harvard economist Derek Scherer comments that:

> There is a centuries' old tradition of gazing with wonder at recent technological achievements, surveying the difficulties that seem to thwart further improvements, and concluding that the most important inventions have been made and that it will be much more difficult to achieve comparable rates of advance. Such views have always been wrong in the past, and there is no reason to believe that they will be any more valid in the foreseeable future.[94]

Such pessimism is especially misplaced now, given that we are in the early stages of a New Economy and can expect perhaps as many as two decades of robust growth until the current techno-economic system is fully utilized. Schumpeter got it right when he stated, 'There is no reason to expect slackening of the rate of output through exhaustion of technological possibilities.'[95] For him, 'Technological possibilities are an uncharted sea.'[96] It is up to businesses and other organizations and policymakers to make the right decisions to ensure that we take advantage of that sea. It is to that task that we now turn.

NOTES

1. There is some evidence that productivity determines stock prices. From 1960 to 2000, there is a 0.65 correlation between growth in non-farm productivity and inflation-adjusted changes in the Dow in five-year intervals, and a 0.64 correlation with the S&P 500. Author's calculation using data at www.globalfinddata.com.
2. One reason is that while it took four farmers to feed ten people in 1990, today four farmers can feed 388 Americans and 128 people in other nations.
3. In 2001 dollars (*Business Week*, 1 April 2002, p. 56).
4. The first Holiday Inn was established in 1952.
5. Levy (1999) p. 2.
6. Bluestone and Harrison (1990) p. 1.
7. Personal consumption expenditures in millions of dollars, 1974 (www.bea.gov/bea/dn/und-pce.exe).
8. Atkinson (1996).
9. Mandel (2004) p. 54.
10. Samuelson (2002).

11. Gordon (2000).
12. Some even argue that the slowdown was caused by a slowdown in electrical productivity. But with electrical output accounting for less than one percent of GDP, it is hard to see how this could have sizeable effects (Alcaly, 2003, p. 72).
13. Dennison (1979).
14. Bowles et al. (1983).
15. Brenner (1998) p. 9.
16. Blinder (2000) p. 2.
17. Samuelson (1999), p. A14.
18. Krugman (1990).
19. Ibid. p. 18.
20. Blinder (1997) p. 58.
21. Mandel (2004), p. xii.
22. This point was reinforced when I sat next to a leading economist, noted for questioning the productivity miracle of the New Economy, at a luncheon during a White House conference on the New Economy in 2000. He argued that technology could not have played a role, because the major two technological innovations of the last two decades, the automatic teller machine and the Sabre airline reservation system, had already had their effect. When I asked him if he thought the new B-to-B web portals like Covisint in the auto industry or B-to-C applications like Orbitz in the airline industry were important, he replied that he was not aware of them.
23. Solow (1987) p. 36.
24. Bluestone and Harrison (2000) p. 68.
25. Dyson et al. (1994).
26. For retail see Klimek et al. (2002). For manufacturing, see US Department of Commerce (2003). See also Brynjolfsson and Hitt (1998).
27. Conference Board (1998) p. 13.
28. US Department of Commerce (2003).
29. David (1989).
30. Motors got more powerful and flexible through the first two decades of the 1900s. More effective AC motors were developed after World War I. In the 1920s, companies developed multi-voltage, more flexible motors, and easy to start push button induction motors, and smoother running motors using ball bearings. In the 1930s, companies developed motors for low speed, high torque applications and constant speed motors with variable speed transmission.
31. For example, an October 1984 ad for the new IBM PC proclaimed, 'hold on to your hat' since the computer had an incredible 20mb hard drive (today most machines come with a 20 gigabit hard drive) and up to 3mb of memory (most come with 256mb) and it was lightning fast, 8 MHz (most today are around 2.5 Ghz).
32. There is historical precedent for focusing on expanding market share. One example was AT&T's reluctance to switch to automated switch boards and manual dial telephones in the 1920s, in spite of the fact that most of its competitors had already done so. The main reason was because phone users were largely upper and middle classes who 'had come to regard telephone operators as a logical extension of their household staff.' The telephone operator, stated AT&T president Theodore Vail in 1915, was the 'servant of every subscriber, as though she was in his office or in his direct employ ... There never can be in my opinion, any way devised to get rid of the "intelligence" which at some point in making up the connection is apt to be required' (John, 1998, p. 198).
33. McKinsey (2001 found a similar pattern in hotels where, despite increased investment in IT since 1995, there has been little increase in hotel productivity. A

large part of the reason is that 'hotels were focused on improving their top-line revenue, and made IT investments primarily to achieve this goal.'

34. US Bureau of Labor Statistics, in *Business Week*, 1 April 2002, p. 58.
35. Ibid. p. 56.
36. Cassidy (2000).
37. Gordon (2000) argues that since semiconductors have become so powerful in the 1990s – according to the Department of Commerce falling in price by 99 percent in the 1990s if quality is held constant – that these huge increases in performance and declines in price account for all the productivity growth.
38. The rapid growth in computer sales closely tracks the adoption of the Internet (www.dallasfed.org/eyi/tech/0306computer.html).
39. According to the Pew Project on Internet and American Life on a typical day in November 2003 54 percent of Internet users went online only from home; 17 percent went online only from work; and 26 percent went online from both home and work. Moreover, as more Americans get high-speed connections from home the frequency of using work connections for personal use is expected to go down.
40. Gordon (2000).
41. Quoted in Armour (2003).
42. (www.irs.princeton.edu/krueger/produc3.htm). Even if this claim were true, it would only be true for a few years, since after a certain point workers cannot speed up more or work more unreported hours.
43. McGinn (2000) p. 51.
44. Ibid.
45. Jorgenson (2001).
46. Schumpeter (1939) p. 37.
47. Testimony before the Senate Budget Committee (1-26-2001).
48. There was some improvement in productivity in services due to computers. For example, the share of clerical workers in banking and insurance declined from 50 percent to 40 percent between 1982 and 1997. As a share of the workforce, clerical workers declined from 16.9 percent in 1983 to 14.1 percent in 1997 (Handel, 2003).
49. Blinder (2000) p. 5.
50. Fine and Raff (2000) p. 4.
51. Roach (2003) states, 'For years, we've all heard about the Promised Land of the New Economy. Loaded up with the latest in new technologies, smart and nimble knowledge workers would ride the productivity curve to a new prosperity. The Information Revolution was supposed to give us all that and more. A funny thing happened on the road to that revolution … for now, call it a failed revolution.'
52. Toffler (1980).
53. Self-checkout scanners pay for themselves in fewer than 15 months.
54. In 2001 there were 38 830 workers in the manufacturing and reproducing magnetic and optical media industry. Employee compensation in the CD and cassette tape reproducing industry is over $860 million. There are over 18 500 video and DVD rental stores and 77 000 music stores, As a result, of the $17 it now costs to purchase a music CD, more than $9.50 is accounted for by distribution, shipping, and store markup, with additional share by the manufacture of the CD itself. Songs could be downloaded online as digital files for almost no production costs.
55. It was not likely that this experiment would work because e-book readers had just appeared on the market and because King was hoping people would voluntarily pay to download his work. In the future, with a 'pay per download' model and the widespread adoption of readers, it is likely that author-to-reader delivery could work.
56. As broadband becomes ubiquitous and home networks let web audio to be sent through stereos, most Americans will listen to radio online, particularly since there

will be many fewer commercials and much greater customization. For example, a user of a service like Music Match can listen to an infinite number of customizable formats that the listener creates based on their own interests. Satellite radio providers like Sirius and XM radio provide a wide range of commercial free radio that listeners can listen to even as they drive long distances (www.nab.org/radio/radfacts.asp).

57. One study examined four storage media (print, film, magnetic, and optical) and four channels (telephone, radio, television, and the Internet). Computers won out in the storage category: 92 percent of newly generated information was recorded on magnetic media. Paper, by contrast, accounted for a hundredth of a percent of the total (www.sims.berkeley.edu/research/projects/how-much-info-2003).

58. www.usmint.gov/downloads/about/annual_report/2002AnnualReport.pdf.

59. It costs US business and banks about $60 billion a year to handle cash and coin. In Europe, the costs of handling cash amount to around half a percent of GDP.

60. Starbucks Cash Card reduced the transaction time with cash from 20 seconds to 4 seconds. In the first two months, customers used the card for 2.3 million transactions, saving over 10 000 hours of customer time.

61. Other countries are farther ahead. Germans can use their smart cards to pay for parking meters. Finns can use their cell phones to transfer digital cash to vending machines to pay for soda, cigarettes and other items.

62. It costs 5 cents to clear a paper check, double that of check imaging (Marlin, 2003).

63. Between 1979 and now, as a share of total payments, checks have declined from 85 percent to 60 percent, and as the Check Clearing for the 21st Century Act is enacted, they will decline even more By 2004, they are expected to be less than half of total payments. 150 million consumers' bills will be presented and paid electronically, up 275 percent from 2003. In 2006, 2.5 billion will be (Unisys Corporation, 2003).

64. Over 50 million federal tax returns were filed electronically in 2003. As a result, the Internal Revenue Service plans to lay-off at least 2400 workers, while retraining and transferring another 4000 to focus more on enforcement.

65. McKinsey (2001).

66. US Airways has announced a pilot program to install automated ticket readers at two airports and expects to be able reduce by 200 the number of gate agents it employs.

67. Doing this would not only eliminate the need for meter readers, it would allow electric utilities to price power by the time of day, significantly reducing electricity demand in peak periods, and reducing the need to build new plants.

68. UCCnet, aims to provide a central registry of product information to retailers.

69. There is also significant potential in the $2.1 trillion construction industry. Daily collaborations among contractors, engineers, architects, and suppliers are based on mounds of paperwork. Companies such as Bidcom, Bricsnet.com and Cephren have collaboration tools that track project specs, cutting costs and reducing errors.

70. ECNs are already displacing some bricks and mortar exchanges. In France, for example, the main futures exchange, MATIF, closed its trading floor and moved to an all-electronic, Internet-based trading platform.

71. Eurex, the Swiss-German electronic futures exchange overtook the Chicago exchange in volume in 2001 going from 109 million shares in 1997 to 543 million in 2000, while the Chicago Board of Trade increased from 242 to 260 million, largely because Eurex is so much cheaper. Chicago traders have to pay exchange fees, floor fees and brokerage fees. The only reason companies trade there is the liquidity. In 2002 the Electronic Trading Island ECN launched its own Island Futures Exchange.

72. A particular item may be of little value to someone, but because of online auctions they can find someone for whom it does have value.

73. Brown and Goolsbee (2000).

74. About 15 percent of users who have been online three months have made a purchase, compared to 60 percent who have been online more than three years (www.gartnerg2.com).
75. Robotics Institute robot pioneer Jo Engelberger says that there have been big advances in artificial intelligence, speech recognition, machine vision, and virtual touch, but no one has put them together to make the giant leap the industry promised ('How robots lost their way', *Business Week*, 1 December 2003, p. IM4).
76. www.frc.ri.cmu.edu/~hpm/project.archive/robot.papers/2003/CACM.2003.html.
77. Advanced on-board computers that track the location of trucks has increased truck utilization by 13 percent (US Department of Commerce, 2003, p. 77).
78. In Wyoming coal is automatically moved along the track to automatic feeders that fill the cars twice as fast as previous automatic loaders. New digital technology lets train agencies be pulled by AC motors, which are much more powerful and reliable. New automated trains can lay ballast along tracks 100 times faster than the old mechanical ways. New laser guided sensors measure track alignment (Philips, 2002).
79. American Hotel and Lodging Corporation (2000) p. 1.
80. *Business 2.0*, 20 February 2001, p. 80.
81. The National Technology readiness survey conducted by the University of Maryland's Center for e-service.
82. The US Postal Service says it costs 24 cents for each dollar in revenue to provide stamps over the counter. The comparable USPS cost for mail with meter indicia is one-tenth of one cent. With 7 million customers visiting post offices each day there exists the opportunity to leverage existing retail kiosk technology to provide low-cost access to these transactions..
83. Atkinson (2001).
84. Ibid.
85. Alorie and Bacheldor (2000).
86. Talmadge (2000).
87. Peltzman (2000).
88. Tassey (1998).
89. One area is the role of robots in providing basic care. For example, it is possible that robots could help care for the elderly at home, by helping to monitor them, reminding them to take their medication and other routine functions.
90. www.healthydelaware.com/hp20101.htm.
91. More than a third of female state prison and jail inmates said that they had been abused as children, as did about 14 percent of male inmates (www.casanet.org/library/abuse/justice-study.htm).
92. Greenspan and Atkinson (2004).
93. Every new Swedish parent is visited by a nurse within a week of coming home from the hospital. If things are not going well parents can get follow-up assistance.
94. Scherer (1999) p. 120.
95. Schumpeter (1942) p. 118.
96. Ibid.

6. The New Economy and its Discontents

The successful implementation of a new technology system and the unleashing of powerful entrepreneurial and competitive forces needed to bring about and sustain a revival of productivity growth is anything but automatic. Because it is seen as a threat to well-established businesses, institutions, regions, and even society as a whole, each new economy calls forth powerful and intense forces in opposition. Enemies of growth and change are capable of not only significantly delaying transformation, but of structuring it so it attains only a portion of its potential. As historian of technology Joel Mokyr notes, 'In every society there are stabilizing forces that protect the status quo. Some of these forces protect entrenched vested interests that might incur losses if innovations were introduced, other are simply do-not-rock-the-boat kinds of forces. Technological creativity needs to overcome these forces.'[1] Schumpeter agrees, 'The resistance which comes from interests threatened by an innovation in the productive process is not likely to die out as long as the capitalist order persists.'[2]

The infamous Luddites who smashed automatic looms at the emergence of the mercantile/craft economy in the 1820s in England are the most notorious enemies of the new, and perhaps were the most direct in their confrontation with change.[3] Luddites were hardly alone, though. Throughout history, opposition, not only to technological change but to the broader social, political, and organizational transformations that accompany it, has been a recurring pattern. Some want nothing more than to protect vested economic interests threatened with 'creative destruction.' Others, like today's opponents of biotechnology, view a particular feature of the new technology system as abhorrent. Others simply oppose change and progress, preferring instead to remain nestled comfortably in established and well-trodden patterns of life. Given the threats to the new, it is a wonder that economic transformation happens at all. As Machiavelli saw:

there is nothing more difficult to execute, nor more dubious of success, nor more dangerous to administer than to introduce a new system of things, for he who introduces it has all those who profit from the old system as his enemies, and he has only lukewarm allies in all those who might profit from the new system.[4]

Economic transformations in the United States have been slowed, but not stopped by opposition. One reason is that the advantages of the new have far outweighed disadvantages of the past. Moreover, unlike Europe and Asia which clung to tradition and resisted disruption, America has consistently embraced innovation. That is perhaps the major reason why the United States has led the past three economic transformations. As Daniel Bell observed, 'The great efforts to industrialize underdeveloped countries, increase worker mobility in Europe, and broaden markets – so necessary to the raising of productivity and living standards – are again and again frustrated by resistance to change.'[5]

However, reflecting Bell's warning, a growing anti-progress, divide rather than grow the pie, movement has emerged in reaction to the New Economy's technological and economic changes. Whether it is anti-globalists protesting at World Trade Organization meetings, privacy zealots raising unfounded alarms about new digital technologies, environmentalists opposing genetically modified organisms, unions resisting automation, or 'bricks and mortar' companies seeking protection from more able e-commerce competitors, as the New Economy has grown, so to has resistance to it. A broad collection of ideological and economic interests now actively works to throw sand in the gears of progress, growth and innovation.

It is more than the fact that today's New Economy discontents are more mobilized than ever, it is that America's faith in the very goodness of progress has diminished. Whereas a generation ago there would have been near universal agreement with the statement 'change is good,' today a host of interests from across the political spectrum would disagree or at least have severe doubts. Whereas in the old economy there was a sense of the inevitability of progress, as reflected in the saying, 'Well, I guess that's just progress,'[6] today the notion of progress is under intellectual attack. Writing in the 1950s, futurist Ernst Morris argued that, 'the drag on progress is the nondreamers.'[7] A vocal set of elites now sees progress as an anachronistic and in many cases oppressive concept.[8]

These are not just interesting social developments. Rather, they go to a central challenge of our time – the need to solve a host of problems, including protecting the environment, boosting health, raising productivity, reducing working time and providing for the baby-boomers' retirement. Solving these and other challenges requires that America makes a collective commitment to embrace policies and practices that support productivity and innovation, even if they challenge entrenched interests. As a result, as the New Economy matures a central task is to redeem the entire idea of progress.

OPPOSITION TO PAST TRANSFORMATIONS

American history is rife with resistance to change. As the mercantilist economy emerged in the 1840s, America was faced with a choice: it could industrialize and in so doing dramatically reorder regional fortunes, or it could remain an agrarian society. Southern agrarians fought northern industrialists and the result culminated in the Civil War. But there were other less dramatic confrontations between past and future. For example, entrenched water transportation interests fought emerging railroads. The 1848 railroad incorporation act in New York required railroads to pay tolls to any canals within 30 miles.[9] In the 1850s, riverboat companies, allied with boat builders and the city of St Louis, sued a railroad company for damages after a boat crashed into a rail bridge over the Mississippi, and sought to have the bridge removed. Because of the persuasive powers of a young lawyer named Abraham Lincoln, who argued for the railroad in court, the shippers lost.

The Factory Era

Forty years later, Americans were of two minds about the emerging factory revolution. On the one hand, they marveled at the inventiveness, power, and output of the new industrial system. So taken up by the outpouring of new inventions was Charles H. Duell, Commissioner of the US Office of Patents, that he was purportedly moved to state in 1899 that, 'Everything that can be invented has been invented.'[10] Likewise, the American Physical Society worried that there would be a surplus of physicists because all the important scientific questions had been answered. As Figure 6.1 illustrates, the technological developments of the era were seen as powering progress.

Yet, the awe for the wonders of the age was balanced by concerns with the excesses and problems that were a byproduct. As new, larger and more powerful industrial corporations displaced smaller companies, while at the same time the agricultural economy was transformed, many saw the new order as a fundamental threat.

Source: http://www.mcny.org/Exhibitions/currierives/progress1.htm.

Figure 6.1   *Poster highlighting key innovations of the nineteenth century: the steam press, the locomotive, the telegraph, and the steamboat*

Nowhere was this more evident than in the concern over excessive corporate concentration and the new trusts and big corporations that were seen as unfairly dominating small business and farmers. More and more Americans began to distrust this new and unprecedented form of corporate organization. Indeed, in documenting the emergence of the large managerial corporation, Alfred Chandler argues that before 1940, these changes were almost certainly opposed by a majority of the American people.[11] As a result, many of the new regulatory initiatives put in place between 1880 and 1920 were spurred by small-business leaders resisting the changes brought on by the factory revolution.[12]

Ida Tarbell's muckraking exposé of Standard Oil made Americans aware of the ruthless practices of John D. Rockefeller and documented his use of legal and illegal means to crush his competitors. Reformers argued that not only did trusts and big corporations unfairly dominate small business and farmers, but they were inefficient. Before he became Supreme Court Justice, Louis Brandies argued in a famous rate case against the railroads that big railroads were economically inefficient. In fact, Brandies argued that medium-sized companies in general were most efficient.[13] In the face of such concerns, Congress was aroused to pass antitrust and monopoly laws.

There was a second, and even more profound, source of opposition that came from those agricultural interests displaced by the new economic order. Industrialization dramatically boosted agricultural output. A farmer in 1860, who might be able to farm a few acres productively, could, by the 1890s, by relying on new equipment, farm many more. Moreover, the rise of the railroad meant that crops like grain could now be produced cheaper in the more fertile Plains states. In addition, the organization of agriculture was changing, with more power going to railroads, manufacturers of farm equipment, slaughterhouses, and other processors. As a result, farm prices fell. As an economy that had been based on farming for over 200 years shifted to one based on factories, great protests arose from rural interests. It was this transformation that provided the spark for the Populist conflagration of the 1880s and 1890s.[14] The Populist movement got its institutional expression with the establishment in 1892 of the People's Party, which challenged the corporate state and its creed of progress. Just as globalization and multinational corporations are the target for new economy animus today, hatred of the railroads, more than anything else, fueled populism. In an attempt to find someone to blame for the dramatic change in their lives, agricultural Populists argued that the railroad barons used monopoly power to squeeze the farmer and control his economic destiny. For example, the affiliated Grand State Farmers Alliance denounced credit merchants, railroads, trusts, and capitalists.

While those left out of the new factory economy were protesting, so too were those who were a part of it but not receiving a fair deal.

Marxist, socialist and anarchist opposition reached its peak. Radical labor organizers, including the Wobblies, Mother Jones, and others sought a dramatic shift in power, and some sought the wholesale overthrow of the capitalist system. Moreover, intellectuals, religious groups and a wide array of social movements expressed opposition. One of the most prominent critics was the philosopher and social critic William James. He stated his case against the emergent new economy:

As for me, my bed is made: I am against bigness and greatness in all forms, and with the invisible molecular moral forces that work from individual to individual, stealing in through the crannies of the world like so many soft rootlets, or like the capillary oozing of water, and yet rendering the hardest monuments of man's pride, if you give them time. The bigger the unit you deal with, the hollower, the more brutal, the more mendacious is the life displayed. So I am against all big organizations as such, national ones first and foremost; against all big successes and big results; and in favor of the eternal forces of truth which always work in the individual and immediately unsuccessful way, underdogs always, till history comes, after they are long dead and puts them on top.[15]

These views were echoed by others who recoiled against the rapid changes swirling about them. The *Independent*, the old abolitionists' magazine, stated, 'The purpose of the trusts, already partly realized, is likely to be more fully achieved in the near future. The middle class is becoming the salaried class, and rapidly losing the economic and moral independence of former days.'[16] In *The Theory of the Leisure Class*, Thorsten Veblen spoke out against the rise of conspicuous consumption, leisure class status, and the building of private fortunes.

Opposition did not just have its roots in economic dislocation, it also stemmed from a cultural unease felt by many who were at the periphery of the new order, either physically or psychologically. In the face of a new society that was cosmopolitan, vibrant, and more sexually oriented, the reaction from those largely in small towns took the form of the temperance movement. With the development of the Anti-Saloon League in 1896, the temperance movement focused the frustrations of traditional small-town Protestant society on the urban, Catholic industrial social system. Like today when many fundamentalist Christians object to a more secular and free-wheeling society, as the factory economy emerged there was also a general anxiety and concern that things were changing too fast.[17]

As with all historical movements fostered by economic transformations, this varied and sundry opposition was doomed to irrelevance, as the factory economy transformed society. This is not to say that the protest movements did not succeed in raising Americans' awareness to real problems, nor that awareness did not lead to needed reforms, especially as reflected by the rise of the Progressive movement. However, as a movement trying to stop the force of progress and turn back the clock, it was largely ineffective. As a result, what started as a movement to stop progress transformed into a movement to tame and humanize the new economy. As Laurence Goodwyn, author of *The Populist Movement*, states:

> This sophisticated despair, grounded in the belief that hierarchical American society could, perhaps, be marginally 'humanized' but could not be fundamentally democratized, became the operative premise of twentieth century reformers. Their perspective acquired a name, and rather swiftly a respectability always denied Populism. In 1900 to 1930, it was popularly recognized as progressivism.[18]

Progressivism became the dominant governing philosophy until the breakdown of the factory-based manufacturing economy during the Great Depression. It was only with the rise of the Progressives 15 years after the emergence of the new factory-based economy that the resistance to change turned into an acceptance of the new, albeit with a justified desire to temper its excesses.

The Corporate Era

As Americans accepted the inevitability of the factory era and its large corporations they turned their attention to attempting to limit its abuses and maximize its promise. As a result, it was not until the emergence of the corporate mass production economy in the early 1950s that widespread opposition reemerged. In spite of the prosperity the new corporate economy ushered in, discontents on both sides of the political spectrum resisted the new order. While the right rejected the growing power of government, the left rejected the growing concentration of power in business and the pernicious effects of a mass society on democracy and individualism. Throw into the mix the disdainful critique of mass society by East Coast elites and it was a wonder that anyone accepted these changes. Yet, in spite of these attacks and resistance to the new, the strength of the underlying techno-economic system meant that a new order was inevitable.

The most vociferous critic on the left was sociologist C. Wright Mills. In his landmark book, *White Collar*, Mills attacked the new corporate economy as a threat to fundamental American values of independence and decentralization. To Mills, the transition to the corporate economy had destroyed the American tradition of independence, craftsmanship, and entrepreneurship, and had given way to alienation and exploitation. Starting a tradition of neo-Marxist critique, Mills argued that workers were exploited as their formerly skilled craft jobs were transformed into unskilled assembly line jobs. Mills also rejected the new social order. In *The Power Elite*, which became a bible of the 1960s New Left movement, Mills defined the new social classes as consisting of the blue collar, white collar, and ruling class power elite. And in a national economy in which corporations run things, 'in so far as national events are decided, the power elite are those who decide them.'[19]

Likewise, urbanist and social critic Louis Mumford attacked the notion of the mass society, complaining that 'our over-mechanized culture' had fallen prey to the 'myth of the machine' and was rapidly moving toward a 'final totalitarian structure.' He argued that:

With this new 'mega-technics' the dominant minority will create a uniform, all-enveloping, super planetary structure, designed for automatic operation. Instead of functioning actively as an autonomous personality, man will become a passive, purposeless, machine-conditioned animal whose proper functions, as technicians now interpret man's role, will either be fed into the machine or strictly limited and controlled for the benefit of depersonalized, collective organizations.[20]

In short, in 1950s the left complained that a mass society, dominated by big institutions, was forcing people into dehumanizing, bureaucratic structures. Man had become a cog in the faceless machine with large-scale organizations creating hierarchy and imposing control. This was all part and parcel of the sociology of the 1950s that focused on the 'mass society' and alienation. Daniel Bell summed it up: 'The theory of mass society no longer serves as a description of western society but as an ideology of romantic protest against contemporary life.'[21] The theory focused on the shattering of the traditional primary group ties to family and local community that was the norm as late as the 1930s. The former social order based on a traditional hierarchical order composed of individuals living in atomistic fashion was breaking down, being replaced by a mass society where achievement was based not on heredity and class, but on education and merit. As Galbraith stated, 'In our time no man of wealth enjoys comparable distinction. Nor is esteem associated with individuals; by the nature of the techno-structure they are submerged in the group.'[22] Economist Robert Theobald complained that, 'many observers feel that the improvement in economic standards during the past fifteen years has been bought at a heavy social cost. They suggest that the attitudes necessary for the most rapid rate of growth are not those which encourage a meaningful life for the individual or a valid sense of community.'[23]

This was not just a concern of a rebellious and isolated left. It reflected liberal thinking as a whole. In 1956 Democratic presidential candidate Adlai Stevenson warned that:

It is not true that the individual rolls around today like a kernel of grain between the upper and nether millstones of Big Government and Big Business – but there is a danger here that is great enough to warrant our keeping such a picture always in mind. Even as we become increasingly vigilant in our battle against the debilitating force of communism we must be aware of another enemy that creeps upon us even more quietly and insidiously: the army of mass mediocrity, with banners flying. We are concerned about a strange, not wholly definable force in which there are at least the identifiable elements of 'government' and technology and massiveness in this age of mass population, mass education, mass communications – and yes, mass manipulation. Indeed it seems that in the mid-twentieth century, mass manipulation is a greater danger to the individual than was economic exploitation in the nineteenth century; that we are in greater danger of becoming robots, than slaves ... Technology, while adding daily to our physical ease, throws daily another loop of fine wire around our souls.[24]

No wonder he lost two presidential elections to the more upbeat Eisenhower. The left may have decried the conformity and lack of control of the techno-structure, but most Americans realized it was responsible for propelling tens of millions of Americans into comfortable suburban middle-class ranks. Such complaints about stifling conformity and mind-numbing stability are especially ironic given that the left today holds up this era as the golden age, in large part because it provided such stability.

While liberals decried the rise of mass society, conservatives were even more despondent, seeing the new economy's big government as destroying the old world where individualism was paramount and government's role was limited. In 1944, Frederick Hayek, the Austrian economist who has attained guru-like status among today's economic conservatives, complained that, 'All we are concerned to show is how completely, though gradually and by almost imperceptible steps, our attitude toward society has changed ... the change amounts to a complete reversal of the trend we have sketched, an entire abandonment of the individualist tradition, which has created Western civilization.'[25] Nine years later Russell Kirk's book *The Conservative Mind* argued against a liberalism that was synonymous with change and saw the emergence of a new, consumer-driven, meritocractic corporate economy as anything but progress. In their search for voices of reason, conservatives found solace in the work of author and intellectual gadfly Ayn Rand, who repudiated the notion of the organization man. Her character, John Garp, an architect in her book *Atlas Shrugged,* gloried in the notion of the great man, who through acts of will would stand up against conformity, rules, and small minds.

Hayek, Kirk, Rand and their fellow travelers railed at the notion of a managed society, in which managers in government and corporations shaped decisions and society's future instead of the seemingly benevolent and mysterious 'invisible hand.' Like a person watching new building developments change his community, Hayek bemoaned that it had become:

> more and more widely accepted that further advance could be expected not along the old lines within the general framework which had made past progress possible but only by a complete remodeling of society. It was no longer a question of adding to or improving the existing machinery but of completely scrapping and replacing it. And, as the hope of the new generation came to be centered on something completely new, interest in and understanding of the existing society rapidly declined; and, with the decline of the understanding of the way in which the free system worked, our awareness of what depended on its existence also decreased.[26]

It was not just that Hayek thought small producers engaged in atomistic capitalism were being swept aside, the new system itself was downright socialistic: 'That socialism has displaced liberalism as the doctrine held by the great majority of progressives does not simply mean that people had forgotten the warnings of the great liberal thinkers of the past about the consequences of collectivism.'[27] ('Liberal' in this context refers to nineteenth-century liberalism, which rejected a strong role for the state.) Rather it was worse because people had been coerced into accepting an alien system. Hayek warned that:

> through all the changes we are observing in the direction of a comprehensive central direction of economic activity, the universal struggle against competition promises to produce in the first instance something in many

respects even worse, a state of affairs which can neither satisfy planners nor liberals; a sort of syndicalist or 'corporatist' organization of industry, in which competition is more or less suppressed but planning is left in the hands of independent monopolies of the separate industries.[28]

He goes on to complain that, 'By destroying competition in industry after industry, this policy puts the consumer at the mercy of the joint monopoly action of capitalists and workers in the best organized industries.'[29] Like Herbert Hoover, Hayek wanted to go back to the days of the early 1900s with small firms and small government. Reflecting today's crop of conservatives, his faith in the old factory economy was so great that he regarded 'competition as superior not only because it is in most circumstances the most efficient method known, but even more because it is the only method by which our activities can be adjusted to each other without coercive or arbitrary intervention or authority.'[30]

Congress and various administrations were not deaf to complaints from the left and right. As large corporations came to dominate an array of sectors, small businesses and their ideological fellow travelers complained that left alone, big business would crush the independent businessmen. One futurist commented that, 'the danger that faces us in the further concentration of business into so few units as to imply absence of essential competition, is the take-over by the government.'[31] As William Whyte noted, 'economically, many a small businessman is a counter-revolutionary and the revolution he is fighting is that of the corporation as much as the New or Fair Deal.'[32] Congress responded, in part by creating the Small Business Administration in the 1950s.

It was not just small businesses that were feared to be at risk from the new corporate and government juggernaut, it was employment itself. When factory automation took off in the late 1950s and early 1960s there was widespread anxiety over the employment effects of automation and productivity. Such concerns entered into the popular imagination of the day, with television shows, news documentaries and reports warning of the loss of work. One particularly telling episode of the television show 'The Twilight Zone', predating the movie *The Terminator*, documented a dystopian world in which a manager replaces his workers with robots, only to end up being replaced by a robot himself.

So great was concern with automation and the rise of push button factories, that Congress's Joint Economic Committee held extended hearings on the matter in 1955. John Kennedy created an Office of

Automation and Manpower in the Department of Labor in 1961, identifying: 'the major domestic challenge of the Sixties – to maintain full employment at a time when automation, of course, is replacing men.'[33] In 1964 President Johnson appointed a National Commission on Technology, Automation, and Economic Progress. Reflecting the still fresh fears of job loss from the Depression just three decades prior, the Commission was so concerned about the disappearance of work that it recommended a guaranteed national income and massive job training efforts. Others at the time even considered schemes whereby the United States would encourage net outmigration of Americans to other nations as the demand for labor contracted.[34]

As the economy boomed and fully automated factories proved to be just a dream, fears of job loss receded. More broadly, in the face of Don Quixote-like opposition, the windmill-like inevitability of the new corporate economy relegated opposition to the sidelines. Besides, the new economy gave Americans prosperity and stability, a potent combination for most Americans after living through the Great Depression and the war.

TODAY'S OPPONENTS TO GROWTH AND CHANGE

As today's new technology system is leading to a New Economy and new society, a growing number of Americans wonder if things might not have been better in the old economy. A host of ideological and special interest forces see the new technology system and New Economy as something that should be stopped, or least resisted, shaped, and controlled. They claim that progress is deleterious to economic stability, environmental quality, privacy, morality, community, and other values. These foes of change have succeeded in reshaping the public's view of the future, transforming it from one where most Americans had faith in the future, to one where resistance to change is legitimized as worthy civic involvement, even when it stems from blatant protectionism or fear. A wide array of interests now work to stop, or at least resist change.

Business

One would expect that business would be the New Economy's vanguard of progress.[35] Unfortunately, for every company developing an innovative and more efficient way of meeting consumers' needs, there are others that view them as a threat. Business persons who spend time and money building businesses are loath to see them disappear because someone has invented a better mousetrap. As Schumpeter argues, 'In capitalist reality, as distinguished from its textbook picture it is not [price] competition which counts but the competition from the new commodity, the new technology ... which strikes not at the margins of the profits of the existing firms but at their ... very lives.'[36] He goes on to state, 'Technological change involves substantial losses sustained by those who own specific assets dedicated to the existing technology.'[37] While those threatened enterprises sometimes build a better mousetrap, increasingly they use political and market power to undercut more efficient and innovative rivals.

A host of industries and professions are fighting back. Gas station owners and their workers have successfully lobbied state legislatures in Oregon and New Jersey to make self-serve gas stations illegal. They have made it illegal in six states for chain stores like Wal-Mart to sell gas. Mom and pop dry cleaners have successfully pressed for local legislation to limit more efficient corporate chains from entering the market.[38] Liquor wholesalers have gained laws in most states that prohibit liquor and wine producers from selling directly to retailers.[39] Car dealers have gained what are innocently called 'relevant market area laws' which carve up territories so other dealers cannot compete. Competition is hard, tiring work, and most businesses would rather not face it.

Business protectionists have been especially animated by the emergence of e-commerce. The Texas Legal Review board, made up largely of attorneys, successfully argued that the software program, Quicken Family Lawyer, should be outlawed on the grounds that the company providing it illegally practices law. Led by the North Carolina Auctioneer Licensing Board, which considers people who sell on eBay auctioneers, three states have passed or are considering laws to require online sellers to be licensed auctioneers or face misdemeanor charges and sizable fines. While consumers can buy a computer online from Dell or other computer manufacturers, thanks to lobbying by car dealers they are prohibited by law from buying a car directly from Ford, GM, Toyota, or any other car manufacturer online. When Microsoft's HomeAdvisor.com set out to establish a web site where agents would accept lower commissions, the National Association of Realtors not only lobbied against Microsoft in its antitrust battle, but also required its member brokerage firms to list exclusively with their own web site, Realtor.com.[40] The list goes on. Optometrists, travel agents, insurance agents, mortgage brokers, investment bankers, securities traders, college professors, music and video stores, radiologists, and even undertakers selling caskets are among the professions and industries that have sought, often successfully, government protection from more efficient and lower cost e-commerce competitors.[41]

Unions

While unions can be a force for progress when they push for improvements in wages and working conditions, they also resist change, particularly when it means automation and fewer jobs for their members. Yet, in the old economy, union leaders often accepted technology-facilitated productivity gains, arguing only that workers should share in them through shorter hours and/or higher wages. Unions often saw their role as helping companies boost productivity.[42] Indeed, it was unions' willingness to support technological progress, while at the same time fighting for better jobs and working conditions, which won them broad public support in the old economy.

However, as union membership has fallen to levels not seen since 1961, many unions see productivity-enhancing technology as a threat. Take the longshoremen's union for example. In the 1950s the West Coast Longshoremen's Union went along with management in what they saw as the inevitable rise of containerization, while securing for its membership generous severance payments.[43] But in the last decade they have sought to derail further port automation even though America's ports are significantly less efficient than many in Europe and Asia and the average annual pay of a longshoreman working more than 2000 hours per year is over $105 000. In 2002 the union called management attempts to increase efficiency 'an attempt to bust the union' and went on strike to prevent them.

Dockworkers are not the exception. In the face of significant job losses due to globalization and automation, the United Auto Workers' special bargaining convention recently set an agenda that calls for income protections that include no layoffs from new technology or productivity improvements. The provisions would reduce the incentives of companies to invest in productivity-enhancing technology – meeting the unions' goal of protecting its members jobs, at least in the short run, but raising costs for consumers. For many unions their promised land is the old economy. Morty Bahr, head of the Communication Workers of America sums up the view:

> The break up of the Bell system threw our members out of their safe cocoon of monopoly. Before the break up, new technologies came out of Bell laboratories at what I would call 'a humane pace.' No one was going to release new communications technology ahead of them. As a result, no one ever lost a job due to changes in technology.[44]

On the other hand, consumers were stuck with black dial phones.[45]

Civil Society

If labor and business are not always productivity proponents, surely we would expect consumer groups to be full-throated advocates, since productivity leads to lower prices and innovation leads to new products and services. But while some consumer groups, like the Consumer Federation of America, fight protectionist actions by business, all of them see their mission as protecting the rights of consumers against business, even if the result is lower productivity. They are interested in boosting consumer surplus, even if it comes at the expense of the rest of the economy.[46]

Perhaps the area where they have been most active in recent years is to try to impose stringent European-style privacy rules on e-commerce. But stringent privacy laws are far from free and would cost the economy millions of dollars as Internet companies would be less able to effectively target advertisements to the consumers most likely to click on them. Without the revenue that targeted advertising would bring, some of the best sites on the Internet would either start charging for access (an Internet death sentence) or close down altogether. Moreover, proposed requirements to give consumers online access to the information that companies have on them would cost companies significant amounts of money, with few benefits for consumers.

Indeed, privacy advocates spanning the spectrum from Phyllis Schlafly's Eagle Forum on the right to the American Civil Liberties Union (ACLU) on the left have made common cause against a number of new digital technologies. For example, they have fought cameras that record a driver's license plate number when they run a red light, even though such systems are vastly cheaper than paying a police officer to sit in his squad car waiting for someone to ticket. Likewise they have fought smart IDs (e.g., putting computer chips on drivers' licenses that would store encrypted information like the owner's fingerprint), even though such IDs are a key tool in the fight against terrorism and would not threaten privacy.[47] The ACLU and other groups are leading the fight against radio frequency identification devices (RFID) that promise to lower the costs of distribution and selling of products.[48]

Many environmental organizations are also strong opponents of new technologies, most notably genetically modified organisms. The biotech revolution promises to dramatically increase crop yields and cut the costs of food and fiber. But that has not stopped groups from fighting so hard against these technologies that some companies refuse to disclose the location of their tree farms for fear of eco-terrorist attacks. Because of the pressure from the Forest Stewardship Council, a group opposed to the use of genetically modified trees, Home Depot, the largest retail lumber seller, agreed in 1999 to sell only wood certified by them, even though the result will be higher prices.

While genetically modified trees are a few years away, the battle now is over genetically modified foods (GMOs). Because of misleading propaganda from environmental groups that has led to boycotts and outright bans on GMOs in some nations, many farmers refuse to use genetically modified seeds, even though they boost yields and lower prices. Opponents are also working to get federal labeling legislation passed that would limit the GMO marketplace.[49]

Anti-progress forces have also mobilized to fight life-saving therapeutic cloning and stem cell research, convincing President Bush to ban federal funding for this research.[50] A coalition of environmentalists, feminists, and other so-called progressives recently sent an open letter to the US Senate opposing therapeutic cloning arguing that,

cloning of any kind is step toward genetic engineering – toward improving human beings. In other words, toward leaving the natural world behind. In that sense it may turn out to be a pivotal battle for the environmental movement, which started a century ago with the effort to save a few Sierra Nevada canyons.[51]

The crux of the matter is summed up by environmental activist Bill McKibben's argument that genetic engineering could 'force us to reconsider liberalism's faith in the onward march of science as well as force a new recognition that political conservatism shares a common root with conservation.'[52]

While a host of interests fights against biotechnology, 'smart growth' advocates fight against the spatial form of the New Economy. The particular focus of their animus are 'big box' retailers like Wal-Mart, who they claim threaten main-street businesses and lead to sprawl. As a result of their pressure some communities have passed zoning ordinances that make it virtually impossible to build such stores, even though such retailers have played a key role in boosting productivity and bringing low cost products to millions of Americans.[53]

Perhaps the most conspicuous source of opposition to the New Economy comes from the opponents of globalization. It was not always this way. In 1956 Adlai Stevenson wrote that, 'as a goal for the future, to be achieved any sooner than distant 1980, I would certainly hope for relaxed restrictions on world commerce – a relaxation not just on tariffs – to the end of freer and freer trade among nations.'[54] Now liberal commentator Bill Moyers describes the North America Free Trade Agreement as a 'trade agreement, supported by two presidents and ratified by the Congress, [that] became an end-run around the Constitution.'[55] As the New Economy has enabled a wide share of information-based service functions, like call centers and back office functions to move to low wage nations, the opposition has gotten even stronger.[56]

Even if opponents became convinced that globalization boosts economic growth, most would still decry it because of its pervasive cultural impacts. Liberal critic Ben Barber warned in, *Jihad vs. McWorld*, that the world is becoming increasingly homogenized into a kind of global consumer culture that devastate indigenous cultures.

While a large number of groups fight growth and change to protect their own self-interest or vision of a good society, they receive intellectual legitimacy from a significant contingent of anti-progress, anti-technology intellectuals. While there has always been intellectual resistance to change, particularly at key turning points from one kind of economy to another, until the 1960s at least, there was a general belief in the inevitability, and even desirability, of social and economic progress. Historian Merritt Roe Smith discusses a sample of books from the period of the 1860s to the early 1900s with titles such as: '*Eighty Years of Progress*; *Men of Progress*; *Triumphs and Wonders of the 19th Century*; *The Progressive Ages or Triumphs of Science*; *the Marvels of Modern Mechanism*; *Our Wonderful Progress*; *The Wonder*

Book of Knowledge; and *Modern Wonder Workers.*[57] The stirring pageant 'Our Country Tis of Thee', written by Walter Ehret in the 1950s, is filled with such optimistic statements as 'there was no stopping a nation of tinkerers and whittlers, long accustomed to making, repairing, improving and changing'; and 'So when you're spellin' the word America, do not forget the "I" for the inventors'; and 'Progress! That was the word that made the century turn.'[58] This optimistic sense was reflected not just in story and song, but in the writings of intellectuals who reveled in the notion of progress and saw technology as a powerful force for liberation and enlightenment. Economist Benjamin Anderson wrote in the 1930s that, 'on no account, must we retard or interfere with the most rapid utilization of new inventions.'[59]

It was not just capitalist-leaning intellectuals who saw the liberating potential of new technologies. Socialist Jack London addressed the working man: 'Let us not destroy these wonderful machines that produce efficiently and cheaply. Let us control them. Let us profit by their efficiency and cheapness. Let us run them by ourselves. That, gentlemen, is socialism.'[60] Socialists, communists, and others on the left embraced technology because they believed that liberation could come about only when the problem of production had been solved, and that could only be done through mechanization and innovation.

While left-wing intellectuals once saw technology as the road to a post-capitalist working man's paradise, many now view it with suspicion and loathing. Since the 1960s these critics have questioned the entire notion of progress, citing economic decline, social and moral disintegration, and environmental degradation. Caught up in their post-modernist pessimism, academics are now more likely to see the 'forces totally new' as 'the forces totally suspect.'[61] As York University historian David Noble puts it, 'Social historians have made great strides ... to redeem (the Luddites).'[62] It shows. The volume *Resistance to New Technology: Nuclear Power, Information Technology and Biotechnology* reflects a movement that interprets technological development in the worst possible light. As described by the publisher: 'Instead of assuming that resistance contributes to the failure of a technology, the main thesis of the book is that resistance is a constructive force in technological development, giving technology its particular shape in a particular context.'

Ohio State University Professor David Hogsette goes even further:

Throughout American history, technology has played a major role in determining and shaping this belief in progress: ships for travel and colonization; weapons for warfare and imperialism; scaffolds and prisons for security, punishment and control; shackles, harnesses, and numerous other implements of containment and torture for slavery; industrial mechanization for increased production and decreased human involvement; printing presses for disseminating and democratizing the spread of information while simultaneously controlling it; telephones for increasing interpersonal connectivity while simultaneously isolating the 'free' subject; computers for data processing and information regulation ...

Makes one long for the good old days when we all worked on the farm.[63] While most are more restrained than Hogsette, left-wing academics now routinely attack the notion of progress as an idiosyncratic reflection of Western rationalism that demeans other cultures. New York University's Neil Postman states:

I think the single most important lesson we should have learned in the past twenty years, is that technological progress is not the same thing as human progress. Technology always comes at a price. This is not to say that one should be, in a blanket way, against technological change. But it is time for us to be grownups, to understand if technology gives us something, it will take away something. It is not an unmixed blessing. We have to go into the future with our eyes wide open ... New technology is sort of imperialistic. It destroys older technologies.[64]

Kind of like the new imperialist bio-tech based cancer drugs that are destroying the older chemical-based ones? David Noble would have us believe that, 'However empowering the new technology might sometimes seem, the appearance is deceiving, because the gains are overwhelmingly overshadowed, and more than nullified, by the losses.'[65] Leo Marx asks in the title of a recent essay, 'Does improved technology mean progress?'[66] The fact that an MIT historian has to even ask the question suggests the deep level of doubt and mistrust in the future and technology. Perhaps the best known anti-progress scribe is congenital critic Jeremy Rifkin. Rifkin's many books include *Beyond Beef: The Rise and Fall of the Cattle Culture*, *The End of Work*, and *The Biotech Century: Harnessing the Gene and Remaking the World*. One review of his recent book states that, 'For years, Rifkin has been asking what the ultimate price will be that we pay for all our "progress".'[67]

In the face of an academia in which many see their mission to 'enlighten' the next generation, college students are told in a myriad of subtle and not so subtle ways that their great-grandparents were dupes to be so taken with technology and to expect a better future. They were not, as Postman would have us be, 'grown ups.' Try telling the farmer who was able to turn in his horse and plow for a Ford tractor, the woman who did not have to haul in blocks of ice to keep the 'icebox' cool, or the family that did not lose their child because of advances in medicine how naive they were to put their faith in these advances. Perhaps it is only a society that has these and other technological advancements that can afford to produce an intellectual class so dismissive of them. It would not be so bad if the views of these irascible scholars were confined to obscure scholarly publications, but they have been teaching an entire generation to distrust technology and the future, and have managed to sow deep doubts in the culture about whether technology is a force for progress.

Resistance to the future has become so widespread that it has almost second nature. One only has to visit the Smithsonian Institute in Washington, DC. Once known as the National Museum of History and Technology, in 1979 its director Roger Kennedy dropped the word 'technology' from its name when technology was equated with nuclear war and Three Mile Island. While symbolic, it reflected the new attitude toward technology. Rather than celebrate technology, the Smithsonian began to focus on 'the social impact of machines and technology,' a euphemism for focusing on technology's negative and disruptive effects. Thus in their 1987 'Field to Factory' exhibit tracing the mass movement of African Americans from the rural South to the urban North, the exhibit ended with the provocative question 'Was it worth it.' Clearly there was dislocation from the mechanization of agriculture, but for an exhibit to focus its message principally on the negative impacts, instead of on the tremendous economic benefits of agricultural mechanization, is to create an ambiguous view toward technology. Likewise after reviewing a 1994 Smithsonian 'Science in American Life' exhibit, one commentator stated, 'there is not much on pure science or the thrill of scientific discovery, and there is a great deal on science's unintended consequences.'[68]

Perhaps the strongest and most animated forces against progress are religious fundamentalists. Fundamentalists have always opposed economic transformations, but today they fight with renewed vigor. Their most energetic efforts have been devoted to restricting the progress of science, starting with how evolution is taught. Publishing books with titles like *Defeating Darwinism by Opening Minds*[69] and *Darwinism: Science or Philosophy?*[70] and passing laws restricting or prohibiting the teaching of evolution in states like Arkansas and Kansas, the Christian right would have high-school students not learn science, but rather theocratic indoctrination.

This is not to say that interest groups like unions, environmentalists, consumer groups, academics and religious groups do not have important and vital roles to play: to work for higher wages and better working conditions, to challenge rapacious polluters and support tax and technology policies that advance cleaner production, to fight against misleading and deceptive commercial practices and egregious privacy violations, to discuss how public policies and corporate practices can ensure that new technologies minimize disruptions, and to speak out against morally corrosive practices in the media and society. But they can do this without opposing automation, technological innovation and scientific progress, and other productivity-enhancing changes that benefit all Americans.

Even though ultimately the liberating forces of the new technology will win out, opponents do slow down change. If the benefits of the New Economy are so compelling, why do opponents win so often? The short answer is money and fear. As Mancur Olsen has documented, the costs of change are usually imposed on a small minority that are willing to be engaged, while the benefits are widely dispersed.[71] Moreover, innovators usually have less power than well-established incumbents.

But it is more than this. It is also that the anti-progress forces are able cleverly to frame their arguments in ways that make it appear that they are fighting for general, as opposed to narrow interests. For example, by equating productivity with corporate profit opponents are able to make it appear that these are simply fights between two interests: big powerful, multinational corporations against honorable civic interests (family farms, mom and pop main street businesses, a safe food supply, privacy, competition, stable communities, 'smart growth,' etc.). When the choice is presented this way, instead of as a choice between proponents of productivity and increased standards of living on one side, and protectionists and ideologues on the other, pro-productivity forces have a much harder time prevailing.

Opponents do not just cast progress as hurting the little guy, they portray it as risky. Casting the future as scary helps mobilize constituencies, gain new members, and raise money. Most opponents are quick to point out that they are not against change, they only want to slow it down, control it, manage it, make sure it is introduced fairly, etc. But such talk is usually just a public relations smokescreen obscuring the real goal of protecting members from change.

Opponents of change want a world in which a worker never loses his job, companies are protected from more nimble competitors, consumer rights trump all else, individuals control all their personal information, the environment is protected whatever the costs, and cities are designed so we live in apartments and take the bus to buy American-made goods from small, local merchants. In short, they want a world in which risk is close to zero, losers are few, and change is glacial and controlled. There is no doubt that in a society buffeted by the winds of change and risk that such a world has significant appeal. But the result of living in such a world would mean that our incomes will go up much more slowly and technological progress to improve health, protect the environment, and improve our lives would slow down significantly. If we want more, we have to risk more. It is as simple as that.

THE POLITICS OF PROGRESS: MODERNIZERS VS. PRESERVATIONISTS

This conflict between stability and progress, security and prosperity, dynamism and stasis, has led to the creation of a major political fault-line in American politics. On one side are those who welcome the future and look at the New Economy as largely positive. On the other are those who resist change and see only the risks of new technologies and the New Economy. As a result, a political divide is emerging between preservationists who want to hold onto the past and modernizers who recognize that new times require new means.

Getting on the right side of progress will be critical for any political party that wants to succeed. In the late 1800s, the Democratic party and its standard-bearer Williams Jennings Bryant, aligned itself with the forces of the past who sought to resist the onslaught of industrialism and preserve small farms and merchants.[72] With the exception of the eight years of the Wilson presidency, the Republican party held the presidency until 1932. In contrast, FDR and the Democratic party became the force for progress in the new corporate, mass production economy with most Republicans looking back longingly at the Robber Baron era. As a result, Democrats controlled Congress for almost all of the era and presidency for much of it.

Today, the parties face a similar question: which will succumb to the forces of protection and reaction and which will embrace progress and prosperity? Both parties have elements that align with the forces of progress and those that protect the status quo. A host of liberal groups see their mission as opposing corporate power – environmentalists, unions, advocates for the poor, consumer groups, and smart growth advocates. But like a color-blind person incapable of distinguishing between a red light and a green light, these groups all too often cannot or will not make a distinction between corporate actions that boost productivity and innovation and those that are not in the public interest. Rather, they reflexively oppose corporate power and prerogative in the belief that 'what is good for General Motors' is bad for everyone else. Thus, if corporations do something that leads to increased corporate profits (e.g. layoffs due to new technology), it must come at the expense of the people. As a result, instead of finding ways to boost productivity and output, the liberal economic agenda is too often one of redistributing economic output to the have-nots and slowing economic change to protect those at risk. The left seems to have forgotten that most workers would like a bigger house, a newer car, a nice vacation, more free time, early retirement, a boat, and more nights out for dinner.

But conservatives are not much better at their embrace of progress. A large swath of social conservatives view the future with fear and loathing, seeking a return to the idealized past as seen in 1950s' television situation comedies. Business-friendly conservatives are often staunch supporters of laws and regulations to protect entrenched business and professional interests. And rather than focus on policies to boost productivity to help raise incomes, conservatives want to take the short-cut – cutting taxes to raise after-tax incomes. Moreover, in their enthrallment with business, conservatives often fail to distinguish between the actions that are good for GM which are also good for the country and those that are only good for GM.

Fortunately, there are elements in both parties aligned to the future. In fact, on some issues free-market Republicans and centrist New Democrats could make common cause as advocates of progress. Both embrace markets, globalization, competition and innovation.[73] Both, at least in their rhetoric, oppose protecting business and professions from economic change and competition. But while New Democrats can find some common ground with free market conservatives, they part ways in two critical areas. While New Democrats believe that collective action through government can be a force for progressive change, free-market Republicans largely reject such a role for government. Typical of the genre is Virginia Postrel, the editor of libertarian magazine *Reason,* and author of *The Future and its Enemies.* While Postrel embraces change, it is change driven solely by individuals and companies acting alone in free markets. For her, anyone who favors collectively trying to shape the future, even if they want government to promote and support change and innovation, as inherently anti-progress. In her view, government support of research on clean technologies to combat global warming is 'stasist' (a term she uses to indicate anyone that resists change) because it tries to shape the future. So are policies to cure cancer or foster education because they impose a central organizing principle oriented to outcomes. Supporters of the V-Chip, air bags, environmental impact statements, mass transit subsidies, antitrust laws, the 1998 Internet copyright bill, Food and Drug Administration drug reviews, the Family and Medical Leave Act, age discrimination laws, and toy safety standards (which 'override fun as a value') are all branded as stasist technocrats. Unless one accepts a future dictated by markets alone, one is a stasist. It would be easy to dismiss this view as extreme, but Postrel's manifesto is now subscribed to by a large share of the Republican party.

Because free-market Republicans are not the only friends of the future, it is clear that a political world divided into just two camps – stasists and dynamists – is too narrow. As Figure 6.2 illustrates, a more realistic framework would include four major political orientations divided along two axes. One axis measures attitude toward change and is divided between stasists and dynamists. The other assesses the orientation toward government as a positive agent for change and is divided between libertarians vs. communitarians. Thus, traditional liberal Democrats are often ambivalent toward change and supportive of a government role. The religious and moralistic wing of the Republican party also rebels against the future, yet with the exception of legislating morality, rejects any role for government. Both groups are stasists who not only want to slow down change, but often want to reverse it – conservative Republicans to the social order of the 1950s and the economic order of the 1920s and liberal Democrats to the social order of the 1960s and the economic order of the 1940s.

Attitude toward government

	Communitarian	Libertarian

Attitude	Stasists	Traditional Democrats	Values Republicans
toward			
change	Dynamists	New Democrats/	Libertarian Republicans
		Moderate Republicans	

Figure 6.2 Political orientations toward change and government

New Democrats, like libertarian Republicans, are dynamists. Both support open trade, technological progress, and free markets and competition. But, unlike libertarians, New Democrats and some moderate Republicans are also communitarians. They believe that government and civil society not only can, but should play a role in helping America advance into the future. In particular, they believe that government has two key roles to play: to foster more and faster progress and to help those hurt by progress.

Unlike many conservatives, centrists believe in a proactive role for government to advance innovation. For example, while Postrel dismisses the Defense Department origins of the Internet as far less significant than its current bottom-up growth, there is no doubt that without government support of this early research and testing, the Internet would simply not exist today. Because of the long-term payoff, high risk, and broadly shared benefits, industry would not have invented the Internet, just as they did not invent the World Wide Web, parallel computing, and the web browser. As a result, while New Democrats generally oppose subsidies that only serve to prop up economic sectors, they support policies such as funding for R&D and education and training that help firms or workers become productive. For example, while the Clinton administration created the Manufacturing Extension Partnership (MEP), a program to help small manufacturers use newer technologies to become more productive, the Bush administration and Republicans in Congress are trying to kill it. While the Clinton administration budgets boosted funding for science and research, the Bush administration has cut it outside of defense and health. There is a world of difference between a program like the MEP that overcomes market failures relating to information barriers and a program like agricultural subsidies. The former leads to higher productivity while the latter leads to inefficient and wasted production.

Thus, New Democrats stake their position clearly, strongly, and unequivocally with the future, and with the fundamentally progressive forces embedded in new technology and innovation.[74] But its not enough just for New Democrats to stand firmly for innovation, competition, productivity and progress, they must also consistently and rigorously oppose those who would seek to stop progress in the name of self-interest or ideological zeal. For their part liberals need to come to grips with the fact that economic efficiency is a progressive force for change. But because their hearts go out to those who are hurt by change, it is hard for them to fully support it.

This leads to the second area that differentiates New Democrats from conservatives: their focus on assisting individuals left behind by change and on ensuring that progress is in fact progressive and not destructive. As Ed Kilgore, the political director of the Democratic Leadership Council, succinctly stated, 'the secret of President Clinton's success can be boiled down to two words, "safe change".'[75] Clinton clearly nailed his flag to the mast of change and progress. In 1992 he asked that Americans make change their friend. But rather than advance an every man for himself ethos held by so many Republicans, he argued that government and civil society should give Americans the tools they need to manage change.

Doing this is important not just because it helps people manage change but also because it helps people accept change. Postrel correctly points out that the future has its enemies and that in times of dynamism and change, which we are certainly in now, their numbers grow. She acknowledges that an 'open-ended future can be genuinely scary, [and] the turmoil it creates genuinely painful.'[76] But her advice to those affected is to just deal with it. New Democrats want to give all people the tools they need to succeed in the New Economy. In this respect President Clinton's 'Bridge to the 21st Century' was the right metaphor. And this is where New Democrats have excelled. They are closer than any other political viewpoint today in American politics at achieving a synthesis which embraces technological innovation while protecting people against its abuses. For example, it means allowing therapeutic cloning to go forward, but not human cloning. It means embracing new information technologies like the Internet and smart IDs, but ensuring that consumers have appropriate privacy protections (e.g. the ability to opt out of data sharing). It means supporting technological innovation and globalization, but also ensuring that programs like unemployment insurance and dislocated worker training programs are adequately funded and effective.

Americans understand that success in the New Economy requires change and adaptation. They just are not willing to leave it up to an every-man-for-himself system. This fact, more than any other, explains the success of President Clinton, and the Third Wayers in Europe, such as UK Prime Minister Tony Blair. This also goes a long way in explaining Al Gore's defeat, for rather than embracing the bridge to the twenty-first century, Gore wanted to build a moat around the twentieth. This suggests that the third way synthesis of the two concepts – growth with security — is the winning political and policy formula. It is only when Americans have to make a false choice between embracing security with stasis and every-man-for-himself with progress, that they choose the latter path. But give Americans a choice that provides an integrating synthesis – change and compassion, innovation and inclusion, growth and security – and they will choose this every time.

There is one other thing that supporters of growth and change have to do to prevail. They have to provide people with a compelling reason to leave their protected island of security and venture out into the ocean of change. In the emergence of the last two economies that reason was clear: exciting new technologies that changed people's lives and economic growth that gave people tangible benefits. In the 1950s people embraced growth and change because they could see the promised land of achieving their middle-class dreams. For most of the era, the gains on the consumer side more than balanced the losses on the worker side. However, when most Americans own homes, have appliances and a car or two, what is the motivation for embracing this scary and uncertain global economy? Social scientists tell us that growth does not make us any happier, for after a certain level, higher incomes do not appear to lead to increased happiness. If we are to convince most Americans to swim to the next island and risk the sharks and dangerous current to get there, we have got to make that island pretty appealing. As Chapter 10 discusses, that next island cannot just be about more wealth. It has got to be about more fulfilling lives. However, to get there we need to make sure that public policies first support robust growth and innovation.

NOTES

1. Mokyr (1990) p. 12.
2. Schumpeter (1942) pp. 132-3.
3. Luddites were not the only ones. One artisan guild in eighteenth-century Prussia went to so far as to issue an ordinance laying down that no artisan 'shall conceive, invent, or use anything new' (Mokyr, 2002, p. 259).
4. Machiavelli (1515).
5. Bell (1960) p. 37.
6. Leading computer scientist, John von Neuman (1956, p. 46) wrote, 'For progress there is no cure.'
7. Morris (1955) p. 290.
8. Schumpeter (1942, p. 147) predicted that intellectuals would bring a growing hostility to what he called the 'capitalist order.'
9. Mandel (2004) p. 145.
10. www.worldofquotes.com/topic/Invention/1/.
11. Chandler (1977) p. 158.
12. John (1997) p. 179.
13. Zunz (1992) p. 35.
14. The utopian movement in the 1880s was a reflection of the belief that change could be resisted.
15. William James, letter to Mrs Henry Whitman, 1899, quoted in Zunz (1992) p. 11.
16. *Independent* (1903), p. 2003.
17. The *Baltimore Sun*'s 29 December 1900 editorial called for refinement before technology proceeds: 'The twentieth century will do an excellent work if it shall make no more discoveries or inventions of any kind, but shall utilize for the good of all men the discoveries and inventions of the nineteenth, and more especially if it shall develop the moral and intellectual forces to keep pace with those material forces that the present century has set to work.'
18. Goodwyn (1978) p. 170.
19. Mills (1956).
20. Mumford (1952) pp. 11-12.
21. Bell (1960) p. 38.
22. Galbraith (1968) p. 187.
23. Theobald (1961).
24. Stevenson (1956) p. 132.
25. Hayek (1944) p. 24.
26. Ibid. pp. 23-4.
27. Ibid. p. 28.
28. Ibid. p. 46.
29. Ibid.
30. Ibid. p. 41.
31. Morris (1955) p. 84.
32. Whyte (1956) p. 22.
33. Quoted in Handel (2003) p. 11.
34. Michael (1962) p. 27.
35. Business has long resisted change. Meat processors argued that refrigerated railroad cars would lead to unsafe meats. In the 1920s the Horse Association of America campaigned to limit the use of trucks on public roads, and conducted a campaign to prohibit automobile parking on principal streets. In the 1930s, the musicians' union, faced with the substitution of recorded music for live orchestras in movie houses, launched a public relations campaign, hoping to convince the public to

demand live music. In the 1950s, the National Milk Producers Federation secured legislation in states preventing margarine makers from selling yellow spread, since it would have made people less likely to buy butter. As a result, margarine was sold in plastic bags with yellow dye pellets that consumers kneaded into the white margarine to turn it yellow. After engineers came to understand that wider spacing of wall studs would not affect integrity of homes, construction workers pressured building code administrators to not make the changes. Retail druggists sought legislation to restrict chain store operations. In fact, economist Joseph Schumpeter, Joseph used the chain store to illustrate what he meant by the 'creative destruction' of capitalism. For a discussion of this see Atkinson (2001).

36. Schumpeter (1942) p. 84.
37. Quoted in Mokyr (1994) p. 564.
38. When Dry Clean Depot, a rapidly expanding low-cost dry-cleaning franchise, tried to expand into the Virginia suburbs of Washington, DC owners of smaller dry cleaners pressured the Fairfax County Council to ban 'Depots' from residential or commercial areas, consigning them to out-of-the-way industrial sites.
39. Newkirk and Atkinson (2003).
40. For a discussion of resistance in the real estate industry, see Ham and Atkinson (2003).
41. We are not the only nation to give in. In France, in an attempt to protect small booksellers, they prevent bookstores from giving more than 5 percent discounts. In Germany sellers have to sell at the price listed on the book.
42. In 1958 Joseph Bierne, president of the Communications Workers of America, wrote about the 'Union's role in helping productivity.' Bierne, the UAW's Walter Reuther, and other labor leaders were members of the 1964 National Commission on Technology, Automation and Economic Progress. While the Commission argued that government should do more to help workers affected by technological change, it was unambiguous in its support of technological innovation and automation.
43. www.eh.net/bookreviews/library/0296.shtml.
44. www.dol.gov/sec/skillssummit/p1s5c.htm.
45. Not all unions are like this. The Singapore National Trade Union Congress declared that 'Singapore trade unions have all along acknowledged that without economic growth and higher productivity, workers' aspirations for better quality of life and improved standard of living cannot be realized. It is therefore essential for trade unions to engage in passive participation in the productivity movement' (Blum and Teick, 1997, p. 44).
46. Consumer groups have fought federal laws allowing bigger and longer trucks, even though they would boost the productivity of the industry and result in lower prices.
47. While the security benefits of smart IDs are significant, the productivity benefits from the ability to digitally 'sign' documents online and automate a wide range of transactions through an electronic purse function would be huge. Because the privacy advocates are so well organized and can inflame inaccurate fears about such technologies (the cards will lead to a police state), they have made many elected officials reluctant to support modernizing of our ID system. If the privacy advocates were as strong in the old economy as they are now, Franklin Roosevelt probably would never have signed the Social Security Act (the creation of a national ID), credit reporting agencies might have been outlawed, preventing tens of millions of Americans from getting consumer credit, and telephone pages might have been prohibited.
48. The Italian clothing maker Benetton group decided it would not use RFID to track inventory, after a consumer group threatened a boycott. The leading group opposing RFID is Consumers Against Supermarket Privacy Invasion and Numbering, a group

that also thinks consumers are exploited when using grocery store frequent buyer cards (www.nocards.org).

49. In a pamphlet arguing against bioengineered food, the natural food company Emerald Valley Kitchen states 'the few arrogant biotechnocrats of our generation must not be allowed to threaten the evolutionary process of 3 billion years.' Although it is okay if a few ideological environmentalists threaten scientific and economic progress.

50. House Republican Whip Tom DeLay (2001) summed up the views of social conservatives when he stated, 'Human cloning perverts science in the name of research. Cloning raises troubling questions and violates a fundamental principle: Every innocent human life is precious and must not be destroyed or manipulated by scientists.'

51. McKibben (2002) p. A23.

52. Ibid.

53. McKinsey Global Institute found that one-quarter of the increase in productivity in the 1990s can be attributed just to improvements in the retail sector. High productivity retailing formats drive out traditional retailers, unless restrained by land-use restrictions or regulations (Baily and Solow, 2001). Churning also boosts productivity. Seventy percent of the least efficient retail stores had gone out of business by 1997 (Haltiwanger et al., 2002). In this sense the smart growth movement is a anti-productivity movement.

54. Stevenson (1956) p. 141.

55. Moyers (2002).

56. Atkinson (2004a).

57. Smith (1996).

58. Ehret (1967).

59. Quoted in Bix (2000) p. 166.

60. Quoted in Noble (1995) p. 12.

61. I recently asked a prominent historian of technology at a major research university to recommend articles that examined opposition to new technology. His email response was instructive, but unfortunately, not all that uncommon: 'In my opinion there has been more irrational and unreasonable support for new technologies than opposition in the past 200 years. If one looks closely at most instances of opposition, and discounts the triumphalist accounts written by the proponents of the new technology, the opponents usually have a pretty good case. This reasonableness is readily demonstrable in the case of the north Yorkshire Luddites, who sought to limit the introduction of water-powered cropping frames.'

62. Noble (1995) p. 7.

63. Students taking his class 'Embracing Technology: America's Love Affair with the Machine' can explore questions such as: 'Are men really better at science than women, or is science a masculinist fantasy (or nightmare) designed to perpetuate patriarchal social designs and to create homogenous masculine cultures that exclude and, in fact, do not require the existence of women? In what ways is medicine gender biased and how do technologies of medicine further subject the female body to masculine control and punishment? ... Are computer technologies actually liberatory, or do they present yet another elaborately veiled attempt to control users?' (www.cohums.ohio-state.edu/english/People/Hogsette.1/descript.htm).

64. www.consciouschoice.com/citizen/citizen1301.html.

65. Noble, (1995) p. xii.

66. Marx (1987).

67. Rouse (undated).

68. Thompson (2002) p. 20.

69. Johnson (1997).

70. Buell and Hearn (1994).
71. Olson (1982).
72. The Gore campaign of 2000 repeated these mistakes, casting itself in populist tones, promising to 'protect the people from the powerful' and from risky changes.
73. See the House New Democratic Coalition (www.house.gov/adamsmith/NDC /ndc.html).
74. See www.ndol.org.
75. Personal conversation with author, May 2002.
76. Postrel (1999) p. 55.

PART II

Modernizing Public Policies for the New Economy

7. Legacy Economic Policy Frameworks

If an economy is to fully benefit from the emergence of a new techno-economic system, economic policy must adapt to fit the new realities and meet the new challenges. However, as new techno-economic production systems emerge a growing mismatch arises with the legacy economic policy system. John Maynard Keynes referred to this failure to adapt in the 1930s when he stated that 'practical men, who believe themselves to be quite exempt from any intellectual influences, are usually the slaves of some defunct economist.'[1]

Today, we are in a similar situation: as the New Economy emerges, our economic policies remain rooted in the old economy. As the economy has become more global, dynamic, and technology-driven, most liberals remain wedded to the demand-side economic policy framework of the mass production, corporate era: big government, a focus on Keynesian management of the business cycle, and economic regulation of key sectors. The left has reacted against creative destruction and the instability of the new global economy, trying to recreate the stability of the old economy, and thinking that the instability is a result of government policies, not of foundational changes in the economic system. For their part most conservatives look even further back for inspiration to the economic policy system of the factory-based economy with its dramatically reduced role for government, less progressive taxation, and limited regulations. While these conservative supply-siders embrace the flexibility, dynamism and competition inherent in the New Economy, they reject need for public investment and economic strategy and a new set of rules of the road.

In the New Economy policymakers of all political stripes need to embrace a new economic framework – growth economics – that focuses front and center on boosting long-term productivity growth. They need to do this by supporting increased investments in knowledge and technology, more robust competition and innovation, fiscal

213

discipline, and governmental transformation. Yet, the fact that both political parties remain deeply influenced by legacy economic policy systems makes it difficult to develop and implement a growth economics framework. Before laying out the principles of growth economics in Chapter 8, it is worth looking in more detail at these legacy economic policy systems.

THE OLD ECONOMY POLICY SYSTEM

The foundations of our economic policy system were laid in the 1940s, when the new corporate economy was emerging. Prior to the 1940s economy policy was, to say the least, ad hoc. Before the Depression there was a general consensus that voluntary cooperation between business, government, philanthropic foundations and labor was the best way to manage the economy. Beyond that there was little accepted understanding of how to manage the economy, or even if the government should intervene. Moreover, the government's capacity to make economic policy was limited.

With the breakdown of the factory economy and the explanation and solution laid out by Keynes in his landmark book *The General Theory of Employment*, it became clear to many, especially progressives, that the old policy framework was fundamentally inadequate for managing a large industrial economy. While FDR tried a variety of experiments (e.g., the Works Progress Administration, the National Recovery Act, and other programs) it was not until after the war that a new economic policy framework became institutionalized. Seeking to avoid another depression following the conversion from a wartime economy, and bolstered by the insights of Keynes, Congress passed the Employment Act of 1946 that established the President's Council of Economic Advisors and the Congressional Joint Economic Committee. The Act stated that it was the 'continuing policy and responsibility of the Federal Government to use all practicable means for the purpose of creating and maintaining conditions under which there will be afforded useful employment opportunities for those able, willing, and seeking to work, and to promote maximum employment, production, and purchasing power.' It went on to state that:

> The President shall transmit to the Congress ... an economic report setting forth; 1) the levels of employment, production, and purchasing power obtaining in the United States and such levels needed to carry out the policy...

2) current and foreseeable trends in the level of employment, production, and purchasing power; 3) a review of the economic program of the federal government and a review of economic conditions affecting employment in the United States or any considerable portion thereof during the preceding year and their effect upon employment, production, and purchasing power.

The goal of the legislation, and indeed the central organizing principle of US economic policy to this day, was not to boost the long term growth of economic output, but rather to make sure that recessions do not cause economic performance to slip below some natural, immutable rate of growth. (In the last two decades the goal of keeping inflation low has been added as well.) When the Act spoke of maximizing production it meant avoiding recessions, running factories at full capacity, and getting to full employment. Government would do this through demand management: by controlling the money supply and federal spending and taxing to boost or restrict consumer spending and private sector investment depending upon the phase of the business cycle. In other words, policymakers and their economic advisors assumed that the overall growth trajectory was immutable and that the best thing government could do was to assure that the economy used all of its potential productive capacities and did not let idle capacity develop. In summing up the intention of the Act, George Soule, the Director of the National Bureau of Economic Research, stated in 1949 that the Act was 'inspired partly by those who wanted a governmental fiscal policy to compensate for the ups and downs of demand originating in the operations of private business, and partly by those who believed in trying to enlist the cooperation of business in stabilizing the economy.'[2] Soule summed up the major challenge of policymakers: 'the most important obstacle to the desired increase which the figures do show (e.g. income) is the frequent recurrence of depression and unemployment. Avoiding depression, therefore, is a most important objective.'[3]

The Act reflected a broad consensus in Keynesian economics. In 1968 Galbraith summed up the view, stating 'The regulation of aggregate demand, it will be evident, is an organic requirement of the industrial system.'[4] He went on to argue that 'the state undertakes to regulate total income available for the purchase of goods and services in the economy. It seeks to insure sufficient purchasing power to buy whatever the current labor force can produce.' It was not just liberal economists who held this view; the business establishment was convinced of it as well. The prestigious 1958 Rockefeller Palen Report on economic policy stated 'public expenditures in support of growth are an essential part of our economy. Far from being a hindrance to progress, they provide the environment within which our economy moves forward.'[5] Because of the strong perceived role of government in keeping up aggregate demand, people spoke of a 'mixed economy' with both government and industry playing important roles.

To fulfill its role in managing demand, government needed to be big. As Galbraith argued, 'If the state is effectively to manage demand, the public sector of the economy must be relatively large.'[6] Heilbroner concurred, claiming that 'government spending can indeed play a decisive role in creating economic expansion, just as private investment spending did in the past.'[7] It was not just spending on social welfare that drove consumer demand, it was also spending on defense. Most shared Galbraith's view that 'defense expenditures in their present magnitude are, in part, an accommodation to the needs of the industrial system and the technostructure.'[8]

There was one other key tenet of old economy policy and it was the assumption that the engine of production was robust and that government's job was to ensure a more equitable distribution of that growing bounty. Galbraith's 1958 best-seller, *The Affluent Society*, made the case that the problem of production had been solved, leaving only one of distribution. The poor needed to gain access to the resources of a rich nation. It was this thinking, in part, that led Lyndon Johnson to launch the 'War on Poverty' in 1964 and Congress to dramatically expand entitlement programs.

With the overriding focus on managing the business cycle and addressing poverty, when it came to the role of government in boosting innovation and productivity, most economists had little to say. The Employment Act of 1946 was silent on productivity – the key to income growth – in part because economists knew little about productivity and even less about how to boost it. While a few maverick economists like Christopher Freeman and Richard Nelson have long toiled in the wilderness of understanding productivity growth and technological change, it is only in the last decade a few mainstream economists have begun to focus on why productivity growth and technological innovation actually occur. To do this they have focused on the special properties and key role of knowledge in creating growth, instead of assuming that simply increasing investment and savings would lead to higher productivity. Notwithstanding this belated interest in productivity, the dominant economic policy approach, and indeed the overriding economic world-view of most policymakers, economists, and pundits remain stuck in the old framework. Indeed, both liberals and conservatives embrace economic policy models from another era.

THE LIBERAL FAITH IN NEW DEAL ECONOMICS

Liberal economic doctrine remains rooted in the old economy. Viewing economic prosperity as largely synonymous with worker well-being, many on the left continue to maintain that it is the demand for goods and services that drives economic growth and that the central goal of economic policy is to keep demand high through robust government spending and measures to keep wages high (e.g. strong unions, minimum wage laws).

Many liberals today do not just look back to the old economy for policy guidance, they oppose the emerging New Economy. For them, the New Economy represents a new threat to economic justice and social cohesion.[9] They emphasize and exaggerate the downsides of the New Economy, while underestimating its benefits. They blame technology and globalization for downsizing of good jobs, stagnant wages, degradation of the quality of work, growing inequality, and environmental destruction. They correctly point out that economic change creates losers as well as winners, but their preferred solution is too often to try to slow or stop the processes of change, a both deleterious and fruitless path. Thus, they prescribe trade protection, top-down regulation, and spending on outdated industrial-era programs. At the end of the day, their land of milk and honey is the old corporate mass production economy made up of large organizations with secure employment, stable markets and limited competition.

Because they draw their inspiration from that era's economic policy framework, it is worth examining how this shapes liberal economic thinking today. While conservatives and moderates have largely rejected the demand-side story that held wide sway in the old economy, liberals continue to embrace it wholeheartedly. In fact, the tight link between economic growth, consumer demand, and government spending is a central aspect of their prevailing economic story and the source of their belief in the primacy of worker's wages and spending as the engine of growth. Never jettisoning Keynesianism, the left stresses that rising consumer demand leads industry to produce goods and services and employ people. Liberals point to the 'golden age' of the old economy when government consciously guided and regulated the market. According to Jeff Faux, former head of the liberal Economic Policy Institute, the Democratic party had crafted a compelling story that was moved by three main ideas: a progressive era idea that the federal government was the only institution powerful enough to challenge the power of big business; a populist idea that income redistribution was a key; and Keynesian economics that said that the key economic role of the federal government was to jump-start consumer demand and through its spending keep it up.[10]

Faux credits the rise in incomes after World War II with 'steady infusion of public spending from the GI Bill, highway, space, and housing programs, and continued large military budgets.'[11] According to this view, government spending, along with a strong labor movement that kept wages growing, was the key to growth. 'Prosperity depended upon maintaining a mass market, which in turn required an activist government and a redistributionist economic policy. This strong consumer spending in turn stimulated production, which led to lower unemployment.'[12] For the left it was consumers' enormous pent up demand coming out of World War II combined with continued high levels of government spending, not the emergence of a new technology system, that led to the long boom from the 1950s to the mid-1970s.

This demand-side model remains the left's focus today. Liberal economist James Galbraith states that 'consumption is also an important and much maligned policy objective. People should have the incomes they need to be well fed, housed, and clothed – and also to enjoy life. Public services can help: day care, education, public health, culture, and the arts all deserve far more support than they are getting.'[13] Former Democratic House leader Dick Gephardt echoes these views saying that 'raising wages does more than help someone buy food or pay for shelter. Remember the Republican nostrum of the 1980s, supply-side economics? I'm a believer in demand-side economics. Raising wages increases the buying power of American workers and that's good for the entire country.'[14] In embracing the demand-led story the left rejects the neo-Schumpeterian analysis that long waves of innovation are the key drivers of economic growth. Liberal economists Barry Bluestone and Bennett Harrison concur: 'what initially energized the post-World War II economy boom had less to do with supply-side factors [like technology] and more to do with extraordinary buoyant demand.'[15] Overlooking the development of the electro-mechanical automation system and science-based develop-ment that drove productivity, they argued 'There was no great technology breakthrough on the supply side like the steam engine or electrification.'[16]

If supply-side factors did not lead to the boom, they likewise, the left argues, did not cause the post-1974 slowdown. Like conservative economic thinkers, the left blames public policies, arguing that when government reduced taxes and cut the growth of spending, starting in the Carter administration and continuing to the first Bush administration, economic growth suffered.[17] Bluestone and Harrison argue 'overall GDP growth would have been sustained at something closer to this record clip in the early 1970s were it not for a total collapse in public sector growth.'[18]

The facts belie their demand-side explanation. Demographic factors actually led to employment growing faster in the last half of the 1970s than it did in the roaring 1960s. However, according to their model, this should have led companies to invest more to meet the growing demand for goods and services. Instead, investment fell. As discussed in Chapter 5, the real reason growth slowed was that the quality of the technology system was not adequate to the task of continuing to boost productivity at its prior rate. To apply this thinking to one industry, increased demand for steel might have boosted investment in more steel mills, but it was not until the steel industry began to invent and bring to market new kinds of steel making equipment and organization of production (e.g. continuous casters, mini-mills) that productivity rates went up.

Moreover, the liberal explanation of the slowdown in the growth of government spending gets cause and effect backwards. The reality was that the productivity slowdown (combined with tax cuts) caused the fiscal crisis, not the other way around, as the left asserts. The slowdown in the rate of government spending growth was only partly the result of a post-New Deal political philosophy, although for the Reagan and first Bush administrations this clearly played a role. Rather it was the slowdown in economic growth that squeezed government revenues, which in turn limited spending growth.[19] Moreover, as wage growth for many Americans began to stagnate, the political pressure to cut taxes as a way to boost after-tax income grew. Once productivity and wages began to grow again in the mid-1990s and the Clinton administration embraced fiscal discipline and debt reduction, the tax issue became a less potent political weapon, and only reemerged in the last few years when pushed by the conservative Bush administration and Congress.

The left's focus on demand-side economics leads many to ignore, or even deny, the robust growth of the 1990s, since the Clinton administration focused on fiscal discipline and not boosting spending. For example, liberal economist Joe Stiglitz simply refuses to admit that the 1990s was as good as it was, going so far to call the decade a 'disaster.'[20] However, the strong performance of the 1990s has forced some on the left to update their traditional narrative while maintaining the underlying focus on the demand side. For example, Bluestone and Harrison still maintain that consumer demand sustains growth by keeping the economy at full employment, but now keeping employment and consumption high is important not because of the old rationale of preventing recessions, but because it leads companies to invest in new machinery and equipment, which in turn boosts productivity.[21]

At its heart, this demand-led economic theory fails to explain the process of technological change. Innovation is driven much more by supply factors (e.g., growth in knowledge) than by changes in the amount of money consumers have to spend. Mark Andreeson invented the web browser not because he calculated that people had more money so they could afford to surf online, but because he was driven to find a new way to surf the Internet (and because he could do the research due to federal research funding to the University of Illinois).

This focus on keeping demand high, and the belief that government spending plays a key role in driving explains why the left remains critical of the Clinton administration's efforts to balance the budget and pay down the debt.[22] Some liberals see balancing the budget as a trap laid for Democrats by crafty Republicans who want to end the era of big government and liberal largess. According to them balancing the budget, even in the long-term, actually hurts economic growth by reducing consumer demand.

As the old Keynesian rationale for spending has become discredited, the left has turned to a new one: using the term 'public investment' to claim that government spending grows the economy. Just as Eisenhower was able to build an interstate highway system by calling it the National Defense Highway System, today it is easier to pass big a spending initiative under the name of 'investment.' However, the left generally does not distinguish between investments (expenditures that provide a payback, such as investments in training or research) and spending (expenditures that are consumed today with little economic payback, such as spending on housing). Thus, the Economic Policy

Institute's growth agenda focuses on 'rebuilding the cities, helping the poor and raising the minimum wage, slowing the pace of economic change, universal health care, more money spent on public education, and slowing globalization, and investing in environmental technologies.' There are legitimate reasons to spend more to revitalize distressed urban areas, but boosting economic growth does not top the list, particularly when it adds to the deficit. Such spending could be justified on social policy grounds but not, as the left is wont to do, as part of an agenda to boost productivity. In short, the left is committed to preserving social outlays, not investment. In other words, they see deficit spending as progressive (as long as it is based on expanded spending and not tax cuts) because it serves the twin purposes of redistribution and Keynesian demand-led growth.

Because of their overriding focus on distributional issues, liberal economic thinkers see increased demand, rather than increased productivity, as the principal reason worker wages increased in the 1990s. Former Clinton administration Secretary of Labor Robert Reich attributes the rise in real incomes of workers at the bottom of the ladder in the late 1990s 'almost entirely to an annually low rate of unemployment – so low that bottom-rung workers could easily find one or more jobs, and put in many more hours than before. But we cannot count on the economy continuing to remain robust forever; it seems doubtful that the business cycle has been permanently repealed.'[23] If it were true that wages were bid up because of low unemployment then it would mean that their gain would have come at the expense of high-income workers or profits. In fact, that was not the case. Profits and incomes went up across the board because high productivity allowed the real economy to produce so many more goods and services.

For the left, wage growth drives productivity and GDP growth, not the other way around. Because of this they fear that production will outrun consumption, as happened during the Great Depression. Liberal economist Robert Theobald states 'To listen to the discussions, one would think that the real issue is how to produce enough. In reality, the core problem has been how to ensure that demand kept up with production so that factories could keep humming and services would be purchased.'[24] Lester Thurow concurs, stating 'name any major product, calculate how much the world could produce if every factory were operating at capacity, subtract what the world is going to buy, and you'll find that the world's production potential exceeds expected consumption by at least a third ... with an excess of production capacity, falling prices are no mystery.'[25] He goes on to state 'systematic deflation is not a certainty, but the third industrial revolution has made it likely enough that there is good reason to think about how standard operating procedures change when prices start to fall.'[26] Never mind that the economy has not experienced deflation in over 70 years.

This focus on keeping labor demand high gets to the heart of the left's ambiguous position toward productivity and their antipathy toward globalization and increased market competition. The only way to boost productivity is to increase the efficiency of production, but this can lead to workers being laid off, particularly if the economy is growing slowly, as has been the case since 2001. Liberal economic thinkers believe that when workers get laid off due to productivity their incomes go down and consumer demand falls. Similar effects result from trade, as it puts pressure on costs, limiting wage increases in some industries. As Gephardt explains in reference to the Mexico trade agreement:

> NAFTA's only accomplishment is to give the United States and other global businesses easier access to low-cost Mexican labor, which helps with profits but little of that lower cost goes to us consumers ... worse than anything, because we missed the opportunity to use NAFTA to get laws better enforced in Mexico we missed chances to build, over time, a huge number of middle class consumers in Mexico. What the world needs now is more able consumers, not just more able producers.[27]

Jeff Faux believes that we are 'engaged in a desperate gamble that ill prepared American workers cannot only survive but prevail in a brutal head to head competition in a world where the supply of productive labor is growing faster than the demand for that labor's production.'[28] According to this view, in a world in which there are more producers than consumers, we should avoid shipping production overseas since that leads to fewer consumers at home and poorer consumers abroad since they are paid so little. The problem with this view is that it equates consumption with wage levels and fails to recognize that if prices fall consumption can increase. Focusing only on wages misses half the picture. If wages go down 10 percent but prices fall 15 percent, workers as a whole are better off. Likewise, low wages paid to workers overseas, while not always improving their standard of living, result in low prices at home, meaning that US consumers can buy more.

The real determinates of standard of living are how many goods and services we produce in a year relative to how much we work. Wage levels only determine how we allocate them. Unless linked to higher productivity higher incomes for some portion of workers is simply a method of redistributing wealth from one group to another. There is no doubt that when the incomes of high earners have been rising, and low and moderate earners' incomes have been stagnant, as has happened in the last two decades, that a more equal distribution of earnings is warranted. But that's not the same as growing the overall economy. While there are compelling reasons to push for a more equal distribution of incomes, that push should be seen for what it is: principally a redistribution, rather than a growth agenda.

A growth agenda focuses on ensuring that the production system is able to produce more per hour of work. In this sense, it is more accurate to say that 'we cannot have consumers unless we have producers,' and that what determines what we consume is what we produce. Over the moderate term, change in wages is in fact closely tied to changes in productivity. From 1963 to 1973, business productivity grew 35 percent while wages grew 31 percent. In that decade, average American workers saw their real incomes go up by almost one-third. In contrast, between 1985 and 1995, productivity grew 9 percent, while wages increased just 6 percent.

This focus on wage levels is what is behind the left's critique of globalization and their belief that trade with developing nations drives down US wage rates. Dick Gephardt states 'ultimately our wages are dependent on workers around the world earning a decent living. We are tied to them whether we like it or not.'[29] But the reality is that as a nation we are not. Over half our trade is with developed, higher wage nations. Even if all our trade were with low-wage nations like China it still would not necessarily lower real wages. Assume a US widget company wants to compete directly with a widget company in China on costs and convinced its workers to take an 80 percent pay cut. Clearly the widget company workers would be worse off, but American consumers would be better off since widgets would be cheaper. Even if the workers would not accept a wage cut and they lost their jobs, the result would still be the same at least in the medium term. Americans would buy cheaper Chinese widgets and the workers who were laid off would find other jobs. Even if the workers' new jobs pay less, total consumption would still be the same, if not higher than before, as long as foreign workers are doing less skilled and less productive work and Americans are doing more skilled.[30] Thus, for the left, trade and globalization are suspect principally because they hurt particular groups of workers, particularly lower skilled factory workers. It is not that the plight of these workers should not be a significant public policy concern, it is just that it is a far different issue than saying that trade with low wage nations automatically lowers our standard of living.[31]

Because the left's focus is largely on boosting worker welfare, a core part of their economic agenda is the promotion of what they call the 'high-performance path.' Business writer Shari Caudron states 'for companies trying to figure out how they will compete there are really only two options: downsizing and cost-cutting, or a high-value added strategy focusing on improving productivity, quality and flexibility.'[32] The left sees the former strategy as anti-worker. There is no doubt that it is, if it focuses on busting unions, cutting wages and benefits, and creating poor working conditions. But that's not just what the left criticizes. Working Partnerships USA, a union-run advocacy organization, talks about the 'wrong way' to change work organizations. It criticizes corporate reengineering efforts, in part because 'most initiatives result in significant layoffs that strain social safety nets and put enormous stress on working families.'[33] Moreover, 'application of new information technologies often leads to deskilling of jobs and increased worker surveillance and stress.' According to the left the way to reorganize work is so it does not lead to layoffs. But boosting productivity can result in layoffs as it enables fewer workers to produce more.

Instead of trying to compete on cost, the left argues that companies should compete on quality, customer service, and customization, as companies like Mercedes, Nordstrom's, and Ritz Carlton do. Productivity would go up if companies boosted training and reorganized work so that it was more satisfying and more highly skilled. Liberal economists Herzenberg, Alic and Wiel argue that boosting industry performance will come largely from improvements in 'humanware,' a term that refers to improvements in the organization of work and skills of workers.[34] They argue that hardware and software cannot give firms competitive advantage, but humanware can. For example, they claim that automatic teller machines 'quickly became commodities, and early returns suggest that home banking will do little to set a bank apart.'[35] Yet, the goal of policy is not to help individual companies gain competitive advantage, it is to boost productivity and innovation in the entire economy. Automatic teller machines and online banking boost productivity, not by fostering better-trained tellers, but by eliminating demand for tellers.

The 'humanware' agenda is proposed to cure all manner of economic problems. Reich maintains that the most effective way to address the wage gap and boost productivity is 'a program that invests in people.'[36] He argues that skills are the most important factor in determining wealth and nations cannot gain competitive advantage by investing in machines and equipment because 'low wage countries can use the same machines and still sell their products more cheaply than we can.' Reich claims that 'American ownership of the corporation is profoundly less relevant to America's economic future than the skills, training, and knowledge commanded by American workers.'[37] Yet developing nations do not use the same machines or organize them in the same way. The fact that technology systems do differ significantly (e.g., the business supply chain is considerably more automated and powered by IT in the United States than in most other nations) and that most of America's wealth is determined by technologies and their use, suggests that an exclusive focus on skills is too simple.[38]

At its heart, the left places workers at the center of its economic policy framework. However, the interests of a particular set of workers are not always the same as the interests of the economy overall. Or, to put it another way, while a worker in a car factory is a worker, he is also a consumer who benefits from productivity gains in other sectors when he buys a television, goes on a vacation, or gets an insurance policy. While the mass production, corporate economy was driven by producers of consumer products and services, today's economy is more fundamentally a consumer-driven economy. Citizens are much more demanding as consumers and increasingly see their identity wrapped up less as a producer and more as a consumer. As a result, as Michael Storper notes, the politics of consumers are different than those of producers or wage earners.[39] Storper states 'consumer interests and identities have played an increasing role in permitting producers to implement productivity strategies that run up against powerful corporatist-producer interests in many countries.'[40] Yet, the left remains committed to a politics that defends the interests of individual groups of workers even if consumers as a group are hurt.

Even when liberals admit that slow productivity growth hurts low-income Americans, they still see redistribution as the answer. Since productivity growth has rebounded in the last few years, some liberals even argue, as they did after the first decade of the corporate mass production economy, that the focus should no longer be on productivity. Rather, policies should focus on ensuring a more equal distribution of the fruits of high productivity. Again, more equitable distribution is needed, but not at the expense of productivity.

Moreover, liberals do not see government as having much of a role in raising productivity.[41] Liberal economist Frank Levy documents how in the 1980s low wage growth for the bottom half of the labor market was due in part to slow productivity growth.[42] Notwithstanding this Levy is resigned to conclude that 'We cannot legislate the rate of productivity growth ... That is why equalizing institutions are so important.'[43] Like many conservatives, many on the left believe that government can do little to grow the pie; that is the job of business. However, government can make sure that the economic pie is divided more evenly.

In a recent book Reich articulates the quintessential New Economy liberal view. While he acknowledges the emergence of the New Economy, he sees the mission of government principally as remedying its downsides, particularly inequity and risk, not to boost growth and innovation. He wants to 'reap the advantages of the New Economy, while preventing its excesses and tempering its injustices.'[44] As a result, his agenda is to cushion people against sudden economic shocks, widen the circle of prosperity by boosting education of lower income persons, give grants to people when they turn 18; raise the pay for human care workers, and reverse the sorting mechanism, with things like school vouchers inversely valued with household income. Nowhere does he mention the need for policies to boost productivity and drive innovation.

Indeed, for Reich, policies that might maximize productivity growth are to be avoided. Reich says liberals could follow a neo-Luddite path, opposing the New Economy, or 'at the other extreme, we could put our foot on the accelerator and let 'er rip. We could choose the path of fastest growth, widest choice, quickest switch ... (but if we did) our incomes would depend on continuous spot-auction bids for our services. All government supports – regulations, insurance, pooled benefits – would be dismantled, as the sorting mechanism became perfectly efficient worldwide.'[45] In other words, churning and innovation need to be managed so that they do not impose too many costs on individual workers, even if doing so would reduce growth.

This focus on stability and equity even at the expense of growth stems from a long liberal tradition. It was perhaps best articulated by the late John Rawls, a well-known social philosopher at Harvard. Rawls's influential 1971 book *A Theory of Justice* sought to establish bedrock principles that people could agree would lead to a just society.

One of them was the principle of 'original position,' where Rawls postulated that we should judge the ethical value of a particular economic arrangement based on no knowledge of our own individual economic or social position. In this position Rawls argues that a reasonable, moral, and self-interested person would support an economy that led to two people getting $1000 more and that this outcome would be just. What if one person gets $1000 while the other gets only half, $500. Would this be just? Rawls answers that it would be, since both parties benefited. What if one person gets $1000 more and the other, nothing. To Rawls, this is an unjust outcome because even though society is $1000 richer, the allocation of that $1000 is based on chance. Rawls's philosophy is the cornerstone of liberal thinking and the source of their focus on distribution. Reich reflects this position when he asserts that 'there's a lively debate about whether Americans at or near the bottom of the income ladder are better off than they were, say, in 1970. Relative to what they could afford to buy before, they are in many ways; relative to what most people in American society can now afford, they're more deprived.'[46] Reich expounded on this view in a dialogue he had with students while he was Secretary of Labor. He stated:

I am concerned about the direction that the country is heading with regard to inequality. Let me ask you for a show of hands. Let's assume that I could offer you a deal, and I want to know how many of you would accept [it] ... 'You have a choice either between the current economy, with all the good news and all the problems it has ... or I will offer you a deal in which the top fifth of income earners get a 25 percent raise and the bottom fifth get a 10 percent raise.' Now the net result is more inequality than we have today, but everybody is better off ... How many like that deal? Put up your hands. Have the courage of your convictions. Hands high in the air. This is a learning experiment here. OK. There are twenty-eight. How many of you do not like that deal? That's interesting. Sixty-three.[47]

Reich was in the latter camp. In other words, even though low income Americans are better off today than they were in 1970, this is not an acceptable outcome because upper income Americans are even richer. Clearly Rawls's first two choices are the best – where both groups gain[48] – but unequal growth is better than no growth, in large part because progressive taxes redistribute some of that growth to the broader society. This is not to suggest that the current unequal distribution of incomes and wealth is fair – it is not. However, being ambivalent about growth is not the answer.

There is one final reason for the left's ambivalence toward high productivity and the competition, innovation, and dynamism needed to achieve it. They worry that trade and productivity will lead to fewer jobs. This view centers on a misconception economists term the 'lump of labor' fallacy. According to this belief there are only a fixed number of jobs and anything that threatens to eliminate a job, means that unemployment will go up and workers will be worse off. Perhaps it is a legacy of the Depression, but most Americans still fear that the economy cannot create enough jobs and that automation risks raising unemployment rates.

This is one reason why liberals oppose prison labor, for they think it steals jobs from 'free' labor.[49] Likewise, automation and offshoring of work are seen as threats to full employment. In his apocalyptic 1995 book, *The End of Work*, social critic Jeremy Rifkin laments that '[technological change] is now leading to unprecedented levels of technological unemployment, a precipitous decline of consumer purchasing power and the specter of a worldwide depression of incalculable magnitude and duration.'[50] Jeff Faux illustrates this view when he describes a dialog between an executive of the Ford Motor Company and UAW president Walter Reuther. As they were touring a car plant in the 1950s, the executive pointed out new automated machines that would replace workers. Reuther countered, 'and not one of them buys new Ford cars, either.' Robert Reich echoed this view in a speech: 'If you [are not skilled] ... technology is taking away your jobs. We used to have a lot of telephone operators in this country. Now we have automated switching equipment. We used to have a lot of bank tellers. I do not know how many of you have tried to find a bank teller recently, but now we have a lot of automated teller machines.'[51] Because automation allows companies to produce the same output with fewer workers, many liberals believe that it reduces consumer demand, and because demand drives growth, this leads to higher unemployment.

However, history has clearly and consistently refuted the notion that high productivity (or trade) leads in the medium to long term to higher unemployment. New technologies boosted agricultural productivity, spurring a decline in agricultural employment. However, as food became cheaper consumers spent the money they saved on other things (e.g., cars, appliances, entertainment), creating employment in other sectors. Thus, what Reuther did not recognize is while auto factory automation would make it possible to produce more cars with fewer workers, it would also lower car prices, thereby boosting demand for cars and creating employment. And as long as auto demand kept increasing from the low prices, more autoworkers would be employed, and this is exactly what happened until the late 1970s. But even when demand for cars grew more slowly than the industry's productive powers, cars continued to get cheaper (when adjusted for inflation and quality). As a result, laid-off auto workers got other jobs and were able to buy cars.

Liberal economic commentators may, when pressed, be willing to acknowledge this, but they argue that things are different now. Because technology is now displacing jobs not only in agriculture and manufacturing, but also in services, there will be no new job-generating growth sectors to employ those who lose their jobs. Rifkin argues that when millions of retail jobs are displaced by e-commerce and a host of other service sector jobs undergo digital automation there will be no new jobs to replace them. But this fails to recognize that savings from a more efficient industry, in this case for example, the insurance industry, would flow back to the economy in one of three ways: lower prices (e.g., lower rates for policyholders), higher wages for the fewer remaining employers, or higher profits (or a combination of the three). In a competitive insurance market, most of the savings would flow back to consumers in the form of lower prices. Consumers use the savings on lower premiums to go out to dinner, buy books, or buy any number of other things. That stimulates demand that other industries (e.g., restaurants, bookstores, movie theaters, and hotels) respond to by hiring more workers.

There is a final reason why the left has been ambiguous about productivity and that is because they are ambiguous about economic growth itself. It was not always like this. In the old economy liberals saw growth as the answer to a host of social problems, not the least of which was poverty. However in the transitional period of the 1970s and 1980s, some turned against growth which they believed was not only no longer the tonic to fight poverty but was also the cause of environmental degradation and a more materialistic society. In the place of growth some turned their attention to distribution. Others, particularly Naderites, environmentalists, anti-globalists, and liberal elites saw growth and technological change as leading to environmental degradation, reduced quality of life, and increased wealth for the rich. They blamed the United States for being too rich, consuming too much of the world's resources, and contributing to more than our share of the world's pollution. Their answer was to simplify our lifestyle, or at least to put bumper stickers on their SUVs encouraging us to think globally and act locally.

There are two main flaws to their argument. First, as much as some may object to growth, the vast majority of Americans and virtually everyone in developing nations want more growth. With the median household income of $42 148 per year in 2000, the average American family would like to be able to afford an addition on their house, college tuition for their kids, a nice vacation, or just the ability to not have to work overtime or have a second job. In this regard, productivity growth is central to the liberal goal of improving the lot for working men and women. Telling Americans that they have to give up on their goals of a better life for themselves and their kids in order to protect the environment is a recipe for political failure. Conservatives promise Americans wealth, liberals tell them to turn down the thermostat.

The liberal framework for economic policy is increasingly out of step with the New Economy realities. But as we will see, the conservative doctrine is no better.

THE SUPPLY-SIDE SIDETRACK

As evidenced by President Nixon's statement, 'We are all Keynesians now,' as late as the 1970s conservatives and liberals shared the old economy policy consensus. In the heyday of the old economy Republicans did not fundamentally challenge the demand-side consensus. Presidents Eisenhower, Nixon, and Ford all believed in government spending to manage the economy, they just believed in spending a little less than Democrats. The reality of the old economic system relegated free market libertarian conservatives to a small, cult-like minority that read Hayek and went to book groups to discuss *Atlas Shrugged*.

No sooner had virtually everyone embraced the demand-side model, than the breakdown of the corporate, mass production economy led to the unraveling of the consensus. Even though most liberals continue to keep the faith, the emergence of high unemployment with high inflation – a phenomena that was not supposed to be possible under the old Keynesian model – coupled with a dramatic slowdown in productivity growth, soon led many to question the prevailing economic doctrine. The disintegration of the old economy created the political opening for a wide-ranging and fundamental critique of the demand-side economic philosophy. What became the supply-side economics movement, initially championed by Ronald Reagan, filled that void.

Like liberals, conservatives ascribed the causes of the slowdown to failures of economic policy. In explaining the great slowdown, supply-side economist Brian Wesbury claims that 'Great Society spending crowded out private sector investment and regulations created rigidities. The entrepreneurial spirit was drained from the economy and potential growth slowed.'[52] Jude Wanniski's influential supply-side bible, *The Way the World Works*, went even further, as it mounted a frontal attack on Keynesian 'demand-side' economic policy. The new supply-side doctrine postulated that the real cause of the nation's economic problems were high taxes, big government, and heavy-handed regulations. Wanniski argued that high taxes reduced incentives for companies and individuals to invest capital, and for workers, particularly high earners and women, to work more hours.[53] The logic went that if the next dollar you earned was taxed at a high rate, people would invest and work less. As a result, he argued that sizable tax cuts, particularly for upper-income Americans and businesses, combined with regulatory relief and the removal of other corporate responsibilities would stimulate investment and growth.

The Reagan-created National Productivity Advisory Commission, which included members such as Paul O'Neil, George W. Bush's Treasury Secretary, fully reflected the new supply-side framework. Launched in response to the drop-off in productivity, the commission was charged with coming up with a national productivity agenda. Their answer was to recommend cutting taxes, including instituting a flat income tax, rolling back clean air and other environmental regulations, extending the retirement age, and cutting corporate health care costs: all nostrums from the supply-side playbook. The report did make the obligatory nod to issues like skills and technology, but to say that the recommendations in these areas were weak would be being kind.[54]

Today, supply-side tax cutting has become an article of faith among conservatives and constitutes almost the entirety of the Bush administration's economic policies. Conservative economic commentator James Glassman contends that 'If you free up supply and you provide higher capacity, you get more goods, higher quality goods, cheaper goods, and you hold down inflation.'[55] Don Evans, Secretary of Commerce in the Bush administration concurs, stating 'If you tax something less, such as work, you will get more of it.'[56]

Conservatives had turned Keynesianism and the liberal consensus on its head, not just because they emphasized supply-side incentives over demand-side management, but because they argued that a key tenet of the old economy consensus – that government not only had to run deficits during economic slowdowns (and surpluses during expansion), but needed to permanently be a large part of the economy to ensure stability – was completely wrong. It was small government that would boost growth.

The new conservatives went further, however, arguing that government spending was not just unnecessary, but was downright harmful. According to the right's view, higher taxes harm the economy by distorting private market forces, and therefore government should raise the least amount of revenues. This article of faith leads conservatives to reflexively oppose anything that can lead to more spending or higher taxes, with the exception perhaps of defense spending and pork barrel spending to benefit their political constituencies, like farmers and corporate special interests. The *Wall Street Journal* editorial page, the house organ of the supply-side movement, sums up the view, 'It is by now an axiom of modern economic thinking that the main engine of growth is the private sector, not government. The more money individuals get to keep, the greater the opportunities for growth.'[57]

Like the left, supply-side conservatives oppose paying off the national debt, but for completely different reasons. While the left worries it will drain money from government spending, the right fears it will preclude further tax cuts. Conservative economist John Makin argues, 'the biggest downside to simply paying off the [national] debt over the next decade arises from the need for taxes and tax rates to be higher than they would be if we aimed just to stabilize the debt-to-GDP ratio.'[58] He goes on to pose the question, 'Spending a trillion to lower tax rates. Is it more likely to benefit the economy than leaving tax rates at current levels in order to cut the federal debt by another trillion dollars?' Like the left's claim that spending spurs growth, the right's claims about tax cuts are simply stated as a matter of ideological conviction. For example, Makin justifies his argument against paying down the debt based on the assumption that since:

Lower taxes, especially lower tax rates, encourage more investment and work efforts, then they are far more stimulative and less inflationary than higher government spending. In contrast, if we assume that higher government spending increases demand for goods and services with no impact on the economy's capacity to produce them, they are unambiguously inflationary. ... it is fiscal stimulus in the form of higher government spending, not lower tax rates, that may require an offset from tighter monetary policy to avoid inflation ... [paying off the national debt] is a preposterous idea.[59]

Larry Lindsey, former director of George W. Bush's Council of Economic Advisors agrees, 'paying off the national debt should not be an end in itself.'[60] It is this kind of thinking that explains why the budget deficit and national debt under the Bush administration have grown to record proportions.

The little appreciated reality of supply-side economics is that in many ways it is just a new form of Keynesianism. Both liberals and conservatives identified the same problems, including the tendency of the old economy to fall into recession. But while liberals embraced boosting demand, supply-siders focused on reducing tax rates to boost the supply of labor and capital. Thus, when the economy is producing below its natural capacity, cutting taxes on workers and investors will get people to work more (since they can retain more of their earnings) and get companies to invest more. As a result, while in one way the supply-siders turned Keynesianism on its head, in a more fundamental way they simply extended it, albeit in a radically new form. For just as the Employment Act of 1946 was silent on productivity, Wanniski's *The Way the World Works* was similarly mute.[61]

There is a more fundamental reason, however, why supply-side economics is a failed guide for growth in the twenty-first century. While correctly a reaction against the economy policy system of the old economy that no longer fit new realities, supply-siders looked for their inspiration not in the emerging New Economy, but in the even older factory economy of the early 1900s – the days of Republican presidents Calvin Coolidge, Warren Harding, Herbert Hoover, and William McKinley, when high earners paid little in taxes, the government provided little in services, and businesses were pretty much free to do whatever they wanted. As a result, today's conservative Republicans sound surprisingly much like Republican leaders from the first few decades of the 1900s. Sounding much like George W. Bush, Calvin Coolidge stated, 'Under this republic the rewards of industry belong to those who earn them.'[62] As a result, 'the method of raising revenue ought not to impede the transaction of business; it ought to encourage it.' He goes on to state in true supply-side fashion, 'I am opposed to extremely high rates, because they produce little or no revenue.' When it came to the role of government, Warren Harding summed it up when he stated, 'I speak for administrative efficiency, for lightened tax burdens, for sound commercial practices, for adequate credit facilities, for sympathetic concern for all agricultural problems, for the omission of unnecessary interference of Government with business.'[63] These are all phrases that are part of the current Republican lexicon.

Because supply-siders are looking back to the factory economy, that era's factors of supply – labor and capital – are central to their economic doctrine. Supply-siders wanted to cut taxes to get workers to work more and investors to invest more. But the key to understanding the failure of supply-side economics is the understanding that it is not the quantity of capital or labor that is the deciding factor in productivity growth, it is quality. New generations of technology and more skilled workers are more productive than older technology and less skilled workers. The quality of capital and labor is determined by knowledge, technology innovation, education and training, competition and innovation, not by meat-axe-like tax cuts.

Even if one were to grant that the supply of capital and labor is the key, it is not clear why reductions in personal tax rates stimulate companies to develop or adopt technologies leading to higher productivity. Supply-siders make grandiose claims proclaiming the economic tonic of tax cuts. Makin argues that 'a reduction in federal tax revenues by a gross amount of $1 trillion would add $3.44 trillion to total GDP available to the economy over the next decade. That is a return of 13.1 percent a year.'[64] But exactly how tax cuts work their magic is not clear because supply-siders fail to offer either a compelling explanation of how tax cuts boost growth or empirical evidence for their claim. For example, they say tax cuts spur people to work more. Given that the top marginal rate was 91 percent in 1960 while the unemployment rate in the 1950s and 60s averaged 4.6 percent and employment growth boomed, it's hard to imagine how a top rate of 39.6 percent in 2000 could have any labor market effects. In fact, there is no evidence that the marginal tax rates in place in the 1990s served as a disincentive to work or that the Bush tax cuts on the top rates induced more people to work more. Indeed, any possible legitimacy supply-side economics once might have had evaporated when, in an effort to balance the budget, President Clinton boosted the top marginal income tax rates, and to the astonishment of supply-siders, investment soared, the economy boomed, and more people worked, including top earners.[65] Moreover, in direct contradiction to supply-side economic logic, the income of the top 5 percent of households facing the higher rates rose more rapidly in the 1990s than did overall income.[66] The new rates did not lead to a new leisure class of rich people on strike protesting the high rates. How many well-heeled CEOs told their boards that they were cutting back to four days a week because the Clinton administration boosted the top rate from 31 percent to 39.6 percent? How many unemployed people sat at home waiting for a tax cut before looking for a job?

The second leg of the supply-side argument is that cutting taxes, especially on dividends and capital gains, gives investors more incentives, thereby boosting the supply of capital, the most important ingredient, they believe, to growth. James Pinkerton, former policy advisor in the first Bush administration, reflects this view when he argues that Republicans should make Americans a 'big offer' on taxation to create 'a system that no longer taxes capital formation at all.'[67] But the logic and evidence behind this claim are as weak as that behind the link between tax rates and work. Putting more money in the bank accounts of wealthy Americans by raising the national debt has little effect on investment for the two reasons. First, investment is driven much more by the availability of investment opportunities and the cost of capital than by tax rates on investors and shareholders. Second, any tax cut effects on increasing net private savings would be more than offset by an increase in net public debt, which in turn would boost rates.

The conservative's mechanistic view of growth – pour more money in at one end and wait for growth to come out the other end – may have made sense in the factory economy of 1904. Then our emerging industrial economy needed to accumulate large amounts of capital to finance huge factories and it did so by tapping the capital of wealthy tycoons. When an inventor needed capital to finance a new company or an entrepreneur wanted to expand a company, they were likely to go hat in hand to a top-hatted tycoon like J.P. Morgan. If Morgan's taxes went up, he would have less money to invest in Thomas Edison's electrical system or Andrew Carnegie's steel mill.

This 1904 approach to economic policy is woefully out of step in a 2004 economy where knowledge and competition drive growth and spur investment much more than lower taxes, and where the cost of capital is much more important than who possesses it. With global capital flows and the proliferation of innovative financing instruments, including huge pension funds, mutual funds and venture capital pools, America has the world's most innovative and liquid capital markets. In

2004 it is not limited financial capital that puts the brakes on growth, but limited intellectual capital. To turn a phrase, there is plenty of capital chasing too few good ideas. In other words, while entrepreneurs with good ideas and good business acumen can usually find capital, capital cannot always find good ideas and innovations to invest in. In fact, it is difficult to find a company with a sound business plan and strong management team that is unable to raise capital. In short, productivity growth comes from innovation, investment in new capital equipment, improvement in skills and adoption of new forms of business organization. Tax cuts on capital and income do little to boost these and, to the extent that they reduce net savings and limit the ability of government to make investments or provide incentives for New Economy growth factors they are actually injurious to growth. As discussed in Chapter 8, this is it not to say that tax incentives for particular kinds of company investments, such as research, new equipment, or training, do not stimulate productivity.[68] However, cutting tax rates does not boost productivity or innovation.

In 2001 Republican supply-siders sold their tonic of permanent tax cuts on income and capital not just with the claim that they promote growth but that they are a remedy for recessions. While tax cuts (and spending increases) can have Keynesian effects writ large (putting more money in the economy), this simply means that the economic machine is more likely to be more fully utilized. It does not mean that the machine will go any faster (e.g., higher productivity). Moreover, this is only true if the tax cuts (or spending increases) are temporary and instituted during economic downturns. But the key to understanding conservatives' tax cut proposals is that conservatives are as likely to make them during an economic slowdown as during an economic boom. George W. Bush proposed his big income tax cut during the 2000 presidential campaign when the economy was booming, and he justified it on supply-side rationale that it would boost work and investment. Then when the economy slowed in 2001 he justified it on the Keynesian grounds that it was needed to get people back to work. The reality is that tax cuts do spur growth, but only when unemployment is high, the cuts are temporary, and most cuts flow to low and middle-income taxpayers who are most likely to spend it. When unemployment is at 4 percent, tax cuts simply fuel inflation. When they are permanent they fuel the deficit and lead to higher interest rates. When greater deficits and higher interest rates are factored in lower tax rates are at best neutral, and are actually likely to hurt long-term economic growth as they starve needed public and private capital investment.[69]

Even if conservatives were to admit the ineffectualness of supply-side economics, many would continue to embrace it for ideological reasons. Just as the left puts equality ahead of productivity, the right elevates individual freedom and liberty. Thus, even if the government could take actions to boost productivity, but had to raise taxes and adopt regulations to do it, supply-side economic doctrine would lead many conservatives to oppose it. Their libertarian opposition to government power, either in the form of taxes or regulations, is so strong that freedom trumps productivity. Senator Robert Taft, leader of the anti-New Deal Republicans, put it this way:

Today the interest of the people has come to center entirely in the field of economics ... and the material welfare of the citizens. Programs are judged on the question of whether they give men more money, more bathtubs, more automobiles, and less time to work. Certainly no one can be against these economic objectives, but it is wrong to subordinate them to the need for greater morality, greater liberty of thought, and greater liberty of action.[70]

No wonder these factory-era Republicans were in the minority throughout the hey-day of the corporate mass production economy.

Friedrich Hayek, the patron saint of economic conservatives, sums up the view: 'personally, I should much prefer to have to put up with some such inefficiency than have organized monopoly control my ways of life.'[71] In a report for the Cato Institute, a libertarian think tank in Washington, T.J. Rogers, the CEO of Silicon Valley-based Cyprus Semiconductors states, 'I do not want more government in Silicon Valley. Government can do only two things: take our money, limiting economic resources; or pass laws, limiting our other freedoms. Even in Washington, alluring subsidies come at a high cost to our industry.'[72]

Conservatives see society as nothing more than an aggregation of separate individuals, who, with the exception of cooperating to protect each other from foreign aggression or domestic lawlessness, have no higher purpose than simply satisfying their needs as consumers and family members. For them, private freedom trumps public interest every time, and one of the most vital aspects of freedom, is the freedom to not have the state take 'your money.'[73] Indeed, beyond national defense and law enforcement, the right sees efforts to even advocate a public interest and employ the public sector to help attain it as a threat to individual liberty. As such, there is no goal, no 'shining city on a hill' to aspire to, no public interest to aspire to, just the amoral workings of a free market where individuals get to 'keep their money'. If President Bush were to give John Kennedy's speech today he might say something like, 'Ask not what you can do for your country, ask what you it can do for you.' Indeed, in his 2004 Republican convention speech, President Bush stated 'government must take your side.' For conservatives, limited government and enhanced 'liberty' is an end in itself.

In the old economy, these kinds of ideas could never get traction, as they were fundamentally in conflict with the big government, stable, mass production, corporate economy. However, the breakdown of the old economy and the emergence of the New Economy has given conservatives new grist for their libertarian idea mills. The right is fond of saying that the New Economy is more like a forest than a machine. Since the old economy was more structured, stable and hierarchical – actually like a machine – conservatives may admit that that era's mixed economy was a necessary evil. But since the New Economy more closely resembles a complex self-adjusting system, they argue that government intervention can now only do harm. They argue that since 'uncertainty is pervasive in the modern economy, a centralized strategy to create growth is not feasible. Growth must be left to the entrepreneurs.'[74]

The emergence of an Internet economy has added another element to conservatives' ideological opposition to government and is why Nobel Prize winner Ronald Coase is another of their patron saints, Writing over 60 years ago, Coase showed how in some cases markets can produce results similar to those that corporations produce. According to conservatives, in an economy in which transaction costs are close to zero (not yet the case), there is significantly less need for big organizations, either public or private. In this ideal world where virtually every interaction can be calibrated and governed by an exchange relationship which reflects the marginal utility of all actors, who needs government? Daniel Bell got it right when he stated that liberal economics ('liberal' refers to pre-Keynesian economics), 'assumed that the market was a sufficient arbiter of the public weal; there were different utilities of individuals and the scarcity of different goods would come to an equilibrium that harmonized the intensity of desire and the willingness to pay the asking price.'[75] Conservatives see the New Economy as having returned us to this promised land. When this is a political movement's overriding ideology, it follows that any kind of government strategy to boost productivity, even if done in ways that fosters competition, relies on market tools, and is industry led, would automatically be dismissed as industrial policy or, even worse, state socialism.

Even if the logic of their positions does not hold up, conservatives can always fall back on history to try to justify their doctrines. It is common for all political movements to believe that the economic conditions of the period when their economic policy framework was ascendant is the vaunted golden era. The left defends Keynesianism and big government because both were in force in the old economy when the Democratic Party was dominant. The right has a huge stake in defending the economic performance of the 1980s when supply-side economics came into its own. If this period can be painted in rosy terms, then supply-side is vindicated. This is why while both centrists and conservatives argue that the economy has entered a long wave of prosperity, conservatives are passionately committed to the interpretation that it started under Reagan. Larry Lindsey would have us believe that 'the current economic expansion, which officials dates from 1991, is better viewed as stretching back to 1982.'[76] John Makin concurs that, 'the 4.5 percent growth for 1982 to 1987 was a full percentage point above the average growth rate of 3.5 percent over the four decades since 1959.'[77]

As economists are fond of saying, statistics can be made to tell any story the analyst wants, and it is no different in interpreting this period. Supply-siders base their case on growth in GDP and growth in per capita income. However, growth in GDP and per capita income are made up of two factors, hours worked and productivity. In the 1980s hours worked grew significantly while productivity did not. Women entered the workforce in unprecedented numbers, increasing from 42 million (42.4 percent of total civilian workforce) in 1980 to 57.5 million (46.1 percent) in 1995. The baby boomers born in the 1950s reached prime working age, adding even more hours worked. And as some workers' wages stagnated or even fell, many felt pressure to work more hours. Moreover, as more workers worked salaried as opposed to hourly wage jobs, yearly hours worked increased, since salaried workers work more than hourly workers. As a result, of the $2.23 trillion increase in GDP (in real dollars) between 1980 and 1995, 27 percent was due to an increase in work hours. When looked at in terms of productivity growth or per capita GDP growth the economic performance of this period was anything but bright. Productivity and wage growth slowed dramatically to around 1.3 percent.

When presented with these kinds of data that cast a dimmer hue on their so-called golden age, conservatives make two arguments. First, they claim that productivity, and by extension GDP, is not properly measured and that it went up faster than officially reported. But productivity went up significantly after 1996 and the way we measured it did not change significantly.

Second, they argue that consumption, rather than wages, is the best barometer of economic well-being. Conservative economists Cox and Alm do not dispute that wages for many workers declined or stagnated, but they counter with a host of statistics to show how much better off American consumers are. For example, they point to the fact that the average size of a home has increased 25 percent from 1970 to the mid-1990s and more households have televisions and computers.[78]

There are two main problems with their rosy analysis. First, they focus on increased consumption of goods (cars, microwave ovens, etc.), not services. But the rate of productivity growth in goods production has been about three times faster than in services, so every year goods get cheaper compared to services and Americans can buy more of them. The story with regard to the 70 percent of consumption that is services is quite different. For example, health care costs have increased at twice the rate of inflation in the past four years.[79]

Second, as described above, as more people work, total income goes up, letting households afford more things. Two-earner households earn more and consume more than one-earner households. In short, it is impossible to separate what Americans consume from what they produce. And at the end of the day, what most determines what Americans consume is the rate at which they can produce it and the 1980s were a period of slow productivity growth.

THE FAILURE OF THE LEFT'S AND THE RIGHT'S ECONOMIC DOCTRINES

In paradoxical ways the left's and the right's economic policy views are not as far apart as most would suppose. For starters, both believe that there is a limited role for government in promoting productivity. The right sees any such action as industrial policy and wants simply to minimize the role of government, in part to support its overarching goal of enhancing freedom. The left sees productivity as the business of business and that the main goal of economic policy is to ensure a fairer distribution of wealth and income.

Neither focus on the keys to growth in the New Economy: technology, innovation, and education and training. Rather, both want to take a short-cut to boost economic well-being. The right wants to cut taxes, principally on high earners, to drive investment. The left wants to give more money to workers to drive consumer demand. As a result, Washington has become the fulcrum of an intense debate about whether investors or low-wage workers should get more money. One side wants to cut capital gains taxes on high earners, the other wants to raise the minimum wage for low earners.

Neither liberal nor conservative economics focuses on the right goal, helping consumers. The conservative strategy for growing the economy is to give businesses and investors what they want: elimination of taxes on investment income, limited antitrust enforcement, and as few regulations as possible. They justify this by pointing to the fact that more Americans are investors now than ever before. But while over 45 percent of Americans are investors, 100 percent are consumers. The liberal strategy is to give low- and middle-income workers what they want: trade protection, a higher minimum wage, transfer payments of all kinds, and regulatory requirements on companies. But while 71 percent of American adults are workers, 100 percent are consumers. As much as the left is reluctant to admit it, the interests of workers are not always the same as the interests of consumers and the overall economy.

Strikingly, both liberal and conservative economic doctrines want to take a short-cut to growth, focusing not on productivity but on redistribution. Conservatives want to raise after-tax income by cutting taxes – taking from public expenditures to boost private incomes. What they fail to see is that people's economic welfare is based not just on their consumption of private goods (their house, car, clothes, foods, etc.) but also on public goods (clean air, parks, libraries, fire and police protection, etc.). Liberals want to boost the incomes of low and moderate income Americans by redistributing money from well-to-do Americans, by taxing the rich more, significantly increasing the minimum wage, and increasing government spending on programs to benefit 'working families.' Neither recognizes that the only long-term answer to improving economic well-being is to boost productivity.

Neither focus on New Economy investments. When liberals recognize the importance of investment, they often focus on old economy investment like physical infrastructure. Liberals do not appear to have met any infrastructure project that they do not like, perhaps with the exception of roads which they claim lead to sprawl. They support infrastructure because it provides high-wage jobs and because it is a way for government to solve a host of pressing social problems and redistribute economic resources, while being seen as supporting growth. But in an economy in which the national physical infrastructure is already largely complete and where knowledge and technology power growth, traditional bricks and mortar infrastructure spending does little to spur measured productivity.

Conservatives are convinced that public spending crowds out more productive private sector spending, and therefore calls for less government spending. But the right fails to recognize that the economic paybacks of many public investments are higher than from many private sector investments. This is because not all private sector investments benefit the economy since a not insignificant share are made for the zero-sum activity of gaining market share, not boosting productivity.[80] Plus it is not as if government spends and people invest – in fact, the lion's share of the Bush tax cuts will go to consumption.

However, the neo-conservative insight that the supply side of the economy is key is right. The only problem is that conservatives focus on the wrong part of the supply-side, taxes and regulation, which do little to spur real growth factors. And, more importantly, their focus is on the supply of capital and labor (at least labor provided by individuals paying high marginal tax rates). But what really constitute the supply side are factors like the skills of the workforce, the amount of research conducted by public and private institutions, and entrepreneurial talents. These and other factors are what determine how productive and innovative an economy is.

Moreover, both liberals and conservatives view with skepticism, or in some cases even disdain, a key player in economic growth. Many liberals view business as the problem, and believe that 'what's good for GM' is by definition, probably not good for the nation. When liberals do want to give the impression of being pro-business, they talk about supporting small business and small farmers, as if somehow small businesses are more virtuous and worthy of help than large businesses. For their part, many conservatives see government as the problem, particularly the federal government, and believe that what is good for government is, by definition, probably not good for the nation. As a result, both the left and right view with significant mistrust public-private partnerships that link the public purpose of government with the entrepreneurial and innovation capacity of the private sector.

Finally, not surprisingly, neither liberals nor conservatives embrace fiscal discipline. Conservatives favor tax cuts while liberals favor increased social spending, even both mean abdicating generational responsibility to significantly reduce the national debt.

This suggests that aligning economic policy with either workers or investors is not always synonymous with economic growth. Policy needs to support a productivity agenda, realizing that in some cases individual workers, firms, and perhaps whole industries, will not benefit in the short run, but that Americans as consumers will benefit.

NOTES

1. Keynes (1936) p. 383.
2. Soule (1948) p. 109.
3. Ibid. p. 41.
4. Galbraith (1968) p. 233.
5. Heilbroner and Singer (1977) p. 215.
6. Galbraith (1968) p. 269.
7. Heilbroner and Singer (1977) p. 207.
8. Galbraith (1968) p. 241. When the federal government cut defense spending at the end of the cold war, many policymakers believed it would make it harder to manage the economy and would lead to recessions.
9. Alcaly (2003).
10. Faux (1997).
11. Ibid. p. 55.
12. Ibid.
13. www.prospect.org/print/V7/25/galbraith-j.html.
14. Gephardt (1999) p. 73.
15. Bluestone and Harrison (2000) p. 33.
16. Ibid. p. 37.
17. A related story holds that wages stagnated because increases in productivity went to profits. In fact, if all of the increase in the share of income going to corporate dividends between 1978 and 1997 went instead to wages and not profits, the former would have only increased marginally faster, 20 percent instead of 16 percent.
18. Bluestone and Harrison (2000) p. 39.
19. Economists estimate that half of the federal deficit of the 1980s was due to a slowdown in the rate of economic growth, with the other half due to the Reagan tax cuts and spending increases, particularly on defense and social security.
20. Stiglitz (2003).
21. Bluestone and Harrison (2000).
22. Stiglitz (2003).
23. Reich (2001) p. 102.
24. Theobald (1998).

25. Like others who predict deflation Thurow was wrong, as inflation continues to grow, albeit at reduced rates (Thurow, 1999, p. 60).
26. Ibid.
27. Gephardt (1999) p. 101.
28. Faux (1997) p. 158.
29. Gephardt (1999) p. 91.
30. In this sense, many free trade proponents who argue that trade always benefits an economy overstate their case. If the US were to lose its higher-skilled, higher-wage industries such as aerospace, software, and advanced business services to low-wage nations, the nation will not benefit economically.
31 A major problem with a large and sustained trade deficit is that it shifts debt to the future, lowering the standard of living for the next generation that must pay off the foreign trade debt in the form of a lower value of the dollar.
32. Caudron (1999) p. 22.
33. www.atwork.org/wp/wc.html#2.
34. Herzenberg et al. (1998-89) p. 56.
35. Ibid.
36. Quoted in www.startribune.com/stonline/html/special/leaky/rei07.htm.
37. Kuttner (1996) p. 83.
38. Even though these companies pay their workers generously relative to their competitors, few of their workers can afford to buy their products or services.
39. Storper (1999).
40. Ibid. p. 18.
41. It is not surprising that discussion of how to promote e-commerce, except as it pertains to equity issues like the 'digital divide,' has largely been absent on the left.
42. Levy (1998).
43. Ibid. p. 4.
44. Reich (2001) p. 242.
45. Ibid. p. 241.
46. Ibid. p. 204.
47. http://ncrve.berkeley.edu/CW73/Reich.html.
48. The Progressive Policy Institute has proposed to keep income inequality from increasing any more than it was in 2000 by automatically raising top marginal rates and lowering taxes on lower and middle income Americans if before-tax inequality widens (Atkinson, 2003).
49. Lafer (1999).
50. Rifkin (1995) p. 15.
51. http://ncrve.berkeley.edu/CW73/Reich.html.
52. Wesbury (2003).
53. Ironically neo-Marxist analysis implicitly endorses a conservative supply-side view of the world. Like supply-siders, Marxists see capital as the driver, and technology, learning and competition as secondary. Like conservatives, they argue that it was high wage demands or the inability of companies to scrap old capital that led to a slowdown in the 1970s and 1980s.
54. The Commission recommended funding 500 graduate engineering fellowships, but it was not willing to allocate funds for this, and instead called for reallocating funding in the National Science Foundation. It made no recommend-ations for education and training, although it called for voluntary industry-labor committees.
55. Institute for Policy Innovation (2000).
56. Winik (2004) p. 7.
57. *Wall Street Journal* (2002) A16.
58. Makin (2000) p. 1.
59. Ibid.

60. Lindsey (2001).
61. Wanniski mentions the term 'productivity' only four times in his 337-page supply-side tome, and in none of these was the focus on boosting it.
62. Coolidge (1925).
63. Harding (1921). Sounding every bit like today's conservative supply-siders, Charles Sumner, in his essay 'The Forgotten Man', states 'Every bit of capital, therefore, which is given to a shiftless and inefficient member of society, who makes no return for it, is diverted from a reproductive use; but if it was put into reproductive use, it would have to be granted in wages to an efficient and productive laborer. Hence the real sufferer by that kind of benevolence which consists in an expenditure of capital to protect the good-for-nothing is the industrious laborer' (www.bluepete.com/ literature/Essays /Best/SumnerForgotten.htm).
64. Makin (2000) p. 3.
65. Over 20 million jobs were created in the 1990s after the higher rates went into effect. For a good summary of the economic literature on tax cuts and growth see Orszag (2001).
66. US Congress (2001) p. 376.
67. Pinkerton (1995) p. 262.
68. Tax incentives to stimulate these lower the cost for companies and lead them to invest more in research, new equipment, and training.
69. The supply-side growth effects are virtually nil because a most of the tax cuts are spent and not invested, and also because they boost the national debt, leading to higher interest rates which in turn reduces investment. This analysis – essentially the final nail in the coffin of supply-side economics ideology – is all the more striking since it employed a dynamic scoring method, long pressed for by Bush's economic advisors, including Douglas Holtz-Eakin, former Chief Economist of President Bush's Council of Economic Advisors, who now heads the Congressional Budget Office. (Dynamic scoring means assessing the budgetary impact of a policy proposal by considering the effects of the proposal on growth and tax revenue.)
70. Quoted in Kirk and McClellan (1967) p. 54.
71. Hayek (1944) p. 217.
72. Rogers (1999) p. 9.
73. In writing about the proper role of the state, eighteenth-century conservative Dublin-born philosopher Edmund Burke argued that 'The power of perpetuating our property in our families is one of the most valuable and interesting circumstances belonging to it [the state], and that which tends the most to the perpetuation of the society itself.'
74. US Congress (2000) p. 18.
75. Bell (1976) p. 26.
76. Lindsey (2000) p. 1.
77. Makin (2001) p. 2.
78. Cox and Alm (1999).
79. www.practicalhealthreform.org.
80. Some studies find that only a small share of capital is spent to boost productivity. In contrast, a large share is spent by companies on activities to gain market share from their competitors, like automated databases. While this spending helps individual companies, in a collective sense it is at best a zero-sum activity that transfers resources from one company to another.

8. Growth Economics for the New Economy

Over the last 100 years, as each new economy has emerged, so too has a new approach to economics and economic policy. With the decline of the mercantile economy in the 1870s and 1880s the discipline of 'classical' economics emerged and began to shape economic policy in the factory era. With the breakdown of that economy in the Great Depression, neoclassical Keynesian economics, with its focus on the business cycle and demand-side factors took hold. With the breakdown of the corporate, mass production economy and the Keynesian consensus, supply-side economics emerged as a reaction against Keynesian economics.

Unfortunately, neither Keynesian economics with its adherents on the left, nor supply-side economics with its adherents on the right, offer the kind of economic policy framework that fits the new economic realities of the twenty-first century. Both focus in an almost Newtonian way on adjusting the demand or supply of capital and labor to keep the economy in equilibrium. Both focus on macroeconomic factors, particularly prices (the former more on wages, the latter more on interest rates), rather than on the institutional factors, particularly technological change, that really drive growth.[1] In fact, neither Keynesian nor supply-side economics has much to say about the complex process by which technological innovation occurs.[2]

Ever since the economics profession became seen as the sole holder of economic truth in the 1950s, the field has not been particularly concerned about messy institutional and organizational issues. Rather, it has preferred to either dwell in the clouds of abstract macroeconomic forces or in the microeconomics forest dictated by simplistic notions of utility maximization. From the day they set foot in their first graduate economics class, most economists are trained to believe that firms and consumers are rational and will behave a certain way depending on the external forces (e.g., interest rates), akin to how atoms behave in particular environments. They take it as a given that firms can be treated as if they are rational profit-maximizing actors and therefore they can ignore the complexities of what goes on inside firms. As economics has become wedded to increasingly complex quantitative mathematical models, it has focused almost exclusively on intermediate variables related to prices – inflation rates, stock prices, interest rates, and other price indicators – believing that if only these variables can be properly adjusted the economy will perform as desired. For most economists, if it cannot be put in a computer model, it is not important. Moreover, the factor that drives all others, is capital. Indeed, *Business Week* Economics Editor Michael Mandel argues that most economists are 'capital fundamentalists' who believe that savings and investment in physical and (sometimes) human capital are the only forces driving growth.[3]

Yet others who toil in the trenches of trying to understand the real economy – organizational theorists, economic historians, planners, business administration scholars, and an emergent school of economists who question the notion of rationality – reject such a view as overly simplistic. For when one gets into the detail of understanding how workers, managers, investors, firms, industries, cultures and national economies actually operate, it becomes readily apparent that the atomistic model of rational actors responding to stimuli does not adequately describe economic reality and that the policy prescriptions built on the model does not effectively drive growth.

THE EMERGING FIELD OF GROWTH ECONOMICS

In part to overcome these limitations a handful of younger economists began to develop a new economic growth model that explicitly recognizes the importance of technological innovation.[4] This 'new growth theory' reformulates the traditional growth model so that knowledge and technology are not simply treated as something that just happens outside economic activity (exogenous). The new growth theory seeks to explicitly understand and model how technological advance occurs, seeing it as a result of intentional activities by economic actors, including government.

One of the reasons for the rise of new growth theory was the growing recognition that the old economic models created in an industrial era dominated by commodity goods production, could no longer adequately explain growth, especially in an economy powered by knowledge and innovation. New growth theory stresses the difference between 'knowledge' and other forms of capital. Previously, knowledge was assumed to be a pure public good that moved freely from person to person, and from firm to firm. New growth theory assumes that technology and knowledge vary in terms of the ability of more than one person to use it at the same time (rivalry) and the ability of someone to prevent others from using it (excludability). For example, a software program is a non-rival good that can be used by more than one person at a time, but is excludable to the extent that intellectual property protections can prevent others from using the program without the permission of the owner of the software. The fact that knowledge can often be used by others means that the economic benefits cannot be captured solely by the innovator. Thus, knowledge is neither a pure public or private good. New growth theory also recognizes the importance of the institutional context of technological innovation and that innovation is not something that comes about simply in reaction to impersonal price signals. It suggests that the development of new institutions to boost innovation will require both experimentation and evaluation of public policies as we attempt to find our way in this new era of knowledge-based economics.

As a result, growth economics is focused on a different set of questions related to how the New Economy creates wealth. Are entrepreneurs taking risks to start new ventures? Are workers getting skilled and are companies organizing production in ways that utilize those skills? Are companies investing in technological breakthroughs and is government supporting the technology base (e.g., funding research and the training of scientists and engineers)? Are regional clusters of firms and other institutions fostering innovation? Are policymakers avoiding erecting protections for companies against more innovative competitors? Are research institutions transferring knowledge to companies? And are policies supporting the ubiquitous widespread adoption of advanced information technologies and e-commerce? In short, growth economics recognizes the fundamental insight that innovation takes place in the context of institutions and as such shifts the focus of economic policy toward creating an institutional environment that supports technological change, entrepreneurial drive, and higher skills.

As such, growth economics shifts the focus from the business cycle and intermediate variables to long-term growth and productivity growth and innovation. In addition to the focus on the individual firm (microeconomics) and the overall economy (macroeconomics) it adds a focus on the industrial system (mesoeconomics). In particular, it focuses on whether entire industrial systems (e.g., health care, real estate, logistics) are structured in ways that enable them to achieve maximal productivity gains. Finally, it recognizes that a host of new policy tools can boost productivity and innovation.

Because of the importance neoclassical economics places on getting prices right there is little place in it for an activist and strategic government role to promote growth other than protecting intellectual property rights and managing the business cycle through fiscal or monetary policy. However, there is beginning to be wider acknowledgement in the economics profession that the traditional neoclassical economic framework has proved an inadequate vehicle for organizing either understanding or action about economic growth. An emerging growth economics model makes it clear that government policies can boost long-term income growth. It recognizes the conservative insight that free markets, competition, and innovation boost growth. Like supply-side economics, growth economics is also focused on the supply side, but not in the sense of reflectively giving tax breaks to companies and wealthy individuals. Rather it recognizes that it is only through the supply side of the economy – the actions taken by workers, companies, entrepreneurs, universities, and governments – that an economy's productive power is enhanced. But growth economics also recognizes the liberal insight that government investments, particularly in science, technology, education and skills, provide a foundation upon which productivity growth depends.

Before discussing the implications of growth economics for specific economic policies (Chapter 9), it is worth first discussing three main fundamentals of growth economics: a focus on the real economy, and not just prices; a focus on growth, not just the business cycle; and a focus on productivity, not just GDP growth.

Principle 1: Focus on the Real Economy – Not Prices

Growth economics focuses on the real economy – the actual output of goods and services – and not on the host of intermediary monetary variables such as consumer prices, interest rates, inflation, wage levels, and stock prices that the business press and policymakers get so caught up with to the point where the reality of the production system is lost. The typical titles of business stories in newspapers and magazines exemplify this focus on the monetary economy: 'Prices up, profits down,' 'Wages up, stock prices down,' 'Inflation grows as Fed looks to raise interest rates.' One would think these intermediate monetary variables are the most important thing in the economy. Yet, these variables are not the economy. In fact, most of the time they are only loosely related to actual economic well-being – growth in real output and productivity. Economic well-being is determined by how productive we are – how many movies, cars, haircuts, insurance policies, etc., we produce per hour of work. All the rest – wage rates, product prices, interest rates, stock prices, currency prices, and others – are just signals to guide the allocation of goods, services, workers and money; they are not ends in themselves. This might appear like simply a semantic difference, but this point is central to how policymakers understand and make economic policy. It is not as if economic thinkers did not understand this in the past. After all in *The Wealth of Nations* Adam Smith stated, 'I thought it necessary, though at the hazard of being tedious, to examine at full length this popular notion that wealth consists in money, or in gold and silver.'[5] But most economists seem to have lost this basic insight.

Consider how most people equate increasing real estate prices and stock prices with increased wealth. The business press regularly points to a rising stock market and real estate market as evidence of increased wealth. But this confuses real societal wealth with asset prices. It is not as if the recent increase in the price of real estate mostly represented an increase in the quality of houses. Most of it came from the fact that the demand for housing grew faster than supply, which drove up prices. But if a home's price goes up 10 percent because demand for housing goes up, society is no richer. After all, the home was the same before and after the price increase. In fact, if anything its use value (as opposed to monetary value) was lower because of depreciation (from normal wear and tear). Thus, while housing may be worth 10 percent more to the owners/sellers, it also cost the buyers 10 percent more. As a result, new homebuyers are able to consume less of other goods and services. The bottom line is that increased house prices make some people (current owners) wealthier, but they make others (buyers) relatively poorer. So, the first insight of growth economics is that there is a difference not only between asset prices and asset value, but also between individual wealth and societal wealth.

This applies equally to the stock market. When stock prices fell precipitously in 2001 and 2002 analysts decried how billions of dollars were wiped out in just a few months. But like housing prices, while stock prices matter to the individuals who own stocks, their rapid rise or fall it does not necessarily represent a change in societal wealth, but rather a redistribution of asset values from one group to another. Amazon.com's stock price fell 96 percent between March 1999 and October 2001 not because Amazon was actually worth less, but because there was a declining demand for its stock. The reality is that when an individual stock increases in value in a few months by 25 percent, the person who sold the stock has 25 percent more money and the person who bought it has 25 percent less than they would have had had they bought before the price increase. Unless that person can sell it for more than he paid for it, he is going to be out of pocket. This is not to say that some of the increase (or decrease) in stock prices does not reflect a real increase (or decrease) in the underlying value and profitability of companies, but those movements of prices stemming from supply and demand factors simply represent a transfer of wealth from one group to another.

This difference between asset price value and real value and between individual and societal benefits is central to the debate over the future of Social Security. While there are 3.3 workers for every retiree today, by 2030 there will be just two workers. As a result, starting in the year 2016, the Social Security system will pay out more in benefits than it collects in payroll taxes.[6] By 2030 it will have exhausted its trust fund surplus. Absent much more rapid growth, at some point taxes will have to be raised or benefits cut.

Conservatives have leaped on this coming demographic train wreck to push Social Security privatization that would let people put their money in the stock market instead of in the Social Security trust fund.[7] After all, they argue, over the long term the stock market has outperformed other investments, so why not let people tap into this source of wealth. Even though most liberals oppose using Social Security funds to create personal private retirement accounts, some embrace the same logic and embrace a version of privatization that would have the government invest the trust fund assets in equity markets.

It is true that if payroll taxes were invested in the market stock, equity prices would rise as the demand increases. However, as soon as baby boomers begin to retire and start selling their stocks to pay their mortgages, medical bills, and other expenses stock prices would begin to fall as the number of sellers exceeds buyers. As this happens the real return to the stocks will fall and the supposed miracle will have evaporated.

A focus on the real economy, as opposed the monetary economy, makes it clear that we should expect this. People do not consume stocks any more than they consume money. They use stocks and money as claims to purchase real goods and services, and driving up the demand for stocks does little to change the economy's output of goods and services. Conservatives will argue that more investment in the stock market will drive growth. The reality is that shifting money from bonds while raising government debt will simply increase rates, offsetting any potential growth effects.

There may in fact be legitimate reasons to shift more control of Social Security to workers in order to make more Americans into owners. However, we should be under no illusion that doing so will make any difference to the coming retirement security crisis, particularly if it is done by boosting the national debt. Shifting Social Security payments to the stock market confuses real wealth that society can draw upon with asset prices that reflect supply and demand factors.

Conservatives are not the only ones who fail to focus on the real economy. Liberals who argue that we should raise Social Security taxes to boost trust fund revenues employ the same faulty logic. Both proposals have one thing in common – they try to save money now to solve a problem that will not become a crisis for at least another decade. The reality is that unless we lend money to other countries that will then pay us back in real goods and services later on, it is not possible for a country to save for the future. How can this be? After all, individuals save for the future. The key is to realize that an individual's savings are not consumed in the future, they are consumed in the present. When someone borrows money to buy a car they are consuming more in the present than they are producing, but they agree to consume less than they produce in later years as they pay off the loan. The person who saves the money and lends it to the car buyer is producing more in the present than they are consuming and as they get paid off in later years, they will consume more than they produce. Just as savings and consumption cancel each other out in the case of the car loan, they do so at the national level as the aggregate savings of a country is generally not saved for the future, but is consumed in the same year in the form of investments. As economist Robert Eisner stated:

> We can take bread out of one mouth today and give it to another today. We cannot save bread to give it to ourselves or our children or grandchildren, 50 years from now. The best we can do to make such a transfer is to build an oven that we hope will still be functioning 50 years from now, or train a new baker who will still be plying his trade then.[8]

Another way to understand this is to consider the source of today's retirees' Social Security incomes. The cars, food, clothes, medical care, and vacations they consume were not produced when they were working. Rather, they are produced today by American workers who, because of the Social Security taxes they pay, consume 15.3 percent fewer cars, food, clothes, medical care, and vacations than they would otherwise. There is nothing wrong with this real-time transfer of consumption – children have always supported their retired parents. What it does mean, however, is that in 2029 we will have to provide retirees with actual goods and services produced in 2029, not with goods and services saved in 2004. The only other ways the retirees in 2029 can consume goods and services that were not actually produced in 2029 is to either: store the goods in an underground mine for 25 years when they would then be brought to the surface; or forgo some consumption now and give it to foreigners (e.g., run a current account surplus) and then collect it later in the form of goods and services. However, given that the United States is already a net foreign debtor and getting more so every year as our annual trade deficit exceeds a record $500 billion dollars, this path is not open to us. In fact, as we eventually will have to run a trade surplus (in other words, produce more than we consume) to pay off foreign debtors, future wage earners will be faced with a double whammy – paying higher Social Security (and Medicare) taxes and paying more for imports because of a lower value of the dollar.

So there are really only two viable ways in the present to prepare for the impending retirement bubble of the baby boom, and neither have much to do with Social Security or the stock market. The first is for the federal government to pay off the national debt which would let it better afford to pay Social Security benefits 20 years from now. In fiscal year 2003 the federal government owed $3.9 trillion to bond holders around the world. As a result, they paid out $318 billion in interest, accounting for 7 percent of federal government outlays.[9] Interest and Social Security payments account for 36.5 percent of the budget. By 2030, Social Security is estimated to account for 34 percent of outlays. If the federal debt was paid off before that, interest payments would fall to zero. The combined share of interest payments (0 percent) and Social Security payments (34 percent) in 2030 would only be 5 percentage points higher than today.

In short, paying off the national debt will allow the United States to use money that is now going to pay off bond holders to pay for Social Security recipients 30 years from now. In essence, this was what President Clinton proposed when he said he wanted to 'save Social Security first' by paying off the national debt. This is why the huge tax cuts pushed through by the Bush administration are so irresponsible, for when the baby boomers begin to retire en masse, money has to be found, and in part will come from raising the taxes of today's children when they get to be workers. Adults today are enjoying the bounty of the Bush tax cuts and asking their children to pay it back when they get older. It is important to note that in addition to paying off the debt, steps can and should be taken to limit retiree's future Social Security benefits, particularly by linking the increase in future retirees' benefits to the rate of inflation, as opposed to the rate of wage increases.

The other major step that can be taken today is to relentlessly focus on boosting productivity so that in 2029 workers produce enough to meet their own consumption needs and the consumption of the increased number of retirees. Even though relatively fewer workers will support more retirees if they produce much more they could maintain or even increase their after-tax income while enabling retiree Social Security payments to stay constant. That is a critical reason why embracing growth economics is key, as it is focused on boosting productivity.

Finally, some will argue that since the number of retirees is going up, why not increase the number of workers, ideally through immigration or financial incentives for people to have children.[10] This solution is prescribed particularly for Europe where fertility rates are especially low. While this seems to make sense, in fact, it is a 'ponzi scheme.' Continuing to get bigger by adding more people simply postpones the day of reckoning. At some point new workers will need to be supported when they retire and they in turn will need an even bigger pool of workers to support them, and the cycle will have to begin all over again. Moreover, there are significant downsides to increasing population, such as higher housing prices, overcrowding, traffic congestion, pollution, and global resource depletion. As a result, it is better to bite the bullet now and focus on boosting productivity, paying off the debt and restraining the costs of entitlements.

Asset prices are just one area where the conventional economic view makes the mistake of conflating the micro with the macro. Another concerns the labor market. For example, because the conventional economic view encourages a focus on the microeconomic, many economists and policymakers warn of an impending labor shortage. In 2001 Elaine Chao, President Bush's Secretary of Labor, warned that, 'Our new challenge is a scarcity in the one fundamental resource that drives every economy in the world: the workforce ... If the coming worker shortage in the next several years is not addressed, the federal budget, the economy, and working taxpayers will pay a huge price.'[11] *Business Week* concurs, stating, 'another big freight train is coming down the track in the US economy. That's the tremendous long-term shortage of labor we are facing.'[12] The same argument has been used to argue that our economy needs the offshoring of jobs to low wage nations to cope with an impending labor shortage.

When looked at from a growth economics perspective it is clear that a worker shortage is not possible, since by definition the output of workers must equal their consumption. It is possible to have a worker surplus, which is what happens when the unemployment rate rises above its frictional rate. But the converse is not possible as there can be no such thing as a negative unemployment rate. That would mean that part of the productive capacity of the economy is being used more than once, which is impossible. In other words, the demand for labor can never exceed the supply of labor because labor demand is determined by what people consume and that in turn is determined by the amount of goods and services the workforce produces. In short, a society cannot consume more than it produces, at least over the moderate to long term.[13] But those who believe in labor shortages believe that if companies had more workers they would produce more. But that is only true because the added workers become added consumers.

This view of labor shortages leads some conservative policymakers to argue that tight labor markets produce all sorts of undesirable outcomes, like higher inflation and lower profits. For example, as the economy boomed in 2000 and the unemployment rate declined to a 30-year low, Federal Reserve Chairman Alan Greenspan warned that one of the only ways to avoid wage-driven inflation would be to increase immigration of workers. Greenspan feared that a shortage of workers would lead companies to bid up wages to attract scarce workers. Therefore, like any case of demand outstripping supply, economists counseled policymakers to simply increase supply (in this case through more immigration) and, like magic, as supply increases relative to demand upward wage and price pressures are abated. Increasing immigration by another 500 000 people a year might alleviate labor shortages in the short term while the newly arrived workers look for work, but once they find jobs they are transformed from being just workers (who happen to be unemployed) to workers and consumers who buy goods and services equal to their wages. Once this happens, and companies have to meet the demand for this new consumption, the demand for workers increases by an equal amount. Thus, the old equilibrium (to the extent that the New Economy is ever in equilibrium) is regained and 'labor shortages' again appear.

Even though employers may not like full employment since they have to pay more to attract workers, this is simply a transfer of income from shareholders to workers. Moreover, because tight labor markets mean more people are working, they are good for the entire economy. If unemployment drops from 5 percent to 4 percent, this means that an additional 1.3 million people are producing goods and services, adding approximately $10 billion to annual output.[14]

Tight labor markets have another key benefit. They induce companies to make investments to boost productivity. Neoclassical economists are right to an extent; when one factor of supply is scarce companies will substitute others for it. Low unemployment makes it hard for companies to find workers and leads them to boost wages (although many economists report this as if they were reporting statistics showing that AIDs increased), which in turn makes it more profitable to invest in labor-saving equipment, leading to increased productivity. Low unemployment also leads companies to spend more on training since they have to take on some of the social functions that in a weak labor market they could let other employers or the government do. From the perspective of the individual employer it may mean added costs, but from the perspective of the overall economy the workforce is more skilled and more productive.

The fallacy of looking at the labor market from the perspective of the individual firm or individual worker as opposed to the economy as a whole, leads some on the left to mistakenly focus on boosting internal company career ladders as the key to economic opportunity for low-skilled workers. Moving up a career ladder makes sense as a way for an individual to gain opportunity, but the gains of a particular individual do not necessarily translate into gains for the economy. The reason is that in the short term the occupational mix of the economy is relatively stable: there are so many managers, so many carpenters, so many janitors, etc. For example, in 2000 there were 14 million managers while there were 4 million retail sales clerks. Training sales clerks to become managers may help individual sales clerks get better jobs, but at least in the short run there will still be the same number of sales clerks and managers and the training programs will have simply re-sorted people within a fixed occupational distribution.

There is one final way in which conventional economic thinking conflates individual and societal welfare. In competition and antitrust policy, the predominant focus has been on limiting market power in the belief that it enables companies to charge higher prices than they would in a more competitive marketplace. But consider cases where mergers result in both higher levels of efficiency and in more market power. Society as a whole is better off because the new company is more efficient, but consumers may be worse off because the new company charges higher prices. Antitrust has tended to give preference to short-term consumer welfare even when it means lower overall productivity. A case in point is the cellular telephone industry. In their zeal to promote competition, in the 1990s the Federal Communications Commission (FCC) allowed up to six cellular spectrum licenses to be issued in each market. As expected, the result was intense competition among providers, but also inefficient investment patterns with companies making duplicative investments not needed in a more rational marketplace. The FCC could have obtained enough competition with much less investment had they issued only five or even four licenses. In short, like prices, competition is a means to an end, not an end in itself.

Principle 2: Focus on Growth, Not Just the Business Cycle

Keynesian policy embodied the goal of eliminating deviations from the natural trend economic growth rate, not the goal of raising the growth trend rate. Listening to economic pundits or reading the business section of newspapers makes it abundantly clear that we still remain caught in the grips of this Depression-era focus on the business cycle. Every utterance of Alan Greenspan is pored over the way Greeks analysed the prophecy of the oracle of Delphi. Every economic blip up is seen as news that economy is back on the right track, while every economic blip down is cause for worry that the economy is heading south. The conceptual framework used by most economic policymakers continues to reflect this notion of fine-tuning the motor of the economy so it goes at the right speed. Indeed the common language such as 'the economy is overheating' or 'there are emerging wage pressures' reflects a mechanistic conception of an economy that must be managed the way a fireman manages the boiler on a train so as neither to blow it up or lose steam. This obsessive preoccupation with the business cycle and the continuing use of analogies to machines are vestiges of old economy thinking. In an economy that is more self-adaptive, the most important challenge is not keeping the boiler at the right pressure, but finding ways to make the boiler more powerful, or to continue the analogy, to invent an electrically powered engine. Growth economics does not judge the growth of the economy by its short-term performance, but rather by its performance over decades.

One indication of the grip the business cycle paradigm has on policymakers and economic analysts is seen in how observers react to signs of an impending economic slowdown. For example, before the 2001 recession Morgan Stanley economist Stephen Roach actually advocated a recession to provide the tough medicine needed to purge the economy of so-called excesses.[15] What are these excesses? Roach complained that 'Americans are not saving enough.' He argued correctly that the expansion of consumption (4.4 percent annually since 1995) in excess of disposable personal income (3.3 percent) could not continue (although it appears that some of this was due to statistical anomalies in how the Department of Commerce measures the economy). Sounding like Andrew Mellon in the 1930s when he blamed shiftless workers for the contributing to the Depression, Roach argues that 'downturns prompt consumers to become more prudent, encouraging them to turn away from speculative investing in the stock market and to start saving sensibly, by putting aside a portion of their wage.' But there is no reason why this 'excess' would not end on its own (consumers will simply not go farther into debt, and as evidenced by the decline in the stock market, will shift their investments to other vehicles like savings accounts), nor why a recession would reverse this. In fact, the recession led to a decline in savings as the unemployed and underemployed drew down savings and ran up debt in order to meet expenses.

Roach's second so-called excess was the stock market bubble. But since this is the flip side of 'excess consumption' – the market goes up because people are investing, not spending – it is not clear why this was a problem. Besides the bubble burst on its own, as one would expect if markets are allowed to work. This leads to his third excess, too much investment in IT equipment by companies. Yet, it is hard to argue that companies spent too much on IT. Sure, capital investment rates were high, particularly as companies spent to respond to the Y2K problem, but it was the high levels of capital investment that drove the higher productivity rates of the late 1990s. Moreover, Roach overlooks the natural contradiction in his argument. How can there be too little saving (e.g., too much consumption) and too much investment at the same time? More to the point, since the capital-to-GDP ratio is at a 20-year low, in spite of the high rate of capital investment, this suggests that capital investment rates are not high enough. The irony of Roach's argument is that rather than focus on the real goal of economic policy, increasing production and productivity, Roach actually advocates having people produce less!

While some incorrectly claimed during the boom years of the late 1990s that the New Economy had led to an outright repeal of the business cycle, there is considerable evidence that the New Economy has lessened its severity. In the old economy recessions were a serious and relatively frequent matter. There were 19 business cycles in the twentieth century, or one every five years. According to Michael Cox at the Dallas Federal Reserve Bank, over the 100 years from 1853 to 1953 the economy was in recession 40 percent of the time. In the mass production, corporate economy things were better, but still there was shrinkage in 21 percent of calendar quarters. No wonder keeping the economy out of recession preoccupied everyone's attention. However, from 1983 to 2003 the economy shrank in only 7 percent of quarters.

One reflection of this new stability is the fact that quarter-to-quarter GDP volatility is down significantly since the mid-1980s. In the three decades preceding 1983, approximately 30 percent of quarterly GDP growth rates were in excess of 1.5 percent while 22 percent were negative. In comparison, the numbers after 1993 were 78 and 10 percent. In short, large movements in GDP are less likely to occur today than in the old economy.[16]

Economists attribute the reduced cyclicality to several causes, including a decline in the change in inventory investments and a greater role of the service sector in the economy. A leading cause of recessions in the old economy was the build-up of inventory, particularly in durable goods industries like autos, steel, and appliances. Because of the inflexibility of production systems, coupled with the difficulty in assuring fast replacement of inventories, companies had a propensity to build up high levels of inventory. When this happened and companies decided to cut production to sell off some inventory, they made fewer products and bought less from suppliers, leading workers to be laid off, which dampened consumer demand, which in turn cut sales even more. This in turn led to more layoffs and the downward cycle would continue until the whole process had worked its way out over the course of a year or two.

Large inventory cycles were really just a reflection of an economy that had difficulty adapting to change. Like an oil tanker that takes 2 miles to change course, the old economy was slow to adapt to changes. However, there is evidence that the New Economy has led to several structural changes that increase the economy's ability to respond to change. In particular, there has been a significant reduction in volatility of inventory investment, particularly in durable goods, and this factor in turn explains a significant share of the overall reduction in GDP volatility. For example, the production of durable goods has become less volatile quarter-to-quarter. In other words the production of durable goods more closely tracks economic demand and is less likely to jerk from feast or famine. One big factor for this is the rise of just-in-time (JIT) inventory systems. Just-in-time involves delivering parts and inputs to the assembly factory much closer to the time that the product is actually being made, instead of shipping large quantities of the product to the factory and storing it on site as a buffer. Because of new communication and transportation technologies the production system operates more in real time. If the old economy was like a US household that shopped every two weeks at a shopping mall and stored food in a large freezer and refrigerator, the New Economy is more like a Paris household where the homemaker goes out every day to buy what she needs for that night's dinner. As a result of JIT, the average production lead-time for supplies has declined from 72 days during the 1961 to 1983 period, to 49 days from 1984 to 1998 period. In other words, in the earlier period, on average, parts (like a car radiator) would be made 72 days before they were actually used in the product (assembled into the car). The inventory-to-sales ratio has been declining since the early 1990s and in 1999 was at its lowest rate since it was first calculated in 1967. The ratio of non-farm inventories to sales fell from about 2.35 percent in 1989 to 1.75 percent in 2002.[17]

Just-in-time is not simply something that companies decided to do, it was enabled by the new production technology, including electronic data interchange (a predecessor to the Internet) that lets companies place orders electronically, overnight air delivery that lets companies get parts rapidly in a crisis, and by more flexible production systems that let companies more easily shift from producing one kind of part to another (for example, shifting from producing tires for an SUV to producing tires for a mid-sized compact). Interestingly, JIT and flexible production systems were first introduced in Japan during the 1970s and they saw a structural break in output volatility in the mid-1970s, earlier than the United States.

The growth in services has been another factor contributing to the stability of the economy. While goods production has gotten more flexible, services production has been inherently more flexible and because most services are produced on demand (e.g., haircuts, bank services, heart surgery), inventory build-up is not an issue.

While the production system is now much more flexible, so too is the labor market. Companies now more rapidly lay off workers in response to any reduction in demand for their products or services. For example, during the boom years of the 1990s, the rate of layoffs exceeded the rate in the 1970s. Moreover, the increased share of the workforce employed as temporary workers and contract workers gives companies more flexibility to quickly adapt. For example, in the slowdown in 2001 30 percent of layoffs were of temporary workers, even though they made up only 2.2 percent of total payrolls.[18] It might seem that a more flexible labor market might make recessions worse, but because companies adapt much more quickly workers can be rapidly redeployed to other firms and sectors where demand is growing.

These changes do not mean the end of the business cycle or that policymakers should abandon efforts to moderate the downward swings of the cycle. In particular, the threat of terrorist attacks do appear to bring a new instability to the economy, as the 9-11 attacks on New York and Washington so clearly demonstrated. However, other changes in the economy suggest that it is time to place more focus on boosting the long-term growth of the economy. Schumpeter got it right when he counseled us to 'judge the performance of an economy not at a given point in time, but over time, as it unfolds through decades or centuries.'[19] Fifty years later some conventional economists are coming around to his way of thinking. The Cleveland Federal Reserve Bank echoes Schumpeter, stating 'an effective policy is one that aims to promote long run national growth, not one that manages movements around a statistical growth trend.'[20] This is economist-speak for focus on long-term growth, not short-term movements of the business cycle.

Finally, what about inflation? Even if recessions are not as much of a problem, economic hard-liners would still argue that the Federal Reserve Board would occasionally have to make preemptive strikes to induce recessions to purge the economy from occasional excesses, particularly inflationary pressures. But there is general agreement that in the new global economy, with increased competition and technology, the risk of inflation is reduced. In the old economy with limited global competition, oligopolies in many industries, and unions that often covered entire industries, it was easy for companies to pass along wage and other cost increases in the form of higher prices. But in an economy with robust global competition, more demanding and informed consumers with access to alternative sales channels, and reduced union bargaining power, companies have more difficulty in passing along price increases, with the result that there is less upward pressure on prices. The New Economy also lets factories operate efficiently at lower capacity utilization rates that in turn let them face production pressures with reduced risks of bottlenecks and inflation.[21] Couple all this with the fact that new technology has enabled companies to increase productivity at a faster rate so they can offset labor and other input cost increases, and it is clear that the risk of inflation is much less than it once was.

As a result of these changes the Federal Reserve should maintain its policy of the last decade of being less trigger-happy about inducing slowdowns to stem inflationary pressures. One of the implications of this is that economic policymakers need to jettison the anachronistic notion of NAIRU (non accelerating-inflation-rate of unemployment – a term economists coined to refer to the rate of unemployment which can go no lower without triggering significant inflation). Growth economics recognizes that the economy can grow much faster without inflation as long as productivity grows as fast. Yet until 1999 most economists postulated that the economy cannot grow faster than 2 to 2.5 percent per year without sparking inflation. But if the economy grew 10 percent in one year it is not inflationary if productivity also grew 10 percent. It is only when growth gets ahead of productivity and the economy is already at full employment (which appears to be around 4 to 4.5 percent) that inflationary pressures might be reignited.

Principle 3: Focus on Productivity, Not GDP Growth

Economists and the economic press generally see changes in gross domestic product (GDP) as the be all and end all of the economy. However, changes in GDP are made up of two components, productivity and hours worked. We could grow the economy through more hours worked if we reduced vacation time, increased overtime, boosted fertility rates and expanded immigration. In fact, these are reasons why per-capita income is higher in the US than in Europe where they work less. However, such a strategy comes at cost of requiring people to work more. In contrast if most of the gain in GDP comes from increases in productivity it means that the economy is producing more per hour of work. Consider an economy where productivity grows 1 percent yet GDP grows 4 percent because immigration and population growth led to a larger labor force. If GDP growth is the main measure of success it would appear that this scenario is better than one where GDP grew only 3 percent, but productivity grew 2 percent. However, the average American would see their incomes go up twice as fast in the latter economy.

In short, the real determinant of a nation's well-being is the extent to which the economy is becoming more productive and efficient year in and year out. Higher productivity growth goes a long way in solving pressing societal problems including Social Security shortfalls, poverty, the national debt, and makes it easier to expand spending in key areas (e.g., transportation, environmental protection, health coverage). Most importantly, as discussed in Chapter 10, if we sustain or even increase productivity growth, within a decade we can expect workers to have not only higher incomes, but also reduced work hours and an increase in the time they can spend with their families and on leisure. As a result, growth economics puts the goal of getting richer (e.g. boosting productivity) at the center, not getting bigger (working more or having more workers), and judges policies on the basis of whether they increase standards of living. In fact, we should set a national goal of doubling living standards in 30 years and towards that end should embrace tax, trade, investment and regulatory policies that advance that goal and reject policies that do not.

As a result, it is time for growth economics to become the dominant organizing framework for US economic policy. The most important economic policy task is to articulate a new progressive economic policy framework that will encourage a new era of higher growth, while at the same time promoting and enabling a broad-based prosperity that produces the widest possible winners' circle. We need to embrace a set of policies grounded in a fundamental reality: faster growth in incomes for American workers stems from expanding the base of knowledge and encouraging innovation. The next chapter will examine how to do that.

NOTES

1. Economist Robert Solow (1957) found that only 19 percent of long-run change in labor productivity was due to increased capital intensity, the remainder was due to what he called 'technical change.' Based on a review of most growth accounting models, Boskin and Lau (1992) estimated that half of economic growth came from technical progress. Jones (2002) comes up with a similar estimate for the period of 1950 to 1993, with an additional 30 percent stemming from higher levels of education.
2. Mandel (2004) documents this, illustrating that most economics classics completely overlook technology. For example, the term does not appear in the index of Milton Friedman's 1979 bestseller, *Free to Choose*.
3. Mandel (2004) p. 47.
4. Arthur (1993), Romer (1990), and Hall and Jones (1999).
5. Smith (1776), Book IV, Section 32.
6. www.ssa.gov/OACT/TRSUM/trsummary.html.
7. For example, the conservative Heritage Foundation claims that if an average 30-year-old could invest their Social Security taxes in a mutual fund instead of the Social Security fund, by the time they retire they would have $500 000 more than if they kept paying social security taxes.
8. Eisner (1994) p. 125.
9. www.publicdebt.treas.gov/opd/opdint.htm.
10. Longman (2004).
11. www.dol.gov/sec/media/speeches/worldeconremark.htm.
12. *Business Week*, 27 August 2001, p. 116.
13. Foreign trade is the exception to this rule, as the United States consumes more than it produces because it runs a trade deficit. But this stems not from the lack of workers but in part from the value of the dollar being too high. When it comes down, Americans will buy fewer foreign goods and services, and foreigners will buy more American goods and services.
14. As the experience of the 1990s showed, it is possible to have full employment and low inflation. It is precisely when productivity is growing rapidly and competition (from globalization, deregulation, and flexible labor markets) is high, that the

economy can take advantage of the talents of all its workers with little risk of inflation.

15. Roach (2001).
16. Kim and Nelson (1999).
17. *Business Week*, 29 July 2002.
18. Cooper and Madigan (2001) p. 27.
19. Schumpeter (1942) p. 83.
20. Cleveland Federal Reserve Bank (1999) p. 17.
21. Bansak, Morin and Starr (2004).

9. Implementing Growth Economics

As we shift from the mass production, corporate managerial economy to a knowledge-based entrepreneurial economy, economic policy must also shift from its old economy concern of stimulating consumer demand while restraining the market power of oligopolies to the new economy concern of boosting innovation and productivity. In *The Wealth of Nations* Adam Smith argued that there were three major inputs to the production process: land, labor, and capital. In the New Economy a fourth component that significantly outweighs the other three, knowledge, needs to be added. To effectively spur growth in the new knowledge economy government must go beyond its traditional roles of spurring consumption Keynesian style or simply cutting taxes on capital supply-side style.

In the new knowledge economy, knowledgeable people, including creative entrepreneurs, skilled shop-floor workers, cutting-edge researchers, innovative companies, and digital-savy 'prosumers' are the drivers of growth. While knowledge and innovation have always been important, they are particularly critical now. As a result, we need an economic framework that supports the new techno-economic system and growth economics is it.

Growth economics is based on what economists have learned over the past 15 years on what drives growth and the role of government in that process.[1] The keys to growth are in some ways profoundly simple. As Nobel Prize winning economist Douglass North summed it up, 'We must create incentives for people to invest in more efficient technology, increase their skills, and organize efficient markets.'[2] As Paul Romer, Stanford University economist and a leader in the field of growth economics, states, the conservative save-more and liberal spend-more

policy prescriptions miss the crux of the matter. Neither adjustments to monetary and fiscal policy, nor increases in the rate of savings and capital accumulation can by themselves generate persistent increases in standards of living ... the most important job for economic policy is to create an institutional environment that supports technological change.[3]

Leading economists now acknowledge that without change we cannot grow, that increases in knowledge and competition drive growth and change, and that government has a key role to play in that process. In short, they are saying that the best macroeconomic policy is microeconomic policy – support for research, innovation, skill building, and digital transformation, all within an environment of competitive markets.

Achieving the full promise of the New Economy requires not just private sector innovation and entrepreneurial drive, but also concerted and strategic public policies to overcome key challenges. At a time when technological innovation is central to boosting productivity, the federal government's investment in research other than the life sciences has been declining. At a time when learning and skill acquisition are keys not only to ensuring that American companies have the skilled workers they need to be productive, but also that American workers have the skills they need to navigate and prosper in the New Economy, there are troubling signs that America's workforce is not prepared for the knowledge economy. At a time when the IT revolution holds the potential to transform entire industries there are signs that the digital revolution is proceeding haltingly.

As a result, if we are to continue to boost productivity, there are four main thrusts for policy: (1) stimulate technological innovation and R&D; (2) foster the transformation to a digital economy; (3) boost education and skills; and (4) promote innovation and entrepreneurship. All this should be done in the context of maintaining fiscal discipline.

STIMULATE TECHNOLOGICAL INNOVATION

Research and development, which yield new products and production processes and add to the knowledge base of industry and the marketplace as a whole, are key drivers of growth in the New Economy. As a result, government needs to develop a twenty-first century growth initiative in which the development of technology, and the associated mechanisms to utilize technology, play a central role.

There are an array of reasons why the marketplace alone does not generate a sufficient level of investment in research. The concept of spillovers and the differences between the private and social rates of return from investment in research may be the most important factor. Since more than one firm can use knowledge, firms can often utilize the results of other firms' research to improve their own products and processes at a fraction of the cost of the original research. For example, the Xerox Corporation invested to develop the windows-icons-mouse paradigm of computing, but Apple and Microsoft made the money from this innovation. When a company comes out with a significant breakthrough product, other companies can reverse engineer it and gain at least some of the knowledge that went into it. Companies try to protect their intellectual property through patents, but not all industries take out patents, and even patents do not protect all the knowledge that went into a product.

This is one reason why studies have found that the social rates of return to R&D are at least twice the estimated private returns.[4] One study found that the average social rate of return from R&D was 123 percent.[5] The overall social return from investment in information technology R&D generally is over 80 percent.[6] When companies do basic research the spillovers are even greater, as high as 150 percent.[7] This makes sense, not only because companies have a hard time keeping secret basic research into how something works, but because such research is so often a building block for much else. Thus when scientists at Bell Labs invented the transistor in the early 1950s, within weeks they published the results in scientific journals and invited researchers in from other companies to examine and learn from their work. Soon scores of companies were using the knowledge to produce and use transistors. Their efforts were the seeds underlying today's IT revolution.

Moreover, while companies like Bell Labs might have readily shared research results in an era when competition and the drive to innovate were so much less, they are much less likely to share knowledge in the New Economy or for that matter, even conduct basic research. Bell Labs could afford to do this because its parent company, AT&T, was a regulated monopoly that was allowed to fold a 'research tax' into every phone call. Nowadays, market awareness is central to the new Bell Labs. Since the early 1990s about half of the laboratories' researchers have worked with business unit colleagues on specific joint projects and as a result are less likely to conduct basic research. Why should a company invest in basic laboratory research and share it with competitors when its stockholders are demanding high profits in the next quarter and when some of the knowledge is likely to flow to competitors?

It is even harder to justify research when the results are uncertain. Many kinds of technological innovations are extremely uncertain, and not just because the technology itself is uncertain. By its very nature conducting research is uncertain. As the pharmaceutical industry knows so well, the results firms hope for may or may not come about. In many cases, the risk is too great, even if the return might justify it. For example, the first company to develop commercial high temperature superconductors would make billions, but the risk of the research efforts failing are so high that few companies are investing in it. Moreover, it is often extremely difficult for companies to predict exactly what the uses and size of the market will be for innovations. Clearly, this was the problem facing Thomas Watson, the chairman of IBM, when in 1943 he predicted that 'I think there is a world market for maybe five computers' or when Ken Olson, founder of Digital Equipment Corp., stated in 1977 that, 'there is no reason anyone would want a computer in their home.'[8]

Benefits from the results are often too far in the future to pass threshold investment criteria.[9] Some research, such as research into solid-state lighting, is unlikely to show payoffs for many years, making it more difficult for companies to fund it. In some cases, like the research needed to develop vaccines for biological weapons of mass destruction, the market is too small for a firm to make a profit from it. In the New Economy there is an additional kind of uncertainty, and that comes from the fact that new technologies increasingly depend on other innovations for their success. For example, if Ford or Toyota want to invest in electric motor technology to develop the next generation of clean cars, the success of their research depends not just on the quality (and luck) of their own efforts, but on a set of variables that may be completely beyond their control. In this case electric motors are worthless without much better battery technology, and it is not clear how successful research in this area will be. This kind of system-dependent uncertainty blocks decision making and shifts investment to short-term R&D projects.

Put this all together and it is not surprising that firms are becoming more reluctant to put resources into basic technological research that is long run, high risk, or both, even though this research could provide significant returns to society. In fact, all these factors combine to lead companies to underinvest in research. Charles Jones found that decentralized, market economies typically underinvest in R&D relative to what is economically optimal.[10] The fact that some economists estimate a 7 percent private return and 30 percent for the social rate of return on R&D, suggests that the optimal level of R&D investment in the US economy is between two to four times larger than the total current level of private investment.[11] This underinvestment means that economic growth will be less than otherwise and the new innovations that will improve our lives will come about more slowly.

As a result, there is an important role for government to support research. Unfortunately, as a share of GDP, government support for non-defense R&D has been steadily dropping, from about 1 percent of gross domestic product in the 1960s to less than 0.7 percent today. As a share of the federal budget, non-defense R&D fell from 5.7 percent in 1965 to 2.7 percent in 2001.[12] As a result, compound annual growth in R&D (public and private) has fallen from around 4.38 percent from 1975 to 1990 to just 3.43 percent from 1991 to 1999. If it were not for the increase in federal funding for biomedical research the decline in the growth rate would have been even greater. Moreover, US government investment in civilian R&D relative to the size of the economy is lower than that of Germany and Japan, and governments in both countries have plans to increase their R&D expenditures. Research and development as a share of GDP is now higher in South Korea and Finland. Moreover, the US ratio has fallen since 1985, while the ratio in Sweden, Japan, Canada, and Australia has risen.

There are a number of reasons for this decline. Budget deficits of the past two decades meant that deficit reduction took priority over research funding expansion. Moreover, once the Republicans took over Congress in 1994, funding cuts took on an ideological nature. These supply-side Republicans took a decidedly narrow view of the federal government's role in research, arguing that it should be limited only to basic research and government mission-oriented research. In other words, government should support research into astrophysics and developing smart bombs, but not much in between.

While conservatives like to point to failed government programs, it is not as if federal research has not shown results. After all, the most important technological innovation of the last 40 years, the Internet, was developed almost exclusively with funding from the Defense Department and later the National Science Foundation. It is hard to imagine a corporation making these investments. The chief scientist would approach the company's CEO and say that he wants hundreds of millions of dollars to develop a completely new way to conduct computer communication and networking for which there is no known commercial application. Moreover, it is by no means certain that they could develop what is needed to make it work. And if it were to be successful most of the benefits would flow to other companies and other industries. Of course, the scientist would be shown the door. Luckily, the program managers of the DOD's Defense Advanced Research Projects Agency (DARPA) were not held to the same standard. As Bob Kahn, one of the pioneers of the Internet in the 1960s stated, 'Without government R&D there would be no Internet today.'[13] Of course it was private entrepreneurs who took the Internet and ran with it, developing thousands of companies and helping to create the economic boom of the 1990s. But the key point is that without the government, the most important technological development of the New Economy would not be here, at least not for another decade or two.

Throughout history the government has played a key role in boosting innovations. The development of interchangeable parts manufacturing has its roots in Eli Whitney's work at the Springfield Armory to develop rifles for the Army. The telegraph got a major boost when Samuel Morse received a government grant to build a 40-mile long telegraph line between Washington and Baltimore in 1843. Herman Hollerith, a former employee of the Census Bureau, developed an automated counting machine using punch cards for the 1890 census, which saved the government $5 million. He later sold his company to a conglomerate that became IBM. The Wright Brothers owed the continued development of the airplane to Department of Navy contracts. Radar was developed with British government funding in World War II. A defense-sponsored microwave research program at Columbia University uncovered the basic concepts the led to the laser. Raytheon developed the microwave oven while doing work on a military radar contract. Electronic data interchange (EDI) was developed by the Air Force to organize the 1948 Berlin airlift. Laser scanning used in stores originally came from the National Aeronautics and Space Administration (NASA). Database technology owes its start to government funding. In fact, the leading database company, Oracle, grew out of a Central Intelligence Agency-funded database software project in the 1970s. The World Wide Web was developed by Tim Berners Lee at CERN, a European government-funded research institute. The web company Akami was developed by MIT mathematics professors who were funded by federal research dollars. Even Google, the popular search engine company, owes its origins to knowledge that was developed with federal funds.[14] More than half the papers cited in computing patent applications between 1993 and 1994 acknowledged government funding.[15] Seventy percent of US biotech patent citations were to papers originating solely at public science institutions.[16] In other words, contrary to what conservative skeptics say, government support of research has been a highly successful undertaking. Studies of academic research consistently show a significant rate of return (RoR). Mansfield found a 28 percent RoR from federally-funded academic research.[17] Studies of publicly-funded agricultural research show a consistent rate of return of around 40 percent.[18] A study of a sample of 14 research projects funded by the Department of Commerce's National Institute of Standards and Technology showed a median RoR of 144 percent.[19] Economists Leyden and Link conclude that government funding complements private R&D and has the effect of spurring additional private funding.[20] Other researchers find a strong link between academic research and patents and corporate technological innovation.[21]

As the old economy emerged in the 1940s, Congress responded by creating the National Science Foundation. However, as Newt Gingrich, former Republican Speaker of the House, noted:

> The United States has been operating under a model developed by Vannevar Bush (a noted MIT electrical engineer) in his 1945 report to the President entitled Science: the Endless Frontier ... With the collapse of the Soviet Union, and the de facto end of the Cold War, the Vannevar Bush approach is no longer valid.[22]

There is widespread agreement among science policy experts that Bush's linear model of research leading ultimately to development is not only overly simplistic, but often – as is the case when development informs research – backward. Moreover, most agree that drawing a bright line between basic and applied research no longer makes sense. Finally, there is increasing agreement that it is better to allocate research funds 'by choice, not chance' so that strategy and public goals guide funding priorities, not solely requests from the research community. As one noted science historian observed, 'The "endless frontier" metaphor, along with its implied research and development paradigm, has reached the limits of its influence and the end of its effectiveness.'[23]

As a result, it is time for a new approach to innovation policy. To start with Congress should establish a National Innovation Corporation (NIC) that would manage a range of innovation investment initiatives described below. The National Science Foundation would be folded into the new NIC as would the Department of Commerce's National Telecommunications Information Administration and the Technology Administration, including the National Institute of Standards. The NIC would also craft overall policies regarding technology policy, including the Internet, telecommunications, the digital economy, nanotechnology, and biotechnology. As the lead organization promoting science and research, the NIC would ensure the government set the right priorities and identified key technology trends. The goal of the corporation would not be to direct innovation or own patents, but rather to work in partnership with universities and the private sector to support innovation.

Congress should also allocate an additional $10 billion per year to the Corporation for several key areas. First, it should fund a $1 billion per year Advanced Cyberinfrastructure Program. The National Science Foundation Blue Ribbon Committee on CyberInfrastructure recently concluded that the science, engineering and educational enterprises would dramatically benefit from major advances in information technology, including building more ubiquitous, real-time, and collaborative digital research environments. An advanced cyberinfrastructure program would fund research and academic research applications to make this a reality. Such research would also lay the groundwork for the next generation Internet to dramatically expand its possibilities.[24]

There is also a critical need to provide increased funding for research infrastructure to universities. As the National Science Board reports, 'Over the past decade, the funding for academic research infrastructure has not kept pace with rapidly changing technology, expanding research opportunities, and increasing numbers of users.'[25] Research infrastructure consists of the equipment, facilities, and installations needed to undertake leading-edge research and develop advanced technologies. Such infrastructure might include DNA analysis equipment for cancer research, nanoengineering research facilities for new materials and systems, and supercomputers to create new media and virtual reality environments.

Because automation (e.g., robotics, machine vision, expert systems, voice recognition) is a key to boosting productivity in both manufacturing and services, government should also increase funds for research at universities or joint industry–university projects focused on increasing the efficiency of industrial or service processes. The fund would support early-stage research in processes with broad applications to boost productivity in a range of industries, not late-stage research focused on particular companies. On top of these investments, annual funding for the NSF functions would be doubled from $5 billion to $10 billion.

While direct government investment in R&D is needed, so too are tax incentives to stimulate R&D. Because the social benefits of R&D outweigh the private benefits, many nations provide R&D tax credits. For example, the Canadian government provides a flat, non-incremental 20 percent R&D credit for large companies, and up to a 35 percent credit for small companies. Provincial government credits can be taken on top of these. Since 1981 companies conducting research in the United States have been eligible for a 20 percent tax credit on research and experimentation investments above what they invested during a 'base period.'

While the R&D tax credit is a key incentive for firms to do more R&D it should be expanded and modernized to make it more effective.[26] First, Congress should make the credit permanent, and expand it from 20 to 30 percent. Second, they should make it easier for small and start-up companies to claim the credit by letting them claim for calculation of their R&D base gross receipts at least equal to $1 million. The total cost would be approximately $5 to 6 billion per year.

Increasing federal support for research is needed, but government also needs to adapt its R&D policies to the realities of the New Economy and in particular support the creation of new institutional models to foster innovation. Now in the New Economy partnerships and alliances, including between the private sector, universities, and government laboratories, play an increasingly important role in facilitating innovation. In short, the key enabler to strengthening innovation, and its dissemination and absorption, may lie as much in increasing the social capital of our productive sectors as in direct investments in science and technology. Federal science and technology policies should support the private sector in reconfiguring itself in ways that advance rapid technological change and diffuse innovation. In particular, policies should recognize that research is now conducted not only on the basis of one-time strategic alliances and partnerships but also through ongoing networks of learning and innovation.[27]

In the old economy where companies conducted most of the R&D within the confines of their corporate R&D laboratories it made sense for federal R&D policy to be focused on individual firms. But in a network economy where innovation occurs at the edges between organizations, such an orientation to research funding makes little sense and can actually be counterproductive by reinforcing existing institutional rigidities. As a result, if a new system of innovation is to fully emerge and prosper, federal science and technology policies, which helped create the broad institutional contours of the postwar R&D system, must be adapted to support the new institutional relationships between industry, universities and government and to build the social capital needed for innovation.

The social benefits from collaborative research are likely to be significantly higher than company-specific proprietary research. Collaborative research, whether in partnership with a university, national laboratory, or industry consortium, is more likely to be exploratory and at an earlier stage than research conducted by a single company. Moreover, because the research is shared from its inception, the benefits are less likely to be fully captured by an individual firm. As a result, because spillovers from collaborative research are greater, firms will tend to underinvest in this even more than in individual research. This suggests that the federal government should support collaborative research through a more generous R&D tax credit. One way to do this is to make all company expenditures, not just incremental expenses, on collaborative R&D eligible for a 30 percent flat credit. Industry investments in collaborative research consortia or investments in research at a US university or federal laboratory would qualify as collaborative R&D.

Tax incentives are not enough. Direct matching funding of consortia is also needed. One way to better link economic goals with scientific research is to encourage the formation of industry research alliances that fund academic research. There are numerous examples of successful university-industry partnerships. For example, 18 wireless communications companies formed a research consortium with the University of California-San Diego Engineering Department to work on advanced research related to the industry. Industry invests because research is performed in areas that are too risky, too long term, and too generic for any one company to invest in. The university invests to ensure that its scientists remain at the cutting edge of their scientific disciplines and work on scientifically and technically demanding tasks.

As a result, Congress should direct the NIC to establish an Industry Research Alliances Challenge Grant initiative to co-invest with industry-led research alliances. Industry members would establish technology 'road maps' and on the basis of these invest in research conducted at universities or federal laboratories. Funded at $2 billion per year, such an initiative could leverage two to four times that amount of money in industry funding. This initiative would increase the share of federally funded university and laboratory research that is market relevant, and in so doing better adjust the balance between curiosity-directed research and research more directly related to societal need.

Such a process would definitely not entail 'picking winners and losers' because industry, in conjunction with academic partners, would identify the broad technology areas critical for research. In fact, because the policy uses market mechanisms to fund R&D, it prevents government from picking winners and losers and scientists from pursuing research interests in isolation from societal need and benefit.

There is one other key change that is needed. Federal innovation policy historically has focused on multinational firms with large R&D units and the approximately 30 first-tier, large research universities (which receive 47 percent of federal research funds to universities), usually in a small number of states (67 percent of federal support for R&D goes to ten states). Both sets of institutions have played key roles in driving technological development. However, small and medium-sized firms have become more important to the nation's innovation system. Moreover, many of the nation's non-top-tier research universities and colleges have developed significant research strengths, often in particular fields. These universities and colleges often play key roles working with industry in their region. Such regional technology collaboration between small and medium-sized firms and higher education is increasingly important.

The Clinton administration and Congress took some positive steps to foster innovation among these firms, in particular by expanding the Small Business Innovation Research Grant program and creating and supporting the Advanced Technology Program. But there is a limit to what can be done at the federal level. States are better positioned to create these kind of regional technology programs. Starting in the early 1980s, several states began to refocus their economic development efforts to promote innovation. They realized that innovation is a key driver of New Economy development, and that state economies prosper when they maintain a healthy research base closely linked to commercialization of technology. For example, under the leadership of Governor Richard Thornburgh, Pennsylvania established the Ben

Franklin Partnership Program that provides matching grants primarily to small and medium-sized firms to work collaboratively with universities. While all 50 states now have initiatives to promote technology-based economic development funding has been limited in part because benefits flow across state lines and accrue in the future. As a result, one way to encourage states to focus more on technology-based economic development would be for Congress to appropriate $1 billion annually to the NIC for a competitive matching grant fund for states to invest in university-industry and other technology and innovation network programs. States would be required to match the federal funds at a ratio of at least one to one and invest in joint university-industry or other collaborative industry-based innovation programs. Industry would be required to match all public funds one to one. Thus, $1 billion in federal funds would be leveraged into at least $3 billion in additional R&D funding, much of it conducted at non-top-tier universities with small and medium-sized firms as partners.

Using Technology

It is not just doing research and developing new knowledge that leads to productivity gain, companies need also to use the new technologies and new knowledge. But some economists have interpreted the findings from growth accounting studies showing that expansion of capital equipment is not central to boosting productivity to suggest that development of technology is more important than its deployment. Yet, growth accounting studies only measure increases in overall capital stock, not replacement of old capital stock with new stock that is embedded with the latest innovations.[28] But much new technology works its way throughout the economy in the latest generations of capital equipment. As economist Paul Romer states, 'when a new type of capital good like the railroad or the digital computer is invented, it takes lots of investment to reap the benefits from these discoveries.'[29] Studies by former Treasury Secretary Larry Summers and economist Brad DeLong show that countries whose industries invest more in machinery and equipment have measurably higher productivity growth than countries that do not.[30] Similarly, companies that invest in newer generations of technology equipment are more productive and pay 10 percent higher wages than companies that do not.

As a result, it is not enough just for government to fund research, it must also make sure that the results of the research are broadly used and that companies buy new capital equipment. Yet, the growth of the stock of business capital has slowed every decade since the 1960s. While it grew 4 percent per year in the 1960s, business capital grew only 2 percent in the 1990s, notwithstanding the significant investments in IT equipment. Part of the reason for this is that IT equipment depreciates quickly and has to be replaced often.

One step policymakers can take is to make sure that interest rates remain low. As Harvard economist F.M. Scherer states, 'policies that stimulate capital investment enhance the rate at which new technology is brought into use and thereby raise the rate of productivity growth. Initiatives that lower the real cost of capital make capital goods investments turn the corner of profitability earlier than they otherwise would.'[31] Eliminating federal budget deficits, which in turn keep interest rates low, spurs investment. In many ways this was the most successful initiative of the Clinton administration. Enforcing fiscal discipline and paying down the national debt helped lower long-term interest rates, which in turn also helped spur investment. However, just as the nation was emerging from the era of budget irresponsibility and beginning to pay down the national debt, the Bush administration passed one of the largest tax cuts in history ensuring that once the economy rebounds to full capacity, interest rates will rise. Moreover, as intended, the Bush tax cut will make it much more difficult to make the kinds of investments in education, training and research needed to boost economic growth. As a result, a first step to implementing growth economics is to roll back the Bush tax cuts while reducing the costs of government by, among other steps, cutting corporate subsidies, reining in entitlements, and reinventing government. Therefore, a core component of growth economics is paying down the national debt while funding new investment in knowledge.

Congress should also adjust tax depreciation schedules to more accurately reflect the depreciation rates of equipment, particularly information technology. Under the tax code companies can depreciate investments in equipment according to depreciation schedules set by the Department of the Treasury. In the old economy, when equipment life cycles were longer, tax depreciation schedules usually reflected the real usable life of equipment and did not slow investment rates. However, today's competitive, information technology-driven economy leads to the rapid development and introduction of new innovations and new generations of equipment that quickly make existing equipment obsolete. Existing tax depreciation schedules have not kept up with the rate of change. For some classes of investments, particularly information technology equipment, these schedules no longer match actual replacement rates. These mismatches can have a negative impact on investment levels. As a result, where appropriate, depreciation schedules should be shortened to reflect actual replacement rates. More broadly, the Treasury Department should develop methods for adding new types of equipment and regularly evaluating existing equipment asset lives. Longer than life cycle depreciation schedules discourage development and deployment of new technologies by raising the true cost of investments.

Direct initiatives can help as well. Government activities in the diffusion of technical information and participation in demonstration projects and test-bed activities go back to the early days of the factory era, with the first demonstration of the telegraph and the creation of the agricultural extension service. Such diffusion activities are even more critical in today's rapidly changing information-driven economy. The Department of Commerce's Manufacturing Extension Partnership supports regionally based, industry-led efforts to help small manufacturers adopt more productive shop-floor technologies and techniques. During its ten years the program has helped over 148 000 firms.[32] Yet, instead of expanding the program the Bush administration has attempted to eliminate it. MEP funding should be doubled to around $200 million with the increases going to support sector-based modernization centers.

Finally, government can play a role in helping industry develop standards, which are a key component of the New Economy's intangible infrastructure. Compatibility standards help to expand market opportunities because they help to increase network effects. Yet there is evidence that companies underinvest in standards relative to the optimal societal level.[33] As a result, government should allow expenses companies incur in developing interoperability standards (as opposed to standards for products) to be eligible for the R&D tax credit.

FOSTER DIGITAL TRANSFORMATION

Just as electro-mechanical and chemical-based technologies were key to boosting productivity in the old economy, digital information technologies are the key to boosting productivity in the New Economy. As a result, policymakers need to pay special attention to crafting a policy framework to foster digital transformation. However, as recently as three years ago, cyber-pundits counseled us that because the Internet was the biggest thing since the printing press, there was little for policymakers to do except stay out of the way and 'do no harm.' However, there are a host of industries and applications, including government, health care, transportation, broadband, and smart cards, where digital transformation has proceeded much more slowly than initially thought. As a result, enabling the IT revolution to reach its full promise will require policymakers to do more than simply do no harm. It will require concerted and strategic government policies. This means crafting a legal and regulatory framework that supports the growth of the digital economy, in such areas as taxation, privacy, digital signatures, telecommunications regulation, and industry regulation (in banking, insurance, and securities, for example). It means using procurement and other direct government tools to help break digital chicken-or-egg conundrums around issues like broadband deployment to help move entire industries faster toward digital transformation.

Ensuring that government does not apply an old economy tax and regulatory framework to the Internet, as well as taking actions to extend the benefits of IT to all people and regions are important to fostering growth of the digital economy. But limiting an Internet and IT agenda to simply a no-tax and deregulatory regime, as the right advocates, or to a digital divide agenda, as the left proposes, will not take us far enough or fast enough toward the goal of ubiquitous digitization. Neither the conservative nor liberal approaches address the real market and political failures that limit the growth of the digital economy.

As a result we need a bold digital economy strategy that seeks to put the US on the leading edge. Other nations are making creative and aggressive efforts to move there. For example, South Korea and Japan lead the world in broadband deployment. And they want to continue to be on the leading edge. Seongnam, a suburb of Seoul, plans to be the first city in the world to do away with cash and credit cards. They plan to equip every citizen with digital cell phones by which they can purchase goods and services at every store in town, including at parking meters, bus stops, and vending machines. Japan is on track to deploy fiber optic cable to every neighborhood that provide speeds of between 20 mbs. to 100 mbs., 20 to 50 times faster than typical speeds in the US. Canada is the leader in e-government and has created a national task force on broadband. The Blair government in the UK has created an E-envoy whose mission is to help advance e-commerce and e-government in the UK. Finland has combined an ID card and health insurance card onto an electronic chip card. The European Union has taken a number of steps to advance policies to foster e-transformation in a number of industries and applications, such as health care, banking and smart cards.

The United States needs to emulate these nations and develop a proactive 'e-conomy' strategy designed to overcoming key barriers. In formulating and carrying out a strategic growth policy for the digital economy, government should act in a number of areas. But this should not be mistaken for a call for government ownership, picking winners and losers, expanded regulation, industry subsidies, or any other 'straw men' that conservatives often erect in response to a more strategic role for government. Rather, government needs to intervene in areas where market failures and other limitations lead to suboptimal outcomes. As a result, there are several key areas that policy should focus on to foster digital transformation.

Work with Industry to Develop Sector Strategies

The application of IT to information-intensive sectors or processes (such as health care, real estate, education, and transportation) that still rely largely on paper and person-to-person interactions holds the potential for the largest productivity payoffs. However, there are a number of barriers to digital transformation in these sectors, including the systems nature of the applications which require the development and adoption of IT by all parts of the industry at once. Take health care for example. Using IT to automate many of the information processes in the health-care system could save tens of billions of dollars per year. Yet, as evidenced by the widespread use of paper forms, handwritten prescriptions, manila file records, and limited use of email and online transactions, health care has been surprisingly resistant to making these changes. President Clinton's Information Technology Committee wrote to newly inaugurated President Bush that 'health care organizations are not well prepared to adopt information technology and applications effectively. Health care is largely a decentralized industry populated by diverse organizations with different motives, resources and incentives.'[34] Fiscal constraints, coupled with a lack of reimbursement for many IT applications, limit the ability of some parts of the industry to make the investments needed to adopt new technologies. Lack of standards and protocols linking all information together in an interoperable way hinders progress. In the face of high levels of uncertainty about future directions of technology and the supporting technical infrastructure, much less whether changes will even happen, technology developers and providers of solutions are hard pressed to justify investments. Moreover, it is not in the financial interest of some players, such as insurers and health maintenance organizations (HMOs), to give consumers and health-care providers the ability to file electronically, since it makes it more likely patients will file claims, while it also speeds up payments.

Similar barriers exist in other industries. For example, in the real estate industry buying a house is nothing if not an exercise in filling out numerous forms and paying endless fees for things like title searches, filing deeds, etc. Realtors have resisted development of direct seller-to-buyer e-commerce sites or even streamlined e-enabled discount brokerage services.[35] Likewise, little effort has been made to digitize the title recording process in spite of the fact that it could virtually eliminate the title search and title insurance industry, saving consumers billions.

Left to its own devices, the market is not likely to transform these industries from paper and face-to-face to digital anytime soon. As a result, government should do several things. First, it needs to work with both technology developers and users to help develop technology reinvention road maps. According to a recent study by the federal National Institute of Standards and Technology, a common complaint from industry managers is that in the face of high levels of uncertainty about future directions of technology and the supporting technical infrastructure that technology road maps are needed.[36] Government could play key roles. For example, the Department of Housing and Urban Development and Fannie Mae (a publicly chartered home financing corporation) should convene a working group in the housing industry, with an eye toward using IT to automate and streamline the process of purchasing a house. The Department of Health and Human Services should do the same in health care, the Department of Transportation (DOT) in transportation,[37] and the Securities and Exchange Commission (SEC) in the securities industry.

Second, the federal government should use its regulatory and purchasing power to move the industries in the direction of full digitization. Consider health care. As purchaser of about half of the nation's health care (through Medicare, Medicaid, the Department of Veterans' Affairs, etc.), the government is in a unique position to catalyse greater adoption of information technology throughout the health-care system. The Department of Veterans' Affairs (VA) has taken the lead in catalysing adoption of information technology for health records. The leaders of the VA have come to realize that any information system that works only in their own system will provide limited benefits. Even VA patients do not stay in the VA system, so if they are to track their patients, they need a system that everyone can use. But more should be done. The President's Information Technology Advisory Committee recommends establishing pilot projects and Enabling Technology Centers to extend practical use of IT to health-care systems.

Finally, Congress and the administration should remove regulatory roadblocks to further digitization in particular sectors. For example, the Department of Education has rules requiring students getting financial aid to put in a certain amount of 'seat time' in classes. Since students enrolled in online courses put in little or no 'seat time', it makes it more difficult, if not impossible for them to get aid. Similarly, if federal requirements designed for credit cards – such as the requirements for return of charges and for detailed reporting of transactions – were imposed on the 'digital cash' function of smart cards, they could effectively kill the market for this technology. Likewise, some developers of proprietary trading systems have suggested that in its continuing attempts to impose on the securities markets its own vision of a 'National Market System' – a vision that is essentially two decades old – the SEC is stifling the development of new and better ways to trade.

Tackle Chicken-or-Egg Issues

In a number of areas, 'chicken-or-egg' issues hold back digital transformation. One of these, for example, is smart cards. Smart cards make it easier to perform a multitude of daily tasks, including digitally 'signing' documents while online and automating payment functions (like parking garages). But there is a chicken-or-egg problem: few people carry smart cards because few applications accept them, and there are few applications because few people carry smart cards.

Public policy can play an important role in breaking through 'chicken-or-egg' issues. For example, in order to significantly boost homeland security and at the same time jump start the smart card market Congress should require states to modernize their driver's license systems by incorporating biometrics and smart cards on the license.[38] Putting a smart card in everyone's wallet creates a network effect that would facilitate widespread adoption of smart card technology. There are other areas such as Internet-based software standards to help users manage privacy (e.g., P3P) and objectionable content (e.g., ICRA) that exhibit similar chicken-or-egg issues. Unless companies make their sites compliant with these standards users will not use them and vice versa.

Perhaps the most important area where the federal government can act is to help stimulate demand for high speed broadband. By encouraging a whole host of new applications, including e-medicine, e-learning and telecommuting, and voice over Internet protocol (VOIP) the government could stimulate the demand for broadband, which would in turn lead to even more broadband applications. The government should support the creation of online adult education materials.[39] Other applications that could be developed include online career aptitude testing,[40] skills assessment, career counseling, and basic skills and English as a second language acquisition. In some cases, these applications exist, but are proprietary and cost money. States and the federal government should consider funding the best of breed programs so that they are available free online. The government can do the same with regard to putting content online. For example, most public television shows could be put online. Likewise, all government reports could be made available in e-book form. Government could also work to create a national digital lending library, allowing local library patrons to 'borrow' electronic copies of books.

Finally, one reason why e-business has been slower to take off is that few companies and governments pass back the cost savings to consumers. Government should lead by example. Congress and the administration should not give in to calls from consumer groups and affected industry groups to prevent companies from pricing their products and services differentially based on the channel by which they sell it. The marketplace, not government, should determine if companies give a discount for online sales or conversely charge a surcharge for offline sales. More directly, governments should give a discount to citizens who interact with government online, or through other kinds of digital automation (such as electronic toll collection) since it saves the government money.

Overcome Middleman Resistance

Finally, resistance to e-commerce competition by those threatened with digital disintermediation is a huge threat to the rapid and widespread digitization of the economy.[41] Given that resisters often enlist government to protect them, policymakers at all levels should not succumb to protectionist pleadings and should oppose actions designed to protect the status quo against e-commerce competition.

But government also needs to be proactive. The federal government should create the position of e-commerce ombudsman to identify, analyse, and advocate for cases where opponents of e-commerce competitors are unfairly trying to use government for protectionist purposes. The Federal Trade Commission (FTC) and the Department of Justice (DOJ) should increase their efforts to prevent retailers and other businesses from colluding to retaliate against companies attempting to sell directly to consumers. As David A. Balto, former assistant director of the Office of Policy and Evaluation of the Federal Trade Commission, has stated, 'When new kinds of competition emerge, one of the first things incumbents may do is to attempt to deny necessary inputs to the innovators by organizing a boycott.'[42] As a result, both the FTC and DOJ should step up their efforts to monitor retailers to determine if they are seeking exclusive dealing arrangements or engaging in other anti-competitive practices against direct selling by the producer. The standard should be a strict one. If retailers communicate in any way with each other, including through their trade associations, or if the retailer has market power to organize what are essentially horizontal boycotts, the FTC and DOJ should investigate and, if the retailers are found guilty, prosecute such cases. In contrast, the FTC and DOJ should take a tolerant position if producers act collectively to sell goods or services online, as long as they are not colluding on the price of the product or keeping out entrants. The FTC and DOJ should develop a legal 'safety zone' that makes it clear that the government does not consider discussions among producers (even if they include all of the market participants or are orchestrated by an industry trade association) to agree to independently launch direct Internet sales efforts or jointly agree on pricing policies toward intermediaries. Policymakers may want to require such collaborators to obtain formal permission for this type of collaboration, as competitors must do to establish R&D consortia.

Finally, Congress needs to think seriously about preempting state laws and regulations governing inherently cross-border e-commerce transactions. States regulate a wide variety of industries and professions whose products and services generally do not cross state borders. For example, most non-bank financial service providers are subject to state laws, and are not eligible for national licensing. However, with the rise of national e-commerce, subjecting companies to 50 different laws raises costs of doing business, and in some cases violate the Commerce Clause of the Constitution. Just as Congress passed national legislation laying out the legal framework governing the acceptance of digital signatures, it should pass legislation developing national frameworks governing business sectors that are now regulated at the state level. Congress should consider developing a national standard based on best-in-class requirements that states currently impose. E-commerce financial service companies would then have only one law to follow.[43] In addition, in areas like Spam, privacy, Internet telephony, spyware, and other Internet policy areas, the presumption should be in favor of national action, instead of a conflicting patchwork of state laws.

FOSTER HIGHER SKILLS

In spite of the promise of digital automation, there are a host of activities that are not amenable to automation because they are too complex. They may involve complex human interactions (a social worker helping a client), non-routine physical work (a maid cleaning a room), or complicated intellectual tasks (a manager planning and executing a marketing campaign). For these kinds of tasks, it is hard to see how technology can be used to significantly automate the work or eliminate the need for it. As a result, if we are to boost productivity in these kinds of jobs, we will need to rely on the soft technologies of skills and work organization – what some have called 'humanware.'[44] Thus, the third leg of a productivity policy has to focus on boosting the productivity of individuals. Increased skills not only enable workers to better perform their jobs, but also enable employers to redesign work to take advantage of those higher skills, further boosting productivity.[45] When companies institute participatory work systems they not only raise productivity and cut costs, but also often provide more rewarding tasks.[46] Firms with more educated workers have higher productivity, and raising the educational level of employees by a year results in an 8 to 13 percent increase in labor productivity.[47]

If we are going to boost skills and help companies move to the kinds of 'high-performance' work organizations that utilize high skills, society will have to make a greater investment in boosting education and skills. Money spent on education and training is an investment, just like any other expenditure made with the expectation that future earnings will exceed the current expenditure.

Unfortunately, there is evidence that society underinvests in skills. Between 1988 and 1999 business investment in training fell 18 percent as a share of GDP.[48] Many larger companies that used to support in-house, dedicated training programs in the 1960s and 1970s have eliminated these efforts. For example, in the 1950s and 1960s it was not uncommon for IBM to spend up to a year training their salesmen. Now, in a much more competitive marketplace they cannot afford to do this.

A major reason for this cutback, even though the economy is more knowledge intensive, is that in a hyper-competitive, ultra-mobile economy it is hard for companies to invest in a resource that is likely soon to walk out the door. During the first ten years of their career, American workers hold up to six jobs.[49] Moreover, when a worker quits, they now often get a raise, giving them more incentive to move on.[50] When workers are this mobile a firm investing in training is at a disadvantage since it has spent money other firms have not, while at the same time providing its competitors with a trained pool of workers to select from.[51]

Because companies train less they are also less likely to put in place high-performance work organizations (HPWO). In fact, HPWO is somewhat like the chicken-or-egg conundrum that affects many digital technologies. Employers do not embrace a high-skills strategy because a not insignificant portion of the labor market lacks the skills to adequately perform in high-performance work organizations. Companies seeking to deploy HPWO practices would not only have to spend the time and money to train workers on needed skills, but also often on remedial skills workers need to for the job. Better to just work with what you have and stay on the lower road of lower wages and lower skills. On the worker side because so many jobs require basic skills, there is less incentive for workers to get additional training.

Jump Starting High-Performance Work Organizations

If our nation is to move more toward a high-performance work organization economy where workers have higher skills and are engaged in work that requires higher skills, we will need to simultaneously address both the demand and supply side of the skills equation. Policies should both encourage companies to reorganize work this way and encourage workers to boost their skills.

In the old economy, the assumption was that workers with basic skills would be hired by companies which would then invest in company-specific skills and the worker would advance up the career ladder. The role of the public sector was to provide an adequate elementary and secondary education, support post-secondary education, and help those individuals not employed get needed skills. Federal training efforts focused on individuals who were not working, but generally ignored workers already in the workforce. Moreover, public training efforts generally were disconnected from private, internal company-run training systems. If government is going to play a meaningful role in skill enhancement, it will need to develop new approaches that recognize these changes in the marketplace.

First, this means boosting funding for adult education and workforce development programs. Federal funding for workforce development fell from 0.083 percent of GDP in 1985 to 0.056 percent in 2003. Second, we have to motivate and assist companies to invest significantly more in skill development. Employers are best positioned to do this because they can identify the skills and knowledge needed for growing jobs. Moreover, by letting employers lead, it is much easier to tie training directly to employment.

There are a number of steps policymakers should take to do this. First, federal and state policies need to encourage and support companies making increased investments in training, particularly in basic skills and remedial education. Because too many workers did not learn basic mathematics, reading, and language skills in school, companies are having to fix these deficiencies before they can train their workers in more advanced skills. Moreover, in most states there are long waiting lists for remedial education. As a result, it makes sense to provide incentives for companies to offer basic skills training. States and the federal government should establish tax credits for company investments in remedial education, literacy training, and English as a second language.[52]

Government should also provide seed funding for collaborative industry training ventures. Inter-firm collaborative solutions are more effective than going it alone. First, by working together, firms in the same or similar industries can pool resources (e.g., information, on-the-job training opportunities, equipment, curricula) that lower costs of training. Moreover, by supporting sector-based alliances (e.g., metalworking, tourism, information technology), firms focus on building a regional training pool, rather than on 'poaching' from other firms to get workers. Second, collaboration allows firms to develop joint solutions and communicate these to educational institutions.[53] In the last several years, a small number of regional and industry-based training alliances have emerged, usually in partnership with state and local governments and technical colleges. As part of the Wisconsin Regional Training Partnership, a number of metalworking firms, in conjunction with the AFL-CIO, used an abandoned mill building to set up a teaching factory to train workers needing further skills. The workers learn directly on state-of-the art manufacturing equipment. The National Coalition for Telecommunications Education and Learning (NACTEL) is an industry-driven alliance of four telecommunications companies and two unions to provide an on-line degree program – an AS degree in Communications IT granted by Pace University.[54]

The federal government can play a key role in fostering industry-led skills alliances. To do this they should create a National Skills Corporation as a publicly chartered government corporation. Its job would be to co-invest with states and industries in industry-led skills alliances. This would be similar to the Blair government's new initiative to support the UK-wide network of employer-led Sector Skills Councils. Because they wanted this initiative to be flexible enough to interact effectively with businesses, trade associations, and unions the Blair government specifically did not place the program in the Department of Education. Rather they established a new Sectoral Skills Development Agency as non-departmental public body with a CEO and an employer-led board.[55]

In the Internet era, there need to be more opportunities to get free or low-cost education and training over the Internet. Yet, most government online sites for people seeking information about finding a job or getting training are poorly designed, hard to navigate and limited in scope. This is because online efforts have usually replicated the fragmented and programmatic nature of the off-line world and have not attempted to create one-stop portals. Government should fund the development of comprehensive online learning and employment portals that contain information on jobs; training and education,[56] including report cards on providers; financial assistance; skills assessment and career counseling; self-paced computer-based learning; and the ability to apply online for benefits. In addition, public Internet access generally should be available in libraries, schools, community-based organizations, public housing complexes, employment centers, and union halls.

Finally, government also needs to make federally funded training and retraining programs easier to access. According to the Upjohn Institute, only 2.4 percent of dislocated workers referred to the US Employment Service received training in 1998. While many dislocated workers do not avail themselves of training because they get jobs within weeks of being laid off, others are deterred from seeking out training grants because the process is time-consuming, bureaucratic, and can carry a negative stigma.[57] To ensure that more people take advantage of the existing training funds available, Congress should replace the current bureaucratic system of training grants with a system of New Economy Work (NEW) Scholarships modeled on current programs to provide scholarships for college. These NEW Scholarships would provide dislocated workers with a scholarship worth up to $4000 that they could use to pay for courses from certified training providers.

FOSTER ENTREPRENEURIAL INNOVATION AND COMPETITION

In conventional economic theory economic growth is seen as a function of the proper level of savings, government spending, and interest rates. Innovation, like changes in fashion, is seen as a 'supply shock' that occurred every once in a while that shifts the supply or demand curves up or down. Left outside the models, innovation and entrepreneurship never enter into the discussion. As Peter Drucker witheringly notes, 'classical economics cannot handle the entrepreneur but consigns him to the shadowy realm of external forces, together with climate and the weather, government and politics, pestilence and war.'[58]

Yet, a few economists like Joseph Schumpeter have focused on the role of the entrepreneur. For Schumpeter, the expansion of industry arose not from the push of capital (e.g., the standard economists' view that raising savings and lowering interest rates creates more opportunity for investment) but from the pull of entrepreneurs. So understanding why entrepreneurs invest and making sure that the opportunities (new technologies, new kinds of organizations, new markets) are there for the entrepreneurs to invest in is a key. Economic growth therefore is not slowed either by reduced demand (the left's critique) or by lack of savings and investment (the right's) but rather by the lack of opportunities for the entrepreneur to break new ground in new areas. As Drucker put it, 'entrepreneurs see change as the norm and as healthy. Usually they do not bring about the change themselves. But – and this defines the entrepreneur and entrepreneurship – the entrepreneur always searches for change, responds to it, and exploits it as an opportunity.'[59]

But it is important to distinguish between entrepreneurship and small business. Many Republicans like to worship at the altar of small business, and are willing to offer up the sacrifices of tax and regulatory relief. Yet, when Schumpeter talked about entrepreneurship he was referring to any type of economic activity that is new and innovative, whether it is from a large corporation introducing a new product or a one-man enterprise developing a new idea. As Schumpeter put it:

> the function of entrepreneurs is to reform or revolutionize the pattern of production by exploiting an invention or, more generally an untried technological possibility for producing a new commodity or producing an old one in a new way, by opening up a new source of supply of materials or a new outlet for products, by reorganizing an industry and so on.[60]

As a result, the key is not to help small business per se, but rather to create a climate conducive to entrepreneurial activities that brings true innovation to the economy.

The New Economy puts a premium on what Nobel Laureate economist Douglass North calls 'adaptive efficiency,' which is the ability of institutions to innovate, continuously learn, and productively change. As markets fragment, technology accelerates, and competition comes from unexpected places, learning, creativity, and adaptation are becoming the new principal sources of competitive advantage in many industries. Enabling constant innovation must become the goal of any organization committed to prospering. Similarly, the goal for public policy in the New Economy must be fostering innovation and adaptation in infrastructure, institutions, and on the part of individuals. These efforts need to be proactive, sustained, and designed for the long term. Growth economics also means not giving in to special interests fearful of change or falling sway to pleading of incumbent firms threatened by competition. These protectionists need to be rebuffed in a host of areas – from their opposition to bioengineered foods that promise dramatic increases in agricultural productivity, to their opposition to mergers that promise heightened efficiencies, to their seeking government intervention to provide shelter from robust e-commerce competitors. The nation that has the least resistance to change is the one that will best succeed economically.

As a result, however, it is not just entrepreneurship that is important, but also competition. Domestically, growth economics means that if government is to promote growth it must facilitate, rather than resist, economic competition. Economists have long acknowledged that competition keeps prices down. The New Economy creates another critical reason for competition: it drives innovation, and ultimately provides the greatest benefits to consumers. Of course, government must continue to provide and enforce commonsense health, safety, and environmental regulations. But as they have done in a host of industries such as trucking, aviation, and long-distance telecommunications, they should resist regulating competitive industries and instead promote competition to achieve public interest goals of lower costs, new products and greater consumer choice.

Because of its effect on competition, global integration is a key component of growth economics. Global integration, open markets, and increased trade allows the US economy to specialize more in the higher-value added activities that it does best. But because it increases the relevant market size, bringing in new competitors, it also increases economic competition, keeping prices down and fostering innovation. However, many free-trade advocates seem to forget that these textbook results only occur if competition is fair, markets are open and subsidies few. Yet, many foreign competitors, particularly in Asia, don't play by these rules. Many nations intervene to keep their currency prices low, provide subsidies to exporters, keep their markets closed, fail to prevent the theft of intellectual property and engage or tolerate a host of other market distortions. This is one reason why the US is running record trade deficits, which have resulted in the loss of over 1.2 million manufacturing and information-based service jobs in the last few years.[61] As a result, just as the federal government needs to enforce rules to keep markets open at home, it needs to aggressively work to keep foreign markets open and free of distortion.

Finally, one way to ensure robust competition is to ensure that prices reflect costs. In the old economy, government often regulated prices when national markets were dominated by oligopolies or monopolies. In those cases, the costs of government intervention were manageable. But in more competitive markets distorted prices are much more likely to lead to economically inefficient decisions by consumers and producers. Therefore, in the absence of clear market failures, markets, not governments, should set the prices of privately provided goods and services. As a result, growth economics distinguishes between programs that address legitimate market failures and those that provide industry subsidies, price supports and regulated prices that foster economic inefficiency. The former include programs that raise the capacity of companies to be more productive and innovative, like the Department of Commerce's Manufacturing Extension Partnership, a program to provide help small and medium-sized manufacturers become more productive. The latter include programs and policies that simply give money to companies with no increase in productive or innovative potential, such as agricultural subsidies. Government should reduce or eliminate the unnecessary price regulations and array of government protections and subsidies that protect entrenched interests without increasing the economy's innovative or productive capacity. For example, agricultural price supports just postpone needed market adjustments while propping up inefficient farm producers and diverting funds that could be better spent on rural development efforts.[62]

CONCLUSION

In the New Economy, innovation and knowledge are the most important factors driving economic growth. If we are to boost both, government cannot consign its role to simply redistributing resources to the needy as liberals advocate, nor funneling resources to rich investors as conservatives advocate. Rather, it needs to invest in knowledge and support competition, but in ways that both preserves fiscal discipline for future generations and helps workers cope with increased risk. By putting knowledge and innovation at the center of our nation's economic policies we can ensure that we can enjoy robust economic growth and rising standards of living for all Americans. What Americans can do with this increased productivity is the subject of the final chapter.

NOTES

1. Jones (2002).
2. www-hoover.stanford.edu/pubaffairs/we/current/north1000.html.
3. Romer (1994) p. 21.
4. Council of Economic Advisors (1995).
5. Coe and Helpman (1995).
6. Studies of specific technologies have shown equally large rates of return. The benefits to society from the development of the CT scanner were significant, not only because of the consumer surplus (e.g., the benefits to consumers that exceed the costs of the technology) but the related technologies it led to. For example, CT scanner technology led to not only a vast array of medical applications, but to devices like baggage scanners in airports. The overall rate of return from the original research in CT scanners was a whopping 270 percent (Brynjolfsson and Hitt, 1993).
7. Mansfield (1980).
8. Heuse (undated).
9. Tassey (1998).
10. Jones and Williams (2000).
11. Ibid.
12. www.nsf.gov/sbe/srs/nsf01309/pdf/tab1b.pdfhttp://w3.access.gpo.gov/usbudget/fy2003/sheets/hist05z1.xls.
13. Speech at American Association for the Advancement of Science, Washington, DC, 9 December 2000.
14. The algorithm Google uses was developed as part of the NSF-funded Digital Library Initiative (www.dlib.org/dlib/july00/arms/07arms.html#ref5).
15. Narin and Olivastro (1997).
16. OECD (2000).
17. Mansfield (1980).
18. Griliches (1992).
19. Tassey (1998).
20. Leyden and Link (1991).
21. Narin and Olivastro (1997).
22. Gingrich (1997).
23. Petroski (1997) p. 211.
24. www.cise.nsf.gov/evnt/reports/toc.htm.
25. The NSF estimates that the future unmet needs of the scientific infrastructure amount to $18.8 billion over the next 10 years (www.nsf.gov/nsb/documents/2003/chapter4.htm).
26. The Congressional Office of Technology Assessment (1995) concluded that 'for every dollar lost in tax revenue, the R&D tax credit produces a dollar increase in reported R&D spending, on the margin. The accounting firm Coopers & Lybrand estimated that if the R&D tax credit were made permanent (as opposed to being repealed), companies would spend $41 billion more on R&D over the next 12 years, which would boost productivity, adding $13 billion (in 1998 dollars) in economic output per year by 2010.
27. Fountain and Atkinson (1998).
28. Scherer (1996) p. 25.
29. Romer (1994) p. 18.
30. De Long and Summers (1991).
31. Scherer (1996) p. 25.
32. www.mep.nist.gov/index2.html.
33. Swann (2000).

34. Presidents' Information Technology Advisory Committee (2001) p. 2.
35. E-realty.com is such a discount model that is trying to penetrate the online market (see Ham and Atkinson, 2003).
36. Tassey (1998).
37. For example, government should invest in intelligent transportation systems (ITS). These involve devices to detect disturbances in traffic flow, real-time traveler information systems, computer controlled ramps and traffic lights, 'on the fly' toll collection systems, and a host of other applications. But many ITS applications that could be provided by the private sector (e.g., on-board traffic tracking systems) cannot be deployed until the public sector deploys basic ITS infrastructure.
38. Ham and Atkinson (2002).
39. For example, the province of Ontario, Canada launched AlphaRoute, an online system providing over 160 hours of online literacy services (for both English and French speakers) via the Internet to help learners in remote areas of Ontario progress from limited skills to the equivalent of Grades 8 and 9.
40. www4.ncsu.edu/unity/lockers/users/l/lkj.
41. Atkinson (2001).
42. Balto (1999).
43. The Gramm-Leach-Bliley Financial Services Modernization Act (P.L. 106-102) used this model to give states four years to have a uniform licensing requirement or reciprocity for insurance, and if they did not act, the federal system of insurance regulation would be imposed.
44. Herzenberg et al. (1988-89) p. 56.
45. A study of 1000 Danish manufacturers found that productivity gains were four to five times higher in companies that introduced new work systems together with ICT, as opposed to those that just introduced ICT (Union of Industrial and Employers Confederations of Europe, 2001).
46. Appelbaum et al. (2000); Black and Lynch (2000).
47. Black and Lynch (2000)
48. Bassi (1996).
49. Acemoglu and Pischke (1998).
50. One study found that workers who changed jobs every other year saw almost the same earnings rise in the late 1980s as workers who kept the same job for 10 years (Cappelli, 1999, p. 150).
51. The Federal Bureau of Labor Statistics found that establishments with medium levels of turnover invested 12.5 hours of training per employee compared to establishments with high turnover who invested only 7.2 hours per year.
52. New Economy Task Force (2000).
53. Collaborative training is one reason why German firms invest more in training than US firms. There, a dense network of industry associations, coupled with the fact that the German federal government contributes half the costs, makes it much easier for firms, most of whom are small, to jointly address training (Hilton, 1991).
54. www.nactel.org.
55. www.ssda.org.uk/about.shtml.
56. www4.ncsu.edu/unity/lockers/users/l/lkj.
57. Weinstein (2002).
58. Drucker (1995) p. 26.
59. Ibid. p. 28.
60. Schumpeter (1942) p. 132.
61. When the multiplier effect is taken into account, the short-term jobs losses from a growing trade deficit are even higher (Atkinson, 2004c).
62. Atkinson (2004b).

10. Building a More Humane Economy

When America last made a transition to a new economy, in the 1950s, most Americans accepted, even embraced, the wrenching changes brought about because they saw the benefits in their daily lives. Today, many fear that the promise of the New Economy is outweighed by its pitfalls, particularly the heightened risk that seems to be part and parcel of today's global, IT-driven economy. To restore the faith in the future so that citizens will be willing to once again accept a new economy it is necessary to offer them a new bargain: accept the change, disruption, and risks inherent in economic transformation in exchange for a significantly better and more humane economy.

To get a sense of what this future economy might look like, it is worth looking to the past, to the writings of John Maynard Keynes. In spite of the fact that much of Keynes's work was a response to the Depression, Keynes was acutely interested in the long run. While he made millions investing in the market in the 1920s, he saw more clearly than most that the ordinary people of England, and indeed of all advanced industrial nations, spent most of their lives toiling under the harshest of conditions for meager incomes. Like Robert Kennedy, who stated 'Some men ask why, I ask why not,' Keynes wondered why people had to be devoted slavishly to work. He thought long and hard as to whether this was mankind's fate, or just a transitory phase before a different kind of economy, and indeed, a different kind of society, emerged.

Keynes gave his answer in 1930 in an all but forgotten essay in the *Saturday Evening Post*. Arguing that technology was steadily boosting output and productivity, Keynes foresaw that as a result there would come a time when:

> I see us free, therefore, to return to some of the most sure and certain principles of religion and traditional virtue – that avarice is a vice, that the exaction of usury a misdemeanor, and the lover of money is detestable, that those [who] walk most truly in the paths of virtue and sane wisdom [are those] who take least thought for the morrow. We shall once more value

ends above means and prefer the good to the useful. We shall honor those who can teach us how to pluck the hour and the day virtuously and well, the delightful people who are capable of taking direct enjoyment in things, the lilies of the field who toil not, neither do they spin.[1]

If these were the musings of some disgruntled bohemian social critic, one might dismiss them out of hand. However, Keynes was not a dreamer, but one of the sharpest economic minds of his time. Still he noted:

> But beware! The time for all this is not yet. For at least another hundred years we must pretend to ourselves and to every one that fair is foul and foul is fair; for foul is useful and fair is not. Avarice and usury and precaution must be our gods for a little longer still. For only they can lead us out of the tunnel of economic necessity into daylight.[2]

Keynes was not the only one, however, who longed for, and indeed predicted, a future focused on life, not just work. Utopians had long dreamed of such a world. In his 1887 classic, *Looking Backward*, Edward Bellamy foresaw a society in which by the year 2000 an individual would spend 20 to 25 years working and then would be free to pursue his own desires. Karl Marx bemoaned that the crushing conditions of the industrial revolution diminished happiness and alienated the human spirit. Like Keynes, Marx believed that the solution to dehumanized work lay in the reduction of hours of work, the automation of labor, and the development of leisure. In an 1846 essay, he blamed capitalism for its dehumanizing characteristics, stating:

> The various stages of development in the division of labor are just so many different forms of ownership, i.e., the existing stage in the division of labor determines also the relations of individuals to one another with reference to the material, instrument, and product of labor ... As soon as the distribution of labor comes into being, each man has a particular, exclusive sphere of activity, which is forced upon him and from which he cannot escape. He is a hunter, a fisherman, a herdsman, or a critical critic, and must remain so if he does not want to lose his means of livelihood; while in communist society, where nobody has one exclusive sphere of activity but each can become accomplished in any branch he wishes, society regulates the general production and thus makes it possible for me to do one thing today and another tomorrow, to hunt in the morning, fish in the afternoon, rear cattle in the evening, criticize after dinner, just as I have a mind, without ever becoming hunter, fisherman, herdsman or critic.[3]

Marx's solution, like that of many other utopians, was to overthrow capitalism. Yet, it was not the fault of capitalism, indeed capitalism at least provided freedom. Until productivity reached a level at which most people could live the good life without excessive hours of back-breaking or mind-numbing work, liberation would be impossible. Unlike the utopians, it was Keynes's genius to realize that liberation would have to wait until productivity grew much more.

Prediction is a dangerous business, never more so than in economics. Notwithstanding this, it is possible that advanced, post-industrial economies are entering a period where it may be possible to think of the organization of the economy, and indeed of society itself, not as an end in and of itself, as it currently is, but rather as a means by which people can live more fulfilled, meaningful, and enjoyable lives. Historically, our economy, workplaces, and built environment have been designed to meet the imperatives of the prevailing techno-economic production system. Many people work in unfulfilling, boring and hard jobs because that work needs to be done and the production system requires the work to be organized this way. But as the economy evolves, this relationship can evolve. Such a vision may seem hopelessly utopian, particularly given that many people seem to be working longer, under greater stress. But today's New Economy is unleashing a host of forces that could enable a more humane economy in which people can enjoy more satisfying work even as they work less.

As the economy gets more productive, companies become more knowledge driven and people become more prosperous, Americans could increasingly expect more rewarding work, more leisure, and more livable communities. Just as we moved from an economy in the first part of the twentieth century focused on production and investment, to one in the last half of the twentieth century focused on mass consumption, it is possible that we are moving to an economy in the first half of the twenty-first century focused on enabling people to live good lives.

There are three main areas where we could see this impact: the creation of more satisfying workplaces and jobs that neither oppress the body nor dampen the spirit; the reduction of work time enabling Americans to enjoy more time away from work, whether in leisure, with their families, or involved in civic activity; and increased choices for people in where they live, leading to the creation of more livable communities.

As the last new economy emerged in the 1950s the challenge was to build an economy that could satisfy Americans' material needs – decent housing, nutrition, medical care and transportation for all. For most Americans, although not all, that challenge has largely been met. As a result, at the emergence of this New Economy, the challenge is to create an economy and society that satisfies our deeper human needs and wants. As Bill Clinton said in his 1992 campaign book, the goal is an economy that 'Puts People First.'

Putting people first entails neither an anti-corporate crusade nor a simple-living, back-to-nature movement. Indeed, the challenge is to find a way to put people first without putting productivity second, for it is robust and sustained productivity growth that will enable people to work less without earning less. As a result, it is time to embrace a new vision and pursue an agenda to relentlessly drive productivity growth, while ensuring that an increasing share of that growth enables people to live better lives.

CREATING MORE HUMANE WORKPLACES

As discussed in Chapter 4, work is increasingly being designed in ways that better meet individual workers' needs. While there are still many oppressive, stifling, or boring work environments, an increasing share of organizations, particularly those that rely on employees' initiative and knowledge, are creating more human-centered workplaces. In the New Economy, more workers identify themselves with their occupation (e.g., computer webmaster, accountant, sales person) than with their employer. They do not necessarily want to belong to an organization, they want work environments that fit them and their unique needs to be themselves and have enjoyable, challenging, and rewarding work. Once a job stops delivering this, they head for the door. Efforts by employers, unions and individual workers will play the key roles in creating more human-centered workplaces. However, government, through its regulations, tax, training, and other policies, can help to foster more satisfying work environments.

One step government can take is to reform labor laws that hinder companies from establishing more worker friendly work practices. The firestorm over a 2000 letter from the Occupational Safety and Health Administration (OSHA) interpreting the application of workplace rules to home offices was a wake-up call to Washington to come to grips with the changing rules of the road for regulating economic activity. In the general hilarity over OSHA's ridiculous suggestion that every home with a telecommuter might need lighted exit signs and ergonomic decorating, the more serious issue was obscured. How can a legal and regulatory scheme designed for industrial age workplaces be applied to information age workplaces? Do we simply abandon workforce safety rules altogether? If not, what weight should we give employer-sponsored arrangements that obviously increase the flexibility and personal satisfaction of employees at the cost of eliminating the old office-and-factory structure that made it easy to set clear rules and offer clear protections for workers?

Clearly, junking all the old rules could enable some old economy employers to coerce some employees into accepting workforce arrangements that are less clear and secure. But on the other hand, millions of workers want flexible hours, non-hierarchical project 'teams,' and the ability to telecommute more than they want the old 'protections' of rigid hours, wages, work conditions, and management–labor bargaining. The dilemma is complicated by the fact that millions of other Americans continue to work, for the moment, in more traditional workplaces where 'freedom from regulation' would look more like abandonment than empowerment.

Labor laws are also at odds with a growing movement to create employee involvement teams. According to a 1994 survey conducted by the Dunlop Commission, 96 percent of large employers use some form of employee involvement teams. But these practices run the risk of being illegal because rank and file employees are involved in managerial decisions and hence these may appear to operate as company-dominated unions. But protections against company-dominated unions were never intended to prevent workplace 'teams,' especially in industries where representation of workers by unions is nearly nonexistent. Employee involvement-sponsored teams are now frequently barred by the National Labor Relations Act (NLRA) from discussing key issues such as work schedules and compensation as part of the NLRA's prohibition against company-run unions.

As a result it is critical that industrial age labor laws should be modernized to reflect today's social and economic realities, facilitating alternative channels for worker empowerment while maintaining and even strengthening traditional protections for the right of workers to organize in collective bargaining units. One step to do this was the TEAM Act, introduced in Congress in 1997. The legislation would have permitted employers in non-union settings to form teams of supervisors and employees to address key workplace issues, through 'employee involvement' programs. However, unions opposed it in part because they were rightly concerned that the bill would weaken unions and give some managers unchallenged dominance. But compromise legislation could be developed that ensures that companies cannot use teams to thwart legitimate union organizing efforts. If properly structured, a TEAM Act compromise could strongly protect union prerogatives where workers show interest in organizing, while strongly protecting worker interests through facilitating teams elsewhere.

Another way out of the logjam over labor law reform would be to create two sets of workplace rules: one for firms committed to the high-performance path and one for other firms. The former set of rules would give employers considerably more flexibility for practices such as employee teams. Companies would be eligible for these high-performance standards if three-quarters of their workers agreed to the standards. Companies adhering to these new standards could be required to let their workers vote anonymously once a year to accept these rules or to revert to the current more prescriptive rules. Moreover, if unions had increased power to organize workers and let them choose whether to be represented by unions, unions would be less likely to resist these kinds of more flexible regulations. One step in that direction would be to pass so-called 'card check' legislation that would make it easier for workers to join unions.

While regulations limit the adoption of high-performance work practices, so does lack of information by companies, particularly by small and medium-sized firms. Many companies, who are often suppliers to larger enterprises, are under tremendous pressure to improve quality and reduce prices. At the same time they frequently operate on very tight margins and have little slack for investing in new processes or reorganizing work. This suggests expanding support for the Manufacturing Extension Partnership to focus more on educating companies about the benefits of high-performance work organization.

High-performance work organizations also require higher skills. But like so many chicken-or-egg issues, if workers do not have the skills to work in the more demanding high-performance work systems, employers will continue to organize production in the old ways that simplify work, giving employees little reason to upgrade their skills. Chapter 9 detailed policies to boost skills. Not only will these boost productivity but they will also encourage more firms to move to high-performance workplaces.

Finally, it is important to remember that high-performance work organization has its limits. Even if all employers wanted to organize work in more satisfying ways, for many jobs this is simply impossible. For example, toll-taking jobs are stressful, mostly boring, and uncomfortable as workers are subjected to the elements and car exhaust. In many cases the best thing for public policy is to support efforts that automate these kinds of bad jobs. For example, if road departments created stronger incentives to use electronic EZ pass systems, most toll-taking jobs would be eliminated within a few years, allowing the workforce to be reduced through attrition or transfer to other transportation jobs. There are a host of other opportunities to automate low-end work. For example, more robust deployment of radio frequency identification devices (RFID) and e-commerce would help automate retail trade jobs.

Some have argued that if technological innovation enables a larger share of lower skill jobs to be automated that this will only reduce the demand for low skill workers, reducing their wages.[4] However, if more low-wage jobs were automated, the occupational mix of the economy would shift toward more skilled and more highly paid jobs, raising incomes for workers. If coupled with better training programs for workers, this shift would lead to increased economic welfare for all Americans, including workers currently in low-wage jobs.

GETTING MORE TIME FOR THE REST OF LIFE

While most workers want more satisfying work, many also want less work. Luckily the New Economy is providing the means for Americans to work less without reducing their incomes. Until the early 1900s most workers put in six-day, 60-hour work weeks, working over 3000 hours a year. Utopians, social reformers and trade unionists dreamed of a day when man would be free of much of the drudgery of work and waged a protracted struggle to realize this vision. In the 1890s the National Federation of Organized Trades and Labor Unions passed a resolution calling for eight hours to be a legal day of work. By the turn of the twentieth century, the popular Eight-hour Day movement emerged, with its slogan, 'eight hours for work, eight hours for rest, and eight hours for what you will.' Unions were not the only ones advocating less work, a number of forward-looking employers were as well. Ford Motor Company made history in 1914 by reducing employees' daily hours from nine to eight while doubling their pay to $5 a day. In the 1920s other leading companies like General Electric and US Rubber joined the movement as they realized that long hours made their workforces less productive. But most workers continued to be employed by companies that stuck to the old ways. As a result, it took the passage of the Fair Labor Standards Act in 1938 to institutionalize a shorter workweek. The Act defined overtime, created the 44-hour work week, and stipulated that wage workers who were required to work more than that were entitled to overtime pay. In 1940 Congress amended the Act, reducing the work week limit to 40 hours. As a result, by 1950 the average work week had fallen from 70.6 hours 100 years earlier to 40.8 hours.

By the 1950s the future of leisure looked bright. The widespread use of automation and the resulting high rates of productivity growth led many to believe that Bellamy's promised land of leisure was around the corner. Not surprisingly there was considerable discussion of how to reduce the work week. Galbraith summed up the prevailing view:

> Over the span of man's history, although a phenomenal amount of education, persuasion, indoctrination and incantation have been devoted to the effort, ordinary people have never been quite persuaded that toil is as agreeable as its alternatives. Thus to take increased well-being partly in the form of more goods and partly in the form of more leisure is unquestionably rational.[5]

The expectations of the coming leisure society were so high that Vice President Nixon, campaigning for Eisenhower's re-election in 1956, proposed a four-day work week, predicting it would lead to a fuller family life for Americans.[6]

However, the large productivity gains of that era's new economy did not yield appreciable gains in leisure. Americans instead chose to consume the increased fruits of higher productivity in the form of more products and services. By the mid-1970s, though, it looked like the hope of a more balanced economy might finally be realized, as 20 years of powerful growth enabled an increased interest in leisure and a post-materialist culture. But just then productivity stalled as the old economy stagnated and the interest in more free time evaporated.

In what would have come as a surprise to many in the 1970s, annual work hours increased from 1883 hours in 1980 to 1966 hours in 1997, creating what some refer to as a crisis of leisure time. This is in marked contrast to other advanced nations. Workers in France put in 1656 annual hours in 1997 (prior to legislation limiting the work week to 35 hours). Germans work even less at 1560 hours. But this is not a reflection of some idiosyncratic European zest for life. Canadians have cut back by more than a full work week during the last two decades, to 1732 hours. Even the Japanese, who were only recently derided as workaholic 'salarymen,' have seen their working hours fall from 2121 in 1980 to 1889 hours in 1995.[7] Americans work almost two weeks a year more than Japanese.

As shown in Table 10.1, compared to Europeans, Americans take few vacation days. While European and Americans got roughly the same amount of vacation time after World War II, after that the Europeans added a week more in the 1950s, 1960s, and 1970s. As a result, with its average of 13 annual vacation days the United States lags behind most European countries. Swedish workers get five weeks off by law, plus another two weeks during the Christmas holidays. The French take an average of 37 days off per year, while the Italians get 42. Unions in Denmark recently staged a nationwide general strike for a sixth week of vacation and settled for two extra days a year, plus three additional personal days for workers with young children. Even the so-called hard-working Japanese take an average of 25 vacation days while the Chinese get 15 days. Until 1998, the United Kingdom was one of the few advanced industrial nations other than the United States without mandatory paid leave, but in that year Prime Minister Tony Blair signed legislation providing working Britons with 20 days mandatory paid vacation days.

Table 10.1   The vacation gap: vacation days by law

Spain	30	Norway	21
France	30	United Kingdom	20
Ireland	28	Germany	18
Japan	25	Canada	10
Belgium	24	United States	0

Source: Robinson (2003).

Americans also work more years. While the average retirement age is 59.3 and 60.5 years in France and Germany, respectively, it is 65.1 years in the United States. Moreover, while the average retirement age went down in the last 15 years in most of Europe, in the United States it went up by 1.2 years.[8] Finally, compared to 30 years ago, a greater share of the population works. The percentage of women in the workforce rose from 33.9 percent in 1950 to 60 percent in 1998. Moreover, women are working more, with their average weekly hours of work increasing from 34.2 hours in 1978 to 36.1 in 1998.[9]

As a result, while the United States has the highest per capita income in the world, Americans earn it by working the most. While Americans are better off materially, modern life is nevertheless characterized by stress, exhaustion, neglected children and the loss of community.

There are a number of reasons given to explain why Americans work so much. One explanation is that workers need the money because of the slow growth in incomes from the mid-1970s to the mid-1990s. To be sure, real median family income rose only 3.1 percent between 1979 and 1994, even though women more than doubled their time in the workforce.

One reason median incomes went up so little was because over one-third of the period's increased economic output flowed to the richest 1 percent of wage earners. Indeed, the earnings of the very wealthy (the top 0.01 percent) went from 50 times more than the average worker's income in 1970 to 250 times by 1998. The average compensation of the highest paid CEOs went from around $1.25 million in 1970 to almost $40 million in 1999.[10] This winner-take-all phenomena has meant that the share of wage and salary income going to the top 10 percent, 5 percent and 1 percent of taxpayers has not been higher since before the Great Depression.[11] Those lucky enough to be in the small elite group, whether it is CEOs, entertainers, professional athletes, attorneys, or doctors, have been able to increasingly live 'lifestyles of the rich and famous.' Were the top 5 percent of earners getting the same share of national income today as they did in 1978 and the economy were the same size, the average worker would earn $6,100 more per year. In this regard it is worth comparing Germany and the United States. During the last half of the 1980s and first half of the 1990s, average incomes went up 15.5 percent in the United States and just 10.4 percent in Germany. But looking at median hourly income reveals a different story. US median hourly income actually went down 2 percent while German median income went up 14.7 percent. In other words, Germany saw somewhat less growth, but a significantly greater number of people benefited from it, enabling them to cut back on their work hours.

Another reason for the increased pressures to work more is that the increase in median worker income was offset by the increased Social Security and Medicare taxes workers and employers paid to support the growing number of retirees. In 1963 they paid just 7.25 percent of wages up to the first $4800 in earnings (equal to $27 100 in 2002 dollars). Today, they pay 15.3 percent on the first $80 400 in earnings. Old age pension and health insurance benefits from government went from 7 percent of wage and salary income in 1970 to 13 percent in 2002. Workers now have to work harder to support a growing number of relatively well off retirees.

Wages did finally begin to grow faster in the mid-1990s but leisure did not. As Americans made more money they used it to purchase more goods and services. A host of new products and services (e.g. wide-screen televisions, cell phones, computers) had been created that people felt they needed, or at least wanted. But consumers are not making these choices in a vacuum. As Juliet Schor notes in *The Overworked American*, social pressures to consume more have became ubiquitous. Today the expectation is to drive to work in a new car filled with the latest features, not a less expensive, but perfectly good 1989 Ford. There is no point living in a small bungalow when everyone else is in a four bedroom McMansion. The vacation to the nearby Poconos is replaced by the vacation to Hawaii. Bottled water replaces tap water. As a result, a vicious circle emerges: as two people work to make ends meet, the 'ends' they expect keep going up, driving them to work even more.[12]

This increase in work stems not just from the collective consumer choices of 130 million workers. Companies and workers face increased competitive pressures to work ever harder. The rise of the 24-hour global company has exacerbated the conflict between corporate values and family values. In a hyper-competitive economy the ideal employee is the one who is always available, not the one who is constantly juggling family responsibilities. In the wired world of ubiquitous communications, the model worker is the one who does not turn off his cell phone and who does check his email. In an economy in which everyone is always looking for the best deal, the ideal company is the one that is open longer and whose employees work harder. As companies face increasingly competitive product marketplaces they get ahead by making sure that their workers work more. As individuals face increasingly competitive labor markets, it is hard *not* to work late nights, go on that out-of-town trip, and bring work home. For if they do not, someone else will. A 1995 survey at Eli Lilly – a company with a reputation as one of the most family-friendly – found that just 36 percent of workers said it was possible to get ahead and still devote sufficient time to their families. In a study of law firms, economist James Rebitzer, found that long hours have become a symbol of commitment and ambition, so that even people who feel neither the need nor the desire to work evenings and weekends get 'stuck in a trap.' He found that even though a majority of lawyers would prefer to work fewer hours, they will not unless their fellow attorneys also cut back.[13] Many workers worry that if they spend less time at the office than colleagues who do not get their work done as quickly, that they might lose out on raises or promotions. These perceptions often are reality. One study found that employees who took family and medical leaves were promoted less and had smaller wage gains.[14]

It is not surprising therefore that the share of people working more than 49 hours a week rose significantly in the late 1980s and early 1990s. Over two-thirds of workers now work 40 hours or more per week, while 8.5 percent regularly put in truly marathon work weeks of 60 hours or more. Managers and professionals in particular have been putting in progressively longer hours on the job and as these occupations have grown, overall work time has gone up. According to economist Dora Costa, at the turn of the twentieth century those in the bottom 10 percent of income worked 600 hours a year more than those at the top. Indeed, one benefit of being at the top was that you did not have to work as hard as the working man. Today's top earners are now the ones putting in the long hours, working 400 hours more per year than low earners. As a result, 29.5 percent of the highest paid workers – managers and professionals – logged marathon work weeks, compared with 24 percent in the early 1980s.[15] This increase explains why 95 percent of workers say they worry that work is taking too much time away from their families, and 87 percent say increased work demands are keeping them from getting enough sleep. It is one reason why the costs of work-related stress are estimated to cost the US economy $300 billion per year.[16]

These pressures to put in more time are not confined to the workplace, they permeate all aspects of society, and increasingly schools. In the old economy, after spending an hour on homework kids would be out playing with their friends in the neighborhood. At the end of the school year they could look forward to an 'endless' summer to wile away the hours doing what kids do, having fun. Now schools are under intense pressure to improve test scores and the easiest way is to give more homework, keep kids in school longer. Because there is such intense pressure to get good grades and test scores so high-schoolers can get into good colleges, parents go along with these trends. In fact, there is a growing trend to lengthen the school day and school year and to even enroll most very young children in full day 'academic' pre-school.[17] For example, because North Carolina education officials worried that they needed to raise the state's test scores, in 2004 they lengthened the school year by two weeks, requiring kids to report for school in mid-August. It is as if as Americans have got so used to working all the time, that we expect our kids to do the same. And of course, kids have no say in these decisions.

Finally, it is not just work and school that are taking up more time, so is traveling there and back. In most large and mid-sized metropolitan areas traffic gridlock is becoming a way of life. According to the Texas Transportation Institute, drivers in the largest 70 metropolitan areas spend an average of 40 extra hours a year stuck in traffic; 150 percent more than in 1982. Whereas ten years ago congestion was confined to rush hours, now it is extended, often to midday and weekend trips. As a result, Americans waste 4.3 billion hours and $74 billion dollars a year stuck in traffic.

Since there are only 24 hours in a day and 365 days in a year, where is all this extra working, schooling and commuting time coming from? The short answer: the family. President Clinton's Council of Economic Advisors reported that, 'Dramatic changes have occurred over the last thirty years in how families combine work and family life.'[18] Clearly one of the most significant is the decreasing amount of time devoted to parenting – the 'parenting deficit.' With more two-earner families, kids are increasingly being raised by nannies, day-care providers, after-school programs, or the television at home alone. Some dads do not see their kids on weekday mornings or nights since they are working long hours or have long commutes. On weekends, when one or both of the parents are not working, it is a frantic rush to get errands and shopping done, along with shuttling kids to soccer games, birthday parties, or tutoring sessions.

One result of the parental time deficit is a decline in breast-feeding. In spite of the evidence that has emerged on the benefits of breast-feeding to both the mother and child, only 29 percent of mothers breast-feed their infants for six months, with 16 percent doing it only for one year, the minimal recommended time according to the American Academy of Pediatrics. Two-thirds of new mothers now return to work within six months of the birth of their child. But it is not just infants who are not spending enough time with their parents, it is kids of all ages. A report from the Carnegie Council on Adolescent Development found that kids spend significantly less time in the company of adults than a few decades ago.[19] About one-third of all adolescents have contemplated suicide; half are at moderate or high risk of abusing drugs, failing in school, getting pregnant, or otherwise seriously damaging their lives. While the risks are exacerbated by poverty, 'in survey after survey, young adolescents from all ethnic and economic backgrounds lament their lack of parental attention and guidance,' the report found.

This is not for lack of parental interest. A survey by *Parents* magazine and the I Am Your Child Foundation found that parents want to spend at least five hours a day with their children.[20] Yet, only half report spending that much time.[21] Another poll found that 70 percent of voters who are married with children say that they do not get to spend enough time with their family and kids. Half of parents blame too long work hours for lack of time spent with their family, while 23 percent cite an inflexible work schedule and 11 percent cite too long a commute.[22] There is a fierce debate over the effects of both parents working, with some arguing that it is detrimental to a child's development and others arguing that the quality of the care kids get is the more important factor, not who provides it. But both sides agree that enabling parents to work less would be beneficial.

This work overload is coming not just at the expense of time spent with our children but from civic activity. Robert Putnam details how since the early 1960s, voter turnout, knowledge about current affairs, and civic organizational activity have all fallen sharply.[23] Among the factors Putnam points to as contributing to the decline in this social capital is reduced non-work time. For example, Putnam found that each additional ten minutes per day in traffic cuts involvement in community affairs by 10 percent for activities on weekdays and weekends alike.[24] Moreover, the increase in work time, especially among women, has deleterious effects on social capital. Many of those women who were homemakers in the 1950s and 1960s were our best social capitalists – keeping school organizations, reading clubs and neighborhood associations afloat. Now when they are not working, they are busy keeping the family going.

Many economic conservatives argue that Americans are working more because they choose to. While a few hard-charging professionals may enjoy 60-plus hour work weeks, evidence suggests that most Americans want to reduce their work hours. According to a *Washington Post* poll, approximately half said they would work fewer hours or fewer days per week, with about 20 percent saying they would not work at all if they could do so and live as well.[25] A survey by the Families and Work Institute found that 64 percent of Americans want to work less, up from 47 percent in 1992. A Mark Penn poll found that nearly nine in ten of married respondents in double-income households with children under age 18 would prefer it if one parent did not have to work outside the house full time.[26] Moreover, while several years ago only about 10 percent of workers would prefer more time off instead of more work, nearly a third now would prefer more time off, while the numbers are even higher among women with kids (41 percent), GenXers (40 percent), those with long commutes (44 percent), and those making more than $60 000 per year (45 percent). Robert Half International asked 1000 workers to estimate the percentage decrease in hours and compensation they would be willing to accept in order to have more personal or family time. Men would reduce their hours and salary an average of 18 percent to get more flexibility; women would be willing to reduce their hours by 23 percent. Seventy-six percent said they would give up rapid career advancement in favor of more flexibility. As a result, if incomes go up due to faster productivity growth and as younger workers become a larger share of the workforce, an increasing share of Americans are likely to want more time off.

One reason why people want to work less is that they are less likely to view work as the center of their lives. While 48 percent of Americans told Roper in 1975 that 'work is the important thing and the purpose of leisure is to recharge people's batteries so they can do a better job,' by 2001 that number had declined to 34 percent.[27] In 1986 just 28 percent of workers said they put too much emphasis on work and not enough on leisure, according to a recent US News/Bozell Worldwide poll 49 percent of Americans felt the other way.[28] The same poll found that 57 percent of Americans now consider leisure important, up from 33 percent in 1986.

In an attempt to help workers better balance work and family, companies are increasingly giving them more flexibility. Forty-three percent of employees have access to flextime, up from 29 percent in 1992.[29] Those offering the option of job sharing increased from 18 percent to 37 percent, while those offering 4-day scheduling rose from 12 to 24 percent. Almost one-third of full-time workers have flexible work schedules.[30] Twenty-six percent of US companies offer telecommuting.[31] This is one reason why the number of telecommuters has grown from 8.5 million in 1995 to 11.1 million in 2002.

Even though many corporations have instituted programs like flex-time or on-site child care, an increasing share of workers are saying that this is not enough. They do not just want flexibility, they want to devote less time to work. For example, a 1999 survey of 1800 workers by Aon consulting found that employees rank paid vacation time and holidays the fourth most important benefit, up from tenth in 1995. The Employment Policy Foundation has found that time off has become the most valued benefit a company can offer its employees. Twenty-eight percent of workers surveyed have seriously contemplated not seeking or turning down a promotion to have more time off. According to a US News/Bozell poll, 38 percent of workers, including 46 percent of managers, have seriously considered cutting back on their hours. Thirty percent say it is likely they will get the option to work fewer hours per day in the next decade. Of those, 54 percent, including 76 percent of managers, say that is because they will personally take steps to cut their hours. A recent survey of male workers aged 20–39 found that having a schedule that allowed them more time for their families was more important to them than doing challenging work or earning a high salary. Around 70 percent said they would be willing to give up some pay in exchange for more family time.[32] More employers are expanding vacation time allowances after fewer years on the job. More employees are getting added weeks of vacation after five to nine years instead of 15 to 20.[33] Paid-time-off banks that lump sick, vacation, and personal days into one category to be taken with their supervisor's approval are now used by 27 percent of employers. As a recruiting tool, work hours have suddenly become an acceptable trade-off for higher pay.

A small share of companies are making even more radical changes, such as adopting a 30-hour work week. Ron Healey, the Founder and CEO of 30/40, has convinced a growing list of skeptical CEOs to cut the work week, including switching to six-hour shifts while still paying workers for a full eight-hour day. Healey says the added expense of hiring more workers pays off because they are more productive, happier and – most importantly – loyal to the company. He argues that absenteeism is eliminated and workers are more productive since they waste less time. For example, employees at sheet-music distributor

J. W. Pepper & Son, in Paoli, PA, work four days a week during slower parts of the year – and still get paid a full-time wage. At Covance Inc., a Princeton, NJ, pharmaceutical development company, managers have found that they can get more work in fewer hours out of employees who telecommute from home. SAS Institute, a North Carolina-based software company, has reportedly saved 'tens of millions' of dollars in turnover costs with an employee-friendly policy of no overtime and a 35-hour week.

Even companies that cannot see cutting below a 40-hour week are making changes. For example, Marriott hotels began a project to increase flexibility while addressing the 'overwork' issue. The corporate culture expected a 50 to 60-hour work week whether there was work to do or not. To fix this, the company worked to define and eliminate low-value work, resolved technology problems that contributed to more work, and eliminated superfluous meetings and unnecessary training. As a result, they were able to reduce hours by an average five per week. The accounting firm Deloitte & Touchè began to think about reducing hours when employees raised the issue by threatening to leave. Now it allows some workers who reduce their hours to stay on an upward career track.

In spite of the growing interest by workers and some companies in reducing work hours, few Americans are willing to see a pay cut to work less. Most still prefer more money to more time. One poll found that just 17 percent of workers would be willing to take a 5 percent pay cut in exchange for a 5 percent cut in work hours. But while most Americans do not want to lose money by working less, the numbers double when workers are asked if they would rather have more money or less time. A Roper Starch Worldwide poll asked people whether, if given a choice, they would prefer more time off or more money.[34] Fifty-seven percent of Americans said they would prefer the money; while 37 percent wanted more time off. The poll asked the same question of people in 29 other countries, and in seven a majority of workers preferred more time off.[35] As productivity continues to grow, it is likely that more Americans will want to take at least some of the increase in the form of more leisure.[36]

Creating an economy in which people will be able to better balance work and family will take more than individuals acting as autonomous agents in the labor market. Conservatives will argue that balancing work and family is a personal issue only individuals can solve on their own. But labor markets are shaped not just by unfettered individual choices, but also by social norms and laws. Most individuals do not have the choice to work a 35-hour week, since the norm, reinforced by federal law, is 40 hours. In an economy in which the needs of people are given at least equal weight with the needs of the production system, decisions about finding the right balance cannot simply be negotiated by individuals in their own workplaces, they require a new social agreement over the relationship between work and family.

The first key to creating a more family-friendly economy is to put productivity growth at the center of our nation's economic policies. Robust productivity growth is the means by which society can afford to consume more leisure while also experiencing rising real incomes. Putting the pedal to the metal of economic efficiency will make it possible for a greater share of workers to earn enough to afford more leisure. However as the history of the last 50 years has shown productivity growth will not be enough. Companies, individuals, and government need to take steps to ensure that a share of increased productivity can go to 'buying' leisure.

To do this government needs to enact policies to help Americans better balance work and family. Such policies do not have to mean giving workers or businesses everything they want. In fact, by giving workers more flexibility and more time off while at the same time giving employers more flexibility in how they can organize work, both can win. As a result, government should start by amending the Fair Labor Standards Act to reduce the amount of time workers work. Should legislation reduce the work week or increase vacations days? When Roper asked people in 1936 if they would prefer a shorter work week or a longer vacation, 69 percent said a shorter week, and 28 percent said more vacation. However, as the work week has declined, a majority of Americans now prefer more vacation days.[37] As a result, government should amend the Fair Labor Standards Act so that after a year on the job employed Americans get three weeks' paid vacation. If productivity continues to go up at a robust pace over the next decade, Congress should expand this to at least four weeks.

Congress should also change laws that prohibit companies from providing time off in exchange for overtime. Currently, time-off options for about the half the civilian workforce who are paid hourly are limited by the Fair Labor Standards Act of 1938 that requires that employers must offer only money in return for overtime. Seventy-five percent of Americans and 83 percent of women with children would like the choice to take overtime in time-off rather than time-and-a-half wages.[38] Legislation in Congress would have allowed employers to offer hourly workers the choice of either one-and-one-half hours of wages or one-and-one-half hours of 'comp time' (additional hours they can take off) for each hour of overtime worked. However, unions and their supporters have successfully fought attempts to change the laws, arguing that companies will simply engage workers in irregular hours, disrupting their personal lives. But there are solutions for this. Legislation can include penalties for employers who force workers into taking time off instead of time-and-a-half wages. In addition, any legislation should bar employers from coercing employees; protect especially vulnerable employees, including part-time and seasonal workers; give employees reasonable latitude over when they can take the time off; limit the accumulation of 'comp-time' hours; enable employees to cash out their unused 'comp time'; and prevent employers from discriminating unfairly in determining who gets 'comp time'.

Telecommuting is another workplace practice that lets people not only balance work and family, but also reduce time spent commuting. However, there are policy obstacles to telework. Under current tax law, for example, employees that receive computing equipment from their employers as an incentive to telecommute must pay income taxes on the value of the equipment. Regulatory uncertainty regarding the status of home offices also acts as a disincentive to companies to formalize their work-from-home arrangements. State tax laws may actually force some teleworkers to pay taxes in two states, the one they work in and the one they live in. Congress should pass legislation that allows employers or employees to take a tax deduction for the costs of home computer equipment and Internet access used for telecommuting. Congress should also pass legislation preventing states from levying double taxes on telecommuters.

Government can also give Americans more time by cutting traffic congestion. Road congestion has worsened for a simple reason: with growing numbers of workers, vehicle miles traveled increased 42 percent in the last 13 years, while lane miles increased 9 percent. As any first year economics student can report, when demand increases faster than supply, shortages occur. In this case, the shortages – space on highways – have led to dramatic traffic delays. While the cause is clear, the solution is equally simple: government needs to expand road capacity and pay for it through either by raising the gas tax or putting in place tolls on new roads.[39]

CREATING FAMILY-FRIENDLY CAPITALISM

While ensuring a better balance between work and non-work activities is important for all workers, it is especially important for families with young children. Yet, the trend over the last three decades has been for new mothers to work. Whereas only 17 percent of mothers of one-year olds worked full- or part-time in 1965, by 2001 58 percent did.[40] In the same period, out-of-home childcare has grown dramatically. Almost 13 million infants, toddlers, and preschoolers – more than half of our nation's 21 million preschool population – are receiving care from someone other than their parents or another family member.[41] More than half of these children in childcare spend 35 hours per week or more in daycare and more than one-third are in two or more child care arrangements each week.[42] In fact, the US is second only to Denmark among developed nations in the percentage of infants and toddlers in day care. One of the major reasons is that many families cannot afford to have one parent stay at home during the first year of the child's life.

These are not simply issues that affect families, they impact society. Good parenting is an investment that brings societal-wide benefits. Children who are raised well are less likely to be a drain on societal resources (e.g., be in jail, have poor health, etc.) and are more likely to become more productive workers.[43] While there are social benefits from the investments good parents make in their children, the cost of raising children (except for public education) are overwhelmingly private and can be significant. A two-parent household earning $36 800 to $61 900 will spend $160 000 to feed, clothe and shelter a child until the age of 18.[44]

There are a number of steps that policymakers can take to address the work-family conflict. The politically easy one, but not the best, is to expand childcare and create universal full-day preschool and after-school programs. This assumes that most parents want subsidized daycare. However, one survey found that 82 percent of parents believe raising children is tougher now than ever before, and 72 percent of parents said they would rather stay home and raise their children than work, if money were not an issue.[45] A survey by the Working Women's Department of the AFL-CIO found that 46 percent of women who are either married or living with someone work a different schedule than their partner, and the percentage is significantly higher (51 percent) for married women with children under 18. The majority of this group chose these separate shift or alternate hours arrangements to accommodate the needs of work and family, which seems to confirm the preference of working parents for avoiding commercial day care if possible. Support for childcare appears to better fit people's needs as workers, as opposed to parents, not to mention what is best for children.[46]

Many of the supporters of universal public day care assume that more time spent in institutional care is best for the healthy emotional development of kids. While this may be true for some families with a problematic home environment, there is evidence that this is not the case for the average child.[47] A substantial amount of research points to the very great benefits both to newborns and to the family from at least one parent staying home with a newborn during their first year of life.[48] The Carnegie Task Force on Meeting the Needs of Young Children reported: 'Experts can now substantiate the benefits of allowing ample time for the mother to recover from childbirth and for the parents to be with their new baby during the first months of life.'[49] Just as importantly, public subsidies for universal child care are unfair to parents who choose to give up the extra income to have one parent stay at home. Parents who make the sacrifice to do the right thing in terms of child rearing get no subsidy, while two-earner families who need the money less get a subsidy.

As a result, at minimum child-care subsidies must be choice neutral, and be available to parents who choose to care for their children at home. One way to do this would be to eliminate tax benefits for paid day care and instead fold the money into creating a refundable $3000 tax credit for parents with children under four.[50] The credit could be revenue neutral if the current credit of $1000 were reduced to $650 for parents of children between four and 17.

While tax credits can help, we also need to make it easier for new parents to take leave to care for newborn children. In a major shift from the previous Bush administration, the Clinton administration signed the Family and Medical Leave Act in 1993. The Act allows 12 weeks unpaid leave after the birth or adoption of a child. But while the Act provided leave, few families take it at the birth of child because they cannot afford to lose the income.

All advanced nations, except the United States, mandate job-guaranteed parental leave and some provision for wage replacement.[51] In fact, according to the International Labor Organization, the maternity and nursing benefits given to working mothers in the US are the least generous in the industrialized world. About 80 percent of the 152 countries surveyed provide paid maternity leave to women workers, and a third permit leave for more than 14 weeks. In Germany a new parent staying home can receive modest financial support for up to one and half years. In Sweden, new parents who have been working receive full pay. Polls show that Americans, whether they have children or not, overwhelmingly support expanding family leave policies. A 1998 survey by the National Partnership of Women & Families found that 83 percent of working parents and 81 percent of working people without children favor expanding unemployment or disability insurance to provide partial wages for workers who need to take family leave to care for a newborn or a newly adopted pre-school child.

There is an easy answer to the problem: use the unemployment insurance system to provide benefits to new parents. Congress should pass legislation that would make parents of newborns eligible for unemployment insurance for up to six months.[52] This is similar to the benefits provided in Canada where new parents are eligible for a basic unemployment insurance benefit rate of 55 percent of average insured earnings up to a maximum of $413 per week. If Congress required all 50 states to adopt this proposal the estimated cost would be approximately $4.1 billion per year, with the federal portion being half. The federal government should lead by example with the President signing an executive order mandating that all federal employees are eligible for 26 weeks paid parental leave to care for a newborn or an adopted child under the age of two.

Finally, while paid leave for new parents would help parents deal with the work/family conflict for the first six months of a child's life, it does not address the need for flexibility after that, particularly during the key years before a child starts school full time. Ideally, families would have the flexibility and financial wherewithal to be able to work less and more flexibility. The key though is to provide families with the abilities to make these choices. Unfortunately, for many workers part-time work is not possible unless they are willing to work in relatively low-pay retail or service jobs often with fewer or no benefits, less opportunity for advancement, and unpredictable work schedules. For many workers with careers, this is not a fair choice and not a balance: they must either give up their career and leave their employer or they must work full time and put their child in full daycare.

Other countries are significantly farther along in creating family-friendly workplaces that support such flexible working. Full-time workers in Sweden have a legal right to work six hours per day (with reduced pay) until their child turns eight.[53] Norway has established a wide range of generous family-leave policies that enable both parents to combine part-time work and partial family leave benefits.

To give parents of infants, toddlers, and pre-school children workplace flexibility employers will need to change. This is particularly true when it comes to middle and higher wage office and white collar jobs, where the choice is often between the career track or the 'Mommy track' (or the 'Mr Mom' track). As a result, it is up to the federal government to encourage companies to become more flexible.

There are several things Congress and the administration should do to increase workplace flexibility for parents with children not yet in full day school. Congress should pass legislation requiring companies to allow parents with children under six to have the right to ask their employer to consider seriously their requests to work flexibly.[54] Under the Blair government in the United Kingdom parents with children under six or disabled children under 18 have been granted the right to ask their employer to consider seriously their requests to work flexibly and this has made a difference in the number of parents with flexible work.[55]

The UK system does several things. First, it places the presumptive burden on employers to consider seriously the requests of workers for flexibility. Employers are allowed to reject requests only on specific and defined business grounds, such as significantly increased costs and health and safety grounds. Employers who do not consider requests seriously risk being taken to an employment tribunal and ordered to consider the request properly and pay compensation. Congress should also clarify workplace legislation that would protect workers from unfair dismissal or detriment if they either seek or take parental leave or flexible work conditions.

Some will argue that employers will ignore a mandate to 'take seriously' requests for work flexibility. The experience in the UK suggests that this has not been the case. Since it was put into place, over one million UK parents of children under the age of six, one in four, have asked for a change in their work hours, and over 80 percent have been granted.[56] Most requests were from women after maternity leave to request working part-time. One way the UK system works is by changing the cultural expectations toward workplace flexibility for parents of young children. More workers expect such flexibility and more companies see it as simply another part of the modern work environment they must provide.

Paid leave, more generous child tax credits and work flexibility are investments in the future of America's families, and most importantly in a healthy start for our children.

CREATING LIVABLE COMMUNITIES

Building a more humane economy will take more than creating more satisfying work environments and ensuring that Americans have increased time for their families and themselves. It will also mean making it easier for more Americans to live in more satisfying places, including smaller cities on a human scale.

Most Americans do not live where they would like to. A recent Gallup poll found that 24 percent of Americans want to live on a farm or in a rural area, with 36 percent preferring small-town life. Surprisingly, these preferences have remained remarkably stable over time, but where Americans live has not.[57] While over 31 percent of Americans lived in rural areas or small towns in 1970, today fewer than 20 percent do. As a result, over one-third of Americans are living in metropolitan areas even though they would prefer to live in less populated areas. You do not need surveys to understand that most people do not live where they want. The fact that many retirees move to 'retirement' spots suggests that many of people spend their working lives living in places that are not their top choices. A large share of Americans would rather be living near the beach, in the mountains, in the desert, or by a lakeside rather than in a crowded city or suburban development in a large metropolitan area and they show that when they retire.

People live in big metros because that is where jobs are. Historically, cities have arisen and grown as centers of commerce, largely because of the need for physical proximity among firms, suppliers, and customers. Agglomerations of people, infrastructure, and industry allowed for the efficient production, transport, and distribution of goods and services. In the factory-based industrial economy a large share of people lived in industrial cities in the Midwest and Northeast because that was where the factories were. In the corporate, mass production economy people spread out in the South and West, with most people in suburbs and central cities of large metropolitan areas. However, just as where people lived and worked changed as past economies changed, this is happening once again. The New Economy is giving people and companies more locational freedom. As an increased share of the economy consists of processing information in digital form, economic activity is able to be physically farther apart, while still remaining functionally close. As more economic activity is in the form of digital bits a growing share of economic activity does not have to be near natural resources or even big population centers.

Where will it be? In the New Economy, companies increasingly look to move to and expand where knowledge workers live. Because they are in greater demand and are able to be particular about who they work for, knowledge workers can live in places that provide a high quality of life in addition to a good job. The result is that for the first time in history it is possible to conceive of a society where a not insignificant share of people live not where the jobs are, but rather where they want, with the jobs following them.

There are steps government can take to help speed this transition. Economic conservatives will argue that the current spatial distribution of economic activity is by definition the most efficient and that intervention will hurt the economy. In reality market forces acting alone are not likely to produce the optimal spatial distribution. The locational decisions made by companies have significant positive and negative externalities that mean that firms will not necessarily make decisions that lead to the optimal outcome for the economy. For example, while a firm may benefit from moving into a crowded metropolitan area, firms already there will pay slightly higher costs because of the added congestion and demand for labor and housing. In addition, there are chicken-or-egg issues involved in regional development. Firms and workers may want to move to a smaller city, but unless both act at once, neither will. Firms may not move to a smaller city because they worry that they cannot get enough workers, and workers will not move there because they worry they cannot get a job.

This would not be the first time that policymakers have sought to influence the spatial distribution of jobs and people. Just as there was an increased focus on leisure studies and self-actualization towards the end of the old economy, there was also an effort to create a national 'balanced growth' strategy. The leadership for such an effort came from, of all places, the Nixon White House. Under the leadership of domestic policy advisor John Erlichman, the administration drew up plans for a national strategy to increase population in smaller towns and rural areas, including 'new towns', in order to cope with increased congestion in large metropolitan areas. But Watergate soon distracted them, and the efforts lay fallow.

There are a number of things governments can do to help create a more human-centered distribution of economic activity. Governments can use the location of government jobs to foster more balanced growth. Where state and federal governments choose to locate their jobs can play an important role in regional development. In addition, when the federal government is making decisions as to closing certain facilities, such as military bases, one of the factors it should use in making the decision is whether the facility is in a large, booming metropolitan area. But governments need to do more than just move their own jobs to smaller cities, they need to establish policies to encourage private companies to do the same. One way to do this is to phase out farm subsidies over ten years and reinvest the savings in a new National Rural Prosperity Corporation.[58] The Corporation would make challenge grants to states for innovative rural development efforts.

ARE A HUMANE ECONOMY AND A PRODUCTIVE ECONOMY IN CONFLICT?

Since at least the factory era, pragmatists and utopians have been at odds. Hard-headed pragmatists have argued that the needs of the economic system and the drive for efficiency trumped all. Idealistic utopians dreamed of organizing an economy around human needs and dismissed the need for efficiency or profits. Today, in the face of growing global competition, pro-business conservatives argue that focusing on living the good life will reduce efficiency and competitiveness. Besides, they argue, the marketplace, not public policies, should decide these matters. In contrast, civil society liberals and progressives argue that the relentless drive toward efficiency dampens the human spirit, fails to meet human needs and spoils the environment.[59] Besides, they argue, efforts to boost productivity support the powerful's interests, not the people's interests.

Luckily they are both wrong. The reality is that the New Economy is enabling a new synthesis where increased efficiency and a more humane economy can go hand in hand. Indeed, the key challenge is to continue rapidly to boost productivity but do it in a way that makes it easier for people to work in more humane work environments and have more time for leisure.

Increased productivity can create a more humane economy. Higher productivity leads to higher wages and lower prices, which allow people to work less while maintaining or increasing incomes. Moreover, automating unpleasant and unsatisfying jobs shifts the overall mix of jobs toward more satisfying ones. Finally, without productivity growth people will not be wealthy enough to afford the kinds of public investments needed to create a more livable society.

Conversely, in an economy that is increasingly powered by knowledge, a more humane economy can boost productivity. People are more productive when they are able to establish a healthier balance between work and non-work activities. Numerous studies show that high-performance work organizations are more successful than more traditional ones. One study of Fortune 1000 firms found that employee involvement is a stronger driver of financial performance than TQM or reengineering.[60] Companies that support flexible work arrangements such as flextime, telecommuting and job sharing had 3.5 percent higher market value than companies with no workplace flexibility.[61] A Boston College study found that flexible work arrangements, including traditional flextime, 'daily flextime' and telecommuting had a positive impact on productivity, work quality and retention, with daily flextime showing the best results by far of any of the three arrangements.[62] The total returns of companies on *Fortune*'s 1993 'Best Companies to Work for in America' list exceeded one index by 80 percentage points over the period 1990–96. The 1998 'Best Companies' total returns beat the same index by 67 percent during the 1995–98 period. Moreover, studies show that both job tenure and productivity are determined by workers' relationships with their immediate supervisor. This is a long way from the days of Frederick Taylor and treating workers like cogs in a machine.

Even if more satisfying workplaces boost productivity, less time working will reduce economic output as people work less. But shifting to shorter hours does not lead to a one-to-one loss of output. According to a US News/Bozell poll, 62 percent of managers surveyed say that shorter work hours would give employees an incentive to be more productive and would have little impact on the country's standard of living.[63] One reason is that when firms cut hours, they also cut out wasted time: lunch hours are reduced or eliminated, breaks are modified, and people are motivated to get to work on time and avoid calling in sick. Another reason is that cutbacks in hours are typically accompanied by an overall restructuring of work and greater autonomy for employees. That was the case at sheet music seller J.W. Pepper. To eliminate time wasted by workers who had little to do during slow periods but were overloaded during the busy season, a group of workers came up with a plan: during the 29 weeks when business was slowest, employees would work four 7-hour days and get paid for five. Pepper would also train employees to handle a variety of tasks, from shipping orders to responding to customer calls so it could shift them to departments where the need was greatest. In the first six years after the plan was implemented, sales doubled – and no extra employees were hired.

Finally, some may argue that such an agenda may be desirable but that with the impending baby boom retirement and the fiscal crisis stemming from increased Social Security and Medicare payments, that we will need to be working harder, not less. However, steps to limit entitlement growth, such as indexing future benefits to prices and not wages, and steps to keep Medicare costs under control would go a long way to ensure the solvency of these programs, precluding the need to work even more.

THE POLITICS OF CREATING A HUMANE ECONOMY

In 1949, George Soule, the head of the National Bureau of Economic Research, argued that 'if we go on advancing at the same rate, it will not be many decades before everyone in the nation has decent housing, adequate nourishment, a good education – in short, the material essentials of a good life.'[64] He went on to say that 'We have within our reach an economic environment that would make it unnecessary for masses of people to be undernourished or ill housed, to work in obsolete plants or shops, or to lack essential medical care, social security or education.'[65] Today, for most Americans Soule's goal of eliminating poverty and satisfying basic needs has been reached. As a result, the progressive agenda today is not just, as the left stresses, to finish the old economy task of boosting the fortunes of the 31 million Americans still in poverty, it is also to help most Americans live better and more fulfilling lives. Obviously government cannot make people happier and more fulfilled, but they can help create conditions in which it is easier for people to achieve these goals on their own. If government is going to help foster the transition to a more humane economy, there will have to be a new political consensus for it. Unfortunately, neither the Democratic nor Republican parties have yet embraced an agenda for a more humane New Economy.

While the Republican party talks about embracing growth they remain yoked to a corporate community whose interests are often at odds to a humane economy agenda. Given that getting to a more humane economy requires some new regulations, such as mandatory vacation time for workers and paid parental leave, business and their Republican allies are likely to oppose such steps. Moreover, dramatically boosting productivity will require a whole new set of pro-productivity policies which some conservatives are likely to oppose as industrial policy. Finally, while the Republican party's corporate supporters have a stake in higher productivity and innovation – as long as it doesn't threaten powerful incumbent business interests – they also have a stake in growing the GDP. Thus, they are likely to be ambivalent towards policies that reduce the number of hours worked since this will lead to a relatively smaller, although not less productive economy.

Moreover, many social conservatives, reflecting their industrial era Calvinist roots, many fear that too much leisure and a focus on living instead of striving will lead to widespread moral decay. As they say, 'idleness is the devil's workshop.' This is not just a recent concern. In 1967 conservative futurist Herman Kahn worried that by the year 2000:

> There may be a great increase in selfishness, a great decline of interest in government and society as a whole, and a rise in the more childish forms of individualism and in the more antisocial forms of concern for self and perhaps immediate family. Thus, paradoxically, the technological, highly productive society, by demanding less of the individual, may decrease his economic frustrations but increase his aggressions against society. Certainly here would be fertile soil for what has become known as alienation.[66]

Such concerns reflect many moral conservatives' deep distrust of people's innate nature. They believe that the only thing that keeps us from turning into a 'nasty, brutish, and short' Hobbesian society is the clamping down on our natural inclinations through such institutions as hard work. If an economy that establishes a better balance between work and families leads people to focus more on their own enjoyment, fun, and leisure then, yes, Kahn is right. But rather than see this as a negative, most people would see it as positive.

If Republicans are beset by pressures leading them to support the current economy, Democrats are also constrained by interests that are not necessarily compatible with a humane economy agenda. Many liberal elements of the Democratic party are ambiguous in their support of both the New Economy and the kinds of policy changes needed. Many still believe that redistribution alone can boost the incomes of low and moderate income Americans. As a result they often place less emphasis on productivity-oriented policies and more on redistributionist ones. Moreover liberal Democrats long for labor market stability and have reacted against the job churning inherent in a dynamic fast-growing economy. As job displacement from digital automation increases, many liberals are likely to side with those who lose their jobs, seeking to protect them from change, even if it means lower productivity growth. Some liberals even question the benefit of productivity. One leading liberal economist recently stated that automation and high productivity in areas such as health care, education, and entertainment are the sign of a poor society, not a rich one, and should be resisted.

Many liberals also focus more on protecting workers against sweatshop bosses or against rapacious big corporations than on crafting policies to ensure that more Americans work in high-performance, more satisfying workplaces. Moreover, many on the left want to preserve the old idealized workplace where workers are employed in large, stable, benevolent organizations. It is for this reason that the left opposes merit pay for government workers and wants to expand union power to determine work rules, even if they result in lower productivity. Workplace security is important but we also need to embrace a progressive agenda to create workplaces that not only do not oppress the body but also liberate the spirit.

Finally, the liberal wing of the Democratic party remains largely focused on completing the old economy's agenda – making sure that everyone could join the consumer economy and satisfy their material wants, especially housing, medical care and transportation, and ensuring that workers are protected from abuses. Now the challenge is to create an economy and society that satisfies our deeper human needs and wants. But many on the left look at the goals of living a better life as the strivings of what political commentator David Brooks refers to as 'bobos' – upper-middle class bourgeois bohemians – who can afford such things. With some Americans still mired in poverty and some workers still exploited on the job, many liberals will see a humane economy agenda as a luxury that diverts attention from the real job of boosting opportunity for those at the bottom of the labor market. They rightly argue that poverty and unsafe jobs are inhumane, but spend little energy pushing to create a society that satisfies Americans' higher needs. The Democratic party cannot be the majority party if its principal goal is to just address the abuses and inequities stemming from the old economy, it has also to be the party seeking to create a more human-centered new economy.

Because of all these factors, developing political support for a humane New Economy strategy will require a new kind of centrist politics in Washington. Moderate Republicans and Democrats from districts with large numbers of progressive knowledge-based firms and knowledge workers are likely to embrace an agenda of higher productivity, a more digital economy, and policies to give workers more satisfying work, more time off and more livable communities. Former Bush domestic policy advisor James Pinkerton is right in saying that the history of American politics can be thought of as a story of a leader and party coming to power by making a big offer to voters. In the past these big offers have resonated when a new economy has emerged and voters were ready for something new. In today's New Economy the big offer is not the Republican vision of a privatized society where the intrinsic forces of capitalism lead to more efficient but not necessarily a fairer or more humane society and where individuals are on their own to get what they can. Likewise it is not liberal Democrat vision of a more bureaucratic society where government programs and regulations lead to a secure and fairer, but ultimately less efficient economy with less choice. Rather, the big offer will come from the party that promises to work to give the American people both freedom and opportunity, high productivity and the good life.

The party that articulates a new American dream, not one of having more money or bigger GDP, but one of more satisfying and rewarding work, a better balance between work and family, and more satisfying communities is the party that could be the majority party for the first quarter of the twenty-first century.

In an address a few months before he was assassinated, Democratic presidential candidate Robert Kennedy may have best summarized the case for creating a humane economy:

The gross national product does not allow for the health of our children, the qualify of their education, or the joy of their play. It does not include the beauty of our poetry or the strength of our marriages; the intelligence of our public debate or the integrity of our public officials. It measures... neither our wisdom nor our learning; neither our compassion nor our devotion to our country; it measures everything, in short, except that which makes life worthwhile.[67]

Like Keynes 75 years ago, Kennedy was ahead of his time. However, given the liberating and productivity enhancing potential of the New Economy, the vision they offered is getting closer, and if we take the right steps, it can be nearer than we think.

NOTES

1. Keynes (1930, 1963) p. 163.
2. Ibid.
3. Marx (1846) Part I, A.
4. For example, see Manning (2004).
5. Galbraith (1958) p. 256.
6. He quickly retracted his proposal after opposition emerged.
7. International Labor Organization (1999).
8. OECD (2001).
9. Bailyn et al. (2001) p. 11.
10. According to *Business Week*, the average CEO of a major corporation made 42 times the average hourly worker's pay in 1980, 85 times in 1990 and 531 times in 2000 (www.aflcio.org/corporateamerica/paywatch/ceou/ceou_compare.cfm).
11. Piketty and Saez (2003).
12. In the widely read book *The Two Income Trap*, Warren and Tyagi (2003) reject the claim made by a number of authors, including Juliet Schor (2001), that many Americans have gotten caught in a trap of overconsumption. They claim that over the past 20 years the financial squeeze on families has not come about because they are buying more things, like designer clothes and eating out more, but because other essentials, like housing and education have gone up in price. While the latter is true, the former is not. The authors make this mistake because to calculate the change in consumption of a particular item they incorrectly use the economy-wide consumer price index (CPI) for it, rather than the specific rate of inflation for it. For example, using the clothing deflator instead of the CPI shows that an average family of four actually spent more on clothes in 2001 ($2081) than in 1984 ($1741), not less as the authors claim. The same turns out to be true for housing, cars, and food (Atkinson, 2004).
13. Cited in Bailyn et al. (2001) pp. 14-15.
14. Ibid. p. 19.
15. Between 1973 and 1991 work hours increased for workers in the top 70 percent of the wage distribution (ibid. p. 14).
16. Schwartz (2004).
17. For example, see a report by the Project on Global Working Families (www. globalworkingfamilies.org).

18. President's Council of Economic Advisors (1999).
19. Carnegie Council on Adolescent Development (1995).
20. Cited in Robertson (2000).
21. Twenty-nine percent of parents spend three to five hours a day with their children, and 18 percent spend less than three hours. Among working parents, two-thirds of fathers (66 percent) and one-half of mothers (51 percent) are unhappy with the amount of time they dedicate to their children.
22. www.ndol.org/blueprint/fall2000/penn.html.
23. Putman (2000).
24. Sagaura Seminar (2000).
25. Morin and Rosenfeld (1998).
26. Penn (2000).
27. Those responding that 'leisure is the important thing: the purpose of work is to make it possible to have leisure time to enjoy life' increased modestly from 36 percent to 40 percent. Quoted in Bowman (2001).
28. Cited in Saltzman (1997).
29. Bond et al. (2002) p. 8.
30. US Bureau of Labor Statistics (1997).
31. 2000 survey by the Society of Human Resource Management in Alexandria, VA.
32. Conducted by Harris Interactive for the Radcliffe Public Policy Center, Washington, DC, *The Washington Post Online*, 5-3-00.
33. Carol Sladek of Hewitt Associates in Lincolnshire, IL.
34. www.roper.com/news/content/news196.htm.
35. www.ncpa.org/pd/gif/pd080700a.gif.
36. Robinson (2003).
37. Cited in Bowman (2001).
38. Penn (2000).
39. Atkinson (2002a).
40. Carnegie Corporation of New York (1994), also US Census Bureau (2002) table 571.
41. Many low-income families don't utilize center-based daycare in part because of the costs, but often utilize family and friend networks (e.g. 'kincare').
42. National Center for Education Statistics, "Characteristics of Children's Early Care and Education Programs," Washington, DC, June 1998, data from Sandra L. Hoffert, Kimberlee A. Shavman, Robert Henke, and Jerry West, National Household Education Survey, 1995, NCES publication 98-128.
43. A study using data from the National Institute of Child Health and Human Development found that children whose mothers spend the first year at home score higher on school readiness at age three and the results persist (Lewin, 2002).
44. Hewlett (2002).
45. Survey by *Parents Magazine* and the I Am Your Child Foundation cited in Robertson (2000).
46 David Blankenhorn (1999) argues that from a child's point of view we have two clusters of 'work-family' policies. One set – paid child care support – is 'designed to free up parents to spend more time as workers' and hence work primarily in the interests of employers rather than families. Corporate managers and public policymakers prefer these over allowing employees more schedule flexibility to take care of family obligations, what Blankenhorn terms 'freeing up workers to spend more time as parents.'
47. Leach (1994).
48. Greenspan and Atkinson (2004).
49. Carnegie Corporation of New York (1994).
50. The Dependent Care Tax credit and the Dependent Care Assistance Plan provide tax benefits to offset the cost to parents of paid day care.

51. Ibid.
52. Atkinson (2003a).
53. www.sweden.se/templates/FactSheet4123.asp.
54. www.demos.co.uk/events/Recentevents/worklifebalance.
55. www.dti.gov.uk/er/wptresponse.pdf.
56. Palmer (2004).
57. A Gallup poll conducted in 1937 found that 30 percent wanted to live on a farm while 28 percent wanted to live in a small town.
58. Atkinson (2004b).
59. Fox (2002).
60. The introduction of Total Quality Management practices was associated with an average return on investment of about 15 percent – no different from companies that did not use it. Companies that pushed reengineering had an average return of 15.4 percent, compared with 13.4 percent for those that did not. But companies that emphasized employee involvement had an average return on investment of 19.1 percent, compared with 15.2 percent for those that made little use of it.
61. www.workfamily.com/open/studies.htm.
62. Of employees surveyed, 87 percent said working one of the three options had improved both their productivity and work quality; 80 percent said flexibility had a beneficial impact on retention. Their managers were also enthusiastic; 70 percent said flexibility improved productivity, 65 percent said it had a positive impact on the quality of work produced and 76 percent felt flexibility had a favorable effect on retention (Boston College, Center on Work & Family, 2000).
63. Cited in Bowman (2000).
64. Soule (1948) p. 51.
65. Ibid. p. 116.
66. Kahn (1967) p. 199.
67. Quoted in Ivanko and Kivirist (2004) p. 219.

Bibliography

Acemoglu, Daron and Jorn-Steffen Pischke (1998), 'Why Do Firms Train? Theory and Evidence', *Quarterly Journal of Economics*, **113**, February, 79-119.

Adams, Henry (1905, 1973), *The Education of Henry Adams*, ed. Ernest Samuels, Boston, MA: Houghton Mifflin.

Adkinson, William, Erik Heinecke and Thomas Lenard (2003), *The Digital Economy Fact Book*, Washington, DC: Progress and Freedom Foundation.

Alcaly, Roger (2003), *The New Economy*, New York: Farrar, Straus and Giroux.

Alderfer, E.B. and H.E. Michl (1957), *Economics of American Industry*, New York: McGraw-Hill.

Alexander, Lamar and Chester Finn, Jr (eds) (1995), *The New Promise of American Life,* Indianapolis, IN: Hudson Institute.

Alorie, Gilbert and Beth Bacheldor (2000), 'The Big Squeeze', *Information Week Online*, 27 March (www.informationweek.com /779/chanel.htm).

American Hotel and Lodging Association (2000), *Hot Topics 2000*, Washington, DC: AHLA.

Appelbaum, Eileen, Thomas Bailey, Peter Berg and Arne L. Kalleberg (2000), *Manufacturing Advantage*, Ithaca, NY: Cornell University Press.

Armour, Stephanie (2003), 'US Workers Feel the Burn of More Hours: Less Leisure', *USA Today*, 18 December (www.usatoday.com/money/workplace /2003-12-16-hours-cover_x.htm).

Arthur, W. Brian (1993), 'On the Evolution of Complexity', Sante Fe, NM: Santa Fe Institute, working paper 93-11-070.

A.T. Kearny and *Foreign Policy Magazine* (2001), *Globalization Index*, January/February.

Atkinson, Robert (1996), 'International Differences in Environmental Compliance Costs and US Manufacturing Competitiveness', *International Environmental Affairs*, **8** (2), 107-34.

Atkinson, Robert, (1998), 'Technological Change and Cities', *Cityscape: A Journal of Policy Development and Research*, **3** (3), 129-70.

Atkinson, Robert (2001), 'The Revenge of the Disintermediated: How the Middleman is Fighting E-Commerce and Hurting Consumers', Washington, DC: Progressive Policy Institute.

Atkinson, Robert (2002), 'Bush Listens to Coolidge, McKinley, and Rove', *Blueprint*, September/October, 35-7.

Atkinson, Robert (2002a), 'Getting Unstuck: Three Big Ideas to Get America Moving Again', Washington, DC: Progressive Policy Institute.

Atkinson, Robert (2003), 'Network Government for the Digital Age', Washington, DC: Progressive Policy Institute.

Atkinson, Robert (2003a), 'Putting Parenting First: Why It's Time for Universal Paid Leave', Washington, DC: Progressive Policy Institute.

Atkinson, Robert (2003b), 'The Bush Manufacturing Crisis', Washington, DC: Progressive Policy Institute.

Atkinson, Robert (2004), 'Vanishing Dreams', *Blueprint*, no. 2, June, 4-5.

Atkinson, Robert (2004a), 'Understanding the Offshoring Challenge', Washington, DC: Progressive Policy Institute.

Atkinson, Robert (2004b), 'Reversing America's Rural Decline', Washington, DC: Progressive Policy Institute.

Atkinson, Robert (2004c), 'Meeting the Offshoring Challenge', Washington, DC: Progressive Policy Institute.

Atkinson, Robert and Randolph Court (1998), *The New Economy Index*, Washington, DC: Progressive Policy Institute.

Atkinson, Robert and Les Garner (1987), 'Regulation as Industrial Policy: A Case Study of the US Auto Industry', *Economic Development Quarterly*, **1** (4), 358-73.

Atkinson, Robert and Paul Gottlieb (2001), *The Metropolitan New Economy Index*, Washington, DC: Progressive Policy Institute.

Baer, Kenneth (2000), *Reinventing Democrats: A Politics of Liberalism from Reagan to Clinton*, Lawrence, KS: University Press of Kansas.

Baier, Scott and Jeffrey Bergstrand (1998), 'The Growth of World Trade: Tariffs, Transport Costs, and Income Similarity', mimeo, University of Notre Dame.

Baily, Martin and Robert M. Solow (2001), 'International Productivity Comparisons Built from the Firm Level', *Journal of Economic Perspectives*, **15** (3), 151-72.

Bailyn, Lotte, Robert Drago and Thomas Kochan (2001), *Integrating Work and Family Life*, Cambridge, MA: MIT Press.

Baker, Dean (2000), 'The New Economy: A Millennial Myth', *Dollars and Sense*, March-April (www.cepr.net/the_new_economy.htm).

Balto, David A. (1999), 'Emerging Antitrust Issues in Electronic Commerce', 12 November, paper presented at Distribution Practices: Antitrust Counseling in the New Millennium, an Antitrust Institute Meeting, Columbus, Ohio (www.ftc.gov/speeches/other/ecommerce .htm#N_26_).

Baltzell, E. Digby (1987), *The Protestant Establishment: Aristocracy and Caste in America*, New Haven, CT: Yale University Press.

Bansak, Cynthia, Norman Morin and Martha Starr (2004), 'Technology, Capital Spending, and Capacity Utilization', Washington, DC: Federal Reserve Board.

Bar, Francois (2000), 'E-commerce and the Changing Terms of Competition', online presentation (http://e-conomy.berkeley.edu/conferences/9-2000/EC-conference2000_papers/barslides.pdf).

Barber, Benjamin R. (1996), *Jihad vs. McWorld: How Globalization and Tribalism are Reshaping the World*, New York: Ballantine.

Bassi, Laurie (1996), 'Expenditures on Employer-Provided Training', Alexandria, VA: American Society for Training and Development.

Bauer, Martin (ed.) (1995), *Resistance to New Technology: Nuclear Power, Information Technology and Biotechnology*, Cambridge: Cambridge University Press.

Bell, Daniel (1960, 1962), *The End of Ideology*, New York: Collier Books.

Bell, Daniel (1976), *The Cultural Contradictions of Capitalism*, New York: Basic Books.

Bellamy, Edward (1887, 1968), *Looking Backward*, New York: Lancer Books.

Benner, Chris, Bob Brownstein and Amy Dean (1999), *Walking the Lifelong Tightrope*, San Jose, CA: Working Partnerships, USA.

Berle, Adolph and Gardiner Means (1932, 1982), *The Modern Corporation and Private Property*, New York: William S. Hein.

Bix, Amy Sue (2000), *Inventing Ourselves Out of Jobs? America's Debate over Technological Unemployment, 1929–1981*, Baltimore, MD: Johns Hopkins University Press.

Black, Sandra and Lisa Lynch (2000), 'What is Driving the New Economy: The Benefits of Workplace Innovation', Cambridge, MA: National Bureau of Economic Research.

Blankenhorn, David (1999), 'Family Friendly or Employer Friendly? A Child's-eye View of Work Family Policies', presentation at 'American Labor and the New Economy', sponsored by Social Democrats, USA, Washington, DC, 22 January (www.newecon.org/famfr_empfr_db.html).

Blinder, Alan (1997), 'The Computer and the Economy', *Atlantic Monthly*, **280** (6), 26-36.

Blinder, Alan (1997a), 'The Speed Limit: Fact and Fancy in the Growth Debate', *The American Prospect*, **8** (34), 57-62.

Blinder, Alan (2000), 'The Internet and New Economy', Washington, DC: Brookings Institution.

Bluestone, Barry and Bennett Harrison (1990), *The Great U-Turn: Corporate Restructuring and the Polarizing of America*, New York: Basic Books.

Bluestone, Barry and Bennett Harrison (2000), *Growing Prosperity*, New York: Houghton Mifflin.

Blum, Albert and Jeffrey Teick (1997), 'Bargaining with Technology', *Business Quarterly*, **61** (3), 40-45.

Bond, James, Ellen Galinksy and Jeffrey Hill (2002), 'When Work Works', New York: Families and Work Institute.

Borchert, John (1967), 'American Metropolitan Evolution', *Geographical Review*, **57**, 301-32.

Boskin, Michael and Lawrence Lau (1992), 'Capital, Technology, and Economic Growth', in Nathan Rosenberg, Ralph Landau and David C. Mowery (eds), *Technology and the Wealth of Nations*, Stanford, CA: Stanford University Press.

Boston College, Center on Work & Family (2000), *Measuring the Impact of Workplace Flexibility*, Boston, MA: Boston College.

Bowles, Samuel, David Gordon and Thomas Weisskopf (1983), *Beyond the Waste Land: A Democratic Alternative to Economic Decline*, New York: Doubleday.

Bowman, Karlyn H. (2001), 'This Labor Day, Workers Have Cause to Celebrate', Washington, DC: American Enterprise Institute (www.aei politicalcorner.org/KB%20Articles/kb010827.pdf).

Brenner, Robert (1998), 'The Economics of Global Turbulence', *New Left Review*, **29**, 1-264.

Brooks, David (2001), *Bobos in Paradise: The New Upper Class and How They Got There*, New York: Simon and Schuster.

Brown, Gordon (2003), 'A Modern Agenda for Prosperity and Social Reform', speech to the Social Market Foundation at the Cass Business School (England), 3 February.

Brown, Jeffrey R. and Austin Goolsbee (2000), 'Does the Internet Make Markets More Competitive? Evidence from the Life Insurance Industry', working paper, Cambridge, MA, Harvard University, Kennedy School of Government.

Brynjolfsson, Erik and Lorin Hitt (1993), 'Is Information Systems Spending Productive? New Evidence and New Results', *Proceedings 14th International Conference on Information Systems*, Orlando, FL.

Brynjolfsson, Erik and Lorin Hitt (1998), 'Beyond the Productivity Paradox: Computers are the Catalyst for Bigger Changes', *Communications of the ACM*, **41** (8), 49-55.

Brynjolfsson, Erik, Michael D. Smith and Yu Hu (2003), 'Consumer Surplus in the Digital Economy: Estimating the Value of Increased Product Variety at Online Booksellers', MIT Sloan Working Paper No. 4305-03.

Buell, Jon, and Virginia Hearn (1994), *Darwinism: Science or Philosophy*, Richardson, TX: Foundation for Thought and Ethics.

Burnham, James (1941), *The Managerial Revolution*, Bloomington and London: Indiana University Press.

Burnham, James (1997), 'The Growing Impact of Global Telecommunications on the Location of Work,' *Contemporary Issues*, no. 87, St Louis, MO: Washington University, Center for the Study of American Business.

Business Week (2002), 'Really Grand Openings', 23 September, 32.

Business Week (2002), 'Restating the 90s', 1 April, 58.

Caplow, Theodore, Louis Hicks and Ben J. Wattenberg (2001), *The First Measured Century: An Illustrated Guide to Trends in America, 1900-2000*, Washington, DC: American Enterprise Institute Press.

Cappelli, Peter (1999), *The New Deal at Work: Managing the Market-Driven Workforce*, Boston, MA: Harvard Business School Press.

Cappelli, Peter, Laurie Bassi, David Knoke, Harry Katz, Paul Osterman and Michael Useem (1996), *Change at Work*, Washington, DC: National Policy Association.

Carnegie Council on Adolescent Development (1995), *Great Transitions: Preparing Adolescents for a New Century*, New York: Carnegie Corporation.

Carnegie Corporation (1994), *Starting Points: Meeting the Needs of our Youngest Children*, New York: Carnegie Corporation.

Carnevale, Anthony P. and Stephen J. Rose (1998), *Education for What: The New Office Economy*, Princeton, NJ: Educational Testing Service.

Carr, Nicholas G. (2003), 'Does IT Matter?', *Harvard Business Review*, May, 5-12.

Cassidy, John (2000), 'The Productivity Mirage', *New Yorker*, 27 November, 106.

Caudron, Sheri (1999), 'The Power of Global Markets', *Business Finance*, April, 22.

Challenger, Gray and Christmas Inc. (2001), cited in 'Dot-com Death Toll Drops in December', *Silicon Valley/San Jose Business Journal*, 31 December (http://sanjose.bizjournals.com/sanjose/stories/2001/12 /31/daily2.html).

Chandler, Alfred D. (1977), *The Visible Hand: The Managerial Revolution in American Business,* Cambridge, MA: Harvard University Press.

Chernow, Ron (1990), *The House of Morgan*, New York: Simon and Schuster.

Claessens, Stijin, Thomas Glaessner and Daniela Klingebeil (2003), 'Electronic Finance: Reshaping the Financial Landscape Around the World', Washington, DC: World Bank.

Cleveland Federal Reserve Bank (1999), 'Annual Report', Cleveland, OH.

Clinton, Bill and Albert Gore (1992), *Putting People First: How We Can All Change America*, New York: Times Books.

Coe, D. and E. Helpman (1995), 'International R&D Spillovers', *European Economic Review*, **39** (5), 859-87.

Conference Board (1998), *Perspectives on a Global Economy*, Washington, DC: Conference Board.

Coolidge, Calvin (1925), Inaugural Address 4 March (www.jfklibrary.Org/ coolidge_inaugural.html).

Cooper, James C. and Kathleen Madigan (2001), 'Labor's New Flexibility Cuts Two Ways While Business Benefits, Temporary Workers are Taking the Hardest Hit', *Business Week*, December, 24.

Corey, Dan (2001), 'Labour's Industrial Policy', *New Economy*, **8** (3), 127-33.

Council of Economic Advisors (1995), *Economic Report to the President*, Washington, DC: US Government Printing Office.

Cox, Michael W. and Richard Alm (1999), *The Myths of Rich and Poor: Why We are Better Off Than We Think*, New York: Basic Books.

Coyle, Diane (1998), *The Weightless Economy*, New York: Capstone.

David, P.A. (1989), 'Computer and Dynamo: The Modern Productivity Paradox in a Not-Too-Distant Mirror', Center for Economic Policy Research, Stanford, CA.

Davis, Bob and David Wessel (1998), *Prosperity: The Coming 20-Year Boom and What it Means to You*, New York: Random House.

DeLay, Tom (2001), Press Release, Tom Delay for Congress, 1 December (www.tomdelay.com/html/prelease.cfm?release_id=191).

De Long, J. Bradford and Lawrence H. Summers (1991), 'Equipment Investment and Economic Growth', *Quarterly Journal of Economics*, **106** (2), 445-502.

Deloitte Research (2003), *Collaborative Knowledge Networks,* Washington, DC: Deloitte Research.

Dennison, Edward (1979), 'Accounting for Slower Growth: The United States in the 1970s', Washington, DC: Brookings Institution.

Dionne, E.J. (2004), *Stand Up, Fight Back: Republican Toughs, Democratic Wimps and the Politics of Revenge*, New York: Simon and Schuster.

Drew, Elizabeth (1996), *Showdown: The Struggle Between the Gingrich Congress and the Clinton White House*, New York: Simon and Schuster.

Drucker, Peter (1993), *Post Capitalist Society*, New York: HarperCollins.

Drucker, Peter (1995), *Innovation and Entrepreneurship*, New York: Harper Business.

Dunning, John H. and Gavid Boyd (eds) (2003), *Alliance Capitalism and Global Business*, Cheltenham, UK and Northampton, MA, USA: Edward Elgar.

Dyson, Esther, George Gilder, George Keyworth and Alvin Toffler (1994), 'Cyberspace and the American Dream', Washington, DC: Progress and Freedom Foundation.

Ehret, Walter (1967), 'Our Country 'Tis of Thee', Pacific, MO: Mel Bay Publications.

Eisner, Robert (1994), *The Misunderstood Economy: What Counts and How to Count It*, Cambridge, MA: Harvard Business School Press.

Fagen, Donald (1982), 'I.G.Y. (International Geophysical Year)', *The Nightfly*, Los Angeles: Warner Brothers.

Farhi, Paul (2003), 'Dean Tries to Summon Spirit of the 1960s', *Washington Post*, 28 December, A5.

Faux, Jeff (1996), *The Party's Not Over: A New Vision for Democrats*, New York: Basic Books.

Faux, Jeff (1997), 'You are Not Alone', in Stanley Greenberg and Theda Skocpol, *The New Majority*, New Haven, CT: Yale University Press.

Figelton, Eamonn (1999), *In Praise of Hard Industries*, New York: Houghton Mifflin.

Fine, Charles and Daniel Raff (2000), 'Internet-Driven Innovation and Economic Performance in the American Automobile Industry', MIT International Motor Vehicle Program.

Fountain Jane E. and Robert D. Atkinson (1998), 'Innovation, Social Capital, and the New Economy: Policies to Support Collaborative Research', Washington, DC: Progressive Policy Institute.

Fox, Nicols (2002), *Against the Machine*, Washington, DC: Shearwater Books.

Freeman, Christopher (1982), *Unemployment and Technical Innovation: A Study of Long Waves and Economic Development*, Westport, CT: Greenwood Press.

Freeman, Christopher and Carlota Perez (1988), 'Structural Crises of Adjustment: Business Cycles and Investment Behavior', in Giovanni Dosi, Christopher Freeman, Richard Nelson, Gerald Silverberg and Luc Soete (eds), *Technical Change and Economic Theory*, London and New York: Pinter and Columbia University Press, 38-66.

Friedman, Milton (1979), *Free to Choose*, New York: Harcourt Brace Jovanovich.

Friedman, Thomas L. (1999), *The Lexus and the Olive Tree*, New York: Anchor.

From, Al and Will Marshall (1998), 'Building the Next Democratic Majority', *Blueprint*, 1 Sept.

Fry, Earl H. (2000), *The North American West in a Global Economy*, Los Angeles: Pacific Council on International Policy.

Galbraith, John Kenneth (1958), *The Affluent Society*, Boston, MA: Houghton Mifflin.

Galbraith, John Kenneth (1968), *The New Industrial State*, New York: Signet Books.

Galston, William (2003), 'After Socialism: Mutualism and a Progressive Market Strategy', in Ellen Frankel Paul, Fred Miller and Jeffrey Paul (eds), *After Socialism*, Cambridge: Cambridge University Press.

Garvin, Glenn (2003), 'He Was Right: Looking Back at the Goldwater Moment', *Reason*, **3** (2), 61-4.

Gephardt, Richard (1999), *An Even Better Place: America in the 21st Century*, New York: Public Affairs.

Giddens, Anthony (2002), *Where Now for New Labour?*, London: Policy Network.

Gingrich, Newt (1997), 'Letter to Science Chairman Sensenbrenner', 12 February, (www.house.gov/science/newt.htm).

Glassman, James K. (1995), 'Secular Politics', *Washington Post*, 22 August.

Golden, Soma (1974), 'The Economy: The Next 25 Years', *New York Times*, 29 December, III-1.

Goldhaber, Michael H. (1997), 'The Attention Economy and the Net', *First Monday*, **2** (4) (www.firstmonday/dk/issues/issues2_4/goldhal).

Goldwater, Barry (1960), *The Conscience of a Conservative*, Shepherdsville, KY: Victor Publishing.

Goodwyn, Lawrence (1978), *The Populist Movement: A Short History of the Agrarian Revolt in America*, New York: Oxford University Press.

Gordon, Robert (2000), 'Does the New Economy Measure up to the Great Inventions of the Past', *Journal of Economic Perspectives*, **14** (Fall), 49-74.

Graham, Otis (1976), *Toward a Planned Society*, New York: Oxford University Press.

Gray, Ralph and John Peterson (1974), *Economic Development in the United States*, Homewood, IL: Richard D. Irwin.

Greenspan, Stanley (2001), *The Four-Thirds Solution*, New York: Perseus.

Greenspan, Stanley and Robert Atkinson (2004), 'Putting Parenting First: Implementing the Four-Thirds Solution', Washington, DC: Progressive Policy Institute.

Greenwood, Jeremy and Ananth Seshadri (2002), 'Technological Progress and Economic Transformation', Research Report No. 3, Department of Economics, University of Rochester.

Griffith, Robert (1982), 'Dwight D. Eisenhower and the Corporate Commonwealth', *American Historical Review*, **87** (2), 87-122.

Griliches, Zvi (1992), 'The Search for R&D Spillovers', *Scandinavian Journal of Economics*, **94**, 29-47.

Grove, Andrew (1999), *Only the Paranoid Survive: How to Exploit the Crisis Points that Challenge Every Company*, New York: Time Warner.

Hagedoorn, John, Albert Link and Nicholas Vonortas (2000), 'Research Partnerships', *Research Policy*, **29** (4), 567-86.

Hall, E. and Charles I. Jones (1999), 'Why Do Some Countries Produce so Much More Output per Worker than Others?', *Quarterly Journal of Economics*, **114** (1), 83-116.

Haltiwanger, John, Lucia Foster and C.H. Krizan (2002), quoted in 'Really Grand Openings', *Business Week*, 23 September, p. 32

Ham, Shane and Robert Atkinson (2000), 'Napster and Online Piracy', Washington, DC: Progressive Policy Institute.

Ham, Shane and Robert D. Atkinson (2002), 'Modernizing the State Identification System: An Action Agenda', Washington, DC: Progressive Policy Institute.

Ham, Shane and Robert D. Atkinson (2003), 'E-Transformation of the Real Estate Industry', Washington, DC: Progressive Policy Institute.

Handel, Michael (2003), *Implications of Information Technology for Employment, Skills, and Wages: A Review of Recent Research*, Menlo Park, CA: SRI International.

Harding, Warren (1921), 'Presidential Inaugural Address', (www.multied.com /documents /Harding.html).

Harrison, Bennett and Barry Bluestone (1990), *The Great U-turn: Corporate Restructuring and the Polarizing of America*, New York: Basic Books.

Haustein, Heinz-Dieter and Harry Maier (1980), 'Basic Improvement and Pseudo-Innovations and their Impact on Efficiency', *Technological Forecasting and Social Change*, **16**, 243-265.

Hayek, F.A. (1944, 1994), *The Road to Serfdom*, Chicago, IL: University of Chicago Press.

Heilbroner, Robert L. (1983), 'The Coming Invasion', *New York Review of Books*, 8 December (www.nybooks.com/articles/article-preview?Article_id =6022).

Heilbroner, Robert L. (1996), 'Do Machines Make History?', in Merritt Roe Smith and Leo Marx (eds), *Does Technology Drive History?*, Cambridge, MA: MIT Press.

Heilbroner, Robert L. and Aaron Singer (1977), *The Economic Transformation of America*, New York: Harcourt Brace Jovanovich.

Henwood, Doug (2003), *After the New Economy*, New York: New Press.

Herzenberg, Stephen, John A. Alic and Howard Wial (1998), *New Rules for a New Economy: Employment and Opportunity in Postindustrial America*, Ithaca, NY: Cornell University Press.

Herzenberg, Stephen, John A. Alic and Howard Wial (1998a), 'New Unions For A New Economy', *The New Democrat*, 1 March, 8-9.

Herzenberg, Stephen, John A. Alic and Howard Wial (1998-99), 'Toward a Learning Economy', *Issues in Science and Technology*, Winter, 55-62.

Hetherington, Marc (2004), *Why Trust Matters: Declining Political Trust and the Demise of American Liberalism*, Princeton, NJ: Princeton University Press.

Heuse, Ron (undated) (www.indwes.edu/Faculty/bcupp/things/computer/gch umor.htm).

Hewlett, Sylvia Anne (2002), 'Have a Child and Experience the Wage Gap', *The New York Times*, 16 May, A 23.

Hilton, Margaret (1991), 'Shared Training: Lessons from Germany', *Monthly Labor Review*, March, 33-8.

Hoover, Herbert (1932), speech given on 31 October, New York City (http://www.search.eb.com/elections/pri/Q00044.html).

Hoover, Herbert (1952), *The Memoirs of Herbert Hoover: 1929-1941, The Great Depression*, New York: Macmillan.

Hufbauer, Gary (1991), 'World Economic Integration: The Long View', *International Economic Insights*, **11** (3), 26-8.

Hummels, David (1999), 'Have International Transport Costs Declined?', mimeo, University of Chicago, Graduate School of Business.

Huntington, Ellsworth and Sumner W. Cushing (1925), *Modern Business Geography*, New York: World Book Company.

Huxley, Aldous (1949), *Prisons, (with the Carceri Etchings by Piranesi)*, Los Angeles, CA: Zeitlin and Van Brugge.

Institute for Policy Innovation (2000), 'New Ideas for the Information Economy', Dallas, TX, event transcript, 18 August.

International Labor Organization (1999), *Key Indicators of the Labor Market 1999*, Paris: ILO.

International Monetary Fund (1998), *World Economic Outlook*, Washington, DC: IMF.

Independent (1903), 'The Fate of the Salaried Man', **60**, 2002-3.

Ivanko, John and Lisa Kivirist (2004), *Rural Renaissance*, Gabriola Island, British Columbia: New Society Publishers.

John, Richard (1997), 'Elaborations, Revisions, Dissents: Alfred D. Chandler Jr.'s *The Visible Hand* after Twenty Years', *Business History Review*, Summer, 151-200.

John, Richard (1998), *The Politics of Innovation*, *Daedalus*, **127** (4), 187-214.

Johnson, Phillip E. (1997), *Defeating Darwinism by Opening Minds*, New York: Rosepubb.

Jones, Charles I. (2002), 'Sources of US Economic Growth in a World of Ideas', *American Economic Review*, **92** (1), 220-39.

Jones, Charles and John Williams (2000), 'Too Much of a Good Thing? The Economics of Investment in R&D', *Journal of Economic Growth*, **5** (1), 65-85.

Jorgenson, Dale (2001), 'Information Technology and the US Economy', *American Economic Review*, **90** (1), 1-32.

Judis, John B. (2000), *The Paradox of American Democracy: Elites, Special Interests and the Betrayal of the Public Trust*, New York: Pantheon Books.

Kahn, Herman (1967), *The Year 2000: A Framework for Speculation on the Next Thirty-Three Years*, New York: Macmillan.

Kanter, Rosabeth Moss (1984), *The Change Masters*, New York: Simon and Schuster.

Kelly, Kevin (1998), 'New Rules for the New Economy', New York: Viking, p. 156.

Kelly, Michael (1998), 'The Child Care Experiment', *Washington Post*, 14 January, A19.

Keynes, John Maynard (1930, 1963), 'Economic Possibilities for Our Grandchildren', reprinted in *Essays in Persuasion*, New York: W.W. Norton.

Keynes, John Maynard (1935, 1964), *The General Theory of Employment*, New York: Harcourt Brace and World, Inc.

Khurana, Rakesh (2000), 'Transitions at the Top: CEO Positions as Open and Closed to Competition', Cambridge, MA: Sloan School of Management, MIT, working paper, cited in Robert Reich, *The Future of Success.*

Kim, Chang-Jin and Charles R. Nelson (1999), 'Has the US Economy Become More Stable?', *Review of Economics and Statistics*, **81** (4), 608-17.

Kirk, Russell (1953, 1986), *The Conservative Mind: From Burke to Eliot*, Washington: Regnery Gateway.

Kirk, Russell and James McClellan (1967), *The Political Principles of Robert A. Taft*, New York: Fleet Press Corporation.

Klimek, Shawn D., Rob Jarmin and Mark Doms (2002), 'IT and Firm Performance in US Retail Trade', US Census Bureau, Center for Economic Studies, CES-WP-02-14.

Kondratieff, Nikolai D. (1935), 'The Long Waves in Economic Life', *Review of Economic Statistics*, **17** (6), 105-15.

Kristol, William (1995), 'The Politics of Liberty, the Sociology of Virtue', in Lamar Alexander and Chester Finn, Jr (eds), *The New Promise of American Life*, Indianapolis, IN: Hudson Institute.

Krugman, Paul (1990), *The Age of Diminished Expectations*, Cambridge: MIT Press.

Kuhn, Thomas (1962), *The Structure of Scientific Revolutions*, Chicago, IL: University of Chicago Press.

Kuttner, Robert (1996), 'Peddling Krugman', *The American Prospect*, September-October, 83-4.

Lafer, Gordon (1999), 'Captive Labor', *The American Prospect*, **10** (46), 66-70.

Leach, Penelope (1994), *Children First: What Society Must Do – and Is Not Doing – for Children Today*, New York: Vintage.

Leuchtenburg, William E. (1963), *Franklin D. Roosevelt and the New Deal: 1932-1940*, New York: Harper & Row.

Levy, Frank (1999), *The New Dollars and Dreams: American Incomes and Economic Change*, New York: Russell Sage Foundation.

Lewin, Tamar (2002), 'Study Links Working Mothers to Slower Learning', *New York Times*, 17 July, A14.

Leyden, D.P., and A.N. Link (1991) 'Why are Government R&D and Private R&D Complements?,' *Applied Economics*, **23**, 1673-81.

Lindsey, Lawrence B. (2000), 'The Seventeen-Year Boom', Washington, DC: American Enterprise Institute.

Lindsey, Lawrence B. (2001), 'Remarks by Dr. Lawrence B. Lindsey to the Federal Reserve Bank of New York', July (www.whitehouse.gov/news /releases /2001/07/20010719-4.html).

Longman, Phillip (2004), *The Empty Cradle*, New York: Basic Books.

Low, William (1984), 'Discoveries, Innovations and Business Cycles', *Technological Forecasting and Social Change*, **26**, 355-73.

Luce, Henry R. (1956), 'A Speculation about A.D. 1980', in *Editors of Fortune Magazine, The Fabulous Future: America in 1980*, New York: E.P. Dutton.

Machiavelli, Nicolo (1515), *The Prince* (www.constitution.org/mac/prince00 .htm).

Madrick, Jeff (1995), *The End of Affluence*, New York: Random House.

Madrick, Jeff (2002), *Why Economies Grow*, New York: Basic Books.

Makin, John (2000), 'The Mythical Benefits of Debt Reduction', Washington, DC: American Enterprise Institute.

Mandel, Michael J. (2004), *Rational Exuberance: Silencing the Enemies of Growth*, New York: Harper Business.

Maney, Kevin (1998), 'The Networked Economy Changes Everything', *USA Today*, November 16, 1E.

Manning, Alan (2004), 'We Can Work It Out: The Impact of Technological Change on Low Skill Workers', Centre for Economic Performance, London School of Economics.

Mansfield, Edwin (1980), 'Basic Research and Productivity Increase in Manufacturing', *American Economic Review*, **70** (4), 863-73.

Marlin, Steven (2003), 'Imaging Counts For Banks', *Information Week*, 24 November, 55.

Marshall, Will (2001), 'Revitalizing the Party of Ideas', *Blueprint*, 23 Jan.

Marx, Karl (1846), 'The German Ideology' (www.marxists.org/archive /marx/works/1845/german-ideology/ch01a.htm).

Marx, Leo (1987), 'Does Improved Technology Mean Progress?', *Technology Review*, January, 33-41.

McGinn, Daniel (2000), 'What is a Shopper to Do', *Newsweek*, 18 December, 51.

McKenna, Regis (1997), *Real Time: Preparing for the Age of the Never Satisfied Customer*, Boston, MA: Harvard Business School Press.

McKibben, Bill (2002), 'Unlikely Allies against Cloning', *New York Times*, 27 March, A23.

McKinsey Global Institute (2001), *US Productivity Growth, 1995-2000*, (*www. mckinsey.com/knowledge/mgi/productivity*).

Meany, George (1956), 'What Labor Means By More', *The Fabulous Future: American in 1980*, New York: E.P. Dutton.

Meyer, Chris (2000), 'What is the Matter', *Business 2.0*, March, 193-4.

Michael, Donald (1962), *Cybernation: The Silent Conquest*, Santa Barbara, CA: Center for the Study of Democratic Institutions.

Mills, C. Wright (1951 1990), *White Collar*, New York: Oxford University Press.

Mills, C. Wright (1956, 1959), *The Power Elite*, New York: Oxford University Press.

Mintzberg, Henry and James Waters (1983), 'The Mind of the Strategist(s)', in S. Srivasta (ed.), *Executive Mind*, New York: Jossey-Bass.

Mokyr, Joel (1990), *The Lever of Riches: Technological Creativity and Economic Progress*, New York: Oxford University Press.

Mokyr, Joel (1994), 'Cardwell's Law', *Research Policy*, **23** (2), 561-74.

Mokyr, Joel (2002), *The Gifts of Athena*, Princeton, NJ: Princeton University Press.

Morin, Richard and Megan Rosenfeld (1998), 'With More Equity, More Sweat', *Washington Post*, 22 March, A1.

Morris, Ernst (1955), *Utopia 1976*, New York: Rinehart.

Moschella, David (2003), *Customer-Driven IT: How Users Are Shaping Technology Industry Growth*, Boston, MA: Harvard Business School Press.

Moyers, Bill (2002), 'Transcript: Trading Democracy', Public Broadcasting System (www.pbs.org/now/transcript/transcript_tdfull.html).

Mumford, Lewis (1952), *Art and Technics*, New York: Columbia University Press.

Nairn, Alasdair (2002), *Engines That Move Markets: Technology Investing from Railroads to the Internet and Beyond*, New York: John Wilely and Sons.

Narin, F. and D. Olivastro (1997), 'Linkage between Patents and Papers: an Interim EPO/US Comparison', prepared for Proceedings of the Sixth Conference of the International Society for Scientometrics and Informetrics, 16-19, June.

National Commission on Entrepreneurship (2001), *Embracing Innovation*, Washington, DC: NCE.

National Commission on Excellence in Education (1983), *A Nation At Risk*, Washington, DC: NCEE.

New Economy Task Force (2000), 'Making the New Economy Grow', Washington, DC: Progressive Policy Institute.

Newkirk, Brian and Robert Atkinson (2003), 'Buying Wine Online', Washington, DC: Progressive Policy Institute.

Noble, David (1995), *Progress without People: New Technology, Unemployment and the Message of Resistance*, Toronto: Between the Lines.

North, Douglass C. (1995), 'Some Fundamental Puzzles in Economic History/Development', Washington University, Economics Working Paper.

Oakley, J. Ronald (1986), *God's Country: America in the Fifties*, New York: Red Dembner Enterprises.

Oliner, Steven D. and Daniel Sichel (2000), 'The Resurgence of Growth in the Late 1990s: Is Information Technology the Story?', Federal Reserve Bank of San Francisco, *Proceedings*.

Olson, Mancur (1982), *The Rise and Decline of Nations: Economic Growth, Stagnation, and Social Rigidities*, New Haven, CT: Yale University Press.

Organisation for Economic Co-operation and Development (OECD) (1995), *Knowledge, Technology and Productivity*, Paris: OECD.

Organisation for Economic Co-operation and Development (OECD) (1997), *Science, Technology and Industry: Scoreboard of Indicators*, Paris: OECD.

Organisation for Economic Co-operation and Development (OECD) (2000), *Science, Technology and Innovation in the New Economy*, Paris: OECD.

Organisation for Economic Co-operation and Development (OECD) (2001), *Society at a Glance: OECD Social Indicators*, Paris: OECD.

Organisation for Economic Co-operation and Development (OECD) (2003), *OECD Science, Technology and Industry Scoreboard, 2003 Towards a Knowledge-Based Economy*, Paris: OECD.

Orszag, Peter R. (2001), 'Marginal Tax Rate Reductions and the Economy: What Would Be the Long-Term Effects of the Bush Tax Cut?', Washington, DC: Center on Budget and Policy Priorities.

Osterman, Paul (1999), *Securing Prosperity*, Princeton, NJ: Princeton University Press.

Packard, Vance (1957), *The Hidden Persuaders*, New York: D. Mackay.

Packer, Arnold E. (et al.) (1987), *Workforce 2000: Work and Workers for the 21st Century*, Indianapolis, IN: Hudson Institute.

Palmer, Tom (2004), 'Results of the First Flexible Working Employee Survey', Employment Relations, British Department of Trade and Industry (www.dti.gov.uk/er/emar).

Peltzman, Sam (2000), 'Prices Rise Faster than They Fall', *Journal of Political Economy*, June, 466-503.

Penn, Mark (2000), 'Why Voters Care about the Quality of Life', *Blueprint*, 1 September, 74-89.

Perez, Carlota (2003), *Technological Revolutions and Financial Capital: The Dynamics of Bubbles and Golden Ages*, Cheltenham, UK and Northampton, MA, USA: Edward Elgar.

Peterson, Jonathan, (2000), 'Unlikely Anti-trade Warrior', *Washington Times*, 2 October, a-10.

Petroski, Henry (1997), 'Development and Research', *American Scientist*, **85**, May-June, 210-3).

Philips, Don (2002), 'Digital Railroad', *Technology Review*, March, 75-8.

Phillips, Kevin (2002), *Wealth and Democracy*, New York: Broadway Books.

Piketty, Thomas and Emmanuel Saez (2003), 'Income Inequality in the United States, 1913-1998', *The Quarterly Journal of Economics*, **118** (1), 1-39.

Pinkerton, James P. (1995), *What Comes Next: The End of Big Government – and the New Paradigm Ahead*, New York: Hyperion.

Plant, Malcolm (2001), 'Critical Realism: A Common Sense Philosophy for Environmental Education?', paper presented at the ATEE Conference, Stockholm (www.lhs.se/atee/proceedings/Plant _RDC_17.doc).

Polanyi, Karl (1944), *The Great Transformation*, Boston, Beacon Press.

Porter, Michael (1985), *Competitive Advantage*, New York: Free Press.

Postrel, Virginia (1999), *The Future and its Enemies*, New York: Free Press.

President's Council of Economic Advisors (1999), 'The Parenting Deficit: Council of Economic Advisors Analyze the "Time Crunch"' (www. newecon.org/ParentingDeficitCEA-May99.html).

President's Council of Economic Advisors (2003), *Economic Report of the President*, Washington, DC: US Government Printing Office.

'The President's Economic Warrior' (2004), *Parade*, 4 January, 7.

President's Information Technology Advisory Committee (2001), 'Transforming Health Care Through Information Technology', Washington, DC: The White House.

Putman, Robert (2000), *Bowling Alone: The Collapse and Revival of American Community*, New York: Simon and Schuster.

Rand, Ayn (1957), *Atlas Shrugged*, New York: Random House.

Rawls, John (1971), *A Theory of Justice*, Cambridge, MA: Harvard University Press.

Reich, Robert (2001), *The Future of Success*, New York: Alfred Knopf.

Reinicke, Wolfgang (1998), *Global Public Policy: Governing Without Government?*, Washington, DC: Brookings Institution.

Rifkin, Jeremy (1992), *Beyond Beef: The Rise and Fall of the Cattle Culture*, New York: Dutton.

Rifkin, Jeremy (1995), *The End of Work: The Decline of the Global Labor Force and the Dawn of the Post-Market Era*, New York: Putnam.

Rifkin, Jeremy (1999), *The Biotech Century*, New York: Jeremy P. Tarcher.

Roach, Stephen (2001), 'The Recession We Need', *The New York Times*, 4 January, op. ed.

Roach, Stephen (2003), 'Global: A Failed Revolution', New York: Morgan Stanley, 17 January (www.morganstanley.com/GEFdata/digests/2030117-fri.htm).

Robertson, Brian (2000), 'Working for Families', *Blueprint*, 1 September, 42-4.

Robinson, Joe (2003), *Work To Live: The Guide to Getting a Life*, New York: Perigee.

Rogers, T.J. (1999), 'Why Silicon Valley Should Not Normalize Relations with Washington', Washington, DC: Cato Institute.

Romer, Paul M. (1990), 'Endogenous Technological Change', *Journal of Political Economy*, **98** (5), 71-102.

Romer, Paul M. (1994), 'Beyond Classical and Keynesian Macroeconomic Policy', *Policy Options*, July-August, 15-21.

Rosenberg, Nathan (1976), *Perspectives on Technology*, Cambridge: Cambridge University Press.

Rosenberg, Nathan (1983), *Inside the Black Box: Technology and Economics*, Cambridge: Cambridge University Press.

Rouse, David (undated), 'Review of "The Age of Access"' (www.bookfinder.us/review8/1585420824.html).

Sagaura Seminar (2000), 'Civic Engagement in America, Better Together', Cambridge, MA: John F. Kennedy School of Government, Harvard University.

Saltzman, Amy (1997), 'When Less is More', *US News & World Report*, 27 October, 78-84.

Samuelson, Robert (1999), 'Boom-Time Battle', *Washington Post*, 22 July, A14.

Samuelson, Robert J. (2002), 'The Myth of the New Economy: The Age of Inflation', *The New Republic*, 13 May, 32-41.

Santayana, George (1905), 'Reason in Common Sense', *Life of Reason*, New York: Charles Scribner's Sons.

Scherer, F.M. (1996), 'Raising Productivity on the Technological Frontier', *Regional Review*, Federal Reserve Bank of Boston, Fall, 25-6.

Schor, Juliet B. (1991), *The Overworked American*, New York: Basic Books.

Schumpeter, Joseph A. (1939), *Business Cycles: A Theoretical, Historical and Statistical Analysis of the Capitalist Process*, New York: McGraw-Hill.

Schumpeter, Joseph A. (1942, 1975), *Capitalism, Socialism and Democracy* New York: Harper Perennial.

Schwartz, John (2004), 'Always on the Job', *New York Times*, 5 September, A1.

Schwartz, Peter and Peter Leyden (1997), 'The Long Boom: A History of the Future', *Wired*, July, **5.07**, 44-56.

Scranton, Phillip (1997), *Endless Novelty: Specialty Production and American Industrialization 1865-1925*, Princeton, NJ: Princeton University Press.

Seigel, Fred (undated), 'The Reader's Companion to American History: Conservatism', Houghton Mifflin (http://college.hmco.com/history/readers comp /rcah/html/ah_019700_conservatism.htm).

Seitel, S. (1996), *Work & Family, A Retrospective*, New York: Work & Family Connection.

Servan-Schreiber, Jean Jacques (1968), *The American Challenge*, New York: Atheneum.

Smith, Adam (1776, 1937), *An Inquiry into the Natures and Causes of the Wealth of Nations*, New York: The Modern Library.

Smith, M.R. (1996), 'Technological Determinism in American Culture', in Leo Marx and Merritt Roe Smith (eds), *Does Technology Drive History? The Dilemma of Technological Determinism*, Cambridge, MA: MIT Press.

Solow, Robert M. (1957), 'Technical Change and the Aggregate Production Function', *Review of Economics and Statistics*, **39**, 312-20.

Solow, Robert M. (1987), 'We'd Better Watch Out', *New York Times Book Review*, 12 July, 36.

Soule, George (1948), *Introduction to Economic Science*, New York: New American Library.

Stevenson, Adlai (1956), 'My Faith in Democratic Capitalism', in *Editors of Fortune Magazine, The Fabulous Future: American in 1980*, New York: E.P. Dutton.

Stiglitz, Joseph (2003), *The Roaring Nineties*, New York: Norton.

Stiroh, Kevin J. (2001), 'Information Technology and US Productivity Revival: What Do the Industry Data Say?', Federal Reserve Bank of New York.

Storper, Michael (1999), 'Rethinking the Economics of Globalization: The Role of Ideas and Conventions', UCLA School of Public Policy and Social Research (www.sscnet.ucla.edu/soc/groups/ccsa/storper /htm).

Summers, Lawrence H. and J. Bradford DeLong (2002), 'Is the "New Economy" a Fad?' (www.j-bradford-delong.net/movable_type/archives/000 773. html).

Swann, G.M. Peter (2000), 'The Economics of Standardization', London: Department of Trade and Industry.

Taft, Charles P. (1956), 'The Familiar Men of 1980', in *Editors of Fortune Magazine, The Fabulous Future: American in 1980*, New York: E.P. Dutton.

Talmadge, Candace (2000), 'Retailers concerned as manufacturers sell online', *Reuters Internet*, 31 December (www.mercurycenter.com/svtech/news breaking /internet/docs7956161.htm).

Taniwaki, Yasu (2003), 'Journal of Interactive Advertising', **4** (1), (http:// jiad.org).

Tarbell, Ida (1904), 'The History of the Standard Oil Company', New York: McClure, Phillips and Co. (www.pbs.org/wgbh/amex/rockefellers/people events/ptarbell.html).

Tassey, Greg (1998), 'The Economics of a Technology-Based Service Sector', Planning Report 98-2, Washington, DC: National Institute of Standards and Technology.

Taylor, Frederick (1911), *The Principles of Scientific Management*, New York: Harper Brothers.

Theobald, Robert (1961), *The Challenge of Abundance*, New York: New American Library of World Literature.

Theobald, Robert (1998), 'The Healing Century', speech to Ontario Arts Council, January (www.nrf.org/RT/HealingCentury.html).

Thompson, Bob (2002), 'History for Sale', *Washington Post Magazine*, 20 January, 15-29.

Thurow, Lester C. (1999), 'Building Wealth', *Atlantic Monthly*, **283** (6), 57-66.

Toffler, Alvin (1980), *The Third Wave*, New York: William Morrow.

Towers Perrin (2001), *Business, People and Rewards: Surviving and Thriving in the New Economy*, London: Towers Perrin.

Tremain, Kerry (2000), 'What Works: Sidney Harman, Innovator Genius on the Factory Floor', *Blueprint*, June, 41.

Trilling, Lionel (1950), *The Liberal Imagination: Essays on Literature and Society*, New York: Viking Press.

Twain, Mark (1897), *Following the Equator: A Journey around the World*, Hartford: American Publishing Co.

Union of Industrial and Employers Confederations of Europe (2001), *The UIECE Benchmarking Report 2001*, Brussels: UIECE.

Unisys Corporation, Unisys Global Financial Services (2003), *Beyond the Decline of the Check* (www.unisys.com/financial/insights/insights_compen dium/Decline_of_the_ Check _-_revised_072503.pdf).

US Bureau of Labor Statistics (1997), 'Labor Force Statistics from the Current Population Survey', May.

US Census Bureau (1993), 'Computer Use and Ownership: Level of Access and Use of Computers, 1984, 1989, 1993, Use of Computers at Home, School, and Work by People 18 Years and Older: October 1997' (http:// landview.census.gov/population/socdemo/computer/ report97/tab06.pdf).

US Census Bureau (2002), *Statistical Abstract of the United States*, Washington, DC: Government Printing Office.

US Congress, Congressional Budget Office (2001), 'Budget Options', Washington, DC: CBO.

US Congress, Office of Technology Assessment (1993), *Rural America at the Crossroads*, Washington, DC: Government Printing Office.

US Congress, Office of Technology Assessment (1995), *The Effectiveness of Research and Experimentation Tax Credits*, Washington, DC: Government Printing Office.

US Congress, Joint Economic Committee Staff Report (2000), *Entrepreneurs Creating the New Economy*, Washington, DC: US Congress.

US Department of Commerce (2003), *Digital Economy 2003*, Washington, DC: US Government Printing Office.

US Small Business Administration, Office of the Chief Counsel for Advocacy (1995), *The Changing Burden of Regulation, Paperwork, and Tax Compliance on Small Business*, Washington, DC: SBA.

US Patent and Trademark Office (2002), *US Patent Statistics Report*, Washington, DC: USPTO.

Useem, Michael (1996), *Investor Capitalism: How Money Managers Are Changing the Face of Corporate America*, New York: Basic Books.

Utsumi, Yoshio (1998), 'IT and Telecommunications in Japan's Economic Recovery', *Journal of Information Policy*, **1** (2), 10-16.

Van Deusen, Edward (1955), 'The Coming Victory of Paper', *Fortune*, October, 130-99.

Veblen, Thorstein (1899), *The Theory of the Leisure Class*, New York: Mentor Books.

Veblen, Thorstein (1904, 1958), *The Theory of the Business Enterprise*, New York: New American Library of World Literature.

Von Hippel, E. (1988), *Sources of Innovation*, New York: Oxford University Press.

Von Neuman, John (1956), 'Can We Survive Technology', in *Editors of Fortune Magazine, The Fabulous Future: America in 1980*, New York: E.P. Dutton.

Wade, Nicholas (2002), 'A Dim View of a Posthuman Future', *New York Times*, April, F1.

Wall Street Journal (2002), 'Slow-Growth Joe', 23 May, A16.

Wanniski, Jude (1978, 1998), *The Way the World Works*, Washington, DC: Regnery.

Warren, Elizabeth and Amelia Warren Tyagi (2003), *The Two-Income Trap: Why Middle-Class Mothers and Fathers are Going Broke*, New York: Basic.

Wesbury, Brian (2003), 'Keeping the Bush Boom Alive', *Wall Street Journal*, 12 December, A12.

Wessner, C. (2003), 'Sustaining Moore's Law and the US Economy', *Computing in Science and Technology*, January-February, 30-38.

Weinstein, Paul (2002), 'New Economy Work (NEW) Scholarships', Washington, DC: Progressive Policy Institute.

Welch, David (2003), 'Ford and Visteon: Ties That Bind', *Business Week*, April 21, 69.

Whitman, Marina N. (1999), *New World, New Rules: The Changing Role of the American Corporation*, Boston, MA: Harvard Business School Press.

Whyte, William H. (1956), *The Organization Man*, New York: Simon and Schuster.

Wiebe, Robert H. (1967), *The Search For Order*, New York: Hill and Wang.

Wiebe, Robert H. (1989), *Businessmen and Reform: A Study of the Progressive Movement*, Chicago, IL: Ivan R. Dee.

Winik, Lyric Wallwork (2004), 'Intelligence Report', *Parade*, 4 January, 7.

Wright, Erik Olin, and Rachel E. Dwyer (2003), 'The Patterns of Job Expansions in the USA: A Comparison of the 1960s and 1990s', *Socio-Economic* Review, (1), p. 289-325.

Wolf, Martin (1998), 'The Bearable Lightness', *Financial Times*, 12 August (www.ft.com /hippocampus/79922).

Yelin, Edward (1999), 'California Work and Health Survey', San Francisco, CA: Field Institute.

Zey, Mary and Tami Swenson (2001), 'The Transformation and Survival of Fortune 500 Industrial Corporations through Mergers and Acquisitions, 1981-1995', *Sociological Quarterly*, **42** (3), 461-84.

Zunz, Olivier (1992), *Making America Corporate, 1870-1920*, Chicago, IL: University of Chicago Press.

Index